WALKING INTEGRITY

WALKING INTEGRITY

BENJAMIN ELIJAH MAYS, MENTOR TO MARTIN LUTHER KING JR.

Edited by

Lawrence Edward Carter Sr.

Mercer University Press
Macon, Georgia

ISBN 0-86554-604-5   MUP/P174

The paper used in this publication meets the minimum requirements
of American National Standard for Information Sciences—
Permanence of Paper for Printed Library Materials, ANSI Z39.48-1984.

Library of Congress Cataloging-in-Publication Data

Carter, Lawrence Edward Sr.,
    Walking integrity: Benjamin Elijah Mays, mentor to Martin Luther King Jr.
/ edited by Lawrence Edward Carter Sr.
        xvii + 428 pp. + 9 pp. of photographs   6" x 9" (15 x 22 cm.)
    Includes bibliographical references and index
    ISBN 0-86554-604-5 (alk. paper)
    1. Mays, Benjamin E. (Benjamin Elijah), 1894-1984. 2. Morehouse College
(Atlanta, Ga..)—Presidents —Biography. 3. College presidents —United States
—Biography. 4. Afro-Americancollege presidents —Biography. I. Carter, Lawrence
Edward, 1941-
LC2851.M72W35   1998
378.1'11'092
[B] —dc21
                                                    98-29611
                                                       CIP

This book is dedicated to

Marva Griffin Carter
Lawrence Edward Carter Jr.
Bernice Childs Carter Johnson
John Henry Carter III
Robert James Branham
Eddie Kate Mays
(1912-1994)
Thomas Kilgore Jr. '35
(1913-1998)
The Martin Luther King Jr. International Chapel Assistants

CONTENTS

ILLUSTRATIONS

A photo gallery appears after page 214. All photographs are used courtesy of the author and Morehouse College.

PREFACE

This book first appeared in 1994 as a *festschrift* to celebrate the centennial of Dr. Benjamin E. Mays's birth. It was commissioned two years earlier by Dr. Leroy Keith Jr., the eighth President of Morehouse College, and published by Scholars Press in a limited hardback edition.

Issued by Mercer University Press for a much wider audience, this edition is designed to document Mays's place in the twentieth century African-American struggle for civil and human rights. Primarily this will be done by tracing Mays's influence, as president of Morehouse College, on Martin Luther King Jr., who called Mays his "intellectual and spiritual mentor." These nineteen chapters represent our gift to the two most outstanding Baptist ecumenical Christians of the century.

Mays's career as a race leader and a college president is in the long shadow of his two mentors John Hope and Mordecai Wyatt Johnson, both of whom preceded Mays calling for the ballot, education, nonviolence and legal redress to end American segregation.[1] In 1993, American historians listed Mays as one of the fifty three most influential persons in Black America, past and present.[2] I first met Dr. Mays in June 1974 in Boston at Twelfth Street Baptist Church when he was crossing the nation autographing *Born to Rebel*, his autobiography. He founded the Psi Chapter of Omega Psi Phi Fraternity at Morehouse College and was hosted in Boston by the Omega Fraternity. I would later be inducted into, Eta Phi, a graduate chapter of Omega in Boston. The next time I met Mays was May of 1979 at Northeastern University's African American Institute when I was ushered into his presence as the Dean Elect of the Martin Luther King Jr. International Chapel at Morehouse College. I knelt down next to his chair behind a desk for what I hoped would be his blessing as I prepared to end my fifteen year stay in Boston and head to Atlanta. Several cameras

---

[1]Leroy Davis, *A Clashing of the Soul: John Hope and the Dilemma of African American Leadership and Black Higher Education in the Early Twentieth Century* (Athens: The University of Georgia Press, 1998).

[2]Columbus Salley, *The Black 100: A Ranking of the Most Influential African Americans, Past and Present* (New York: Citadel Press, 1993), 192-194.

began flashing as I got in place. I asked Mays what he could say to me as I anticipated beginning my work as the first Dean of the Morehouse College Chapel. He said, "Be Yourself." "Give the students the best you have to offer." "If you get 200 students to come to Chapel on Sunday, you are doing a good job. If you get 400 to come, you are doing an excellent job, but if you get 500, you will have triumphed."

Mays delivered a brilliant and sincere invocation at my installation service as the first Dean of the Martin Luther King International Chapel on Sunday, October 7, 1979. Calvin Anderson Brown Jr. '52, president of the Morehouse College National Alumni Association is the first person to call Mays "a candle in the dark." E. A. Jones chose Brown's metaphor as the title of his new history of the College and dedicated it to Mays upon his retirement in 1967. Jones died in 1980 as I was preparing to fly to Ohio to visit my parents and then to Illinois to spend most of the summer with my wife, who was a doctoral student at the University of Illinois in Urbana-Champaign. Because I was so new to the college and did not know Jones well, President Hugh M. Gloster did not think it was necessary for me to remain in Atlanta for Jones's funeral. With some pain of conscience I decided to take along a copy of Jones's book, *A Candle in the Dark: A History of Morehouse College*.

As the plane was ascending over Atlanta I started thumbing through the 380 page tome, and I came across Appendix G which listed four pages of writings of Mays. As my finger went down to the bottom of page three I was about to turn it when I noticed item No. 44 which said, "Since 1946, Mays has written 1,040 weekly articles for the *Pittsburgh Courier*. Few college presidents in America have written so much and so widely."[3] When I noticed that the articles continued to the bottom of the next page, totaling seventy-two articles, I sat up straight up in my seat. I had discovered a pearl of great price and the answer to a frequently asked question: "What did Dr. Mays say in his legendary chapel talks every Tuesday morning to the Morehouse student body?" As fate would have it, the home of my stepfather and mother in Columbus, Ohio was surrounded by the world's largest single campus university, The Ohio State University, with its William Thompson

---

[3]Edward A. Jones, *A Candle in the Dark: A History of Morehouse College* (Valley Forge: Judson Press, 1967), 325.

Memorial Library being less than a mile from our front door. I was bursting with excitement, and the moment my mother's car arrived in my back yard, I quickly deposited my luggage in the family room, grabbed the keys to my stepfather's truck, and announced I was headed to the OSU Library.

On arriving I ran up to the second floor to the African-American Studies Division, and asked if they had the national edition of the *Pittsburgh Courier* on microfilm. The clerk said, "Yes," and pointed me toward the files. I immediately found the spool for June 1, 1946 and started reading Mays's weekly *Courier* articles. The more I read the stronger my hunch became that I had found the treasure and perhaps the only documentation of "the seeds of revolution" that Mays planted in the Sale Hall Chapel at Morehouse. After looking at about fifteen of the articles, I abruptly jumped up from the microfilm machine and ran to a pay telephone to call Mays's home on Pamlico Drive in southwest Atlanta. The great moral educator answered the telephone himself.[4] With a little anxiety in my voice, I identified myself, told him where I was and what I was doing and asked, "Is it possible, Dr. Mays, that your weekly *Pittsburgh Courier* articles influenced your weekly chapel talks, and your chapel talks influenced your *Pittsburgh Courier* articles?" Without hesitation Mays said, "Yes, that's right!" "So this is perhaps the only remaining documentation of what you said in chapel every Tuesday," I exclaimed. "That's right." Thanking Dr. Mays, I informed him that I would see him in one month, I hurried back to the microfilm machine and copied some of the articles.

When I arrived in Urbana-Champaign, Illinois my wife, Marva, was required to be in class most of the day. Hence, I made a decision to spend from 9 a.m. to 9 p.m. in the University of Illinois Library annotating Mays's *Courier* articles. Little did I know, that this would begin a research period that would land me in the basement of Mays's home for days, weeks, and months close to the date of his passing in 1984. Most of this time was spent in his three newspaper albums reading and summarizing 1,871 articles. He even permitted me to carry the albums to my apartment on the Morehouse campus where I would work into the early morning hours. Mays wanted me to publish all of the articles. Written permission was granted also

---

[4]Thomas Kilgore Jr. with Jimi Kilgore Ross, *A Servant's Journey: The Life and Work of Thomas Kilgore* (Valley Forge: Judson Press, 1998), 108.

by the publisher of the *Pittsburgh Courier*, the late Mr. John Sengstacke. I spent many hours talking with Mays in his family room, his more formal living room on Sundays, in his basement study, in his back yard and with his loyal secretary, Sally Warner.

Mays also wrote a letter on my behalf to Michael Winston, the former head of the Moorland-Spingarn Research Center at Howard University, granting permission for me to have full access to his personal papers which he gave to the University in 1976.

The name of Mays's most famous student, Martin Luther King Jr. is synonymous with the philosophy of nonviolence and the Civil Rights Movement in the United States—a philosophy and a movement profoundly influenced by the example and teachings of India's Mohandas K. Gandhi. Not so well-known, however, are the names of four other men associated with King and his alma mater, Morehouse College in Atlanta, and their vital role in establishing the historic and philosophical link between Gandhi and King—a link that altered forever the social and political fabric of the United States. These Morehouse men were Howard Washington Thurman '23, Benjamin Elijah Mays '67 (hon.), Mordecai Wyatt Johnson '11, and Samuel Woodrow Williams '37. Through their efforts, Martin Luther King Jr., '48, was introduced to the philosophy of "nonviolence." The collective efforts of these five ordained Christian ministers of the Baptist tradition, self-described "servant-scholars," introduced and shaped the philosophy of nonviolence that became a pillar of the American civil and human rights movement.

With the help of eighteen other scholars, we get a clear picture of the man who taught Thurman, Williams, and King (through his Sale Hall Chapel talks), and whose contributions reflect the genius of Hope and Johnson. This volume sets forth issues that remain relevant today. Such issues include Mays's concern for equality, access, race relations, activist ministers, social conscious churches, humane theology, social change, nonviolence, ecumenism, scholarship and funding of good education, irrespective of whether it is by a majority or minority institution. Mays wanted an inclusive philosophy that would be "accepted by philanthropic America and governments."[5] Other areas yet to be addressed in writings about Mays should deal with him as journalist and preacher.

The following people either contributed or facilitated some aspect of the work that has resulted in this publication. All share some admiration for Mays. I shall always be grateful for their help. Special thanks go to Wiley A. Purdue, Acting President of Morehouse College, for making the publication of the centennial collection of essays possible. Deep gratitude must be extended to Harry W. Gilmer of Scholars Press, whose encouragement and belief in this project made all of the stress and strain easier to endure. I am also in the debt of Dennis Ford of Scholars Press, whose careful reading of this manuscript demonstrated the patience of Job. Sara Foster of Scholars Press gave tremendous creative skill in her assistance with the promotional materials. The festschrift was reviewed with attention to all of its details by Robert J. Clemente, whose commitment evolved to the point of sacred duty. The manuscript was twice read by William Garfield Pickens a member of the Morehouse Class of 1948. His thoroughness will forever be appreciated. The Reverend Samuel T. Ross-Lee '92 helped me do research at the University of South Carolina in Columbia. He patiently copied 600 pages of microfilmed material on "Benjamin E. Mays vs. The Southern Railway" and rendered similar assistance at South Carolina State University in Orangeburg. My gratitude goes to Toby D. Sanders for critically reading the entire manuscript and helping with the computer work. The greatest amount of editorial assistance for the second edition came from Andrew Manis of Mercer University Press. He deserves the lion's share of the credit for the books reorganization and fine tuning. Andy is an excellent teacher and full of patience. I willingly accept responsibility for any shortcomings found on these pages.

Our son, Lawrence, has sacrificed many games of chess and movies with me because of the work involved in this book. My wife, Marva, willingly gave me all the love, support, and understanding that such an undertaking requires.

My greatest debt is perhaps to Dr. Mays himself. In addition, I am also forever in debt to the following people: Charles G. Adams, James Theodore

---

[5]Benjamin E. Mays, "Preface to the Issue . . ." *A Journal of Research on African American Men, Challenge* 6 (August 1995): vi-ix.

Anderson, Samuel Banks, III, Lerone Bennett Jr., Barry Beckham, Esme Bhan, Robert H. Bolton, Charles A. Bowman, Robert James Branham, Anibal Bueno, Noel C. Burtenshaw, Orville Vernon Burton, James Campbell, Richard J.B. Campbell, Doris J. Clark, Clayborne Carson, Marva Griffin Carter, Obie Clayton, Robert Clemente, Freddie C. Colston, Samuel DuBois Cook, Sylvia F. Cook, Maceo C. Dailey, Illya E. Davis, Caroline Fike, Charles S. Finch, III, Dennis Ford, Sara Foster, John Hope Franklin, Doris Levy Gavins, Harry W. Gilmer, Hugh Morris Gloster, Yvonne King Gloster, Henry Goodgame, Donald W. Harward, the late Butler Henderson, Edwin L. Herr, Asa G. Hilliard III, John H. Hopps Jr., Theda Jackson, Randal M. Jelks, Barbara Jenkins, Freddie Johnson, Mimie Johnson, Leslie Jones, Gretchen Keiser, Leroy Keith Jr., Barbara Sue K. Lewinson, Fred C. Lofton, Shirley Manor, Walter E. Massey, Verner Randolph Matthews, Oscar McCloud, Thomas J. S. Mikelson, Terrence Moore, Otis Moss Jr., Maceo Nance, Clarence G. Newsome, the late Gibran Marvin Borders Patterson '95, Bernice Mays Perkins, the late Samuel D. Proctor, John Raminsky, Lewie C. Roache, Charles Shelby Rooks, Dereck J. Rovaris, Harriet Joseph Scarupa, Barbara H. Sizemore, Kate Stevens, Lela Swell, Charles E. Taylor, James C. Tazel, R. Roosevelt Thomas, Lyndon Wade, Barbara A. O. Wardlaw, Clinton Warner, Sally Warner, Anne Wimbush Watts, Beverly Wheeler, Jerome C. Williams, Charles V. Willie, Gayraud S. Wilmore, and Vincent L. Wimbush.

The following articles are re-presented in these pages and used with permission: Lerone Bennett Jr., "The Last of the Great Schoolmasters," *Ebony* 32 (Dec. 1977), 74-79; Noel C. Burtenshaw, "Mays Planted Seeds of Revolution in the Chapel at Morehouse," *The Georgia Bulletin* (October 14, 1982), 8; Orville, Vernon Burton, "Foreword," to Benjamin E. Mays, *Born To Rebel: An Autobiography* (Athens: The University of Georgia Press, 1971), ix-liv; *Congressional Record*, Extensions of Remarks, "Presidential Medal of Freedom for Benjamin Elijah Mays," the Honorable Wyche Fowler Jr. of Georgia, the Honorable Julian C. Dixon of California, the Honorable Paul Simon of Illinois, Monday, January 13, 1983; Miles Mark Fisher IV, Speech delivered on the occasion of the occasion of the Tenth Annual Martin Luther King Jr. College of Ministers and Laity Conference, Religious Emphasis Week, March 3, 1995, Morehouse College, Atlanta, Georgia; Doris Levy Gavins, Chapter 3 of "The Ceremonial Speaking of Benjamin Elijah Mays: Spokemans For Social Change, 1954-1975,"

(Ph.D. dissertation, Louisiana State University, 1978); Hugh M. Gloster, "Dr. Mays' Successful Career Comes to Triumphant End," "Dr. Benjamin Elijah Mays, President Emeritus of Morehouse College, Passes," "Campus Memorial Program Tribute to Dr. Benjamin E. Mays," "Funeral Tribute to Dr. Benjamin E. Mays, *Morehouse College Bulletin* 46 (Winter 1984): 2, 4-6, 10-11, 18-19; Barbara Sue Kaplan Lewinson, "Chapter 2 of "Three Conceptions of Black Education: A Study of the Educational Ideas of Benjamin Elijah Mays, Booker T. Washington, and Nathan Wright," Ed.D. dissertation, Rutgers University, 1973; Fred C. Lofton, "A Messiah of the Messiah," A sermon delivered on February 18, 1990, Martin Luther King Jr. International Chapel, Morehouse College, Atlanta; Verner Randolph Matthews, Chapter 3 of "The Concept of Racial Justice of Benjamin Elijah Mays (1895-1984) and its Relevance to Christian Education in the Black Church," (Ph.D. dissertation, New York University, 1991; Thomas J. S. Mikelson, "The Negro's God in the Theology of Martin Luther King, Jr.: Social Community and Theological Discourse, " (Ph.D. dissertation, Harvard University, 1988); Charles Shelby Rooks, *Revolution in Zion: Reshaping African-American Ministry, 1960-74* (New York: Pilgrim Press, 1989), 48-75; Dereck Joseph Rovaris, Chapter 6 of "Developer of an Institution: Dr. Benjamin Elijah Mays, Morehouse College President, 1940-1967," (Ph.D. dissertation, University of Illinois, 1990); Charles V. Willie, "The Education of Benjamin Elijah Mays: An Example in Effective Teaching," *Teachers College Record* 84 (Summer 1983): 955-562.

Benjamin Elijah

The words, the monuments
a grateful people raise
to Benjamin Elijah Mays
will stand
as markers in time
and the land.

But those markers will not be for him
Heroes are their own way.
The markers will be for us
who wander less sure
having no North Star to follow.

The markers will make known to us
and to the years,
our Benjamin Elijah journeying
to show where hand-holds
were on the mountain steep and smooth.

The markers will tell to us
and to other men,
how he was lone,
far forward in the hostile land
when we
could not cover him
when we
were organized for sortie
or march

And when other men
sing of their heroes,
we will know to speak our brother's name
argue for his admittance
into the pantheon.
Enemies are enemies not always

because they hate us
but because
they love their own.

The markers will remind us.
We love our own.
Our heroes will no more be nameless
and forgotten
because we did not record them.
Sing of them.
We know how.
What goes forward,
into tomorrow,
into remotest time,
is not what the hero does
but what the legend sings.

The markers will be our song,
our memory of Benjamin Elijah
sung loud
so that time
will not dim him,
so that he
will not die.

—Henry Blakely

1

THE LIFE OF BENJAMIN ELIJAH MAYS

Lawrence Edward Carter Sr.

Benjamin Elijah Mays was born in Ninety Six, South Carolina, August 1, 1894, to formerly enslaved parents, S. Hezekiah and Louvenia Carter Mays. Mays lived between the end of the first Reconstruction and the beginning of the second Reconstruction. Two years after his birth, the United States Supreme Court declared that racial segregation was legal, as long as the facilities for both races were equal. His father was a farmer and a heavy drinker who was given to spousal abuse. The elder Mays was not a champion of education for young Bennie. African Americans in the rural areas of the South usually received seven months of school rather than nine. This shortened school year permitted students to work in the cotton and tobacco fields. Mays reported in his autobiography, *Born To Rebel,* the effect of this abbreviated school year:

> In the seventeen years since I entered the first grade at the age of six, I had spent only seventy-three months in school—the equivalent of eight nine month years of schooling. Had I been able to complete each year without being taken out for farm work, I would have graduated at fourteen instead of twenty-one. I regret those lost years.[1]

His mother was deeply religious, oriented to a serious prayer life, and encouraged Bennie to go to school. Louvenia's spirituality had a profound effect on the Bennie's dreams and hopes. Benjamin Elijah was baptized, licensed to preach, and ordained to the Christian ministry at the Mount

---

[1]Benjamin E. Mays, *Born To Rebel: An Autobiography* (Athens: University of Georgia Press, 1987), 40.

Zion Baptist Church. He attended the high school department of South Carolina State College in Orangeburg, completing the course in three years and graduated as class valedictorian in 1916. Mays informed his mother that, given the conditions in his native state, he needed to leave South Carolina "to seek a new world."

THE EDUCATION OF BENNIE MAYS

Mays spent his freshman year of college at Virginia Union University, in Richmond, Virginia. The following September he transferred to Bates College, in Lewiston, Maine, because he wanted to compete with white students. At Bates the young Mays was a leading campus figure, scholastically as well as in extracurricular activities. When Donald W. Harward, the current President of Bates College, spoke at Morehouse College in recognition of the Centennial Anniversary of Benjamin E. Mays's birth, he told of how Mays was accepted at Bates College on academic probation. He concentrated in economics, English literature, history, philosophy and religion. His scholarship was supplemented by multiple part-time jobs on and off campus. Mays's outstanding achievement at Bates and beyond were rewarded when he was inducted into the Bates Chapter of Phi Beta Kappa fifteen years after earning his bachelor's degree; received an honorary degree of Doctor of Laws from Bates's in 1947; and became the first recipient of the Alumnus of Merit Award, thereafter known as the Benjamin Elijah Mays Award in his honor [Bates's highest honor.] Additionally, Bates's annual intercollegiate debate tournament is named in his honor, and in 1993 the North American Parliamentary Debate Championship Tournament, held at Bates College, was dedicated to Mays's memory. [2]

After receiving his bachelor's degree in 1920, he was ordained a Baptist minister two years later. On 3 January 1921, he arrived at the University of Chicago for graduate study. While in Chicago, Mays served as a student assistant to Lacey Kirk Williams, pastor of the historic Olivet Baptist Church and president of the National Baptist Convention, U.S.A., Incorporated. Another student assistant to Williams was Cornell Everett

---

[2]Donald W. Harward, "Benjamin Mays and Bates College" in *Walking Integrity: Benjamin Elijah Mays, Mentor to Generations*, ed. Lawrence Edward Carter Sr. (Atlanta: Scholars Press, 1996), 478.

Talley, who also had graduated from Morehouse. Mays began his role as mentor by taking Talley under his wing, showing him how to study and to negotiate the difficult requirements at the University of Chicago. Later, Talley recalled once arriving at the threshold of Mays's classroom just as the bell sounded. Mays stopped him and announced, "Mr. Talley, your right foot is on time and your left one is late and you can't come in." Such was Mays's seriousness as a teacher and respect for time was a hallmark of his professional career.[3]

Mays was eventually recruited to Morehouse by President John Hope in 1921 to teach higher mathematics and to coach the debating team. He also served as acting dean. During Mays's third year at Morehouse, he met his most esteemed mentor, Mordecai Wyatt Johnson, then pastor of the First Baptist Church of Charleston, West Virginia. Johnson had been invited by president John Hope to speak in Chapel. The occasion made a lasting impression on Mays, who later recalled:

> I shall never forget that address. He spoke to us and challenged us so eloquently, that we were led to believe that this man was called of God to do his work. I can see Mordecai years later, walking across the Howard campus, walking with a sense of dignity and freedom. Strangers on the campus had to know he was the President. . . . Surely God called Mordecai Wyatt Johnson to expound the social gospel to America and to make Howard University a truly great university.[4]

Johnson went on to earn a B.A. from Morehouse in 1911, a second B.A. from the University of Chicago, a Bachelor of Theology from Rochester, and a Master of Theology from Harvard University in 1923. Later, Johnson profoundly impressed Mays when as president of Howard University he prevailed upon the federal government to make Howard a

---

[3]Cornell Everett Talley, in conversation with the author. Talley, Morehouse Class of '32 later became one of the great Baptist preachers of his time. The Morehouse College pulpit is named in Talley's honor. The pulpit was a gift of a college trustee, Charles Gilchrist Adams, pastor of Detroit's Hartford Memorial Baptist Church. Adams claims Talley as his mentor.

[4]From Mays's unpublished eulogy of Mordecai Wyatt Johnson.

federal institution, in reparation for 350 years of slavery, segregation, and denigration. Mays agreed with Ralph Waldo Emerson's assertion that "an institution is the lengthened shadow of one man." Howard University was indeed Johnson's long shadow. Mays respected Johnson's refusal to "cringe and kowtow" and his example. His example made it possible for the civil rights movement to be motioned by the Howard University Law School and seconded by Morehouse College.

Mays manifested his mentor's courage in the unorthodox subject of his 1925 Master's thesis from the University of Chicago. His thesis was entitled, *Pagan Survivals in Christianity*. Within the first two paragraphs of his introduction, Mays wrote bluntly that the only people who can deny there are heathen survivals in Christianity are those who had not investigated the subject.

> Furthermore, they reject the conclusions in an attempt to elevate Christianity, give it a purely heavenly origin, and free it from all earthly influences. Those who deny it think that Christianity is too noble, too sacred to be associated with "heathenism." They take the attitude that everything pagan is bad and should be rejected, and that everything Christian is good, and should be accepted. But traditional views of this kind do not conform with the facts, and are not in accord with sound reasoning.[5]

Mays then identified the ancient prototypes behind the Nativity, the miraculous birth, the deification of Jesus, the resurrection and immortality, baptism, the allegorical interpretation of the Bible and the influence of Stoicism upon New Testament writers, chiefly, Paul. He concluded by arguing that "heathen" origins do not destroy their Christian usefulness. In fact, they were the means by which Christianity absorbed vital elements of its pagan environment and "met the needs of the heathen world far more effectively" than any other agency, religion, or philosophy in the Roman Empire.[6]

In 1925, he received his M.A. degree from the University of Chicago

---

[5]Benjamin E. Mays, *Pagan Survivals In Christianity* (Chicago: The University of Chicago, 1925), 1.
[6]Ibid., 89.

and became an instructor of English at South Carolina State College. As young professor, he cut so commanding a figure that young ladies followed from his classes to the trolley car, hoping that he would notice them.[7] He had sadly been rendered eligible by the untimely death of his wife Ellen Harvin, who died in 1923 after an operation in an Atlanta hospital. On 9 August 1926, he married Sadie Gray, a teacher and social worker, who had also received her M.A. from the University of Chicago.

The couple worked together wherever Mays's work took them. In 1926, he was appointed executive secretary of the Tampa, Florida Urban League. From this position, Mays in 1928 published an article in the *Tampa Bulletin*, entitled "It Cost Too Much." In what Mays called a "sanely restrained, objective expression of my attitude toward segregation," he drew a distinction "between obeying unjust laws through necessity and the voluntary acceptance of a law which one did not have to accept." This inaugural article began an a long career as an editorial writer, which eventually distinguished Mays as one of the most important but least recognized public theologians of the century.

MAYS THE THEOLOGIAN

After two years at this post, he became National Student Secretary of the YMCA, headquartered in Atlanta. During their stay in Atlanta, Mrs. Mays joined the faculty of the Atlanta University School of Social Work. From 1930 until 1932, he directed a study of the Negro churches in the United States under the auspices of the Institute of Social and Religious Research in New York City. Out of this work grew his book, *The Negro's Church*, written in collaboration with Joseph W. Nicholson and published in 1933. This volume is an exhaustive sociological survey of the Negro church in America, based on a firsthand study of 609 urban and 185 rural churches in twelve cities and four rural areas. Carefully documented, the book treats various aspects of the African-American church with scholarly thoroughness. In later years, Mays discussed this subject in magazine

---

[7]Maceo Crenshaw Daily Jr., "Benjamin E. Mays on Aspects of Black History: Booker T. Washington, W. E. B. DuBois, Mordecai Johnson, Emmett Jay Scott, and Howard University" in *Walking Integrity: Benjamin Elijah Mays, Mentor to Generations*, (Atlanta: Scholars Press, 1996), 335.

articles. This volume stood unrivaled for 35 years.

His research for *The Negro's Church* revealed to Mays how desperately the black church needed trained leadership. He became aware of a lack of interest in the intellectual development of clergy. The seeds of his future career as a seminary dean were planted by what he learned writing *The Negro's Church* and by his three year experience as pastor of the Shiloh Baptist Church in Atlanta.

The educator's next position took him to Washington, D.C., where he became dean of the Howard University School of Religion in 1934 at the invitation of Mordecai Johnson. On December 17, 1935, Mays was awarded his Ph.D. degree by the University of Chicago. His dissertation on "The Idea of God in Contemporary Negro Literature," later published as *The Negro's God*, was one of the first analyzes to argue that African American ideas of God grow out of their social situation. He held that most African Americans think about God in terms of either "Compensation" or "Constructive development." Compensatory thinking about God was "traditional" in the sense that it was "set forth in the Bible, with primary emphasis upon the magical, spectacular, vengeful, and anthropomorphic nature of God revealed in the Old Testament." "Ideas are compensatory," wrote Mays, "when used or developed to support, uplift, and console, even though the belief or ideas does not fit observed facts." This compensatory understanding of God has had a significant negative effect on black people. It convinces them that "the fight is fixed," which has a dangerous undercurrent of predestination or fatalism.

Mays's theological orientation was influenced by the Social Gospel theology of the 1920s and 1930s. His constructive views were primarily universal, addressing the needs of African Americans and their feelings of inferiority. One of Mays's motivations for selecting his dissertation topic may have been the 1930 Pulitzer prize-winning play *Green Pastures* by Marc Connelly. After the great flood of Noah's time, Connelly has "De Lawd" say to the angel Gabriel:

> It ain't right for me to give up trying to do something with them. [human beings] Dog gone mankind must be alright at the core or else why did I bother with them in the first place. . . . Gab there isn't anything worth while no where that didn't cause somebody some worry... The more I know I have to keep on improving

things. The main trouble is, mankind takes up so much of my time. He ought to be able to help himself a little... Gabriel, did you notice that every now and then mankind turns out some pretty good specimen? The Good man is the man who keeps business.[8]

Vincent Harding notes that the God reflected in the literature of black people rarely had been an "other worldly" God who made them detached from the world. Rather, Mays saw "the Negro's God" as actively participating in struggles against slavery, segregation, and discrimination. That understanding of God did not advise leaving events in the hands of God. It found in God values that needed to be infused into the human situation, and human beings were expected to participate in that transformation. Sometimes that meant transforming the lives of individual persons and sometimes it meant changing the larger social, political and economic structures which order human life. This was indeed a bold and rebellious subject for a 1934 dissertation from the University of Chicago, and was a forerunner of Black Liberation Theology—conceived at Chicago, born at Howard, matured at Morehouse, and explicitly expressed by at New York City's Union Theological Seminary by James H. Cone.

Related to this was his theological balancing of "rebellion" with "the responsible society." In 1948, President D. V. Jemison sent Mays to the founding session of the World Council of Churches of Christ to represent the National Baptist Convention, U.S.A., Inc. in Amsterdam, Holland. During this first assembly, Mays helped to hammer out a middle axiom, called the "idea of the responsible society." Influenced by Mays's views the Amsterdam Assembly explained:

Man is created and called to be a free being, responsible to God and his neighbor. Any tendencies in State and society depriving man of the possibility of acting responsible are a denial of God's intention for man and his work of salvation. A responsible society is one where freedom is the freedom of men who acknowledge freedom and public order, and where those who hold political authority or

---

[8]Marc Connelly and William Keighley, *The Green Pastures*: Digital Video, (MGM/UA Home Video 1936).

economic power are responsible for its exercise to God and the people who see that welfare is affected by it.[9]

A careful analysis of this statement, according to Walter G. Muelder, reveals crucial themes in contemporary world society, which also permeated Mays's writing before and after 1948: (1) The role of religious norms in a just and free society, particularly the creative purposes of God and his concern for person and social salvation; (2) the conception of man, his dignity, rights, and self-realization in community with others; (3) the nature, authority, and scope of the modern state and its functions in relation to the community; (4) the interpenetration of the political, economic, and social spheres of society; (5) the tension of polarity of such ideals as equality, freedom, and justice in both economic and political life and as inherent in the idea of responsibility; (6) the accountability of power groups within nations; (7) the responsibility of persons to domestic and international orders of freedom and justice as well as to God, the source of persons and community; and (8) the responsibilities of nations to one another and to the future of human welfare.[10]

The social sciences, disciplines we use to make things right, study both human and personal *responsiveness* as social and psychological facts which underlie *responsibility* as an ethical reality. Responsiveness is the focus of behavioral science; responsibility is the focus of ethics. Both responsiveness and responsibility are functions of a holistic personality. Real interests are those of responsible action for the entire community. False interests do not serve the best interest of the group and, consequently, do not subordinate personal gain to social gain. Muelder emphasized that, "Through the idea of a responsible society, we relate the theological idea of the Kingdom of God to contemporary social issues." Mays was fond of telling youth:

You are young and beautiful, you are not responsible. If you were born with physical defects, you are not responsible. If you were born with a brilliant mind, you are not responsible. If you live in slums,

---

[9]Amsterdam Assembly, *The Church and the Disorder of Society* (New York: Harper, 1948).

[10]Walter G. Muelder, *Moral Law in Christian Social Ethics* (Richmond: John Knox Press, 1966), 45.

you are not responsible. If you live in a high class neighborhood, you are not responsible. Therefore, you have no reason to boast and become arrogant because you were born privileged or to feel ashamed and unworthy because you were born poor. You are only responsible for how you use your God given talents."[11]

At first glance, the pairing of rebellion and responsibility appears to be contradictory. Without them, however, time would become the ally of social stagnation. Mays's concept of rebellion meant being in a constant search for justice. Justice for Mays is a right and a responsibility, a principle and a practice. Legalized, religious, traditional, and state-sponsored oppression demands a rebellion. An ethically based nonviolent rebellion represents a response of poetic elegance. It is so insofar as it involves respect for the enemy as a person, the use of means that reflect the ends you seek, the clear intent to win the opponent over, rather than merely win over him. Mays could rebel because he was "disturbed about man," as the title of one of his books indicated. In the words of one of his favorite poets, Thomas Carlyle,

Life is not a May-game, but a battle and a march, a warfare with principalities and powers. No idle promenade through fragrant orange groves and green flowery spaces waited on by the choral muses and the rosy hours; it is a stern pilgrimage through the rough burning sandy solitudes, through regions of thick-ribbed ice.[12]

This view grounded Mays in the Christian moral law tradition of a rational will and universal principles reflected in theology of a personal God, as seen in his doctoral dissertation later published as *The Negro's God*. When one analyzes the main emphasis of *The Negro's God* or "the development of the idea of God in its relation to certain trends revealed in contemporary Negro literature," one finds

. . . Such appeals, norms, and ethical factors as: (1) available alternatives, (2) consequences both immediate and long-range, (3) scope

---

[11]Sylvia F. Cook, "Memories of Dr. Benjamin Mays," in *Walking Integrity*, 494.

[12]Benjamin E. Mays, *Quotable Quotes of Benjamin E. Mays* (Atlanta: Vintage Press, 1983), 10.

or range of values to be considered, (4) controlling ideals, (5) the values of the concrete or specific situation, (6) ultimate and proximate goals, (7) individual responsibility, (8) an ideal of community, society, or culture, (9) the social role of the decision-maker, or the differentiation of roles, (10) a conception of the most inclusive end, and (11) devotion to the community.[13]

Orville Vernon Burton was the first to refer to Mays's life as a "rebellion of poetic elegance," for Mays was a conscientious resistor of institutionalized and traditional injustice of any kind. Mays lived a life of nonviolent caring-respect for friends and foes alike. Orville Burton said, "Mays had a capacity to see the humanity in his oppressors." His mission was to enhance human dignity and not degrade it. He believed in the sacredness of all human personality. He was temperamentally "undiscourageable." President Florence Reed of Spelman College discovered this after she had appeared to have thrown cold water on Mays's idea of a Phi Beta Kappa Chapter at Morehouse. He followed always the habits of industry and probity with a certain moral and intellectual virtue. His mother is credited with fortifying his belief in God and his belief in the efficacy of prayer, and for strengthening his conviction that the universe is essentially moral—never sustaining exploitation, war, and injustice.

Mays developed a responsible ethical pedagogy of poetic rebellion. Mays and Hope called their students "young gentlemen," in rebellion against negative facts inherent within the larger social order. In recognition of his responsible ethical nonviolent rebellion, Georgia State University and the University of South Carolina endowed professorial chairs named in honor of Benjamin Mays. The responsible society said there was no Mason-Dixon line between the kingdom of God and social issues. If Mays helped at all in understanding social responsibility it was because he knew how, when, and over what to rebel. While trying "to seek a new world" he could say, "not failure, but low aim is sin."

---

[13]Muelder, 8-9.

MAYS THE PREACHER

Perhaps Mays's most important influence was as a preacher-advisor in his weekly chapel talks: At Chicago, he had been influenced by university president Robert Maynard Hutchins. Mays was particularly moved by Hutchins's 1935 commencement address, in which he warned against moral corruption that came from the great American aspiration of "getting on":

> The way to get on is to be safe, to be sound, to be agreeable, to be inoffensive to have no views on important matters not sanctioned by the majority, by your superiors, or by your group. We are convinced that by knowing the right people, wearing the right things, holding the right opinions, and thinking the right thoughts, we shall all get on. . . . Do not let "practical" men tell you that you should surrender your ideals because they are impractical. Do not be reconciled to dishonesty, indecency, and brutality because gentlemanly ways have been discovered of being dishonest indecent and brutal. As time passes, resist the corruption that comes with it. Take your stand now before time has corrupted you.[14]

Like Hutchins, Mays never accepted the notion that morality was, "none of education's business," and his later commencement charges contained echoes of John Hope, Mordecai Wyatt Johnson, and Robert Maynard Hutchins. To the class of 1963, for example, Mays said:

> Whatever you do, wherever you go, I hope you will perform so well in your chosen work and stand so high in depth of character that when positions open up or promotions are in order, your credentials will be so impressive that those authorized to recommend persons for the new jobs or for promotions will be compelled to examine your credentials. Whether you, or someone else, gets the position is not important. But it is important that you be so outstanding in your field and so noble in character that you cannot be ignored.

---

[14]Milton Mayer, *Robert Maynard Hutchins: A Memoir* (Los Angeles: University of California Press, 1993), 3-4.

Perform so well that when your name is called, no one will be able to dismiss you with a wave of the hand or a shrug of the shoulder. As a Morehouse man I want you to stand for something worthwhile. I want you to count.[15]

The new president used his Chapel pulpit to advocate a stubbornness about segregation:

We would make talks in Chapel and even the students would make talks against going to segregated theaters and segregated anything. *Every year* I talked to my students and told them that I did not want to see them go up in the "buzzard's roost" to see anybody's show, any theatrical performances. And I made it very strong. I said, "Even if God Almighty came to preach at a white church, I wouldn't go to hear Him. I would not go to a segregated theater to see Jesus Christ, Himself."

Mays was also fond of telling his Chapel congregations at Morehouse, "I would rather go to hell by choice than to stumble into heaven following the crowd."

He walked into a powerful prophetic preaching tradition at Morehouse that had already been established by C. T. Walker, A.D. Williams, Charles DuBois Hubert, J. Pius Barbour, Peter James Bryant, E. R. Carter, Mordecai Wyatt Johnson, Benjamin Brawley, Sandy F. Ray, Williams Holmes Borders, Cornell E. Talley, Howard Thurman, Martin Luther King Sr., and religious scholars George Kelsey, Richard I. McKinney, and James Hudson.

Mays believed the adage that injustice triumphs only when good people are silent. Mrs. Mays was correct when she suggested "Born To Rebel" for the title of his autobiography. This prophetic discontent with the status quo Mays passed on to a generation of change-agents in his Chapel talks at Morehouse as he planted the seeds of sedition. According to William G. Pickens, class of '48:

---

[15]Edward A. Jones, ed., "The President's Charge to the Class of 1963," *Morehouse College Bulletin*, 31, July, 1963, 32.

Students might have tried to cut Chapel, but never on Tuesdays because at 9:00 a.m., President Mays spoke to us . His voice almost sounded like the voice of Heaven; many wondered if God Himself could have spoken more brilliantly, pointedly, interestingly or inspirationally.[16]

Otis Moss Jr., a 1956 Morehouse graduate and the current chair of the College's Board of Trustees, noted one of Mays's most powerful admonitions:

If you become a teacher, teach so well that your students will never be able to talk about good teachers unless they call your name. If you become a doctor, practice medicine so well that your community cannot talk about good doctors unless they call your name. If you are a minister, preach and practice the religion of Jesus Christ so well, that even those who do not like you will say, "he is a man of God." Never allow the world to dismiss you because of lazy, sloppy, half-done, mediocre work. Whatever you do, do it so well that the living, the dead, or the unborn could not have done it better.[17]

Mays always preached before a full-house. He wore a black cut away with striped trousers. With his crown of premature gray hair, deep chocolate complexion, and keen features, the March 1948 South Carolina State College newspaper, *The Collegian*, described Mays sitting "majestically and imperturbably, facing a capacity audience waiting for the 'On The Air' sign of WRNO." Mays's annual Easter sermon was based on Luke 23:46, "Father into thy hands, I commend my spirit." All of his work on the road was also heard in the Chapel at Morehouse on Tuesday mornings. Martin Luther King Jr. more than likely heard this sermon in the spring of his senior year.

The sermon stressed that "Jesus died challenging God," and that one

---

[16]William G. Pickens, "Strolling Down Memory Lane," *The Maroon Tiger* 70 (14 May 1998): 5.

[17]Otis Moss Jr. "Dr. Benjamin Elijah Mays: A Voice for the 20th Century and Beyond," in *Walking Integrity*, 497.

need not feel sorry for a great man's glorious death. Mays told of how bravely great men have died, true to the cause for which their lives had been dedicated, such as Mohandas K. Gandhi or Socrates. "Feel sorry for the man," said Mays, "who dies running away licked, a coward, fearfully having failed to fight for justice for all peoples of the world." At different stages of his work on earth, Jesus was plagued by injustice, tyranny, condemnation, and the almost insurmountable forces of the Sadducees, zealots, the Romans, and the Pharisees. "Was Jesus fanatical and mistaken? Let history speak for itself." Mays ended his Easter message with the words, "Jesus challenges the people of earth while they work, yet, fight, all the while having faith in the consequences. That's the conquering faith."[18] This 1948 Easter sermon is the prototypical echo and shadow of Martin Luther King Jr.'s prophetic faith. Mays is credited by King for making the profession of the Christian ministry intellectually respectable.

Mays's sermons and speeches clearly marked him as an unbiased "race man" who was psychologically predisposed to the sounds of the black preacher. He acquired among his arsenal of gifts a cultured cadence so measured, mesmerizing, and poetic that it created an antiphonal response between the pulpit and the pews, thereby transmitting echoes reminiscent of the untutored and unlettered rural African-American preachers.

In 1982, when Mays delivered what was to become his final sermon to Morehouse College in the Martin Luther King Jr. International Chapel, as was typical, he had great effect on the congregation. His sermon that evening was entitled "You Shall Reap What You Sow." Mays told the author that in the early 1930's, before the age of the tape recorder, the nature of his sociological study of *The Negro's Church* forced him to transcribe by hand the sermons of hundreds of black preachers who had neither the benefit of education nor had come under the tutorial influence of white teachers. Mays reported how he unconsciously imbibed his measured speaking rhythm from listening to and transcribing the sermons of these non-lettered black preachers. His was a didactic preaching style. He never used large words in his speaking or writing so that persons with limited learning could understand what he was saying. It appears to have been a

---

[18]Editor, "Doctor Mays In Twelfth Annual Easter Address," *The Collegian*, South Carolina State College, Orangeburg, South Carolina, March 1948, 1.

principle with Mays, never to entertain in his sermons, lectures or addresses. He seldom, if ever, told jokes or deliberately made people laugh.

Of his power as a preacher, John Hope Franklin once noted:

> Dr. Mays already belonged to that select group of speakers—of which Howard Thurman and Mordecai Johnson were prime examples—who could pack the chapel an hour before the services began. Although the chapel was compulsory, there was no need to enforce the rules when Benjamin Mays was scheduled to speak. There he was - tall, slender, handsome in morning attire - mesmerizing and inspiring the undergraduates with his exclamation that he was "worried about man." For subsequent weeks on end, we went about he campus emulating Mays adding that we, too were "worried about man!"[19]

On April 25, 1982, Phillip Potter, the first black General Secretary of the World Council of Churches of Christ in Geneva, Switzerland, stood in the Morehouse College Chapel pulpit and announced that he was 18 years old at the 1948 Amsterdam Assembly, and that he heard Mays spontaneously participate in the debate concerning the responsibility of the World Council to prevent South African churches from coming into the WCC segregated. Secretary Potter told us that Mays's contribution in that debate launched his career in Christian ecumenism and culminated in his election to the position of General Secretary making him the spokesman for four hundred million Christians.

From within his teaching positions and administrative post, Mays produced four generations of "hell-raisers:" James Nabrit Jr. and Howard Thurman, James Farmer and Samuel Williams, Martin Luther King Jr., Floyd McKissick, and Phillip Potter, Maynard Jackson, Louis Sullivan, Walter E. Massey, Michael Lomax, David Satcher, George Haley and Major Owens are just a few examples.

MAYS THE WRITER

---

[19]John Hope Franklin, "To Fill the 'House' With Pride" in *Walking Integrity*, 347.

Mays published nine books in his lifetime: *The Negro's Church*; *The Negro's God*; *Seeking to be Christian in Race Relations, A Gospel for the Social Awakening, The Christian in Race Relations* (pamphlet); *Disturbed About Man* (his only published volume of sermons dedicated to Martin Luther King Jr.); *Born to Rebel* (his autobiography); *Lord, The People Have Driven Me On* (proof that we are by nature communitarian beings with spiritual aspirations and needs); and *Quotable Quotes*, (which Mays approved but did not edit).

Mays published 1,871 articles in the national edition of the *Pittsburgh Courier* from 1946 to 1982. Mays wrote over 800 unpublished addresses, lectures, eulogies, and sermons. Articles by Mays also appeared in newspapers like the *Tampa Bulletin, The Norfolk Journal and Guide, The Atlanta Constitution, The Christian Science Monitor*, and *Chicago Defender*. Mays found time to publish in scholarly journals and popular magazines for the academy, church, and society. Mays's many writings include nineteen chapters in books and 232 articles in such publications as the *Crisis, Christian Century, Journal of Negro Education* (in which he was a contributing editor). Other journals and magazines were *the National Educational Outlook Among Negroes, The A.M.E. Zion Quarterly Review, Encyclopedia of Religion, Howard University Bulletin, Journal of Religious Thought, Highroad, Religion in Life, Georgia Observer, The Pulpit, Church Social Worker, International Journal of Religious Education, Phylon, Woman's Mission, The Methodist Woman, Prophetic Religion, Negro Digest, Our World, Child Study, Presbyterian Survey, World Call, Presbyterian Life, The Y.W.C.A. Magazine, Intercollegian, Wesley Quarterly, The Journal of Educational Sociology, The Atlantic Monthly, Saturday Review, Ebony, Together, Teachers College Record*, and the *Morehouse College Bulletin*.

Mays's autobiography, *Born To Rebel*, sold more than 25,000 hardback copies. This book was based on his global observations of race relations. In 1954 at the Evanston, Illinois, the Second Assembly of the World Council of Churches of Christ, he internationalized the Civil Rights Movement in his now famous address, "The Church and Racial Tensions." This speech resulted in his receiving more hate mail than any other speech he delivered in his entire career. He also read the speech to the students and faculty in the Morehouse College Chapel.

Mays's ethical, educational, social and theological criticisms permeated his writings, from *The Crisis and The Christian Century* to the *Journal of*

Educational Sociology and The Christian Science Monitor. There exists no modern-day parallel among college or university president. It should be noted, however, that Robert Maynard Hutchins, president of the University of Chicago from 1929 to 1951, is believed by many to be the greatest university president of the twentieth century.

As Hutchins was the University of Chicago, Mays was Morehouse College. Like Hutchins, Mays's unblinking realism never yielded to cynicism or nihilism. Both men were constant optimists. But, unlike Hutchins, Mays was not just heard—he was honored as an unarmed prophet who disarmed Jim Crow and created Black leaders in a laboratory of freedom. Lerone Bennett says, "Mays did with pennies, nickels and dimes, what Harvard, Yale, and Chicago did with millions." Indeed, there are enough parallels between Hutchins and Mays to suspect a significant influence.

(1) Hutchins was a good debater. He learned his method at Oberlin and relied upon it throughout his life. Mays was a champion debater at Bates, where he was also captain of the team in his senior year. He later taught debating at Morehouse for three years to teams that were never defeated. (2) Hutchins got rid of intercollegiate football at Chicago; Mays wanted to end it at Morehouse. (3) Hutchins spoke publicly about educational problems, politics, freedom and democracy, delivering nearly eight hundred public addresses from the 1930s through the 1950s. His dynamism and oratory shaped the public image of the University of Chicago; Mays addressed the issues of segregation, politics, and religion, education and democracy, delivering over 800 public addresses from the 1940s through the 1970s. The power of his eloquence stamped the Morehouse mystique. (4) Hutchins authored twelve books on democracy, education, freedom and the world state; Mays authored nine books on the church, God, race relations, and the social gospel. (5) In 1937, Hutchins convinced the faculty and trustees to admit high school juniors; in 1942, Mays established an early recruitment program, which lured Martin Luther King Jr. and Maynard Holbrook Jackson to Morehouse after their junior years in high school. (6) Hutchins created an atmosphere in which everyone around him was moved to do his best work, because it was expected of him. Mays was known for saying,

There is an air of expectancy at Morehouse College. It is expected that the student who enters here will do well. It is also expected that once a man bears the insignia of a Morehouse Graduate, he will do exceptionally well.

(7) Hutchins defined the ends he sought according to an ideal as did Mays. (8) Hutchins was described as a "Man of Honor," who "tried to live up to his convictions." Mays was called "Walking Integrity." (9) Clark Kerr called Hutchins, "the last of the giants" to rule American universities; Lerone Bennett called Mays "the last of the Great School Masters." (10) The faculty at the University of Chicago did not want Hutchins to leave in 1951; the faculty of Morehouse refused to accept Mays's decision to retire in 1965 and asked him to stay on for two more years, until the Centennial of the College. (11) Hutchins quoted heavily from the Great Books of the Western World; Mays quoted from the Classical Literature of African Americans and from the Harvard Classics. (12) "I have assumed," Hutchins wrote in 1956, "that the duty of an educator is to try to change things from the way they are to the way they ought to be." On becoming president of Morehouse, in 1940, Dr. Mays announced "I intend to draw more than my breath and my salary."

MAYS THE ECUMENIST AND PEACE ADVOCATE

In December 1944 Mays was elected vice-president of the Federal Council of the Churches of Christ in America, the first member of his race to hold that office; he served with United Methodist Bishop G. Bromley Oxnam. Even as vice-president of the Federal Council, Mays was the object of racial discrimination within the Council, as he reports in his autobiography.[20] Although Mays lived in Atlanta forty-three years and was invited to speak to white and black groups all over the nation, he was not invited to Atlanta's white pulpits. There were three exceptions: Emory University's Glenn Memorial Church, Trinity Presbyterian Church of Atlanta, and Saint Paul United Methodist Church in Marietta.[21]

He belonged to several organizations, including the Commission on Interracial Cooperation, the Southern Regional Council, the Commission

---

[20]Mays, *Born to Rebel*, 252-253.
[21]Ibid., 252.

on the Basis of a Just and Durable Peace, and the Commission on Christian Strategy for Post-War Planning. Mays was a member of three fraternities, Delta Sigma Rho, Delta Theta Chi, and Omega Psi Phi; he was also a member of the national board of the YMCA. A well-known lecturer, he was frequently called to speak before Southern white audiences, as well as many African-American audiences; and he lectured at hundreds of colleges in the United States. In 1944 Mays was named on the Schomburg Honor Roll of Race Relations as one of twelve Blacks who had done outstanding work in building better race relations in America. In the mid-1950s he was cited by the *Pittsburgh Courier* as one of the twelve most powerful men in America.

MAYS THE ADMINISTRATOR

In 1940, after six years as the dean of Howard University's School of Divinity, Mays was offered the presidency of Morehouse College. Mays became president of Morehouse College on 1 August 1940. Howard Thurman had turned down the presidency and William Holmes Borders had been eliminated because he did not hold a doctorate. Mays accepted the post largely because of "the Morehouse spirit." He later wrote:

It was a few able, dedicated teachers who made the Morehouse man believe that he was 'somebody . . . This [Morehouse] spirit, and the challenge to preserve and perpetuate it, clinched my decision more than anything else to accept the presidency. It was good for Morehouse that it had such inspiring black men on the faculty in the beginning of the twentieth century. Salaries were miserably low, but devotion was correspondingly high.[22]

Some clergy thought Mays "was not orthodox enough, for a college that was Baptist-born and Church-related," though Morehouse had become non-sectarian in 1929. The University of Chicago Divinity School was looked upon by conservative Baptists as a hotbed of heresy and peopled by agnostic professors, infidels, atheists, and avowed secularists. The May 15, 1940,

---

[22]*Born To Rebel*, 173.

The Georgia Baptist called Mays "a scientific Christian, not a religious one," and a notorious modernist, who "believes in everything in general and nothing in particular." In spite of these views, when Mays arrived at Morehouse for the second time in the summer of 1940, he hit the ground like a one-man renaissance. Mays ended his opening chapel talk by promising no miracles:

> But I do promise you one thing as I close: I promise you before my maker, before God, that I will give Morehouse College all that I have. I will give to the institution and to you the best of my mind, heart and soul. I will give to this institution my money until it reaches the sacrificial point. In other words, I will serve this institution as if God almighty sent me into the world for the express purpose of being the sixth president of Morehouse."[23]

It was not going to be easy for the 46-year-old Mays who found Morehouse the weakest link in the Atlanta University system, with an inadequate physical plant, a shrinking faculty, a small endowment, low morale among alumni, faculty, and students, and the second world war beginning to reduce the size of the student body.

During Mays's wartime presidency, a period of difficulty for all colleges, the school's enrollment remained satisfactory because he had the foresight to create an early recruitment program in which high school students were admitted to the College at the end of their tenth or eleventh grade year. Martin Luther King Jr. was one of many early admittees in September of 1944 at the age of fifteen. Mays also increased the tuition, which earned him the nickname from the students, "Buck Bennie."

One of the little known facts in the history of black higher education is that through the persistent urging of Benjamin E. Mays, Margaret Mitchell, author of *Gone With the Wind,* financed the college and medical school educations of over twenty African-American doctors. From June 22, 1942, to June 20, 1957, over fifty-three letters were exchanged between Mays, Mitchell, her husband, and others.

Mays was legendary for his letter writing. His secretaries were known to

---

[23]Mays, *The Alumnus*, Morehouse College Bulletin, 10 (February 1941).

groan under the burden of his prolific correspondence. In October 1944 Mays wrote a letter complaining about his treatment in the dining car of the Southern Railroad between Atlanta and Greenville, South Carolina. NAACP attorneys, led by Thurgood Marshall, took the railroad before the Interstate Commerce Commission, which rejected their plea for $2,500.00 in damages. The Commission reprimanded The Southern Railroad and issued Mays a "feeble apology," promising that his rights would not be violated again aboard The Southern Railroad. Eventually the objective of Mays's letter was achieved in the celebrated case of *Elmer W. Henderson vs. United States, et al.* (339 US 816,1950), which ended the infamous dining-car curtain, which had humiliated Negroes by separating them from white passengers aboard trains.

According to Shelby Rooks, before 1960, Bennie Mays was one of the few college presidents among historically black schools to direct student toward graduate education and for seventy-six years Mays operated on the leading edge to create a collective vision, a new spiritual renaissance, that would transform American culture, social history and theological education.[24]

A LEGACY OF CHARACTER

One of Benjamin Mays's favorite nieces, Bernice Mays Perkins of Cleveland, Ohio, served as an executor of his estate. She told the author the story of borrowing money from her uncle to make a down payment on her and her husband's first home. Mays agreed to loan the money, without interest, and the Perkins agreed to repay the money by a certain date. The loan was paid in full. Mays then said he was pleased that they kept their promise to repay the loan on schedule because he deposited it in a special savings account as a little nest egg for their future. Mays rewarded his niece and husband for keeping their promise. Honesty was everything for Mrs. Perkins' uncle. He trusted her enough to make her co-executor of his estate.

Silvia Cook, former first lady of Dillard University whose wedding to Samuel DuBois Cook was performed in the Mays home, found Mays unpretentious, easy to entertain, and happy to be a part of family life on his

---

[24]See Rooks's article in this volume.

frequent visits to their home in Durham, and on the Dillard University campus in New Orleans. Cook also reported that Mays told her that he didn't intend to dig his grave with his teeth. His diet was very simple. He preferred foods common during his youthful life in South Carolina, such as, turnip greens, sweet potatoes, black-eye peas and pea soup. He diluted his coffee with half a cup of water. Cook added:

> The last trip that Dr. Mays took before he died was to our home at Dillard for Thanksgiving weekend in 1983. He had become feeble and frail. His niece, Ms. Cordelia Blount; and his secretary, Mrs. Sally Warner, reminded us that Dr. Mays had to be coaxed to eat. Since he was always such a high-achiever, I decided to use a grading system to entice him to eat. I served him his food; and after he finished eating; he asked, "How did I do?" And I replied, "You did pretty good. I would give you an A-." Dr. Mays said, "Give the food back to me. I want to make Phi Beta Kappa," and he finished all of his meal.[25]

Mays's secretary, Sally Warner, described him as precise and orderly. Some have said Mays paid close attention to picayune details. Hugh Gloster said, Mays could be counted on to dot every "i" and cross every "t." Mays was also a very cautious man as observed by James Edward Haines Jr. a student driver for Mays during his years at Morehouse. Haines said that the brake pedal in Mays's car was badly woven, almost to the metal. The reason for this was that Mays drove with his left foot constantly on the brake and his right foot on the gas. The objective was to be in constant control at all times.

Mays was a rebel by nature and circumstance as revealed in his *Pittsburgh Courier* articles. He sought the unity of all Christians in love as one body in Christ, not a disunity based on economics, education, gender, nationality, race, religion, or region. A headline in the national edition of the *Pittsburgh Courier* on August 5, 1950 read, "Dr. Benjamin Mays Heads Attack on Bias in Churches." B. H. Logan reported that at the eighth session of the Baptist World Alliance meeting in Cleveland, Ohio, Mays

---

[25]Sylvia F. Cook, "Memories of Dr. Benjamin E. Mays" in *Walking Integrity*, 495.

chaired the Commission on Social Justice calling for the removal from their worship and fellowship all forms of segregation and discrimination. The Mays resolution differed from previous resolutions where "it added that discrimination based on religion, culture, color and race provides fertile soil for the development and spread of communism, fascism, and other anti-social programs."[26]

Meeting in the mammoth lakefront stadium, with a 4,000-voice choir, 50,000 Baptists from forty-eight nations, including 5,000 Negro delegates, heard the Morehouse College president emphasizing the points of the resolution in an address, "Christian Light on Human Relationships." Logan wrote that Mays's address was rated as one of the most brilliantly delivered of the six-day gathering.

In what would please scholar Cornel West, Mays avoided the hopeless nihilism that pervades contemporary black life. He began his autobiography, *Born to Rebel* with one of his earliest childhood memories, an incident particularly meaningful in light of his later status in the world community. He recounts,

> I remember a crowd of white men who rode up on horseback with rifles on their shoulders. I was with my father when they rode up and I remember starting to cry. They cursed my father, drew their guns and made him salute, made him take off his hat and bow down to them several times. They rode away. I was not yet five years old, but I have never forgotten them . . .That mob is my earliest memory.[27]

Early in life young Bennie realized that academic degrees or popular acclaim were empty and short-lived if one is made to submit to those unworthy of respect. It is surprising, considering what Mays lived through, that he remained all his life a man of character, civility, and compassion, who retained warmth for the white race, while never losing sight of the ever-present gulfs of despair in both this nation and the world. The potential of all races in these United States will be helped by the example of this

---

[26]B. H. Logan, "Dr. Benjamin Mays Heads Attack on Bias in Churches" in *Pittsburgh Courier* (August 5, 1950).
[27]Mays, *Born to Rebel*, 1.

extraordinary man, "born to rebel."

END OF HIS TENURE

Mays stood before a capacity crowd in the Archer Gymnasium on 18 February 1967 for the Centennial Convocation. He had himself dedicated this gym with the financial help of many alumni, including Martin Luther King Jr., in 1956. The audience included 329 representatives from colleges and universities, 37 from various learned societies, and 24 from foundations, corporations and government agencies. Some 306 institutions sent greetings and certificates. In his convocation statement, titled, "Et Facta Est Lux," the College motto, Mays described the founding of the College in Augusta, Georgia and its achievement in a segregated century as "tantamount to a miracle" and "an act of God." He then announced, "But we are not naïve. We know that despite the record of a hundred years, there are those who think of the predominantly Negro colleges as being good enough for Negroes in a segregated century but not good enough for people in a desegregated century." Seven sentences later Mays declared:

> If Morehouse is not good enough to educate all the people, it is not good enough to educate Negroes. We make no apology for what we have been in the first century and we make no apology for what we aspire to be in the second century—a college serving all students irrespective of class, race, culture, religion, and nationality. So as we move into the second century, we go with faith, fortitude, hope and determination that the second century will be more glorious than the first.[28]

Three months later on Tuesday, May 30, 1967, in the third and final Centennial Convocation, Mays stood for the first time hoodless before a Morehouse College Commencement to deliver the keynote address and receive an honorary Doctor of Humane Letters from the school he had led for twenty-seven years. His commencement address was titled "Twenty-

---

[28]Jones, ed., "Dr. Mays' Centennial Convocation Statement 'Et Facta Est Lux'," *The Alumnus*, Morehouse College Bulletin, 36 (Spring 1967): 60.

Seven Years of Success and Failure at Morehouse." In the first paragraph Mays said, "When Morehouse was founded in 1867, virtually all of science, religion, and statesmanship were speaking with an unanimous voice declaring that the newly emancipated people were a little less than human."[29]

Using his debater's style, the Morehouse president marshaled fourteen powerful "authorities" throughout American history who shared this view. He then concluded: ". . . how fallible, how finite, and how wrong the most brilliant mind can be when it plays the role of God and speaks ex-cathedra about the future of Man.

Implying that his 1940 arrival at Morehouse was like a wedding ceremony, Mays told his audience that he had kept his vow, and that after twenty-seven years at the helm he had not cheated. "No dishonesty is so reprehensible as that dishonesty where one cheats on a job when great responsibility has been placed on his shoulders. Listing eight successes and nine failures was the heart of Mays's self assessment. The successes included: (1) Enrollment increased by 300 percent, from 358 to 962. (2) The number of students going on to graduate and professional schools increased to 56 percent, at 34 universities. (3) Faculty holding the Ph.D. degree increased from two in 1940 to thirty-four out of sixty-five full-time teachers, or a 52.3 percent rise. The Morehouse percentage of doctorates exceeded the percentage of doctorates at Albion, Allegheny, Bates, Colby, Cornell in Iowa, Kalamazoo, and Lawrence College, and equaled the percentage at Bowdoin and Earlham. Mays's point in citing these statistics is that less training does not make one a better teacher nor a more honest person. "There is no virtue in an academically weak faculty." (4) The physical plant was enlarged since 1940 in housing, worship and academic facilities from eight to twenty-five buildings. (5) The land areas increased from 10.6910 to 20.1771 acres. The additional 9.4861 acres cost the College $379,444 or $40,000 per acre. (6) The endowment increased from $1,114,000 to $4,500,000. (7) The lowest salary was six and two-thirds times greater than it was in 1940-41. (7) Mays played a large role in the founding of the Interdenominational Theological Center.

For twenty-seven out of a 100 years Mays and Morehouse had tried to develop a free man in a racially circumscribed nation. The College's first

---

[29]Program, Morehouse College Commencement 1998, 29.

Ph.D. president stated the school's pedagogy:

> The Morehouse philosophy was and is that a man does not have to
> accept the view that because he is a Negro certain things were not
> meant for him. He can be free in a highly segregated society. Long
> before demonstrations and Supreme Court decisions abolished
> segregation, the Morehouse students were taught to accept no
> segregated situation except that which was absolutely necessary; and
> that though their bodies were segregated, their minds could be free.
> Students who broke faith with this principle and went to segregated
> theaters, restaurants, and Churches went there without administra-
> tive sanction.... The philosophy drilled into them [Morehouse
> graduates] [is] that the Morehouse man can succeed in the world
> despite crippling circumstances under which he had to live.
> Morehouse was built on the faith of Negroes and a few white leaders
> like Joseph T. Robert, Morehouse's first president, a South
> Carolinian, who went North rather than rear his children in a land
> of slaves.

Mays also had some failures. (1) His naïveté in believing that he could
create a scholarly atmosphere at Morehouse within ten years so strong that
the desire to pursue excellence should be so contagious that most of the
students would pursue excellence and those without purpose could not
survive. (2) Mays also believed that by moving the College forward he could
raise the percentage of alumni givers to fifty percent. (3) He failed in his
attempt to get someone to head a campaign for a million dollars in
recognition of Morehouse's centennial anniversary. (4) The effort to get the
historically black colleges of Atlanta recognized by whites as significant
employers and financial contributors to the health of the city and the South
failed. (5) He said, "We believed when we came that each and every person
would do his work so well that constant follow-up would be unnecessary. It
isn't so." (6) Mays concluded that the Morehouse faculty was a very able,
but educationally conservative and afraid of experimentation. (7) The last
failure Mays listed was his failure to communicate in a lonely presidency his
dreams and aspirations for Morehouse to the lovely, loyal and devoted
faculty, students, trustees and alumni.

It was clear to Mays that the private and public power structures in economics, education, and politics never intended to make schools for African Americans first-rate. He felt the future of the College would depend on two things, the ability of the institution to "buy" the intellectually talented students, and on whether or not the alumni cared.

On May 31, 1967, the Atlanta Alumni honored Mays and his wife Sadie Gray Mays at a banquet in the Grand Ballroom of the Marriott Motor Hotel before 1,000 enthusiastic, formally garbed admirers. Each paid $10.00 a plate to hear tributes to the Mayses from a host of dignitaries.

Ivan Allen Jr. called Mays one of Atlanta's truly great all-time citizens. John Wheeler described Mays as a distinguished citizen of the world who could never have attained the remarkable success in building Morehouse without his high standard of personal integrity and inner strengths in times of crisis. Lucius Tobin, professor and Mays's pastor at the Providence Baptist Church, speaking for the faculty,

> Mays has been the protector of academic freedom. We were given the freedom to teach the truth as we understood it. Freedom is so precious and so vulnerable in this provincial Southland, in this country of mass hysteria and thought control. . . . There never was any attempt to curtail this freedom and justify the treason because of pecuniary needs of the institution... Dr. Mays never sat uncomfortable on the moral fence. . . . Fidelity to religion does not require surrender of critical intelligence. We were admonished to maintain the dialectic between the community of faith and the community of learning. Dr. Mays knew how easily teachers and professors become 'prisoners of procedures; victims of arteriosclerosis.' Nothing is worse than the 'hardening of the categories.' We were admonish to be creative without being dictatorial, forceful without the misuse of power of someone who did not want to change, it has been said, "the skirt of his personality is so short that his erudition is indecently exposed.[30]

Upon his retirement, the trustees honored him by permitting Mays to choose his own successor. He chose his former faculty member, editor of his

---

[30]Ibid., 37-38.

speeches, articles, and the College's *Alumnus* magazine, a powerful fund-raiser and textbook author, alumnus Hugh Morris Gloster '31. A summa cum laude, Phi Beta Kappa, Fulbright Scholar, Ph.D. from New York University, Gloster had formerly served as dean of faculty at Hampton University, where he had raised twenty-one million dollars. Gloster was also the founder of the College Language Association and its journal. As president of Morehouse he would sextuple the endowment, found the Morehouse School of Medicine, the Martin Luther King Jr. International Chapel, and raise one hundred and thirty million dollars in twenty years.

It had been agreed for some time that if Martin Luther King Jr. predeceased Mays, the latter would do King's eulogy and vice versa. The funeral procession marched four miles through the streets of Atlanta from Ebenezer Baptist Church to the Morehouse campus. Mays stood to speak before an estimated crowd of one-hundred and fifty thousand. He stood on a $16,000.00 platform, anonymously given by Robert Woodruff, President and CEO of Coca-Cola. In his weekly *Pittsburgh Courier* article, April 27, 1968, "They Came From Everywhere," Mays described the crowd before him as including White House staff, Supreme Court justices, and dignitaries from all over the world. In his eulogy Mays poignantly dramatized a potent need for justice. He remarked,

> The Memphis officials must bear some of the guilt for Martin Luther's assassination. The strike should have been settled several weeks ago. The lowest paid men in our society should not have to strike for a more just wage. A century after Emancipation, and after the enactment of the 13th, 14th, and 15th Amendments, it should not have been necessary for Martin Luther King Jr. to stage marches in Montgomery, Birmingham, and Selma, and to go to jail thirty times trying to achieve for his people those rights which people of lighter hue get by virtue of their being born white. We, too, are guilty of murder. It is time for the American people to repent and make democracy equally applicable to all Americans. We, and not the assassin, represent America at its best. We have the power . . . to make things right.[31]

---

[31]Mays, *Disturbed About Man*, 14-15.

CONCLUSION

The universal admiration which Mays commanded was easily seen in the politicians who often rushed to stand next to him to be photographed. Twice I saw Mays, in the early 1980s, enter the great nave of the Martin Luther King Jr. International Chapel unescorted and late for Baccalaureate and Commencement, aided only by a walking cane: once, while the Morehouse Glee Club was singing and a second when Hugh M. Gloster was presiding at the lectern. When Mays came into full view of the audience, a spontaneous standing ovation of 2,500 people interrupted the proceedings, continuing until Mays took his seat. He smilingly acknowledged the applause by waving his cane.

On Mays's final day before the National Baptist Convention, USA Inc. in the Los Angeles Coliseum in September 1983, President T. J. Jemison, the son of D.V. Jemison, introduced him by saying, "My brothers and sisters, it is my privilege to present to you the greatest teacher Black Baptists have ever produced . . ." Before Jemison could complete the sentence, twenty thousand Baptists jumped to their feet waving white handkerchiefs and screaming, "Dr. Mays, Dr. Mays, Dr. Mays…!" It was one of the most inspiring days of the author's life, as I and a great host of Morehouse College alumni clergy wheeled Mays down the great center aisle of The Coliseum.

The Ninety-eighth Congress voted in 1983 to recommend to President Ronald Reagan that the highest civilian medal of the United States, the Medal of Freedom, be conferred on Mays. Reagan refused to sign House Resolution 17 recommending The Presidential Medal of Freedom for Benjamin Elijah Mays that had been sponsored on Monday, January 3, 1983, by the Honorable Wyche Fowler Jr. of Georgia, the Honorable Julian C. Dixon of California, and the Honorable Paul Simon of Illinois.

Mays received 55 honorary degrees in his lifetime, and his fifty-sixth degree posthumously, from Columbia University. Butler Henderson received this degree on behalf of Mays. Seven academic buildings and an Atlanta street are named in Mays's honor. Mays received over 500 awards and honors in his lifetime, and died March 28, 1984, at 7:30 a.m. in the Hugh Spaulding Hospital at the age of eighty-nine, lauded as the first citizen of Atlanta. His body lay in state at Danforth Chapel at Morehouse, the Providence Baptist Church, his home Church, and the King Chapel.

Mays's funeral was held in the Martin Luther King Jr. International Chapel on the Morehouse College campus on a rainy day before a capacity congregation of over 2,600 persons. William V. Guy presided over the solemn service. Among the eleven speakers were former President of the United States, Jimmy Carter, and Samuel DuBois Cook, '48, President of Dillard University, who delivered the eulogy. Mays's funeral program consisted of five printed pages—the cover, the order of the service, two hymns, and a listing of the active and honorary pallbearers and honor guard. There was not one line of biography.

Mays was buried in the Southview Cemetery next to his wife, Sadie, in a white, Georgia marble crypt they both selected. In further recognition, Mays and his wife Sadie, were disinterred from the Southview Cemetery in Atlanta and reinterred on the Morehouse College campus Monday, May 15, 1995. The epitaph on the Mays's crypt reads as follows:

MAYS

Benjamin Elijah	Sadie Gray
August 1, 1894	August 5, 1900
March 28, 1984	October 11, 1969
Born to Rebel Against Ignorance, Oppression and Social Injustice	She Had Special Concern for the Young, the aged, the disadvantaged, the poor. She did what she could to help them.

The Thurman and Mays international campus memorials are not unlike those at Stanford University, Duke University, Tuskegee University, the University of Illinois, Benedict College, Talladega College, Clark Atlanta University, Georgetown University, and Boston University, where deceased academicians are buried on campus.

In addition, returning the remains of Hope, Thurman, and Mays to the Morehouse campus recalls an ancient African view of human existence that is expressed in the simple words, "Let the circle be unbroken." There is also a Biblical precedent recorded in Genesis

50:25; "And Joseph took an oath of the children of Israel, saying, God will surely visit you, and ye shall carry up my bones from hence.' " (KJV)

Congressman John Lewis of Georgia is leading the sponsorship of a commemorative stamp honoring Mays by the United States Postal Service with more than 75 Congressional sponsors in the United States House of Representatives.

Mays built fourteen buildings at Morehouse, but he was not known as a builder of buildings. He raised millions of dollars, but he was not known as a fund-raiser. Like his mentors, Mays was an eloquent motivator who gave strong challenges. These qualities have made him legendary.

2

"Born to Rebel"

Orville Vernon Burton

The afterglow of Reconstruction had almost faded by 1894. In that year Benjamin Elijah Mays was born, about four miles from the crossroads settlement of Rambo (now Epworth) and ten miles from the village of Ninety Six, South Carolina. The rights of blacks—especially the precious right to vote—had been seriously curtailed, although two African Americans sat in the General Assembly and one represented the state in Congress. Some thirty years after the Civil War, most blacks in the South depended on white landowners for employment as sharecroppers, tenant farmers, and wage laborers. The chains of racial segregation were fastened more securely each year. In these difficult circumstances Mays, the youngest of eight children of former slaves, distinguished himself as a preacher, teacher, administrator, scholar, author, newspaper columnist, civil rights activist, and presidential adviser.

Mays was tirelessly active in important organizations and movements that exemplify changes in the South from the turn of the century until his death in 1984. He was coauthor of the influential 1942 Durham statement, which initiated a series of discussions resulting in formation of the Southern Regional Council. He served as vice-president and on the Board of Directors of the National Association for the Advancement of Colored People and became a member of the Committee of 100, which formed and supported the more activist NAACP Legal Defense and Education Fund. Mays served on the executive committees of the International Young Men's Christian Association and of the World Council of Churches, as president of the United Negro College Fund and of the Atlanta School Board, and as chairman of the National Sharecroppers and Rural Advancement Fund. He was a guiding force in the Urban League and a host of other social justice and liberal organizations, such as the Southern Conference for Human Welfare, the American Crusade to End Lynching, the Southern Conference Educational Fund, Civil Rights Congresses, and the Peace

Corps Advisory Committee.

In his best-known role, as president of Morehouse College from 1940 to 1967, Dr. Mays transformed a struggling black college into perhaps the most prestigious African-American institution of higher learning. In that office he trained and inspired a brilliant cluster of leaders, of whom Martin Luther King Jr. was the shining star. Mays not only lived to see the "Second Reconstruction," the civil rights movement of the 1950s and 1960s, he also launched and sustained it. A 1971 article in the *Harvard Theological Review* pronounced Mays one of three "outstanding Black clergyman who have exerted a tremendous impact upon American life."[1]

Mays's distinguished career was a continuing response to the black southern experience; the early years of his rural life paralleled that of many black youths who grew up the children of tenant farmers. Born during the heyday of "Pitchfork Ben" Tillman, Mays was a year old when South Carolina's constitution disfranchised African Americans. The following year, in *Plessy v. Ferguson*, the Supreme Court of the United States declared segregation legal. Mays's earliest memory was an encounter with whites in the Phoenix Riot of 1898. A group of armed vigilantes galloped up and cursed his father, making him salute, remove his hat, and bow. In 1901, when Mays was seven years old, Booker T. Washington dined with President Theodore Roosevelt in the White House, and South Carolina Senator Benjamin R. Tillman raged, "The action of President Roosevelt in entertaining that nigger will necessitate our killing a thousand niggers in the South before they will learn their place again." In 1909, when the NAACP was founded, Ben Mays was fifteen years old and had never received more than three to four months of schooling in any one year. At the Epworth post office in 1915—the year of Booker T. Washington's death—a white doctor cursed and struck Mays because he was dressed in clean, neat clothes, and stood tall with pride. That summer Mays became a Pullman porter and learned about Yankee racism: he bought a drink in Detroit, and when he

---

[1]Richard I. McKinney, "The Black Church: Its Development and Present Impact," *Harvard Theological Review* 64, 4(October 1971): 477; Doris Levy Gavins, "The Ceremonial Speaking of Benjamin Elijah Mays: Spokesman for Social Change, 1954-1975" (Ph.D. diss.,Louisiana State University, 1978), 185. Quotations and information derived from *Born to Rebel* are not cited.

returned the glass from which he had drunk, the white waiter smashed it.

During World War I African Americans fought to make the world safe for democracy even though they could not vote in the American South. Ben Mays registered for the draft, but, determined to finish his college degree, he informed authorities that he was studying for the ministry. Mays also expanded his theology to include some of the ideas of Eugene V. Debs, president of the American Railway Union and organizer of the Social Democratic party of America. Debs was in prison for his defense of those charged with sedition in World War I. Mays explained,

> I'm deeply impressed with the words of Eugene Debs writing while a prisoner in a federal prison in Atlanta. These are the words: "As long as there is a lower class, I'm in it. As long as there is a man in jail, I'm not free." Eugene Debs inspired me greatly. To me, Eugene Debs has shaped my sensitivity for the poor, the diseased and those who have given their lives for the good of those sick and poor, the great and the small, the high and the low.[2]

Red scares and lynchings followed the wave of racial hatred that accompanied the beginnings of the great black migration after World War I, when blacks moved from the farms to the cities, especially the northern cities. While farm-reared Benjamin Mays was residing in Richmond, Lewiston, Chicago, Tampa, and Atlanta, Marcus Garvey's Universal Negro Improvement Association's Back to Africa movement caught the attention of many African Americans. Mays, however, became more committed to Christianity and to expanding democracy to include blacks in America. By the 1929 economic crash and the Harlem Renaissance's urban "New Negro," Benjamin Mays had published "The New Negro Challenges the Old Order," an article about South Carolina's primarily rural race relations. As historian I. A. Newby wrote, "One of the New Negroes was Benjamin E. Mays." In 1926, speaking at Benedict College, Mays announced, "I cannot

---

[2]Editorial, *The Colored American*, November 1901, 78; Donald Norton Brown, "Southern Attitudes Toward Negro Voting in the Bourbon Period, 1877-1890" (Ph.D. diss., University of Oklahoma, 1960), 151; Mays, Address at the Ceremony Dedicating the Historic Marker at Mays Crossroads near Mays's Birthplace, Epworth, SC, November 7, 1981, 5.

and I would not apologize for being a Negro. We have a great history; we have a greater future. . . . we have a rendezvous with America." He continued, "I will live in vain, if I do not live and so act that you will be freer than I am—freer intellectually, freer politically, and freer economically." Mays implored the students: "Seek to serve your state, not as a Negro but as a man. Aspire to be great—not among Negroes, but among men! God knows I want to be a great teacher. I want no racial adjective modifying it. I want to preach the gospel of peace, good will, justice, and brotherhood—not to Negroes and for Negroes, but to men and for men." The editor who reported the speech added, "There was terrific applause following Mr. Mays' address but, outside, the Editor heard a representative of the 'Old Negro' saying: 'The young man has much to learn: he is quite radical.' "[3]

As the depression destroyed the tenant-farming economy of millions of African Americans, Mays grappled with the effects of poverty and discrimination in a southern city and researched the meaning of the African-American experience through the black church. During World War II, when blacks were again asked to die for American democracy, Mays, by that time president of Morehouse College, searched for a way to save his school, whose enrollments were depleted by the draft. In 1948 Mays got philanthropic support for a program to allow gifted high school students to enter Morehouse as freshmen.

After World War II, when America became obsessed with communism and McCarthyism, Mays spoke out bravely and forthrightly about the injustices in American society. "For us in the South, the maintenance of segregation is more important than democracy; than the Christian religion; than, I was almost about to say, than keeping communism out of the country. I dare say a vast majority in the South would have preferred a Hitler victory to the elimination of segregation." In the 1940s and 1950s, when prejudice was ingrained in churches throughout the country, Mays, the first black to serve as vice-president of the Federal (now the National)

---

[3]I. A. Newby *Black Carolinians: A History of Blacks in South Carolina from 1895 to 1968*, Tricentennial Studies, No.6 (Columbia: University of South Carolina Press, 1973), 232-34; Mays, "The New Negro Challenges the Old Order" and "Address Delivered at Older Boys' Conference, Benedict College, February 26, 1926," both in Asa H. Gordon, *Sketches of Negro Life and History in South Carolina* (1929; reprint, Columbia: University of South Carolina Press, 1971), 192-212.

Council of Churches, cried out for integration and justice. Speaking at the World Council of Churches' Assembly in 1954, he warned, "It will be a sad commentary on our life and time if future historians can write that the last bulwark of segregation based on race and color was God's church."

After the Supreme Court ruled against segregated schooling in *Brown v. Board of Education,* the Southern Historical Association in 1955 asked Mays to present his views on the recent decision. Mays took the opportunity to speak on "The Moral Aspects of Segregation." He told the historians:

> No group is wise enough, good enough, strong enough to assume an omnipotent and omniscient role. . . . To do that is blasphemy. It is a usurpation of the role of God. . . . We are morally obligated to abolish legalized segregation in America, or reinterpret the Christian Gospel, the Old and New Testaments, and make the Gospel say the noble principles of Judaism and Christianity are not applicable to colored peoples and Negroes. Tell the world honestly and plainly that the Fatherhood of God and the Brotherhood of Man cannot work where the colored races are involved. Make no mistake—as this country could not exist half slave and half free, it cannot exist half segregated and half desegregated. If we lose this battle for freedom for 16 million Negroes, we will lose it for 145 million whites and eventually we will lose it for the world. This is indeed a time for greatness.[4]

In the 1960s, when African Americans protested their lack of civil rights in the American South, Mays was consulted as a longtime leader in the fight against segregation. By 1977 Mays was an adviser and confidant to President Jimmy Carter, a fellow southerner and a born-again Baptist with whom Mays felt a spiritual kinship. Mays reflected, "How can you explain Jimmy Carter? God must have sent him." Mays believed Carter did more for civil rights than any other president, particularly in appointing forty-one blacks to the federal courts. President Carter described Mays as

---

[4]*Columbia Record,* 3 May 1949, 1, 4; *Editorial Reprints from the Petal Papers* and personal comments by P. D. East, editor (Petal, MS); James W. Silver, "The Twenty-First Annual Meeting," *Journal of Southern History* 22 (February 1956): 61.

"my personal friend, my constructive critic, and my close advisor."[5]

Just as events influenced Mays, so did Mays influence events. Leading in the struggles against segregation, actively involved in the civil rights movement, writing a weekly newspaper column, pioneering in African-American scholarship and education, presiding over the desegregation of Atlanta's public schools, Benjamin Mays helped inaugurate a new era of race relations. Lerone Bennett Jr., in a tribute entitled "The Last of the Great Schoolmasters," aptly labeled Mays the vanguard of the civil rights movement. He was one of the African Americans who were "bold enough, wise enough, and selfless enough to assume the awesome responsibility" of bridging the gap between the first Reconstruction and the second. According to Bennett, "None tilled more ground or harvested a more bountiful crop than Benjamin Elijah Mays, a lean, beautifully-black preacher-prophet who served as Schoolmaster of the Movement."[6]

In this age of the antihero, it is perhaps difficult to grasp fully the heroism of Mays's rebellion; it was a rebellion of poetic elegance, both pertinent and passionate. According to Mays's former student Samuel DuBois Cook, former president of Dillard University, Mays understood that "the heart of the ethical consciousness is the cry of the human heart and soul for something better, nobler, higher, and richer." Mays was "a philosopher of the heroic life. The heroic life is defined in moral, religious, intellectual, humanistic and institutional terms." Heroism demands tough choices, and Mays once said, "I would rather go to hell by choice than to stumble into heaven by following the crowd." Charles V. Willie, a professor of education and urban studies at Harvard University and a former student of Mays, explained that Mays had found satisfaction in a life where he responded effectively to constant challenges; for Mays, to live was to struggle. Writing about the endemic racism in white society in 1977, Willie drew upon the theory of the social philosopher Rene DuBos and the example of Benjamin E. Mays. According to DuBos's theory, society needs rebels who become the "standard bearer of the visionaries who gradually increase man's ethical stature"; rebels provide "hope that our societies can be saved."

---

[5]Mays, Address at Epworth, November 17, 1981, 5; Remarks by Senator John Drummond, Mt. Zion Baptist Church, Greenwood, SC, April 1, 1984, 2-3.

[6]Lerone Bennett Jr., "The Last of the Great Schoolmasters," *Ebony* 32 (December 1977):74-79.

Willie argues that this is why the redoubtable fighter Mays entitled his life story *Born to Rebel*.[7]

Though Mays's mother could not read, she instilled in her son the belief that he was inferior to no one. As Mays grew older he fortified that belief with the strength of his religious convictions and education. His travels exposed him to a cosmopolitan view of race relations. So vehement was his conviction that white and blacks were equal that he startled some African Americans who had been degraded by segregation. He understood issues and struggles on the grand moral plane, but the beauty of his life was that he immediately applied his principles to everyday problems. He lived in a segregated society, but he refused to support or be a part of segregation. He climbed stairs rather than ride a segregated elevator; he walked rather than support a segregated mass-transit system.

Born to Rebel contains an abundance of historical material about the values and culture of rural South Carolina. Chronicling his life until 1970 and offering a commentary on race relations in America, his autobiography is an important story of the black experience in America, and a significant component of the American experience as well. The *Presbyterian Survey's* assessment of Mays in 1954 applies to his autobiography also: "No one has more right to speak on race than Dr. Benjamin Mays. . . . because of his own integrity and understanding, ... no one . . . says it with the simplicity and effectiveness with which Dr. Mays speaks." *Born to Rebel* provides a vivid glimpse of twentieth-century history from the African-American perspective, too often ignored or incorrectly interpreted in history books. Mays's life provides insight into the transitional years from Booker T. Washington's accommodationist philosophy to the Black Power radicalism of the late 1960s and early 1970s.[8]

All his life he felt cheated by the lack of opportunities for schooling and the constant reminders of his second-class citizenship. To understand Mays one must understand the different perspectives of African Americans and

---

[7]Samuel DuBois Cook, Introduction to *Quotable Quotes of Benjamin E. Mays*, by Benjamin E. Mays (New York: Vantage, 1983), xviii; Charles V. Willie, *Black/Brown/White Relations* (New Brunswick, NJ: Transaction Books, 1977), 214.

[8]Rachael Hende, *Presbyterian Survey*, June 1957, photocopy in Benjamin E. Mays file, South Caroliniana Library, University of South Carolina, Columbia, SC (hereinafter cited as SCL).

whites on the history of South Carolina. I. A. Newby, in *Black Carolinians*, explained:

> To white Carolinians from Calhoun to Strom Thurmond states'
> rights and "local self-government" were rallying cries against
> tyranny and synonyms for individual liberty and local democracy.
> To blacks they were code words for white authoritarianism, the very
> existence of which depended upon denying liberty and local
> democracy to blacks. . . . Tillmanism is the nearest thing to a
> genuine mass movement in the history of white Carolina, and
> whites in the state paid homage to it for over a generation. To
> students of black history and racial equality its most striking
> features are the extent to which it expressed the desire of white
> Carolinians to dominate blacks and the fact that much of its unity
> and force derived from its antiblack racial policies.

Newby elaborated:

> The central fact in the history of black Carolina has been the
> racism of white Carolina. Black Carolinians have been black folk in
> a society dominated by whites. Race was the criterion used to
> identify them, define their role, restrict their advancement, thwart
> their hope, limit their horizons. Their society isolated them as a
> racial group, educated (or failed to educate) them as a racial group,
> worked them as a racial group, exploited them as a racial group.[9]

From slavery to the more subtle institutional racism of the present day, scholars have found that South Carolina politics has chiefly revolved around the issue of the status of black people, and ever present in antebellum South Carolina was the fear of a black revolt. Fearful that political conflict would somehow undermine slavery, South Carolina had a less democratic form of government than any state in the union. Candidates for the legislature had to own property. White citizens could not vote directly for president, governor, or United States senator; and blacks could not vote at all. South

---

[9]*Black Carolinians*, 12, 15-16.

Carolina was the hotbed of nullification, "fire-eaters," and secession. Even after the Civil War the fear of black insurgency continued to dictate. Reconstruction and Redemption set the stage for Mays's life. The first South Carolina constituti nal convention of Reconstruction, held in 1865, opposed extending the franchise to African Americans. "This is a white man's government," Governor Benjamin F. Perry asserted, "and intended for white men only." The South Carolina legislature also introduced a "Black Code," which imposed on African Americans a condition as close to slavery as was possible after emancipation.[10]

In response to the notorious black codes and to the terrorism accompanying the first year of emancipation Congress enacted the Civil Rights Act of 1866. Under military supervision South Carolina convened its second constitutional convention of Reconstruction in November 1867. More than half the delegates, 76 of 124, were African Americans. The new constitution gave the right to vote to every male resident of South Carolina twenty-one years of age or older "without distinction of race, color, or former condition."[11]

If Reconstruction could have succeeded anywhere, it was in South Carolina. Blacks formed a majority of the population, and Reconstruction lasted longer than in most southern states. Public education from primary level to college was suddenly opened to former slaves; blacks served in nearly every office at county and state levels (except for the governorship); blacks won half the seats of the lower house of the General Assembly and held a majority in the House for six years (longer than in any state at any time in American history), although never a majority in the Senate; and more land was distributed to former slaves than in any other state. From 1868 to 1877, eight blacks were elected to Congress and two became lieutenant

---

[10]"Speech of B. F. Perry," *Journal of the People of South Carolina, Held in Columbia, South Carolina, September 1865*, (Columbia: Julian A. Selby, 1865), 14; South Carolina, *Constitution of 1865*, art.1, sec.14, and art. 4; SC, *Laws*, 1865, 271, 276, 293, 295-296, 299, 303-304. My discussion of discrimination and the history of voter dilution draws heavily upon Laughlin McDonald, "An Aristocracy of Voters: The Disfranchisement of Blacks in South Carolina," *South Carolina Law Review* 37 (Summer 1986): 557-582, and upon unpublished testimony in voter-dilution trials given by expert witnesses J. Morgan Kousser and Peyton McCrary.

[11]U.S., 14 *Stat.*, 27, 428, 15 *Stat.* 2, 14, 41; *The Constitution of South Carolina, Adopted April 16, 1868* (Columbia: John W. Denny, 1868).

governor. African Americans served on the South Carolina Supreme Court and as secretary of state, adjutant general, secretary of the treasury, Speaker of the House, and president pro tem of the senate. At the local level, blacks were state representatives, sheriffs, probate judges, magistrates, postmasters, and school commissioners. All of this occurred, however, because federal troops were enforcing federal laws. During Reconstruction South Carolina experimented briefly with idealism in the form of interracial democracy and responsive government, but most whites preferred racial discrimination, low taxes, and few government services.

Because white South Carolinians were never willing to share citizenship, let alone political power, with African Americans, violence accompanied Reconstruction. The Ku Klux Klan, active at least as early as the 1868 election, violently opposed black enfranchisement, and systematic terror reached a new intensity during the critical 1876 election. Even with federal troops in the state, Martin Witherspoon Gary coordinated a campaign of terror to "redeem" the state and return it to the orthodox conservative white leadership that had governed South Carolina before the Civil War. Massacres throughout the state reflected the principles expressed in the twelfth and sixteenth points of Gary's "Edgefield Plan":

12. Every Democrat must feel honor bound to control the vote of at least one negro, by intimidation, purchase, keeping him away as each individual may determine, how he may best accomplish it.

16. Never threaten a man individually—if he deserves to be threatened the necessities of the times require that he should die.

Cold-blooded executions were common. As Benjamin Tillman later explained, "The struggle in which we were engaged meant more than life or death. It involved everything we held dear, Anglo-Saxon civilization included.[12]

Redemption put the "moderate" Democrat Wade Hampton in the governor's office. Moderation meant that he preferred fraud and intimida-

---

[12]"Plan of the Campaign of 1876," in the papers of Martin Witherspoon Gary (SCL); Benjamin R. Tillman, "The Struggle of 1876: How South Carolina Was Delivered from Carpet-Bag and Negro Rule," speech at the Red-Shirt Reunion at Anderson, SC, 1909.

tion to meticulously planned multiple murders of African Americans. In 1878 Martin Witherspoon Gary explained: "We regard the issues between the white and colored people of the State, and of the entire South as an antagonism of race, not a difference of political party. . . . White supremacy is essential to our survival as a people." Gary proposed that African Americans be excluded from the political process by barring them from the Democratic party primary. Thus, the white primary was used informally after 1878 to resolve disagreements so that whites could present a united front to black foes in the general election. Because the Democratic primary was open only to whites from 1878 until 1944, it was the real election in most races. Blacks were effectively disfranchised for the next sixty-five years.[13]

In 1895 the state adopted Governor "Pitchfork Ben" Tillman's plan to disfranchise African-American citizens permanently. First the legislature passed a re-registration act that was carefully administered in a racially discriminatory manner to prevent blacks from defeating a call for a constitutional convention. The resulting 1895 constitution kept blacks from having any real influence in the electoral process by establishing a literacy (or property) test, a poll tax, and an understanding clause.[14] African Americans challenged both the literacy test and the poll tax that southern states enacted after Reconstruction, but the Supreme Court upheld both disfranchising tactics. The effect of disfranchising legislation was profound: only three thousand blacks, or 0.8 percent of voting-age African Americans

---

[13]*Charleston News and Courier*, 4 June 1878.

[14]David Duncan Wallace, *The South Carolina Constitution of 1895* (Columbia: Bureau of Publications, University of South Carolina, No. 197, February 15, 1927), 35; George Brown Tindall, "The Question of Race in the South Carolina Constitutional Convention of 1895," *Negro History Bulletin* 15 (January 1952); *Journal of the Constitutional Convention of the State of South Carolina* (Columbia: Charles A. Calvo Jr., 1895) 10 September 1895, 1-2; *Constitution of the State of South Carolina, Ratified in Convention, December 4, 1895* (Columbia: R. L. Bryan, 1909), especially art. 2, sec. 4; Susan Bowler and Frank T. Petrusak, "The Constitution of South Carolina: Historical and Political Perspective," in *Government in the Palmetto State*, edited by Luther F. Carter and Davis S. Mann (Columbia: Bureau of Governmental Research and Service, University of South Carolina, 1983), 27-44.

in South Carolina, were registered to vote in 1940.[15]

After *Smith v. Allwright* overturned the white primary in 1944, the Democratic party, which included practically all the white voters in South Carolina, organized itself into private clubs. African Americans could vote in primaries only if they swore to uphold separation of the races in education and society, if they took an oath that they believed in states' rights, and if they swore opposition to federal employment-discrimination laws. Judge J. Waites Waring, the aristocratic Charlestonian who had ruled against the white primary, declared the oath unconstitutional. Representative Mendel Rivers vilified Waring in Congress. "He is as cold as a dead Eskimo in an abandoned igloo. Lemon juice flows in his frigid and calculating veins. . . . Unless he is removed there will be bloodshed."[16]

In 1952 Waring (the first federal judge to rule against segregated schools) retired and left South Carolina for the more secure environs of New York City. Benjamin Mays, however, remained in the South, even though he received at least fourteen offers of prestigious and important jobs in the North, where "there was less segregation, where Negroes in the North thought they were free." He explained in 1957, "I stay in the South because I believe my best work can be done in the South. I plan to continue to live here." He stayed in the South marching forth from Morehouse's comfortable and protective walls of ivy into this hotbed of racism, and, like Daniel staring down the lions, he confronted an integrated South Carolina audience. "Inherent in segregation is injustice; inherent in segregation is inequality. Segregation says to every white child in the South 'there's a man

---

[15]James F. Byrnes to William Watts Ball, 18 January 1920, in the papers of William Watts Ball, Perkins Library, Duke University; Arnold Derfner,"Racial Discrimination and the Right to Vote," *Vanderbilt Law Review* 26, (1973): 523-584; Newby, 291.

[16]For details see V. O. Key, with the assistance of Alexander Herd, *Southern Politics in State and Nation* New York: Knopf, 1949), 130-55; Jack Bass and Walter DeVries, *The Transformation of Southern Politics: Social Change and Political Consequence Since 1945* (New York: Basic Books, 1976). Key entitled chapter 7 "South Carolina: The Politics of Color," and when Bass and DeVries updated Key, they called their South Carolina chapter "The Changing Politics of Color"; McDonald,"An Aristocracy of Voters," 573-576; U. S., 94th Congress, *Congressional Record, House*, 9, 752; *Charleston News and Courier*, 22 July 1948,1; Robert Lewis Terry, "J. Waites Waring, Spokesman for Racial Justice in the New South," (Ph.D. diss., University of Utah), 1970; S.C. *Journal of the House of Representatives*, 88th General Assembly of the State of South Carolina, 2d Session, H. B. 2177, 15 February 1950, 440.

you can kick around.'" In 1949 Mays called upon South Carolinians to "support the civil rights movement." He admonished, "We need to get rid of fears in the South. Fears of democracy and Christian religion. But we are a scared people. . . . We are scared to abolish segregation." The *Charleston News and Courier* complained that Mays was "inciting animosity of the rougher elements of the white population."[17]

Rougher elements made sure that racial violence did not cease. A gruesome measurement of racial terrorist activities is lynching. Twelve African Americans were lynched in South Carolina in 1889, eight in 1895, six in 1897, fourteen in 1898. In 1933 a black man, Bernie Thompson, was lynched in Mays's home town of Ninety Six. Writing about the lynching of a black man in Greenville, South Carolina in 1947, Rebecca West explained that some white southerners believed "that lynching is a social prophylactic." Table I summarizes the reported lynchings of blacks from 1882 to 1950 in states where Benjamin Mays had lived. Every black man knew that standing up to whites put life itself in jeopardy. Yet Mays, from the time he was a young man, proclaimed loudly and eloquently that African Americans should be, had to be, truly free and equal—that the pernicious institution of segregation, based on the implicit premise of black inferiority, must be destroyed.[18]

Mays's fearlessness freed him; he always spoke out forcefully against lynching and called for anti-lynching laws. In South Carolina he also attacked segregation and lynching. Legal segregation, he charged, was "worse than lynching. Segregation breeds lynching, injustice, and all kinds of discrimination . . . and advertises to the world that here is a group of people unfit to live as normal human beings." Moreover, he defiantly criticized southern politicians who claimed to oppose a federal anti-lynching law on the grounds that it interfered with states rights:

> If . . . men who filibuster on the floor of the Senate against Civil Rights are honest, let them come back to Georgia, South Carolina,

---

[17]Mays, Address at Epworth, SC, 17 November 1981, 6; Mays, "Full Implementation of Democracy," *New South* 12 (March 1957):10-12; *Columbia Record*, 3 May 1949, 1,4; *Charleston News and Courier*, 8 May 1949, 4.

[18]*New York Herald-Tribune*, 10 October 1933; Rebecca West, *A Train of Powder* (New York: Viking Press, 1955), 77.

Mississippi, Alabama, Virginia and let them stand up like men and say 'We don't want any federal anti-lynching bill. We'll have our own anti-lynching bill. We will abolish the poll tax. . . . We will do something about discrimination in employment," and I'll never believe they are honest until they do that.[19]

TABLE 1

Number of African Americans Lynched in States Where Mays Lived

Years	SC	GA	VA	FL	IL
1882 - 1903	109	241	70	115	10
1904 - 1908	14	52	4	13	2
1909 - 1913	18	75	2	44	4
1914 - 1918	10	79	4	23	2
1919 - 1923	10	58	3	34	0
1924 - 1927	4	5	2	18	1
1928 - 1932	3	8	0	6	0
1933 - 1937	3	13	0	8	0
1938 - 1942	1	6	0	7	0
1943 - 1946	lynchings not reported by state; total of 13				
1947 - 1950	1	2	0	0	0
Total	173	539	85	268	19

Source: Walter White, *Rope and Faggot: A Biography of Judge Lynch* (New York: Alfred A. Knopf, 1929), 254-258; Jack Simpson Mullins, "Lynchings in South Carolina, 1900-

---

[19]Bass and DeVries, 253; *Columbia Record*, 3 May 1949, 1,4.

1914" (M.A. thesis, University of South Carolina, 1961); Annual Report of the National Association for the Advancement of Colored People, each year has a different title (New York: NAACP, in named years). *Note:* Years are not equally grouped. No black was lynched in Maine from 1882 to 1950.

Governor Strom Thurmond declared in his 1948 acceptance of the Dixiecrat presidential nomination, "There are not enough laws on the books of the nation, nor can there be enough laws, to break down segregation in the South." When South Carolina gave her native son 72.1 percent of the vote in the presidential election that year, Mays warned, "Today the South worships at the shrine of segregation"; before democracy could be realized, southern whites had "to get a new God to worship."[20]

As long as segregationist politicians controlled the political processes, educational opportunities for African Americans were extremely limited. Mays summarized the situation: "We can never have justice in education under a segregation law." Discrimination in schooling was blatant. In his 1911 inaugural address Governor Cole Blease explained.

> I am in favor of building up the free school system so that every white child in South Carolina may be given a good common school education. . . . I am opposed to white people's taxes being used to educate Negroes. I am a friend of the Negro race. . . . The white people of the South are the best friends to the Negro race. In my opinion, when the people of this country began to try to educate the Negro they made a serious and grave mistake, and I fear the worst result is yet to come. So why continue?

In *Born to Rebel* Mays dwells on the lack of educational opportunities for African Americans in the South, opportunities that black Americans have always seen as especially important. African Americans yearned to read the Bible. They also valued literacy because it was closely associated with freedom. Education shows clearly and measurably how political discrimination affects people's lives. In Appendix A of *Born to Rebel*, in a section entitled "Discrimination with a Vengeance," Mays reviews the discriminatory funding for black and white children in the South. Table 2 shows the

---

[20]*Columbia Record*, 3 May 1949, 1,4.

expenditures of Mays's home county and of South Carolina in white-to-black ratios from 1896 to 1960, the last year for which figures for segregated expenditures were available.

In 1900, for example, the state of South Carolina spent 4.21 times more on each white child in school than on each black child. If the ratios had been calculated according to the proportion of total number of black and white children instead of by the number that attended school, the dis-

TABLE 2

Racial Discrimination Ratios of Educational Expenditures in Greenwood County and in South Carolina, 1896-1960

Year	Greenwood County	South Carolina
1896	—	1.2
1900	3.9	4.2
1901	27.0	4.3
1902	5.8	4.2
1903	4.3	4.2
1904	7.5	4.8
1905	7.2	4.3
1906	6.4	5.3
1907	7.9	5.0
1908	9.8	5.7
1909	3.4	6.1
1910	6.3	5.4
1915	7.2	8.7

1920	10.4	8.5
1925	11.7	8.4
1930	9.3	7.4
1935	6.2	5.0
1940	4.2	4.4
1945	3.4	3.2
1950	1.7	2.4
1955	1.2	1.6
1960	1.3	1.5

Source: Annual Reports of South Carolina Department of Education in named years.

Note: From 1901 to 1910 Mays was enrolled in Greenwood County schools. Ratios were obtained by dividing (total educational expenditures on whites divided by white public school average attendance) by (total educational expenditures on blacks divided by black public school average attendance). For a few years, enrollment figures had to be substituted for attendance. Every year was computed, but except for the years Mays was in Greenwood County public schools, I reported five year intervals. 1896 is the first year separate statistics for blacks and whites are available. Greenwood County's expenditures are first recorded in 1899. 1960 is the last year for which segregated expenditures are available.

crepancies would have been even greater. Ironically, in 1896, the year of *Plessy v. Ferguson*, the expenditures were less unequal than in later years. As the century progressed, the "separate but equal" system resulted in expenditures of more than eight times as much per white child as per black child in the state. During Mays's first year in the Greenwood County schools, the county spent only $6.29 for each white child attending school compared to 23 cents for each black child, a white-to-black expenditure ratio of twenty-seven to one! In the last year before segregated statistics (but not segregated schools) fell into disuse, half a decade after *Brown* had replaced *Plessy* as the governing constitutional law in the United States, the state still spent 50 percent more on each white pupil than on each black. A

large portion of the discrepancy was due to differences in teacher-pupil ratios
and teachers' salaries: black teachers were paid less than white teachers to
teach more children. The discrimination in the state's segregated institutions of higher education was even more flagrant.

Mays's life as a student and as an educator reflected the difficulties
inherent in a segregated society. In early twentieth-century upcountry South
Carolina, cotton regulated the rhythms of life. As tenant farmers, Mays's
family had to put picking cotton before schooling. School for blacks in the
Ninety Six area ran from November to February. At the age of fifteen Mays
left the neighborhood "Brickhouse" School (misnamed; it was clapboard)
and traveled twenty-four miles from home to the better Baptist association-
sponsored McCormick School; yet he still received only four months of
schooling each year. Two years later Mays entered the eighth grade at State
College, which was also a high school. The decision to transfer was not easy.
Mays's pastor and his teacher at McCormick wanted him to remain there to
help instruct the younger children, and his father was vehemently opposed
to his son's attending high school because he, like many farmers, believed
that too much education made people foolish and dishonest. The fare from
Ninety Six to State College at Orangeburg, 125 miles away, was three
dollars and five cents. With his mother's prayers and blessings, and a ten-
dollar bill his father had angrily thrown at him (ten dollars was a considerable sum for a black tenant farmer in 1909), Mays attended his first "real"
school. His brother sent what money he could spare and Mays worked his
way through school. He picked up paper on campus, worked as a janitor,
painted houses, washed dishes, and after midnight, when other students
slept, he cleaned outhouses. During his junior year, determined to continue
his education, Mays rebelled against his father's authority and did not go
home to help with the spring planting.

Mays was inspired by African-American teachers at State College.
When his math class had difficulty, Professor Nelson C. Nix challenged
them: "You boys can't work these problems? The white boys at the
University of South Carolina are eating these problems up!" Nix encour-
aged Mays and assured him that he knew as much as any white student, but
Mays craved the best education he could get; he needed to prove to himself
that he could compete with whites in education, an impossibility in the
South. Nix planted in Mays's mind the idea of graduate school at the
University of Chicago, and that idea took root.

Mays was twenty-one years old when he graduated from high school at State College. He tried to get into a northern college, but the best he could do was Virginia Union, another black school in Richmond. The following year Bates College accepted him. Mays was determined to go even though his friends, especially the Yankee Pullman porters, warned that he would freeze in Maine. While working his way through college, Mays, an honor student, won the sophomore declamation contest and was on the debate and football teams. Bates College did not emancipate Mays, he professed, but "it did the far greater service of making it possible for me to emancipate myself, to accept with dignity my own worth as a free man." At Bates, Mays made his first white friends.

After Bates, Mays applied to Newton Theological Seminary but was rejected because he was black. Instead, he attended the University of Chicago. The contrast between Chicago and Bates College was enormous. At Bates teachers had never refused to acknowledge their black students, and all restaurants served blacks; in Chicago most cafes near campus would not serve blacks, white students did not eat at the same tables with blacks, and some white teachers did not speak in public to their African-American students.

After only three semesters, John Hope, president of Morehouse, lured Mays away from Chicago to teach math and algebra at his college in Atlanta. After graduation from Bates, Mays had married Ellen Harvin, a schoolmate at State College, and Morehouse gave Mays the opportunity to be near his wife, who was teaching in South Carolina. Their time together was short, however; Ellen died in an Atlanta hospital less than two years after Benjamin had moved to Atlanta.

Mays began teaching math, psychology, and religion at Morehouse in 1921 and earned a reputation as a fair but demanding teacher. He accepted nothing less than a student's best effort, whether the student was an athlete or a member of the debating team (which he coached), light- or dark-skinned, from a deprived background as he had been or from the brown bourgeoisie.

As pastor of the small congregation of Shiloh Baptist Church, Mays also fought segregation from the pulpit. Working with people in his congregation kept him in touch with the lives of those African Americans who were not sheltered in the elite world of the college-educated. As a preacher, Mays had to speak their language. He was proud to be from the rural proletariat and never insulted their intelligence or underestimated them. His people were always part of his heart, and he drew strength from them. Mays entitled his last book, written in 1981, *Lord, the People Have Driven Me On.*[21]

After three years at Morehouse, Mays decided to resume his studies for an advanced degree from the University of Chicago. In 1924 Chicago was still rife with racial prejudice, but here, at the age of thirty, Mays made his first southern white friend, W. O. Brown.

In 1925 Mays finished his M.A. He considered remaining at Chicago as a candidate for the Ph.D., but once again he was lured away—this time to his high school alma mater, South Carolina State, to teach English. Here he met his second wife, Sadie Gray. The two were married during the summer of 1926, while they both did graduate work at the University of Chicago.

Since married couples were prohibited from working together at South Carolina State, the newlyweds took jobs with the National Urban League, which in 1926 sent Mays farther south, to Tampa, Florida. Working with both black and white communities was difficult for a man of integrity who opposed segregation. While the Mayses struggled with problems of poor housing, low pay, poor recreational facilities, and second-class citizenship in Tampa, they continually reached out and cared for others. When an African American appeared in juvenile court, either Sadie or Benjamin Mays were there too, and soon delinquent black youths were sent to the Urban League instead of the home for juvenile offenders. In a newspaper article entitled "It Costs Too Much," Mays challenged the segregation laws that confined blacks to balconies and rear seats, carefully laying out the important distinction between "obeying unjust laws through sheer necessity and the voluntary acceptance of a law which one did not have to accept." Mays kept this distinction clear in his life and encouraged his students to do so. As he wrote later in *Seeking to Be Christian in Race Relations*,

Segregation crushes manhood, creates fear in the segregated and makes him cowardly. It develops in the person segregated a feeling of inferiority to the extent he never knows what his capabilities are.

---

[21]Mays, *Lord, the People Have Driven Me On* (New York: Vantage, 1981).

His mind is never free to develop unrestricted. The ceiling and not the sky becomes the limit of his striving.[22]

In Tampa, Mays and his wife went beyond the job description of improving the "lot of Negroes in employment, recreation, housing, health, education and juvenile delinquency." This Mays did and did well, but what challenged the Tampa community was his earnest belief that his job was also to help "Negroes build respect for and pride in themselves despite the strangling chains of segregation." Believing they would eventually be dismissed because of their refusal to accept the status quo, the Mayses resigned from the Urban League in 1928 and moved to Atlanta, where they lived for the next six years. Benjamin became the student secretary for the National YMCA, a job that involved working with African-American students in South Carolina, Georgia, Florida, Alabama, and Tennessee, while Sadie found employment first with the Georgia Negro Child Welfare Department and later with the Atlanta University School of Social Work. The YMCA, segregated in the North and the South, became partially integrated under Mays's secretariat.

In 1930 Mays left the YMCA to study the black church in the United States. Under the auspices of the Rockefeller Institute of Social and Religious Research, Mays and fellow minister Joseph W. Nicholson began their pioneering study of 609 urban congregations and 185 rural churches. They spent fourteen months researching and another ten months writing *The Negro's Church* (1933).

Studying and writing stirred again Mays's dream of a doctorate, and he re-entered the University of Chicago in 1931. Returning to Chicago at thirty-seven years of age, Mays protested campus discrimination and demanded equal seating at public affairs and equal housing in the dormitories. His wife received an A.M. degree from the School of Social Science Service, and Mays finished his classwork in 1934 and received his Ph.D. from the University of Chicago Divinity School in December 1935.

In the summer of 1934 Mays became dean of Howard University's School of Religion. Howard, situated in Washington, D.C., admits students

---

[22]*Tampa Bulletin*, 7 April 1928; Mays, *Seeking to be Christian in Race Relations* (New York: Friendship Press, 1957), 46.

of any race, color, and national origin but has always been a black university
whose special role has been the education of African-American students. It
is jointly supported by congressional appropriations and private funds.
Because the United States Constitution requires the separation of church
and state, the School of Religion was in a particularly vulnerable situation.
Mays recounts both his successes and his failures as dean. He guided the
school toward its accreditation by the American Association of Theological
Schools; Howard was the second black seminary to qualify. The distinguished faculty Mays gathered and the number of black leaders who
graduated from Howard prove that his accomplishments were nothing less
than extraordinary.

Mays's success as dean of the School of Religion at Howard brought
recognition to the former South Carolina farm boy. On his travels to
Europe and India Mays broadened his understanding of race, discrimination, and segregation, and discovered that prejudice against African
Americans was not confined to the United States. On ships he had a double
cabin to himself and was seated alone at dinner. When a letter mistakenly
informed a London hotel he was the distinguished president of Howard
University, he was treated well; but when he returned to the same hotel
without a letter, he discovered that for a black man there was no room at the
inn.

On his travels Mays also learned that the plight of blacks was even worse
in South Africa than in the United States. He found that, because the
profoundly different religious views of Muslims and Hindus in India
produced a strong sense of unity within both groups, Muslims could not
understand why Christians would segregate or lynch other Christians in the
United States. Mays studied the plight of the Indian "untouchables" and
concluded that their situation paralleled that of American blacks.

In India, Mays met with Mahatma Gandhi, who made Indians proud of
their culture and history, who identified with the "untouchables," and who
used the techniques of nonviolence to start a movement for India's
independence that eventually led to the dissolution of the British Empire.
Mays urged Gandhi to oppose the entire caste system and not just
"untouchability." Although Mays had practiced nonviolent protest for most
of his life, Gandhi introduced him to a broader perspective. Gandhi
articulated implications for change beyond Mays's individual challenges to
segregation and advocated mass campaigns of passive resistance to bring

about change. When Mays later gave his famous Tuesday morning Morehouse talks, he drew upon his discussion with Gandhi to encourage young black men who had to live in a prejudiced society.

On 1 July 1940 Mays became the sixth president of Morehouse College. Morehouse, established in 1867 and named in honor of Henry Lyman Morehouse, secretary of the American Baptist Home Mission Society, was "dedicated to the task of building men: first by enlightening their minds, then by freeing them from the shackles of a psychological conditioning brought about by nearly two hundred and fifty years of slavery." Mays believed in the need for African-American colleges only because of the discriminatory effects of segregation. Mays asserted,

> If white historians had cared enough, had been knowledgeable enough, had been sensitive enough, good enough—and if the Founding Fathers had had the black man in mind when they wrestled the thirteen colonies from England and founded this country, there would have been no need . . . of Negro colleges.

If it were not for black colleges, Mays argued in 1976, the education of minority students would have been "blotted out." Schools such as Morehouse provided "images, the things that tell people they are somebody, that they count."[23]

At Morehouse, Mays found morale low, the endowment on the point of losing a million dollars, and the school in the least favorable position among the colleges that formed the Atlanta University Affiliation. Morehouse, "the stepchild in the Affiliation," was "fast becoming a junior college." Atlanta University controlled Morehouse's budget and finances, Morehouse students ate meals on the Atlanta University campus, and Spelman provided medical care for them.[24]

Soliciting the cooperation of students, faculty, trustees, alumni, and friends of the school, Mays promised to "give to Morehouse College all that I have . . . the best of my mind, heart, and soul. . . . I will give . . . my

---

[23]Benjamin Brawley, *History of Morehouse College* (Atlanta: Morehouse College, 1917); Edward A. Jones, *A Candle in the Dark: A History of Morehouse College* (Valley Forge, PA: Judson Press, 1967); *Presbyterian Outlook* 158 (April 26, 1976).

[24]Jones, *Candle in the Dark*, 137-138.

money until it reaches the sacrificial point. . . . I will serve this institution as if God Almighty sent me into the world for the express purpose of being the Sixth President of Morehouse College." After accepting the presidency, Mays immediately planned for the expansion and growth of Morehouse. His program included raising four hundred thousand dollars to match an endowment offer; securing annual contributors; constructing a new dormitory, dining hall, chapel, gymnasium, and classroom building; encouraging alumni to recruit new students; providing faculty housing; collecting past-due debts from students; increasing faculty salaries; and improving the credentials of the faculty. Not only did Mays accomplish his initial goals, but during his twenty-seven-year tenure he raised over fifteen million dollars. In addition to the five buildings included in the original plan, Morehouse constructed thirteen others, including seven dormitories, a music building, and a science laboratory.

Mays did not, however, focus on buildings. These accomplishments were minor compared to the creation of a special spirit at Morehouse College. Samuel DuBois Cook believed that "Mays's genius was as an inspirer and motivator as well as a transformer of young men. . . . the Mays legacy is one of the great possessions of Black people and America." Under his leadership, the faculty and teaching improved, student participation in extracurricular activities increased, the curriculum was constantly strengthened, available resources were used wisely and additional resources were steadily acquired, and full accreditation was obtained. Mays used honorary degrees to instill pride in young black men; in 1943, Morehouse became the first black college to award an honorary degree to Paul Robeson. At the ceremony, Mays introduced Robeson as

> a man who embodies all the hopes and aspirations of the Negro race and who, despite crippling restrictions, breathes the pure air of freedom. . . . You represent in your person, in your integrity, and in your ideals the things for which this college stands and for which it shall continue to stand.

In 1968 the most prestigious of academic honor societies, Phi Beta Kappa, established a chapter at Morehouse. When Mays accepted the presidency of Morehouse, he protested, "If Morehouse is not good enough for anybody, it's not good enough for Negroes." By the time of his retirement,

Morehouse was an excellent college by any standard.[25]

Mays never lost sight of his goal, to create the best possible environment for the coming age of young black men. According to the historian David Lewis, "The personality of the statuesque and white-maned Dr. Mays permeated the milieu of the college with firm but unobtrusive moral guidance." The July 1965 *Morehouse College Bulletin* devoted a twenty-page supplement to Mays's administration. Included in the appraisal of his service was the following: "Under the far-reaching leadership of Benjamin E. Mays, Morehouse College has gone beyond mere academic respectability. Morehouse's bigness is not in student populations nor financial resources, but in the quality of an educational program that has led to earned recognition as a front-rank liberal arts college.[26]

At a Founders' Day address in 1963, the speaker gave Mays credit for nurturing Morehouse "from young adulthood to maturity." Predecessors laid the foundation, but Mays molded and gave to the great institution the form it is today. The celebrated 'Morehouse man' is very much the Benjamin E. Mays man. Mays fulfilled his initial promise; he served as if heaven-sent, gave as if his very existence depended upon it, and led Morehouse toward success.[27]

Every Tuesday morning for twenty-seven years, President Mays addressed Morehouse students on the state of the college and answered their questions. Again and again in his Tuesday talks, Mays encouraged Morehouse students to be men, not "black" men who had to play second fiddle to white men, but rather black men who were not afraid to walk side by side with whites. Mays's most famous disciple, Martin Luther King Jr., realized when he entered Morehouse that "nobody there was afraid." Mays encouraged students to fight fear and racism. "If you are ignorant," Mays told students, "the world is going to cheat you. If you are weak, the world is going to kick you. If you are a coward, the world is going to keep you

---

[25]Lerone Bennett, "Last of the Great Schoolmasters," 73; Dorothy Butler Gilliam, *Paul Robeson: All-American* (Washington: New Republic, 1976), 113, 159; Marie Seton, *Paul Robeson* (London: Dennis Dobson, 1958), 141-143.

[26]David Levering Lewis, *King: A Biography*, 2d ed. (Urbana: University of Illinois Press, 1978), 19; *Morehouse Alumnus*, July 1965 (special supplement), Jones, *Candle in the Dark*, 267.

[27]*Morehouse Alumnus*, April 1963, 5; Jones, *Candle in the Dark*, 265.

running."[28]

Admired by many, Mays also had critics. When he was a youngster, others found him too studious and serious. As a preacher, the young Mays was sometimes perceived as a hopeless modernist who strayed from the conservative doctrines that black Baptists accepted as orthodox. Some faulted what they believed to be inconsistencies in Mays's fusing of civil rights, social gospel, democracy, and Christianity in theology. As a college teacher and administrator, he was criticized as too demanding—he graded too strictly.

Both blacks and whites found many of his actions as a civil rights leader threatening. When President John F. Kennedy named Mays to the Civil Rights Commission, the Senate refused to confirm the appointment because Mays was a desegregationist and therefore unable to make "impartial" decisions. Georgia's two senators, Richard B. Russell and Herman E. Talmadge protested that Mays's strong stance on integration was too narrow-minded! Like many who challenged the social hierarchy of a segregated society during the 1930s and 1940s, Mays was wrongly accused of being a Communist. Because of Mays's association with groups interested in social justice, groups that may have had Communist members, the Georgia senators claimed that Mays had Communist leanings. They cited *Communism and the NAACP,* published by the Georgia Committee on Education in 1958, where the Mays's entry included thirty-one "Communist" actions such as his sponsorship of a dinner honoring W. E. B. Du Bois, his support of the American Crusade to End Lynching, his chairing a conference on discrimination in higher education for the Southern Conference Educational Fund, his membership on the nominating committee of the Southern Conference for Human Welfare in 1947-1948, and, of course, his leadership in the NAACP. Mays, who perceived communism as anti-Christian, was outraged to be labeled a Communist. Although Mays denied the allegations, Kennedy withdrew the nomination and tried to compensate by appointing Mays as one of the initial members of the Peace Corps Advisory Committee.[29]

---

[28]Lewis, *King,* 21.

[29]Ted Poston, "Mays and King," *New York Post,* 10 April 1957; *America's Betrayal: Martin King, Red Tool; Report of Hearings by the Louisiana Joint Legislative Committee,* 6-9 March 1957, 57, and the *Congressional Record,* 23 February 1956, 2,831, photocopies of

Some African Americans thought that Mays should have confined his critique of American society to black-wh te issues. Mays's opposition to the Vietnam war and his broad views on social justice sometimes upset more conservative civil rights leaders who believed that blacks should be supportive of President Lyndon Johnson's foreign policy because Johnson was supportive of civil rights legislation. Mays, however, as at his 1968 commencement address at Michigan State University, argued that Americans had to battle three major enemies of man: war, poverty, and racism. He warned, "Make no mistake: We will abolish war or war will abolish mankind."[30]

Mays was principled but practical. As chairman of the Atlanta school board he made decisions that angered people, blacks and whites, on both sides of the political spectrum. In order to make integration work and to keep Atlanta from becoming an all-black city surrounded by white suburbs, Mays accepted what has become known as the Atlanta Plan as a compromise. Although the Atlanta Plan is generally hailed as one of the most successful school desegregations in America, some civil rights leaders believe Mays could have demanded more according to the law of the land.

Mays did not give blind support to all black causes. The civil rights movement was divided, and Mays's unwavering support of Martin Luther King Jr., angered conflicting leadership. An old-line integrationist, Mays disappointed some young black separatists in 1967 when he criticized the Student Nonviolent Coordinating Committee for absence of "constructive ends. . . . Anything that tends to set white against black, I think, does harm." He later said, "I don't think the Black Panthers are going to emancipate the black people from the problems of hunger, housing and more economic stability." Many younger activists advocated violence or (reared in an increasingly secular urban culture far removed from Mays's origins) rejected Christianity, which they considered the opiate of the black masses in America. To this later generation the aging warrior Mays appeared dated. But even some of the most vociferous of these black activists still acknowledged the greatness of Mays and pointed to him as a positive role

---

above in Mays's Folder (SCL).

[30]Mays, "The Universities' Unfinished Work," Commencement Address, Michigan State University, East Lansing, 9 June 1968; Gavins, "Ceremonial Speaking of Mays," 229.

model, a mentor, and even as a "cultural hero."[31]

Mays's abolitionist-temperance tradition at times offended those from more sophisticated backgrounds. He spoke his mind, often giving unsolicited advice. For example, he advised his faculty to observe three don'ts—don't drink, don't smoke, don't borrow money. Mays's only indulgence was the five or six teaspoons of sugar he heaped in each of the several cups of coffee he drank every morning. Richard Barksdale suggests that the coffee and sugar may have provided Mays's legendary energy.

Indeed, his energy was a legend. In 1981 Mays talked about "the spirit of urgency" and how "I worked all my life as if eternity was in every minute." Many people attribute Mays's nickname, "Buck Benny," to his quick pace; he seemed to bounce as he sped from one place to another. Others ascribe it to his determination to "buck" the system. Mays, however, said that he acquired the sobriquet during his early days at Morehouse, when he initiated austerity programs to save the college and insisted that students repay outstanding debts.[32]

Although *Born to Rebel* demonstrates clearly why people honored and respected Mays, the autobiography, with perhaps too much reserve, omits many of the incidents that inspired devotion. Stories about the "puritan" Mays mislead one into thinking he was ascetic in his emotions as well. As president of Morehouse, he met and got to know every student, inviting them into his home for visits. He was intelligent, witty, a wonderful conversationalist, and a great raconteur. A classmate from the University of Chicago described Mays as "one of the greatest personalities in the world." Yet he was a very modest man. In 1980 as he received numerous honors, Mays explained, "I have never done anything for the purpose of being honored, to have my name on the front pages of the newspapers. I have done what I believe I was sent into the world to do: worship my God and serve my Fellowman." Even after all the recognition and awards he could say" we all travel the same road from our mother's womb to the grave. So there's no need of anybody getting chesty. We travel the same

---

[31] "A Black Thorn in the White Conscience," *Atlanta Journal and Constitution*, 18 January 1970, sec. M, 9; Charles V. Willie, "The Education of Benjamin Elijah Mays: An Example in Effective Teaching," *Teachers College Record* 84 (Summer 1983), 955; Nathan Wright Jr., "Education of Black Youth," *Newark Star Ledger*, 9 May 1971, 27.

[32] Mays, Address at Epworth, SC, 17 November 1981, 4.

highway."[33]

Mays does not relate that he offered to pay fines incurred by Martin Luther King Jr. and others involved in civil rights work. He discusses how he firmly required Morehouse students to pay defaulted debts, but he neglects to mention his generosity in paying for students' educations. A former Harvard Divinity School student who was a Danforth Seminary Intern at Morehouse remembered, "After receiving personal financial favor from Dr. Mays during a crucial and critical phase of my academic career, I tried to repay him. He refused my attempt by simply saying, "If I have helped in any way, pass it on.' And for the rest of my life, I will try to pass it on."[34]

Mays was devoted and loyal to family, friends, and institutions. He always returned to Ninety Six for family reunions, celebrations, and funerals. He served loyally as president of the alumni association of South Carolina State, and a speaker at the 84th Founders Day said that Mays was "remembered in the Orangeburg community for his outstanding speeches at the annual Easter service held in the old White Hall campus for twenty-five years. This event drew a capacity audience each year."

Another example of people's devotion to Mays and Mays's reciprocal loyalty is in the small country black school in Pacolet, South Carolina. In 1953 this school adopted the name Ben E. Mays High School. The students voted to have a Ben E. Mays day each year in honor of the school's namesake, and Mays never missed the day. The superintendent of the school said, "We think it noteworthy when an internationally known figure takes time out from a busy schedule to spend a day with boys and girls in a small rural school. Dr. Mays's presence annually should serve as an inspiration to the students of this institution." Teachers felt "that the presence of Dr. Mays is serving as an aid to the holding power of the high school" and more and more students stayed in high school and graduated. Mays also established ranking male (who, of course, went to Morehouse) and female

---

[33]Ibid., 5; Mays, typescript of speech at Mays portrait unveiling, State Capitol, Columbia, SC, 12 July 1980, 7; George A. Singleton, *The Autobiography of George A. Singleton* (Boston: Forum Publishing, 1964), 142.

[34]Charles G. Adams, "Benjamin Mays: An Amazing Man," *Michigan Chronicle*, 7 April 1984, A6.

scholarships for the senior class.[35]

Mays was democratic in his personal life just as in his political beliefs. Everyone—students, faculty, administrators, politicians, and endowment donors—wanted some of his time, and he was open to all, on a first-come first-served basis. If he had agreed to speak to a small rural congregation on a particular day, he would not break his commitment to make room for a more prestigious engagement. In 1980, when an African-American congregation in Ninety Six renamed their church Mays United Methodist, he was more touched by that honor than by any other he had ever received.

For Mays, religious faith lay at the very center of his life. In *Disturbed About Man* he wrote, "The first Christian light, therefore, to shine upon human relationships is the conviction that God is the author or all life, the source of human life is not blind mechanistic force, not blind chance, not natural laws; the source of human life is God." Greatly inspired by the faith of his father and the piety of his mother, the young Mays plowed a row, hitched his mule to a tree, and prayed, asking "the Lord to make it possible for me to get an education. I used to go out at night in the light of the moon and do the same thing—praying for God to help me get an education." In later years Mays the theologian wrote, "Man cannot leave God alone, and God cannot leave man alone; so someday, man will yet learn that the ways of the Lord are just and righteous altogether and that in obedience to God's command man will make the earth a place of love, brotherhood, justice, and peace."[36]

Being at peace with his omnipresent, omniscient, and omnipotent God enabled Mays to walk fearlessly in the land of prejudice and segregation. In "The Obligations of the Individual Christian" Mays argued,

> The Christian cannot excuse himself by saying, "I cannot go against tradition; I cannot buck the mores; I cannot jeopardize my

---

[35]Letter from Mays, Class of '16 alumni president, 1925, Mays file (SCL); "Mays Honored," *Black News*, 16 February 1980; "Ben E. Mays School, Pacolet, SC," *Journal of PEA* 10 (September 1958):12.

[36]Mays, *Disturbed About Man* (Richmond: John Knox Press, 1969), 17, 19; Barbara Lewinson, "Three Conceptions of Black Education: A Study of the Educational Ideas of Benjamin Elijah Mays, Booker T. Washington, and Nathan Wright Jr." (Ph.D. diss., Rutgers University, 1973), 18-30,128-132.

political, social, or economic future." The true Christian is a citizen of two worlds. Not only must he answer to the mores, but he must give an account to God. and with God's help he can be loyal to the highest and to the best he knows.

Expounding on freedom, he again turned to the individual's relationship with God. "The free man, walking the high road moves on faith in the rightness of his position, takes the next step, trusting where he cannot prove, leaving the consequences to God." With God as his friend Mays feared no white man and no white man's unjust law.[37]

As a Christian Mays understood the humanity of his oppressors, whom he was always ready to forgive. He argued that the "chief sin of segregation is the distortion of human personality. It damages the soul of both the segregator and the segregated. . . . It is difficult to know who is damaged more—the segregated or segregator." He believed that people had the power to change for the better. He was always happy to award an honorary degree from Morehouse to someone who had once been an oppressor of black rights but had become a champion of civil rights because he understood how difficult and courageous such changes were. Such actions illustrate why Julian Bond said of his college president, "I am kneeling at the feet of a giant. Making friends of enemies has been the lifelong mission of Benjamin Mays."[38]

An extremely proud man, Mays was also meek, meek in the biblical sense, as Jesus and Moses were meek. Like Jesus, who drove the moneychangers out of the temple and challenged the Pharisees, and like Moses, who confronted Pharaoh and led his people out of Egypt, Mays followed his God and his conscience to fight injustice and segregation throughout the world and especially to free his people in the American South from the oppression of racism. Mays said during a commencement address at Bucknell University:

---

[37]Mays, "The Obligations of the Individual Christian," in *The Christian Way in Race Relations*, ed. William Stuart Nelson (New York: Harper, 1943), 225; Mays, "Each in His Time," Eulogy of Emory O. Jackson, Sixth Avenue Baptist Church, Birmingham, Alabama, 16 September 1975, Gavins, "Ceremonial Speaking of Mays," 281-287.

[38]*Editorial Reprints from Petal Papers; Greenwood Index-Journal*, 6 January 1984.

The test of good religion is not how we treat our peers and those above us, but how we treat those beneath us, not how we treat the man highest up, but how we treat the man farthest down . . . the real test of my religion would be how I treat the man who has nothing to give me—no money, no social prestige, no honors, Not how I treat the educated, but how I treat the man who can't write his name.

Mays took the text on Lazarus and Dives to call for social conscience among Bucknell's graduates. He told his audience,

we must be concerned about the plight of other people. Whether we like it or not, our destiny is tied up with their destiny, and their welfare is ours. Jesus, in the twenty-fifth chapter of Matthew, makes it clear that our relationship to God is dependent upon our relationship to man. "Inasmuch as ye did it unto the least of these, ye did it unto me." Dives goes to hell not because he was rich and not because he was bad. Dives was a good man, a decent respectable, law-abiding citizen. He went to Hell because he had no social conscience. He did not care.[39]

Mays never hid his deep and abiding faith in God. Whether giving a sermon or delivering a speech before a secular audience. Mays never failed to use "a series of related biblical references." Mays never criticized without providing constructive suggestions, no matter whether his audience was a graduating class at a huge Midwestern state university, the congregation of a tiny rural black church, or a president of the United States. "We should begin in the kindergarten to develop people who believe in our Christian principles and democratic ideals. Goodness is as important as literacy. An honest heart is as important as a brilliant mind."[40]

Although he had been tutored in speech and became one of the most celebrated educators and orators of the twentieth century, he never rejected

---

[39]Mays, "His Goodness Was Not Enough," Commencement Address at Bucknell University, Lewisburg, PA, 13 September 1954; Gavins, "Ceremonial Speaking of Mays," 205-211.

[40]Mays, "The Universities' Unfinished Work"; Gavins, 24, 235.

his roots. Charles V. Willie maintains that Mays took his inspiration from the Bible and incorporated the "wisdom of the folk in his speeches and sermons." He integrated "folk wisdom and formal knowledge" so that each informed the other. Mays used literary sources, psychology, philosophy, "everything I have learned," and "the experiences of the people sitting out in front of me, experiences I know they have had. We are all bothered by the same things—birth, courtship, marriage, sickness, death, anxiety." According to Mays, a successful speaker "must first have a message to give with the ultimate purpose to teach, not teaching so much to learn, but teaching to make people think. The speaker must first believe in what he is saying. . . . The truth is essential." Mays aimed "to not only make them feel, but to think deeply as well."[41]

Whatever the occasion, Benjamin Mays prepared meticulously for each speech, but he never used written notes before he was forty-five, and he was sixty before he relied on a manuscript. For Mays, speaking was a creative act and he prepared for every audience accordingly. Mays always talked with people, rather than reading speeches. Encouraged at the age of nine by a standing ovation from the congregation for his recitation of the Beatitudes, Mays captivated and inspired audiences until his death. He also relied on reason over emotion. He retained the grace of simplicity and the charm of the farm boy but was as much at ease addressing heads of state as delivering a sermon to the members of a small black congregation. Partly because Mays treated all audiences with respect, his speaking impressed his listeners with its "sheer power." Robert Brisbane described Mays's appearance as "regal," and Daniel Thompson, vice president of academic affairs at Dillard University, stated, "His presence was so great that anything he said would have gone over well." Bell Irvin Wiley, president of the Southern Historical Association, described Mays's 1956 talk on segregation as an

impassioned commentary on these moral inequities; the eloquence and the force with which the speaker stated his views was evidenced by the fact that he was twice interrupted by vigorous applause—a phenomenon without precedence in the Association's history—and

---

[41]Willie, in foreword to *Quotable Quotes*, ix; Gavins, 24-27.

by the tremendous ovation that he received at the conclusion of his remarks.[42]

Mays demanded perfection of himself in his scholarship just as in his speeches and his educational work. His account of the Phoenix Riot in Appendix A of *Born to Rebel* is first-rate historical investigation combining techniques of oral history with more time-tested traditional sources. Although he lived through the Phoenix Riot in 1898, Mays did not depend on memory for his account; he did extensive research. His work pointed to the economic underpinnings of the riot and made important distinctions between renting and sharecropping that most historians miss today. Mays understood rural society, and his writings and research reflect a unique perspective on the agrarian South.

Mays's greatest contribution as a scholar lies in his combination of the study of race relations and religion. Contemporary scholars of African-American religion still utilize *The Negro's Church*, by Mays and Joseph W. Nicholson, and Mays's *The Negro's God as Reflected in His Literature*. According to Mays and Nicholson, the origin of the black church clearly distinguished black from white religion in the United States. Five themes underlay the origins of the black church: various periods of growing racial consciousness, group and individual initiative, splits and withdrawals from established churches, black migration, and mission of other churches. Both books pioneered the analysis of the liberating aspects of the black church. Mays argued that the black church provided a safe haven and an escape from the segregation and discrimination that marked every day in the lives of African Americans. To

be recognized and to be "somebody," has stimulated the pride and preserved the self-respect of many Negroes who would have been entirely beaten by life, and possibly completely submerged. Everyone

---

[42]Gavins, 30-31; *Editorial Reprints from Petal Papers*; Silver, "Twenty-First Annual Meeting," 61.

wants to receive recognition and feel that he is appreciated. The Negro church has supplied that need. [43]

The book also criticized the poorly trained ministers who often encouraged socially irrelevant patterns of escape by preaching compensatory, your-reward-is-in-heaven, pie-in-the-sky Christianity. Again reflecting his own upbringing in rural South Carolina in his understanding of black religion, Mays wrote in *The Negro's God* that he had

> heard the Pastor of the church of my youth plead with the members of his congregation not to try to avenge the wrongs they suffered, but to take their burdens to the Lord in prayer. . . . invariably after assuring them that God would fix things up, he ended his sermon by assuring them further that God would reward them in Heaven.
> . . . Being socially proscribed, economically impotent, and politically browbeaten, they sang, prayed, and shouted their troubles away. This idea of God had telling effects upon the Negroes in my home community. It kept them submissive, humble, and obedient. It enabled them to keep on keeping on.

While Mays opposed the concept that religion should keep people "submissive, humble, and obedient," he thoroughly approved of a religion that helped a downtrodden people endure—"to keep on keeping on." His analysis was not one-sided.[44]

Mays was more than a scholar of black religion, and his view of religion was more than a vague anthropological explanation for the world. For Mays, religion and Christianity were vital forces. Conducting his research during the Great Depression, Mays was able to capture the pulse of the black church. As a result Mays accurately predicted the later needs and feelings of the African-American community. He suggested consolidation to relieve economic problems of the black church and to encourage more cohesiveness in congregations and better leadership from the black community. He

---

[43]Mays and Joseph W. Nicholson, *The Negro's Church* (1933; reprint, New York: Russell and Russell, 1969); Mays, *The Negro's God as Reflected in His Literature* (1938; reprint, New York: Russell and Russell, 1968), 15.

[44]Mays, *The Negro's God*, 26.

criticized the static, nonprogressive nature of the church and noted that it had failed to retain the loyalty of many of the most critically minded African Americans. His list of the shortcomings of the black church is long: pastors were poorly educated; too many sermons betrayed a magical conception of religion; teachers in church schools too often lacked college educations; there were too many black churches for the number of black churchgoers; the churches struggled under a heavy load of indebtedness; they were too little concerned with social problems such as juvenile delinquency.

Mays asserted, however, that the positive outweighed the negative in the black church. The church was the first area of life outside the family where African Americans enjoyed freedom. *The Negro's Church* also discussed the preacher's importance in African-American society. Black preachers were leaders, politicians, orators, bosses, and idealists. The ministry was one of the few professions open to talented African-American men in the nineteenth and early twentieth centuries. In 1930 blacks accounted for less than a tenth of the population of the United States, while African Americans accounted for nearly a fifth of the total number of preachers. The black church was, and still is, a foundation of pride and self-respect for African Americans, and they can become leaders and hold responsible positions within its administration.[45]

Mays intrigued students by pointing out how the black church could foster social change. The pulpit of a black church provided a forum for discussing world problems, including racial difficulties, and for dispensing practical advice. Through adult education the church could reach poor and uneducated African Americans. For generations of African Americans the church had been the center of intellectual life as well as religious and moral teaching. Mays remarked that whites practiced politics in government while blacks practiced politics in the church.

For the rest of his life Mays continued to research and write about black religion. In *Seeking to Be Christian in Race Relations*, written three decades after *The Negro's Church* and *The Negro's God as Reflected in His Literature*, Mays discussed the value of nonviolent protest and noted that Martin Luther King Jr. drew upon his Christian and African-American heritage in

---

[45]Mays and Nicholson, *The Negro's Church*, 3.

preaching his gospel of nonviolent change. Mays maintained that nonviolent protest took root in African-American culture the first time a slave sang a spiritual. Songs of protest about slaves' suffering and pain, spirituals refuted the white myth that African Americans were satisfied with life in white America. Spirituals helped blacks bear the burden of racism in America. Mays argued that these songs helped to prevent the hatred and bitterness that otherwise would have developed into violence and race wars. Mays pointed to the black abolitionist Frederick Douglass and Harriet Tubman as practitioners of nonviolence in their efforts to free slaves. Mays discovered nonviolence in the quiet persuasiveness of Booker T. Washington and the eloquent bitterness of W. E. B. Du Bois. Mays pointed out that, since 1935, when Donald Murray won a court case enabling African Americans to attend the University of Maryland Law School, the NAACP had been peacefully using the courts to gain larger citizenship rights for African Americans. The courts were also used to lessen the disparity between blacks and whites in salaries and educational facilities. Change came slowly through legal channels, but the people persevered, gaining strength of spirit from their relationship with God and their nonviolent efforts for change.

"Among all things," as Julian Bond insisted, "Dr. Mays is a teacher. It is his reason for being. His teachings are based on his faith and his faith is based on the feeling that man is a rational being able to build a better world." Mays once described his motivation in his weekly newspaper column:

> I behave as I do because I know that as long as I am treated as a Negro, a caste man, this thing isn't right, and until my dying day I shall insist first on being a human being and incidentally, a Negro. In my protest, I am not fighting to be *with* anybody. I just want to be human and allowed to walk the earth with dignity.

Mays's unrelenting opposition to racism was a logical consequence of his belief in the unity of the human family, a family with kinship to God. He strongly believed that segregated schools denied the God-given unity of mankind. The purpose of education was to strengthen human dignity and kindness. "I think the great need is an education with a social conscience; science has made the world a neighborhood. It is left for all of us—leaders in education and religion—to make it a brotherhood."[46]

Mays's influence reached far and wide. *Roots* author Alex Haley once told a "Benjamin E. Mays Day" audience how his father had driven over a hundred miles so that young Haley and his brother could see the great educator. Local black leaders in many southern towns and urban centers, working for civil rights in their own communities, testify to the crucial impact Mays had on their own lives. As I researched the era from Reconstruction to the modern civil rights movement, I was told by African-American descendants of Reconstruction political leaders that many black activists learned from Mays "behind the veil," to use W. E. B. Du Bois's phrase. In 1982 Andrew Young, mayor of Atlanta and former ambassador to the United Nations, said essentially the same thing; in every city in the United States, the leading black doctor, the most important black attorney, "most certainly one of the key preachers and probably most of the black elected officials owe where they are to Dr. Mays." Coretta Scott King said to Mays, "Most of the black male leadership in our country during the last forty years has in some way been inspired by you . . . . Martin Luther King, Jr. called you his spiritual mentor and was greatly influenced by your life and example. . . . you've been a great inspiration to me."[47]

Mays's relationship with King is the most famous example of how he encouraged others. Stephen B. Oates wrote in *Let the Trumpet Sound* that at Morehouse King "found his calling" under the inspiration of Benjamin Mays, who

> as a preacher and theologian was out to renew the mission of the black church. . . . At Morehouse chapel, this tall and erudite man, with his iron-gray hair and hypnotic voice, mesmerized his young disciples by preaching stewardship, responsibility, and engagement. "Do whatever you do so well," he counseled, "that no man living and no man yet unborn could do it better." Here at Morehouse, he

---

[46]*Greenwood Index-Journal*, 6 January 1984; Mays, "My Views," *Pittsburgh Courier*, 7 May 1966, 13, and April 1955, reprinted in *New South*, January, 1964, 45, copy of second article in Mays file (SCL); Lewinson, "Three Conceptions of Black Education," 31.

[47]Leonard Ray Teel, "Benjamin Mays: Teaching by Example, Leading Through Will," *Change* 14 (October 1982):15; *The Ninety Six Star and County Review*, 11 November 1981; *Greenwood Index-Journal*, 3 and 11 November 1981.

was not turning out doctors or lawyers or preachers, Mays said. He was turning out *men*." Accordingly, King saw in Mays what he wanted "a real minister to be"—a rational man whose sermons were both spiritually and intellectually stimulating, a moral man who was socially involved. Thanks largely to Mays, King realized that the ministry could be a respectable force for ideas, even for social protest.[48]

It would be human nature for a teacher to claim credit for a former student who achieved greatness. But Mays was extremely modest about his relationship with King, saying that he did not realize his influence until King wrote about it in *Stride Toward Freedom*. Martin Luther King, Jr., symbolized hope and courage for African Americans, but Mays was a symbol to King. King turned to Mays for advice, and Mays often helped King in the struggle for civil rights.

Mays's influence on his most distinguished disciple could be a book unto itself. Their friendship lasted from King's collegiate days to his death in 1968. In 1944, when Mays was forty-five years old and in the fourth year of his presidency, King entered Morehouse at the age of fourteen in Mays's special program for gifted high school students. A powerful pulpiteer with impeccable academic and scholarly credentials, Mays stirred his college students with addresses based on commonplace observations but spurred by intensity and intimacy. King often stayed behind to discuss the sermon, and by the time he was in his junior year at Morehouse, the two men talked regularly in Mays's office. Whether they agreed or disagreed, these discussions, which Mays encouraged with all Morehouse students, influenced King greatly. From their days together at Morehouse, through the years of the civil rights struggle, and until King's death, the pair shared the same philosophy and goals.

Describing the "insistent call to the ministry" that her husband felt, Coretta Scott King explained:

---

[48]Stephen B. Oates, *Let the Trumpet Sound: The Life of Martin Luther King, Jr.* (New York: Harper and Row, 1982), 19.

From first to last Dr. Mays took a great interest in Martin. It was not that he deliberately guided him towards the ministry as that he influenced Martin by his example. For although Dr. Mays was brilliant, he was not removed from the heart of the people. In the pulpit he talked a great deal about social justice; you might say he preached a social gospel. This conformed exactly with Martin's views, and it helped to form them. . . . At Morehouse listening to Dr. Mays preach . . . Martin came to see that the ministry could be intellectually respectable as well as emotionally satisfying. When he accepted this fact, it opened the way for him to go into the church.[49]

Mays was crucial in his support of King and the Montgomery bus boycott in 1956. Word had reached King at his parents' home in Atlanta that under an antiquated anti-boycott law he and eighty-eight others had been indicted and that he would be arrested if he returned to Alabama. Distressed because his son would be part of mass arrests, because he might be harmed, and because as a black civil rights leader he would not receive due process in the Alabama courts, the elder King invited his most trusted friends to counsel against his son's returning to Montgomery. Attorneys, educators, and newspapermen, fearing that Montgomery was ready to explode, advised King against returning to the city. King, however, announced that he had decided to go back. He later wrote:

In the moment of silence that followed I heard my father break into tears. I looked at Dr. Mays, one of the great influences in my life. Perhaps he had heard my unspoken plea. At any rate, he was soon defending my position strongly. Then others joined in supporting me.[50]

---

[49]Coretta Scott King, *My Life with Martin Luther King, Jr.* (New York: Holt, Rinehart and Winston, 1969), 85-86.

[50]Martin Luther King Sr., with Clayton Riley, *Daddy King: An Autobiography* (New York: William Morrow, 1980), 170-171; Howell Raines, *My Soul Is Rested: Movement Days in the Deep South Remembered* (New York: G. P. Putnam's Sons, 1977), 64-65; Lewis, *King*, 73-74; Oates, *Trumpet*, 92-93.

King was arrested, but the boycott became a major cornerstone of the civil rights movement. In June 1956 a United States district court ruled that racial segregation on city bus lines was unconstitutional, and in November the Supreme Court affirmed the district court's ruling. By December, the buses in Montgomery were integrated and the Second Reconstruction was underway.

The next year, Mays honored King at the Morehouse commencement. "You did not betray that trust of leadership," the college president began.

> You led the people with quiet dignity, Christian grace and determined purpose. While you were away, your colleagues in the battle for freedom were being hounded and arrested like criminals. When it was suggested by legal counsel that you might stay away and escape arrest, I heard you say with my own ears, "I would rather spend 10 years in jail than desert people in this crisis." At the moment my heart, mind and soul stood up erect and saluted. I knew then that you were called to leadership for such a time as this. You are a symbol of hope and courage for oppressed people everywhere.[51]

In 1964, when King won the Nobel Peace Prize, Mays initiated a plan to have the entire city of Atlanta celebrate their distinguished native son. Mays recounts how he was able to overcome jealousy and division within the black community and the objections of white racists to organize a committee for the gala. Pressure from the *New York Times* and encouragement from Mayor Ivan Allen turned the tide; the dinner was a great success for both King and publicity-conscious Atlanta. Four years later, after King's assassination, Mays delivered his eulogy. It has been said that when Mays preached King's funeral, he "extracted the essence not only of Martin but also of Benjamin. Either man could have been speaking of the other."[52]

Mays struggled against great adversity to gain an education and to maintain a sense of self-worth while living in a society that at every turn

---

[51]Coretta King, 158-59.
[52]Teel, "Benjamin Mays," 22.

expressed its belief that he was worthless. He spoke out firmly but peacefully against the injustices of race relations in America. Mays could have contended, as many others did, that things have improved vastly since the 1890s, that we should count our blessings, that we should not rock the boat, but he steadfastly refused to do so. Having lived through some of the worst times that racism spawned in America, he looked back through seven decades of social progress and concluded that we must not be satisfied with that progress. He continued active in educating, advising, and encouraging others to democratize America.

At the age most people retire, the indefatigable Mays began a whole new career as chairman of the Atlanta School Board for twelve years. Mays also remained active in support of reform. Typical is the letter that he and Martin Luther King Sr. wrote in support of the boycott of J. P. Stevens and Company in 1977. "Racial justice today is dependent on economic and social justice" and an "issue of conscience has arisen which demands our involvement." Workers, black and white, male and female, young and old, "need our help urgently if justice is to be served." When black children were being murdered in Atlanta, the *Christian Century* interviewed the "long-time national black leader and highly respected president of Atlanta's school board." Mays informed the reporter

> the situation should be a challenge to the churches. Take our black churches—almost every one, however beautiful it may be, is only a stone's throw from youngsters not going to Sunday school, maybe selling dope, maybe becoming thieves. . . . Housing projects are very near my church; we ought to bring the children into our church and let them know we care. The church could give them incentive.

The writer commented, "When the 86-year-old educator sees a youth out of school during school hours, he marches right up to inquire why." In 1983 he was the co-chairman of South Carolina Senator Earnest Hollings's presidential steering committee. When at eighty-seven he retired as "the oldest board president in the United States. . . Mays said, 'I have several things to do before I die.'" He started working on three books, a collection of his articles, a recounting of his twenty-seven years at Morehouse, and a history of *Brown v. Board of Education*. "I plan to die in the harness," said Mays.[53]

The life of Benjamin Elijah Mays illustrates the ironies of southern history. Born in an area known as the "dark corner" of a county notorious for its extremism, Mays emerged as the great advocate of nonviolence. This area of the South Carolina upcountry has produced many national, regional, and state leaders of distinction. John C. Calhoun, the great defender of slavery; Martin Witherspoon Gary, the "Bald Eagle of the Confederacy"; and "Pitchfork Ben Tillman, the agrarian firebrand, all were born in the area. A marker in Ninety Six commemorates one of the largest gatherings in the history of the state, when throngs of supporters presented canes to Congressman Preston S. Brooks to replace the one he had broken in the U. S. Senate chambers while thrashing the Massachusetts senator and abolitionist Charles Sumner. The Edgefield Chapter of the United Daughters of the Confederacy maintains the Gary home as a shrine that houses memorabilia for the Red Shirts, the paramilitary group that violently "redeemed" South Carolina. This area is also the home of Senator J. Strom Thurmond, who used his presidential nomination by the "white supremacist" Dixiecrat party in 1948 as a starting point from which to maneuver his way into a political dominance unmatched in the state since the days of John C. Calhoun. A life-size statue of Thurmond faces the Edgefield courthouse. One can tell much about what a people value by what they select to preserve as historical and by the sites they deem significant enough to mark with plaques and monuments.[54]

In the Ninety Six in which I grew up in the 1950s, no statue or plaque memorialized the great educator and apostle of peace Benjamin Elijah Mays. The world in which I grew up had not changed much from the segregated world into which Mays was born, and I remained unacquainted with the African-American oral tradition regarding Mays. As a senior at Furman

---

[53]*Christian Century*, 26 October 1977, 975; Linda Marie Delloff, "It Is Clear," *Christian Century*, 1-8 July 1981, 692-693; "Atlanta Educator to Retire," Associated Press article [1981?] in Benjamin Mays file, Greenwood County Regional Library.

[54]Richard Maxwell Brown, *Strain of Violence: Historical Studies of American Violence and Vigilantism* (New York: Oxford, 1975), 67-90; the chapter is entitled "South Carolina Extremism and Its Violent Origins: From the Regulator Movement to the Edgefield Tradition, 1760-1960"; Orville Vernon Burton, *In My Father's House Are Many Mansions: Family and Community in Edgefield, South Carolina* (Chapel Hill: University of North Carolina Press, 1985).

University in 1969, I went to hear Mays speak; upon meeting him I was amazed to learn that we were from the same home town. The greatest South Carolinian in the twentieth century was from Ninety Six, and I had not even known who he was!

Readers sense in *Born to Rebel* a deep hurt. As a young man Mays believed: "I could never do what I hoped to do or be what I aspired to be if I remained in the state of my birth. I had to seek a new world." In his preface Mays wrote of the "indignities" and the "injustices and brutalities heaped upon Negroes during my lifetime." One purpose of his writing *Born to Rebel* was "to expose the snail like progress which we have made in Negro-white relations in the South and in the nation." Mays was constantly aware of the racial inequities in the American South. In fact, it was almost as if he were always taking notes and seeing everyday experiences through the prism of the racial problem. Yet this is not a bitter book, fraught with pent-up rage at the circumstances of life in the segregated South. It is instead a quiet, rational insistence that all is not well in America.

But the American South is changing. Mays helped it change for the better and recorded that struggle in *Born to Rebel*. One of the major accomplishments of the civil rights movement was the passage of the Voting Rights Act of 1965, which abolished most of the qualifications and other legal impediments to black voting. The Voting Rights Act and the Poll Tax Amendment outlawed the literacy test and the voting tax, and the civil rights movement emboldened blacks to register to vote and to exercise the franchise; nevertheless, the lower socioeconomic status of African Americans reduces their political participation, and the apathy produced by a lack of candidates representing their interests makes matters worse. African-American voter registration and voter turnout therefore remain lower than that of whites. Interest in voting is acquired as a consequence of what scholars call "political socialization." The children and grandchildren of black citizens who were discouraged from voting in the years before the Voting Rights Act are less likely to register and vote than whites of similar ages whose parents and grandparents did vote.

Mays asserted that "the right to vote is the most sacred thing a man can have." Before blacks could vote he often told audiences, "My father voted, so what's all the argument about? It's nothing new. And 25 years from today your children will be amazed at all this hullabaloo about nothing." He wrote his autobiography partly to help offset these lingering effects of past discrimination. Legal barriers are in fact breaking down, and the psychological restraints that minimized black participation during the Jim Crow segregation period are now dissipating. Blacks today register about as freely as whites in South Carolina. Mays advised black youth that they were "standing on the shoulders of others who have endured and fought through the ballot and the courts." About those who did not break the obstacles to voting, Mays charged, "Any man who is ashamed of his background is a slave."[55]

The South Carolina of today is not the South in which Mays grew up. Many younger blacks and whites do not remember the old blatant segregation. Issues of at-large elections, staggered terms of office, numbered-post provisions, reapportionment plans designed to keep white incumbents in office and exclude minorities, bloc voting by race, majority vote requirements, and other discriminatory practices not banned by the Voting Rights Acts remain prevalent today and continue to dilute blacks' voting strength. Mays opposed these and earlier forms of discrimination, but he understood the differences among the past, the present, and the hope for the future.

Mays completed his autobiography in 1970 (most of the writing was done years before). At that time he wrote that he never felt "at home in my native county." His experiences—watching the Phoenix Riot, "observing the way my people were treated, noting the way in which they responded to this treatment, never having had a white friend from Greenwood County, and having always lived in a rented home"—left him with "a feeling of alienation from the county of my birth. The chasm was so wide between black and white in my day that I never felt that any white person in Greenwood County or in South Carolina would be interested in anything I did."

Mays, however, lived to see the South's acceptance of him and of the kind of life he preached. In 1977 Richard Raymer, a white member of the Atlanta school board, said of Mays, "He is the most widely respected citizen in Atlanta today. If you took a poll he would come out on top. He is the kind of man we would like our kids to grow up to be." In 1974 Lander College in Greenwood awarded Mays the thirty-fourth of his fifty-six

---

[55]*Greenwood Index-Journal*, 15 July 1980; *Columbia Record*, 3 May 1949, 1, 4; Mays, "The Road to Blessed Immortality," *The Pulpit: A Journal of Contemporary Preaching* 28 (January 1957): 30-31.

honorary degrees, and Representative W. J. Bryan Dorn entered the tributes and Mays's acceptance speech into the *Congressional Record*. Furthermore, Dorn added,

> Greenwood County has produced no more illustrious son than Dr. Mays, who was, I am proud to say, born only a short distance from where I now live. . . . [He is] one of the world's most renowned and distinguished educators. Dr. Mays, a superb orator and gentleman, has been an ambassador of culture, good will, brotherhood and understanding throughout the world.

On a later occasion Dorn listed some of the world's leaders he had known, including presidents and generals, and said, "The greatest man I have ever known is my friend and neighbor, Dr. Benjamin E. Mays." In 1979, when South Carolina named a new veterans administration hospital in honor of the thirteen-term congressman, Mays was asked to address the assembly. The black man who had believed no white from Greenwood County could be interested in anything to do with him, who had thought he would never have a white friend from his home county, told the gathering, "With all due respect to you great people who have assembled here today, I'm here for one purpose, because I'm a friend of William Jennings Bryan Dorn." Speaking at Ninety Six in 1981, Mays said, "Yes, Lord, South Carolina has changed. I, myself, have changed." [56]

In the end, Mays the prophet was honored in his own country. In July 1980 his portrait was hung in the South Carolina State House in Columbia; he was the second African American (after Mary Bethune McCloud) to be so honored. On that occasion Mays exulted, "I am no longer an alien in my native state, I feel as free as the wind that blows, free as the birds that fly." He was also inducted into the South Carolina Hall of Fame. On a crisp Friday in early November 1981, dignitaries including Coretta Scott King, together with white and black home folk, gathered at a ceremony to name the intersection of Scott Ferry Road with U.S. Highway 178, six hundred feet from his birthplace, "Mays Crossroads." A

---

[56]*Greenwood Index-Journal*, 15 July 1980, and 18 June 1974, 4; Bennett, "Last of the Great Schoolmasters," 79; Mays, Speech at the Dedication of the Dorn VA Hospital, 14 June 1979.

tall granite marker pays tribute to Mays as "one of the state's most distinguished native sons/ one of the great forces for civil rights not only in this country but around the world." Although *Born to Rebel* ends with an indictment of the South, Mays, in the decade after its publication, found a special peace with the homeland that had treated him and other African Americans so badly for so long: "I am happy, I am glad, in fact I am extremely proud that my native state has done so much to honor Benjamin Mays, son of the soil, son of the farm, son of slaves."[57]

He continued, "My father was born into slavery nine years before Lincoln issued the Emancipation Proclamation and my mother was born into slavery before Congress made slaves citizens." Mays reminded the crowd gathered to honor him that he was fifty-two years old when he was first allowed to vote, that African Americans in South Carolina could not vote until 1946. "Yes, Lord, the people have changed for the better in my native state of South Carolina." Mays recounted the Phoenix Riot, his first childhood memory, and told the crowd that the mob of white vigilantes murdered his cousin. "There was a time when I hated my native state, not the people but for what the politicians did—segregating me so that I could never rise to be what God intended all men to be—free." He said that for most of his life he had not sung "Dixie," but now he could. "'Dixie is no longer to me the world of the segregated society." He concluded by telling the integrated crowd that

> the South is destined to play a great role in democratizing the United States. . . . Yes, I can sing "Dixie" but I can also sing, "My country 'tis of Thee, sweet land of liberty." . . . I love my friends, I love my South Carolinians. . . . I shall not, and I can not and I would not even if I could, let my native state down."[58]

At a memorial service for Mays on April 1, 1984, at Mays Crossroads, the state senator for Greenwood and McCormick counties, John

---

[57]Mays, Speech at portrait unveiling, 6, and address at Epworth, 7 November 1981; *The Ninety Six Star and County Review*, 11 November 1981; *Greenwood Index-Journal*, November 3 and 11, 1981.

[58]Mays, Address at Epworth, 6-7; *Ninety Six Star and County Review*, 11 November 1981; *Greenwood Index-Journal*, 3 and 11 November 1981.

Drummond, said:

We are glad that history will always link his name to this church, to my home town of Ninety Six, and to the little community of Epworth where he entered this world. We will say with pride that we were his home folks. And we will be the beneficiaries of the works of a man who found this world a troubled place, and made it better.[59]

His obituary in the *New York Times* extolled Mays, "teacher and preacher! It was a noble and powerful combination," Charles G. Adams, pastor of the Hartford Memorial Baptist Church in Detroit and president of the Detroit Central Branch of the NAACP, wrote of Mays:

The epitome of manhood, Benjamin Elijah Mays was tall, stalwart and wise. Having perfected the art and diplomacy, refinement, taste, style, common sense, faith, thrift, diligence, discipline, patriotism and total dedication to human betterment, Dr. Mays was the Benjamin Franklin of Black America. His indomitable faith, personal integrity, capacity for hard work and concern for others fueled and fired his meteoric rise from abject poverty and mean obscurity to the highest-ranking scholar, author, activist and educator that one could know. Without a doubt, he was the most distinguished pulpiteer and educator that America has ever produced. . . . [He instilled] faith and character. . . . Never before has America seen a more perfect blend of faith, intelligence and courage. . . . At 89, he died, still dreaming, still writing, still fighting for justice, still striving for excellence. May his memory and his character live long in the hearts and minds of those whose lives he touched.[60]

---

[59]Drummond, "Remarks at Mt. Zion Baptist Church," 3.
[60]*New York Times*, 1 April 1984; Adams, "Benjamin Mays."

3

"EMANCIPATING MYSELF":
MAYS THE DEBATER

Robert James Branham

Benjamin Mays is generally remembered as an outstanding
orator whose wisdom and eloquence shone from the pulpit
and the platform. To Mays, wrote Marcus Boulware in *The
Oratory of Negro Leaders*, "the pulpit is a place for adjusting man's
relationship to other men and to God," and the platform a place "to
uplift and improve the condition of his fellowman."[1] But throughout his
long career, Mays embraced opportunities for debate, occasions in which
his views would be heard and judged in direct confrontation with others.
Formal debate played an important role in his intellectual development,
in his efforts to influence the direction and tactics of civil rights
campaigns, and in the policy deliberations of the many organizations in
which he assumed positions of leadership. Even Mays's individual
speeches were often framed in clear response to positions advanced by
others, joining in debate with adversaries not present.[2] What did Mays
see in debate? Why did he favor it as a medium for persuasion and
deliberation?

In this essay, I trace the development of Mays's knowledge and
practice of debate and its importance in his public career. I first examine
Mays's early training and competition in debate as a student at Bates
College, where he was among the best debaters in what was perhaps its
most successful period in intercollegiate competition. His undergraduate

---

[1] Marcus H. Boulware *The Oratory of Negro Leaders, 1900-1968* (Westport, CT: Negro
Universities Press, 1969), 188.

[2] Robert James Branham, *Debate and Critical Analysis: The Harmony of Conflict*
(Hillsdale, NJ: Erlbaum, 1991), 2-3; Robert James Branham, "Debate and Dissent in Late
Tokugawa and Meiji Japan," *Argumentation and Advocacy* 30 (Winter 1984), 132.

records offer insight to the content and philosophy of his debate instruction and clues to its place in his later thought and work. Second, I examine an aspect of Mays's college debate career omitted in published accounts of his life: his exclusion on the basis of race both from the national honorary society for intercollegiate debate and oratory, Delta Sigma Rho, and from the Bates chapter of that organization. Mays's collegiate years marked the beginning of an ultimately successful eighteen-year effort by the Bates chapter to amend the national constitution of DSR, which culminated in the belated admission of Mays and, eventually, in his receipt of the national organization's highest award. Finally, I discuss the role of debate in Mays's career after Bates, from his years as debate coach at Morehouse to his public advocacy for social justice, as he engaged in widely publicized debates on desegregation, the use of non-violent confrontation, and South African apartheid, among other subjects. Benjamin Mays understood himself to be a "rebel," committed to resistance and transformation. Throughout his life, debate was one important means through which he sought to challenge injustice and promote social change.

"ON THE SIDE OF TRUTH"

When Mays came to Bates in the fall of 1917, the widespread practice of intercollegiate debating was only a quarter-century old. The first highly publicized meeting between Harvard and Yale in 1892 ignited an explosion of debating activity among the nation's colleges and universities. "A new kind of literary activity has arisen," wrote Ralph Curtis Ringwalt in 1897, "which, while possessing some of the best elements of sport, and at the same time enlisting the good-will of those who were most strenuous in their opposition to the prominence of athletics, has taken firm hold on undergraduate life: I mean, of course, intercollegiate debating." By 1902, the practice had spread "throughout the college world." Leagues were formed, rules were promulgated, and audiences thronged in great numbers to see the contests.[3]

Although debate was popular at many colleges, it was accorded an extraordinary degree of significance and institutional support at Bates. The college's first intercollegiate teams were coached by President George C. Chase, who viewed debate as emblematic of the educational mission of the college.[4] Indeed, under Chase's direction, Bates modified its curriculum so that all students, male and female, were required to complete at least one course in argumentation and debate. Many students, including Mays, completed additional coursework in advanced argumentation. Competence in oratory and debate was regarded at Bates and elsewhere as a hallmark of intellectual achievement.

More pragmatically, Chase viewed intercollegiate debate as an opportunity for his small school to compete successfully with much larger and more established colleges and universities. "The administrators of colleges liked to feel that excellence was demonstrated by the college if its teams proved successful," writes E. R. Nichols, and "the large college has never had the supremacy over the small college in debate that it has had in athletics." Bates's upset victories over Colby and Boston University in its first year of competition (1896) seemed to confirm Chase's vision. By the time Mays joined the team in 1917, Bates had won all but ten of its debates. Indeed, from March 1917 (the spring before Mays's arrival) through 1923, Bates debaters were undefeated, and Bates was described in *The American Magazine* as "the tiny college that has beaten the world

---

[3]The Harvard-Yale debate was by no means the first intercollegiate debate, although it has often been cited as such. Debates between college literary societies, such as that between the Adelphic Society of Northwestern U. and the Atheneum Society of the University of Chicago in 1872, had long occurred. But the Harvard-Yale debate, billed as a match between the universities' selected representatives, attracted far greater publicity and was responsible for the explosion of intercollegiate debating in the 1890s. See Otto F. Bauer, "The Harvard-Yale Myth," *The AFA Register* 11 (Winter, 1963), 20; Ralph Curtis Ringwalt, "Intercollegiate Debating," *Forum* 12 (January 1897), 633; Egbert Ray Nichols, "A Historical Sketch of Intercollegiate Debating: I," *The Quarterly Journal of Speech* 22 (April, 1936), 217.

[4]George M. Chase, *George C. Chase: A Biography* (Boston: Houghton Mifflin, 1924), 116-117.

at debating." Debate became a crucial part of the College's self-definition and of its public reputation.[5]

Similarly, at this point in his life Mays viewed participation in intellectual competition, including speech and debate, as a chance to confirm his abilities to himself and to others. He noted:

> I wanted to go to New England primarily for one reason: my total southern environment proclaimed that Negroes were inferior people, and that indictment included me. . . . Although I had never accepted my assigned status—or lack of it—I knew that I had to prove my worth and ability. How could I know that I was not inferior to the white man, having never had a chance to compete with him? Since such competition was impossible in the South, the arena had to be elsewhere.[6]

Mays later rejected the need to "prove himself" through competition. But as a college student, whatever the stated topics of his competitive debates, Mays understood himself to be confronting and refuting racist notions of black intellectual inferiority through his own performances; "I needed to prove this widespread feeling to be a false one," he wrote.[7]

Mays took little time to make his mark at Bates. He had nearly twenty years of experience in public speaking by the time he enrolled. Eight weeks after his arrival he won the prestigious sophomore declamation contest, the most important oratorical competition held at the college and the culmination for most students of the previous year's required work in oral and written expression. Mays recited "The Supposed Speech of John Adams," which he had rehearsed during the previous summer while working on the Pullman cars of the New York

---

[5]Nichols, "Historical Sketch," 219, 217; Rex Stuart, "This Tiny College Has Beaten the World at Debating," *The American Magazine* 46 (September 1923), 32; Robert James Branham, *Stanton's Elm: An Illustrated History of Debating at Bates College* (Lewiston, Maine: Bates College, 1996), 11-12.

[6]Benjamin E. Mays, *Born to Rebel* (New York: Scribner's, 1971), 50.

[7]Benjamin E. Mays, Lord, *The People Have Driven Me On* (New York: Vantage, 1981), 18.

Central Railroad. "My victory in the declamation contest also attracted the attention of A. Craig Baird, professor of English and Debating coach," Mays remembered, "the same afternoon that I won first prize in the contest, Professor Baird visited my room to urge me to try out for the debating team.[8]

Albert Craig Baird had come to Bates in 1913 after completing divinity studies at Union Theological Seminary, where his instructors in speaking had included Henry Sloane Coffin and the great preacher Harry Emerson Fosdick, who, like Mays himself, was to bear a profound influence on the speaking of Martin Luther King Jr. Baird insisted that debate was the art of "selling ideas" and propagating the "social gospel." It was not simply a process for discovering truth, but an opportunity "to make truth prevail."[9] Baird told his debaters:

> First, you are to have genuine intellectual integrity. . . . Second, we expect you to have social integrity and outlook. . . . Thirdly, your personality reflects moral integrity. You are on the side of truth.[10]

In Baird, Mays found an instructor who is now widely regarded as one of the most important scholars and teachers of debate in this century. The year after Mays's graduation, Baird and Bates achieved their greatest debating fame, as three debaters traveled from Lewiston to Oxford University for the first intercontinental collegiate debate. Baird was hailed as a "genius" in *The American Magazine* and was in great

---

[8]Mays, *Born to Rebel*, 57.

[9]Orville Hitchcock, "Introduction," *American Public Address: Studies in Honor of Albert Craig Baird* (Columbia: University of Missouri Press, 1961); Keith Miller, *Voice of Deliverance: The Language of Martin Luther King, Jr., and Its Sources* (New York: Free Press, 1992); A. Craig Baird, *Public Discussion and Debate* (Boston: Ginn & Co., 1928), 13; A. Craig Baird, "The Educational Philosophy of the Teacher of Speech," *The Quarterly Journal of Speech* 24 (December, 1938), 548-549.

[10]A. Craig Baird, quoted in frontispiece to Leroy Cowperthwaite, et al, *On the Side of Truth: A Century of Intercollegiate Debate, Remembrances of A. Craig Baird* (Iowa City, IA: U of Iowa Baird Debate Forum, 1993).

demand and a speaker and writer.[11] In 1925 Baird left Bates for the University of Iowa, where he became chair of the department, national president of the Speech Association of America, and the author of several standard texts in graduate and undergraduate communication studies. Baird served as editor of the annual editions of *Representative American Speeches* from 1937-1959, and included Mays's sermon on "The Inescapable Christ" in the 1944-1945 volume. "It was Baird," Mays writes, "who made me believe I could debate."[12]

Newly-arrived at Bates, Mays received his first formal instruction in argumentation and debate under Baird's direction in a course (English III) required of all second-year students. The argumentation course was developed in 1901 by debating coach and English instructor William Trufant Foster, who became the first president of Reed College. Mays read Foster's landmark textbook, *Argumentation and Debate*, in English III,[13] supplemented by materials written or provided by Baird, as reflected in Baird's *Outline of Argumentation and Debate Prepared for Students in Bates College*. This surviving outline provides a glimpse of the actual principles, topics, and exercises employed in Baird's remarkable course.

---

[11]Waldo Braden, "A Symposium on Liberalizing Influences: Great Teachers," *The Southern Communication Journal* 47 (Winter 1982), 107-108; Owen Peterson, "A. Craig Baird," *Southern Communication Journal* 47 (Winter 1982), 130-134; The 1921 Bates-Oxford meeting is often cited as the first international debate and Baird as the founder of international debating. Baird's predecessor, Bates coach A. K. Spofford, actually arranged the first known international debate, between Bates and Queen's College, Canada, in 1908; Rex Stuart, "This Tiny College Has Beaten the World at Debating," *The American Magazine* (September, 1923), 32; see also Branham, *Stanton's Elm*, 37-39.

[12]Baird's most important works include *Public Discussion and Debate* (1928), *Speech Criticism* (with Lester Thonssen, 1948), and *American Public Addresses*, 1740-1952 (1956); Benjamin E. Mays, "The Inescapable Christ," in A.C. Baird, ed., *Representative American Speeches: 1944-1945* (New York: H. W. Wilson, 1945), 298-306; Benjamin E. Mays to Gladys Hasty Carroll (May 19, 1951). Mays Papers, Installment No. 3, Box 9. Moorland-Spingarn Research Center, Howard University.

[13]*Annual Report of the President, 1901-1902* (Lewiston, ME: Bates College, 1902), 22-25; "William Trufant Foster," *The National Cyclopaedia of American Biography*, v.15 (New York: James T. White & Co., 1916), 300-301; William Trufant Foster, *Argumentation and Debating* (Boston: Houghton Mifflin, 1908).

The recurrence of racial topics and illustrations in Baird's *Outline* is striking. All Bates sophomores were required to read and discuss Moorfield Storey's essay on "The Negro Problem," for example, and to analyze Lincoln's refutation of the Dred Scott decision and Douglas's claim that the Declaration of Independence does not include black Americans. The "appeal to prejudice" is identified in the English III outline as the characteristic and fallacious method of *ignoratio elenchi*, or "ignoring the question," and Baird's illustration of the "chain of reasoning" begins with the premise that "All negroes are men."[14] Baird's students were taught to question generalizations, to demand and scrutinize evidence, to seek common ground, and to equip themselves for moral suasion.

The sophomore argumentation course was among the pillars of the Bates general education requirements in the early decades of the twentieth century. It also provided an extraordinary training and recruitment ground for Bates's famed intercollegiate debating team.[15] Colleges in this period held only a few debates each year, usually attended by large audiences. Only a handful of outstanding students were chosen to represent their schools in intercollegiate contests and the competition for these coveted positions was keen. During his year at Virginia Union before coming to Bates, Mays served as an alternate for a debating team that included Everett Eugene Smith, future pastor of Atlanta's Ebenezer Baptist Church, and Charles H. Thompson, who would become a professor of psychology and education at Howard University and editor of the *Journal of Negro Education*. Similarly, Mays and his teammates at Bates and his own debating students at Morehouse were among the most distinguished students of their institutions. To be selected for an intercollegiate debate was to be accorded a great academic honor, but also

---

[14]Probably referring to Storey's lecture condemning "Race Prejudice," published in *Problems of To-Day* (Freeport, NY: Books for Libraries, 1920, rpt. 1967), 103-148; A.C. Baird, *Outline of Argumentation and Debate, Prepared for Students in Bates College, English III* (Auburn, ME: Merrill & Webber, c.1920), 67, 49; "A is B; All negroes are men; B is C; All men are vertebrates; C is D; All vertebrates are animals; D is E; All animals are mortal; Therefore, A is E; All negroes are mortal." A.C. Baird, *Outline*, 35.

[15]Chase, *George C. Chase*, 117-118.

to be invested with an enormous responsibility and commitment. Mays at first resisted Baird's request that he try out for the team "on the grounds that I needed all my time for study, particularly since I had to do other work," including shoveling snow at President Chase's house, "in order to meet my expenses." Baird, however, did not easily accept Mays efforts to decline. After repeated inquiries by Baird, Mays finally agreed.[16]

To Mays's surprise he was selected as a member of the varsity team during his first semester at Bates and was named an alternate for the Sophomore Prize Debate. According to his senior yearbook, Mays appeared "in many speaking contests and debates on campus," but the opportunities to debate in the prestigious intercollegiate contests were very limited even at Bates. In a hand-written postscript to a letter sent to Bates debating coach and former teammate Brooks Quimby in May 1935, Mays recalled:

> I was a member of the varsity team during my three years at Bates. But circumstances over which I had no control kept me from debating my sophomore and senior years. You recall the war cut down our number of debates during the academic year 1917-18.[17]

When Mays was finally selected for an intercollegiate debate, his scheduled opponent withdrew.[18] In the spring of his junior year, however,

---

[16]Mays, *Born to Rebel*, 57.

[17]Mays, "Why I Went to Bates," *Bates College Bulletin* (January 1966), 21; *The Mirror* (Lewiston, ME: Bates College, 1920), 48; Letter from B.E. Mays to B. Quimby (6 May 1935), Bates College Special Collections.

[18]In Baird's program design, twelve debaters were selected for training. This squad spent months in research and practice before a scheduled debate. From these twelve students, only a few (usually three to six) were selected to compete in actual intercollegiate contests. Through this system, Baird believed, the benefits of debate training would be extended to more students than the few able to compete; at the same time, he reasoned, competition for the actual debating slots would be more keen. The selection of debaters to meet other colleges was, however, a subjective process which Mays believed to be prejudiced. Not chosen for the Bates teams to face Cornell and Harvard in the 1918-1919 season, Mays was "furious": "It may be that race had nothing to do with the selections. It is difficult to prove that it did. It is even more difficult to believe that it did not." *Born to Rebel*, 59.

Mays participated in one of the most important debates of the season.[19] On 25 April 1919, in Medford, Massachusetts, Mays and two teammates faced Tufts University as part of the annual triangular competition among Bates, Tufts, and Clark. Bates opposed the often-debated proposition "Resolved: That the United States should adopt the cabinet form of government modeled after that of Great Britain." On the same evening, another Bates team supported the proposition against Tufts in Lewiston. Manuscripts for the speeches of the Bates debaters were rediscovered in 1994.[20] Mays and his teammates worked for two and a half months in preparation for the debate.[21]

Mays faced more than the burden of these labors, however, while preparing for the debate. Mays was acutely aware of the racial violence that swept the nation in the aftermath of the First World War, in which 200,000 African Americans had served overseas. Many returned home in the spring of 1919 with a determination to "make the world safe for democracy" in the U.S. as well as in Europe. But as Mays would later write, "the black man's participation in World War I did not improve his condition one iota," and demands for equal treatment were met with increased violence.[22] Seventy-eight African Americans were reported lynched in 1918 and eighty-three in 1919, including several black veterans in uniform, some of whom were burned alive.[23] In the "Red Summer" of 1919 that followed Mays's debate, twenty-six race riots erupted throughout the United States as white mobs attacked and black citizens fought back. In Omaha, Nebraska an African American man was dragged through the streets, shot more than a thousand times, and hanged in the middle of town. A white mob killed twenty-five African

---

[19]Mays mistakenly recalls that he participated in no debates during his junior year. See *Born to Rebel*, 59.

[20]I am grateful to Mary Riley, librarian of the Bates College Special Collections, for bringing this transcript to my attention.

[21]"Bates Wins Championship," *The Bates Student*, 1 May 1919, 1.

[22]Benjamin E. Mays, "Crises in Public Education Since 1954," *The Pursuit of a Culture and Human Dignity* (New Orleans: Dillard University, 1971), 11.

[23]Langston Hughes, Milton Meltzer, and C. Eric Lincoln, *A Pictorial History of Black Americans* (New York: Crown, 1973), 267.

Americans in Arkansas; blacks and whites fought in the streets of Washington for three days after white troops raided black residential areas; riots killing nearly forty and injuring five hundred raged for nearly two weeks in Chicago. Federal troops were called out to quell riots in Omaha, Knoxville, Norfolk and Chicago.[24]

Working as a Pullman porter during the "Red Summer" between his junior and senior years at Bates, Mays witnessed first-hand the terrible wake of the Chicago riots. Mays saw his achievements in college in relationship to the events unfolding elsewhere in America. In the middle of a page in his school scrapbook, Mays placed the program of a theater production in which he had performed. Below it, he pasted a border of newspaper articles reporting racial violence ("Hooded Band Flogs Alabama Girl, 17;" "Predicts U.S. Race Wars Will Finally Bring Class Strife"). Next to the *Boston Globe* report of his graduation from Bates, he placed a clipping on the violence three weeks later in Hazelhurst, Mississippi: "Whites Drive Negroes From Southern City."[25] His own extraordinary accomplishments were literally framed by his awareness of the bigotry these achievements defied.

Although Mays's April 1919 speech against Tufts makes no explicit mention of the racial violence and injustice that raged beyond the walls of the debating chamber, his opposition to the cabinet form of government is rooted in concerns at the center of America's social crisis. Addressing Tufts' claim that the British system would produce greater efficiency in government operations, Mays explains that "efficiency is more than speed in legislation and administration"; it demands that the government adhere to principle and be "active in safeguarding the civil liberties of all."[26] By this standard, the U.S. Congress might in fact be judged grossly inefficient, having failed to secure the life and liberty of its

---

[24]Lerone Bennett Jr., *Before the Mayflower. 5th ed.* (New York: Penguin, 1982), 352-353.

[25]Scrapbook in Installment No. 3, Box 12, Mays Papers, Moorland-Spingarn Research Center, Howard University. I am grateful to Esme Bahn for providing me with this material.

[26]Benjamin Elisha (sic) Mays, "Third Speaker for the Negative," *Bates-Tufts Debate*, 25 April 1919, 1. Bates College Special Collections.

black citizens through such measures as anti-lynching legislation, first introduced twenty years earlier.

Mays's primary objection to the cabinet form of government lies in the degree to which it would enhance the power of Congress over the executive and judiciary. From the departure of George White in 1901 until the election of Oscar DePriest in 1929, the U.S. Congress had no African American members, a result of numerous voting barriers erected after Reconstruction. Investing some prescient confidence in the Court and the President to act in ways contrary to prevailing popular sentiment long before the legislature would do so, Mays decries the prospect of "a Supreme Court under the thumb of Congress," which would mean "political control by legislators, as is the case in England."[27] Mays's negative team won the contest with a unanimous decision.[28]

By winning the debates against Tufts in both Medford and Lewiston, Bates claimed the annual championship of the triangular league. "Success has again crowned our efforts in intercollegiate debate," Bates President Clifton Daggett Gray crowed in his annual *Report*, "making the account stand at present as thirty-six victories and ten defeats" since the beginning of intercollegiate debate at the college. But the tiny report of Mays's victory in the *Lewiston Evening Journal* was dwarfed by the advertisement in the same issue for the downtown Empire Theater's showing of *Birth of a Nation*, D. W. Griffith's racist apologia for lynching.[29]

During his years at Bates, Mays won every significant award in debate and public speaking. He won the sophomore declamation contest and sophomore prize debate; the junior and senior exhibition prizes. He served as president of the Bates Debating Council and of the Bates Forum, a public issues discussion organization. He was the Class Day Speaker. His senior yearbook explained: "If you hear him once, you will always remember him."[30] His success furnished "proof that superiority

---

[27]Mays, "Third Speaker," 4.

[28]"Bates Wins Championship," *The Bates Student* (1 May 1919): 1.

[29]Clifton Daggett Gray, *President's Report* (Lewiston, ME: Bates College, 20 June 1919), 8; *Lewiston Evening Journal*, 26 April 1919.

[30]*The Mirror* (Lewiston, ME: Bates College, 1920), 48.

and inferiority in academic achievement had nothing to do with color of skin." He noted:

> One of my dreams came true at Bates. Through competitive experience, I had finally dismissed from my mind for all time the myth of the inferiority of all Negroes and the inherent superiority of all whites—articles of faith to so many in my previous environment. I had done better in academic performances, in public speaking, and in argumentation and debate than the vast majority of my classmates. . . . Bates College made these things possible. Bates College did not "emancipate" me; it did me the far greater service of making it possible for me to emancipate myself, to accept with dignity my own worth as a free man.[31]

DELTA SIGMA RHO

Mays has written of his time at Bates and in Maine as remarkably free from racial prejudice and discrimination.[32] Yet despite his great success in debate and oratory at the College and the many awards bestowed upon him, he was excluded on the basis of race from membership in Delta Sigma Rho, the national debate honorary society whose local chapter was for fifty years the governing body of Bates debate. Mays does not write of this exclusion in his autobiography, but his time at Bates marked the beginning of the national campaign by the college to integrate DSR. Fifteen years after his graduation, Mays was the first African American admitted to the society.

DSR was founded in the Midwest in 1906 in an effort to bring to forensic competitors the prestige and honor associated with Phi Beta

---

[31]Mays, *Born to Rebel*, 58, 60.

[32]Mays, *Born to Rebel*, 55. I am indebted to Thomas Connolly for his groundbreaking research and insight on this issue. In several instances cited below, copies of original correspondence have been lost since the time of his research and the transcriptions provided in his thesis provide the only surviving record of the words of key participants in the dispute. Thomas J. Connolly, *A History of Bates Debate*, unpublished thesis, Bates College, Lewiston, ME, 1979.

Kappa.[33] The bearer of the DSR emblem, representing the oratorical "key to power," according to first national secretary Judge Loevinger, was certified to have "had his moral and social fiber trained and tempered."[34] Fifty chapters had been chartered by Mays's graduation in 1920 and others eagerly sought admission. Most of Bates's principal competitors in the Northeast, including Harvard, Yale, Amherst, Mt. Holyoke, Cornell, and others, joined DSR.

When Bates joined in 1915, it was with the expectation that all students who met the qualifications for membership, stipulated in the 1911 national constitution as "any person who has been an authorized and fully participating representative of a university or college . . . in an intercollegiate debate or oratory," would be eligible to enter DSR if nominated by their chapter. The Bates chapter's own constitution, adopted 21 June 1915, stated accordingly that membership would be open to "any person of good moral character" who "displayed a high degree of ability and efficiency as a speaker."[35]

But these statements proved hollow. Within the first year of DSR's operation at Bates, the chapter was informed that in practice, if not by constitution, the national office would not admit black applicants. For Bates, whose Debate Council president and best debater was an African American (Arthur Dyer) and whose founding principles proclaimed equality of access, the segregated society provoked a moral crisis. The Bates chapter petitioned the National Committee on 30 March 1916, for permission to admit black students for membership. DSR National Secretary-Treasurer Stanley B. Houck denied the request. "With reference to exclusion of Negroes from membership in Delta Sigma Rho," he insisted, "this provision must be adhered to by all chapters." Houck explained that exclusion had "always been the unwritten rule." DSR's principal rival, Tau Kappa Alpha, was also segregated, as Article

---

[33]H.L. Ewbank, "Bits and Pieces of Delta Sigma Rho History," *Delta Sigma Rho 1906-1956 Golden Anniversary* (Boston: Wayne Davis, 1956), 7.

[34]"History of Delta Sigma Rho," *The Gavel* 15 (January 1933): 12.

[35]"Constitution of the National Society of Delta Sigma Rho," *The Gavel* 1 (15 October 1913): 6; Article II, "Constitution, The Bates Chapter—Delta Sigma Rho, Adopted 21 June 1915." Bates College Special Collections.

VIII of its Constitution limited membership eligibility to "male, white persons who have participated in at least one intercollegiate debate or oratorical contest."[36] Houck expressed the concern of the·DSR National Council that any potential admission of black students would lend support to competing societies and hinder the efforts of DSR to gain new chapters among Southern colleges and universities:

> It was accordingly decided that the possible injury done to a few Negroes by excluding them from membership would be offset by the good which the society could do in the South, and that there be no split between the Northern and Southern chapters on this issue. The Southern delegates made it clear that however unreasoning their prejudice might be, the fact remained that Southern institutions would not affiliate with any society that admitted Negroes on the basis of equality with whites.[37]

Faced with this stark pronouncement, the Bates chapter faced a difficult decision: to withdraw from DSR, thereby foregoing not only its perceived honors but also diminishing Bates's influence in the organization; or to remain in DSR and initiate a national campaign to eliminate its race-based exclusion. Bates chose the latter course. At its first annual meeting, held on 26 June 1916, the Bates chapter of DSR admitted an all-white slate of new members, including all participants in intercollegiate debates except Arthur Dyer. At the same time, Secretary Harry Rowe "was instructed to write S. B. Houck, the National Secretary-Treasurer concerning Bates's feeling in the matter of the exclusion of negroes from membership."[38]

---

[36]"Eligibility," *The Speaker* 7 (February 1923), 1. This explicit exclusion was removed by 1926, when the TKA constitution's eligibility provision opened membership to "persons who have participated as speakers in at least one intercollegiate debate or oratorical contest." *The Speaker* (May 1926), 35.

[37]Stanley B. Houck to Harry Rowe, 6 April 1916, quoted in Connolly, *History of Bates Debate*, 83.

[38]*Minutes of Delta Sigma Rho*, 26 June 1916, Bates College Special Collections.

Rowe, campus YMCA secretary and a debater from the Class of 1912, took this charge seriously. Throughout the spring of 1917 he wrote to other DSR chapters explaining that Bates "has a definite problem on its hands in that one of our best and most experienced debaters is a Negro, and according to the regulations of the last Council is not eligible." Rowe asked for their "moral and active support in presenting a re-opening and reconsideration of the matter at the National Council meeting."[39] At the National Council meeting in New Haven, Rowe drafted, circulated and submitted a petition to re-open discussion of the policy and personally protested the Council's ruling. Rowe's efforts failed to overturn the policy but did gain support among other chapters. Because National Council meetings were held only once every five years and dominated by adult faculty officers, the opportunities for chapter-led reform were minimal. Yet the prospect of such reform was accepted by the Bates chapter as justification for its own continued segregation.

A few months after the failure of the Rowe petition at the 1917 meeting, Benjamin Mays entered Bates and, like Dyer before him, made plain the gross injustice of his exclusion through superior performance. Throughout Mays's career at Bates, the college's chapter of Delta Sigma Rho, including current debaters, faculty, and distinguished alumni, met in segregated gatherings to conduct business and initiate new white members.

Rowe repeatedly wrote the national office with new arguments, new proposals and new supporters. At a meeting of New England chapters in Cambridge, Massachusetts in 1920 (the year of Mays's graduation), Rowe formed a bloc of New England chapters willing to pressure the national office in concert. But finances prevented Rowe from traveling to the 1922 national convention in Iowa City and the Bates petition for local autonomy in membership selection was presented by DSR National Secretary Mabel Mason Carlton, who reported back to Bates in a letter read at a special meeting of the college's chapter on 19 May 1922: "As

---

[39]Harry Rowe to Paul O'Donnell, 25 April 1917. Quoted in Connolly, *History of Bates Debate*, 85.

your voting delegate I supported the petition and of course voted for it, but it was lost. The action of the Council was based on a practicable, workable, administrative problem, and not on any question of race prejudice."[40]

While denying that it bore racial prejudice, the National Council of Delta Sigma Rho in 1922 amended its constitution to formalize its policy of race-based exclusion. Article II, Section II now explicitly limited membership to "any person not a negro" who has represented a university or college in intercollegiate oratory or debate. The oath of initiation was modified to require that a new member swear not to be a "member of any other intercollegiate forensic honorary society and not a negro." Moreover, a rule was adopted requiring a four-fifths vote to amend Article II, so as to withstand future efforts by Bates or other chapters to strike the "not a negro" provision.[41]

Yet Bates retained its chapter, excluding Theodore R. Pinckney '23 and the Debate Council president who had represented the College in its 1925 British tour, John P. Davis '26. Davis, later Executive Director of the National Negro Congress, refused to accept his exclusion or the Bates chapter's excuses for administering it. The Bates chapter voted in its annual meeting in June 1926 to petition the national office to accept Davis. When the national office predictably rejected this request, Davis dispatched a letter to Bates trustee and DSR member Louis Costello, editor of the Lewiston newspaper. Bates, Davis charged, was "sailing under a lying flag" when it claimed its organizations to be open to all students yet denied access to black students in practice. On 15 September Bates DSR President and Professor John Murray Carroll expressed the decision of the chapter to continue its affiliation with the national organization. The exclusion of black debaters, he argued, "is not the fault of Bates, but rather part of the general disability under which Negroes labor, and if Bates takes this course [of withdrawing, as suggested by

---

[40]Quotation from letter of Mabel Mason Carlton to the Bates Chapter, D.S.R., recorded in the *Minutes of Delta Sigma Rho*, 19 May 1922, Bates College Special Collections.

[41]Ewbank, "Bits and Pieces," 11.

Davis] it will only deny her students the advantages of affiliation with this honor society without in any degree furthering the rights of the Negro."[42] Carroll nevertheless reaffirmed the Bates chapter's commitment to press for reform at the national level.

Bates's next opportunity to press for an amendment of the national DSR constitution came at the 1931 council meeting held at Northwestern University. As always, the deliberations on black membership were conducted by whites only; neither Mays nor any other African American was ever permitted to argue on their own behalf. The Bates chapter submitted a petition "to strike out from the constitution and oath of Delta Sigma Rho, the clause 'not a negro' wherever it appears." The outline of arguments presented by the Bates representative, Randolph Weatherbee '32, survives. It notes that "the Bates College varsity teams have used two negro speakers in intercollegiate debates of the past" who "have demonstrated high forensic ability and should not be barred from membership because of color alone." The Bates petition argues that "the clause is undemocratic" because "it places merit below color in membership selection" and that it is "inconsistent with the purposes and policies of Delta Sigma Rho," for "to deny to any persons the reward granted to others in the same institution for equal services is not conducive to the encouragement of effective and sincere public speaking." The Bates chapter, however, placated delegates who wished to continue to exclude black debaters from their own chapters. Striking the "not a negro" clause from the national constitution, Bates argued, would leave the issue to local chapters. "Such action," the Bates petition reassured racist

---

[42]John P. Davis to Louis Costello, 18 August 1926). Quoted in Connolly, *History of Bates Debate*, 80; In his *History of Bates Debate*, Connolly wrongly states on p. 94 that the Bates chapter defied the national constitution by inducting John P. Davis '26 in its 1927 annual meeting. Actually, Bates inducted John F. Davis '28, a white debater; John Murray Carroll to the Trustees of Bates College, 15 September 1926). Quoted in Connolly, *History of Bates Debate*, 93.

delegates, "in no way works injustice on those Chapters to whom local membership of negroes would be objectionable."[43]

Even this grievously qualified petition met with enormous resistance from the faculty who occupied the national offices of DSR. On the first day of the convention, Weatherbee, the Bates delegate, was "accosted by Mrs. Gilbert Hall, wife of the national vice-president, who demanded to know if we realized that the reason that the negro wanted to get into the D.S.R. was so they could mate with white women." "This knowledge left us aghast," Weatherbee wrote to Bates coach Brooks Quimby; "It was the kind of stuff we faced all day." Weatherbee and the twenty chapters he had assembled in support of the Bates petition joined forces with a similar group led by the Yale chapter. Saying that "he feared a breakup of the organization," national president Stanley Houck pleaded with the Bates and Yale delegates not to introduce the amendment and to let him bring the matter to the floor instead. In fact, as Quimby later complained, "both Houck and Hall did all they could to prevent the vote."[44] Only when the Cornell representative rose to say that if the resolution to call for a vote was not passed, Cornell and six other colleges would leave DSR immediately, was the opportunity to vote approved.

But when submitted to the individual chapters for their approval, the amendment to strike the "not a negro" clause failed to gain the four-fifths majority necessary for passage.[45] But one crucial obstacle was removed. Two months after the convention, on 18 August 1931, Houck resigned as DSR president and was replaced by H. L. Ewbank, who supported the amendment and pledged to resubmit it for chapter approval until it passed. Brooks Quimby of Bates was elected national vice-president.

---

[43]"A Petition to the General Council of Delta Sigma Rho: To Strike Out From the Constitution and Oath of Delta Sigma Rho, the Clause 'and Not a Negro' Wherever It Appears," (n.d.). Bates College Special Collections.

[44]Randolph Weatherbee to Brooks Quimby (1931), *DSR Correspondence*, Bates College Special Collections, "DSR Correspondence," 3; Brooks Quimby to H.L. Ewbank, (October 6, 1931), *DSR Correspondence*, Bates College Special Collections.

[45]H. L. Ewbank, "Announcement of Vote," *The Gavel*, March 1932, 7.

At last, on 15 April 1935, Ewbank received the fifty-three votes necessary to amend the constitution and asked "all chapters . . . to govern themselves accordingly." On May 22 Bates chapter president Clarence Quimby informed Harry Rowe that "three Bates graduates [Arthur Dyer, Benjamin Mays, and John P. Davis], as a result of this change, are eligible and have been recommended by the coach of debating for formal election at our June meeting, and have been approved by the national society."[46] Notified of his long-overdue election to Delta Sigma Rho, Mays, by then Dean of the School of Religion at Howard University, responded in a letter:

Dear Professor Quimby:
I thank you for your letter of May 1. It was my impression when I was in college that Bates had tried to make it possible for Negroes to become members of the National Forensic Society of Delta Sigma Rho. It is gratifying to know that Bates has kept on the job, and that after many years of effort she has won.

Mays enclosed a check for his membership and initiation fees. At its annual meeting in June the Bates chapter of Delta Sigma inducted seven new members, including Benjamin Mays '20, the first African American initiate approved for membership in the national society in over twenty years.[47]

In its 1956 celebration of its Golden Jubilee, Delta Sigma Rho selected "for special recognition a few members who have made notable contributions in various fields." Joining his former coach, A. Craig Baird, and fellow Bates debater Erwin Canham, Benjamin Mays was among the fifteen distinguished members honored by DSR. In the citation of his achievements, no mention is made of his race-based

---

[46]H. L. Ewbank, "We Amend Our Constitution, *The Gavel,* November 1935, 8; Clarence P. Quimby to Harry Rowe, 25 May 1935), *DSR Correspondence,* Bates College Special Collections.

[47]Letter from B. E. Mays to B. Quimby, 6 May 1935, Bates College Special Collections"; Annual Meeting Delta Sigma Rho, 12 June 1935," *DSR Chapter Minutes,* Bates College Special Collections.

exclusion from DSR for seventeen years. Instead, the last line of his citation reads: "His social philosophy is that racial discrimination is to be solved through education and patience."[48]

DEBATE AFTER BATES

Mays's involvement with debate did not end at Bates, but continued in his career as an educator and his work as a public advocate for social justice. In 1921 Morehouse President John Hope visited Mays at the University of Chicago Divinity School and hired him to teach mathematics and coach the college debating team. Debate had long held an important place at Morehouse. The college's Ciceronian Lyceum met in alternating weeks during the 1880s and '90s to stage extemporaneous and prepared debates. Their topics included contemporary political issues (such as prohibition and women's suffrage), literary disputes (e.g., "Which is the most noble character in *Enoch Arden*?"), and theological matters.[49]

With the advent of intercollegiate debating competition in the 1890s, like many other colleges (including Bates), Morehouse shifted its debating activities from the literary societies to an Academic Debating Club, established in 1903, that drew from the entire student body and represented the college in its meetings with other schools. Morehouse's first intercollegiate debate was held in 1906 with students from Talladega College, and the two schools joined with Knoxville College in 1911 and Fisk University soon after to stage an annual quadrangular competition.[50]

John Hope, the first black president of Morehouse, placed a greater premium upon training in speech, composition, and argument. Although

---

[48]Canham was a member of the Bates team, including John P. Davis, that debated at Cambridge, and later served as editor of *The Christian Science Monitor*; *Delta Sigma Rho, 1906-1956*, 22, 27.

[49]Ridgely Torrence, *The Story of John Hope* (New York: Macmillan, 1948), 237-238; Quoted in Benjamin Griffith Brawley, *History of Morehouse College* (College Park, MD: McGrath Publishing Co., 1917, rpt 1970), 121-122.

[50]Brawley, *History of Morehouse College*, 124, 126.

the teams selected to represent Morehouse in intercollegiate debates were generally drawn from the top students of the senior class, Hope insisted that every Morehouse man possess a proficiency in oratory before graduation. Howard Thurman recalls that at Morehouse during the years of Hope and Mays,

> No man could get a degree from the college until he had conceived and memorized an original oration. We were required to write one each year for four years and were not permitted to graduate until we had given our orations in Friday chapel in front of the student body and the faculty. . . . We were thus trained in public speaking before what was the most critical audience for us—our classmates and professors. . . . We learned to think on our feet and extemporize. Later, during my post-graduate years, members of the audience would frequently come up to me after one of my talks and say, "You're one of John Hope's men, aren't you?" The Morehouse training was unmistakable.[51]

Mays prepared his students for their intercollegiate and intramural debates and traveled with them to the matches at other colleges. Perhaps his most notable team was that of Thurman and James Nabrit during the 1922-1923 season. Thurman, the great mystic and theologian, was later to be joined by Mays on the faculty of the Howard University School of Religion and, like Mays, would journey from Howard to India in the mid-1930s to discuss with Gandhi the applicability of confrontational non-violence to the American struggle for civil rights. Nabrit would become dean of the Howard Law School, president of Howard University, a member of the NAACP legal team that challenged segregation on the road to Brown, and United Nations Ambassador for the United States, appointed by President Lyndon B. Johnson.[52]

---

[51]Howard Thurman, *Lay Bare the Heart* (New York: Harcourt Brace Jovanovich, 1979), 36-37.

[52]Richard Kluger, *Simple Justice: The History of Brown v. Board of Education and Black America's Struggle for Equality* (New York: Vintage, 1977), 518-523.

When Mays took Thurman and Nabrit to debate against Fisk University in Nashville in the spring of 1923, he discovered that Fisk President McKenzie had struck all black candidates from an integrated list of prospective adjudicators submitted by Mays.

I protested this display of rank discrimination, but to no avail. Once I had submitted my list, I was bound to accept any three names chosen by the host college; there was no higher court of appeal. I was furious, but I was powerless. I told Thurman and Nabrit that they had no choice either: they had to win that debate! When the judges gave the decision to Morehouse, I was (and still am!) accused of making one flying leap from the first floor of the Fisk University Chapel to the rostrum to congratulate Nabrit and Thurman.[53]

Mays left Morehouse in 1924 to resume his studies at the University of Chicago. Although no longer involved with competitive academic debate, his career as a public debater on social, religious and political issues was just beginning. Mays's undergraduate debating coach, A. Craig Baird, had promoted the "free and full discussion of matters about which opinion differs" as "the great ally" of truth and an engine for social reform. Baird and Mays viewed debate not as an isolated academic exercise but as invaluable preparation for civic life. "The student," Baird told his pupils, "who is learning in the classroom and on the platform the technique for an honest defense of these right convictions and intelligent policies is committed to a most practical and worthy task."[54]

Yet black debaters, no matter how talented and well-trained, who sought to apply their skills to the task of influencing public policy faced enormous obstacles. Largely barred from the legislature, African Americans developed and participated in alternative institutions for policy debate and deliberation. "Local churches, associations, conventions, and conferences," wrote Mays and Nicholson in *The Negro's*

---

[53]Mays, *Born to Rebel*, 93.
[54]Baird, *Public Discussion and Debate*, 14.

Church, became "the Negro's Democratic and Republican Conventions, his legislature and House of Representatives."[55] As an active and respected leader in religious organizations such as the National Baptist Convention U.S.A., Inc., the YMCA, and the Federal and World Councils of Churches, Mays employed his skill in argumentation, oratory and debate to help shape their policies.

One of the most remarkable series of debates in Mays's public life was conducted in the First, Second, and Third Assemblies of the World Council of Churches, held in Toronto in 1950, in Evanston, Illinois, in 1954, and in Amsterdam in 1958. Decades before most U.S. organizations began to reassess their relationships and responsibilities toward the apartheid regime of South Africa, Benjamin Mays was among those who sought to use the WCC to dismantle the unholy alliance between apartheid and the powerful Dutch Reformed Church. Mays found in the WCC an organization that could most effectively denounce the Dutch Reformed Church's claims that racial discrimination was grounded in the Bible and intervene against the Church's public support for apartheid. It was also an organization in which he could directly and with equal standing engage the representative of the Dutch Reformed Church in extended debate.

At the 1950 conference, several delegates proposed to the Central Committee of the WCC that a delegation be sent to South Africa to confer with the churches of that nation on racial issues, particularly with the dominant Dutch Reformed Church. The official representative of the South African church, Ben J. Marais, insisted that any delegation sent should be an all-white one, so as not to offend the white South Africans with whom they would meet. A two-hour debate on the wisdom of sending a delegation and the question of such a delegation's composition then ensued between Marais and his most vocal opponent, Benjamin Mays. "It was absolutely mandatory that I oppose him," Mays explained; "I felt that I was in a better position to do so than any white delegate."[56]

---

[55]Benjamin E. Mays and Joseph W. Nicholson, *The Negro's Church* (New York: 1933; rpt. New York: Arno Press and the *New York Times*, 1969), 9.

[56]Mays, *Born to Rebel*, 257.

Mays offered a lengthy formal refutation of Marais's remarks and criticized the Council itself for timidity on the issue. Mays ridiculed the oft-repeated claim from Marais and other defenders of apartheid that "outsiders cannot understand" South Africa's need for segregation and should not get involved. Noting that such arguments always came to the Council from white supporters of apartheid, Mays wondered aloud what different viewpoint might be heard from a Christian Bantu. Mays reminded the Council that the South African voices they heard were by no means "the voice of South Africa" and that even his own powerful voice could not possibly represent the experiences of the black majority, "who never have an opportunity to speak for themselves anywhere in the world." Mays denounced the white claim that apartheid is "for the good of all" as virtual "blasphemy."[57]

Marais sought to exploit Cold War anxieties by portraying the South African communist party as the chief indigenous opponent of apartheid. Mays forcefully turned Marais's argument to his own advantage. If the churches and their interpretation of the scriptures and theology are aligned with apartheid and only the communists oppose the evils of segregation and injustice, Mays observed, "then you have laid the foundation for communism in South Africa." Mays embraced both the base value of his opponent ("the spread of communism is undesirable") and his claim that communism was a threat in South Africa. But Mays reversed the link to Marais's claim, arguing persuasively that were the Council to follow Marais's advice, the communist position would be strengthened, not diminished. To Marais's claim that sending an ecumenical delegation would worsen the situation in South Africa, Mays responded succinctly: "I don't think it can get worse."[58]

Mays carried the day, as the Central Committee voted to support his position. In practice, however, the interracial delegation was not sent and four years later, when the World Council of Churches met in Evanston, Illinois for its Second Assembly, Mays again debated with Dr. Marais on

---

[57]*Buffalo Evening News*, 15 July 1950.

[58]George Dugan, "Church Unit Plans South Africa Trip," *New York Times*, 15 July 1950, 14.

racial segregation. "My position and Marais's had not changed since our debate in Toronto four years earlier," Mays noted. Marais claimed to be personally opposed to segregation, but believed it was a "practical necessity" in South Africa. Echoing earlier American opponents of the immediate abolition of slavery, Marais urged the Council to go slow and pursue gradual change. Mays, on the other hand, denounced segregation as immoral and insisted that the Council take immediate action to eradicate it. In his 1954 address to the Council in response to Marais, Mays offered a detailed scriptural case against segregation. Because Marais and others used Biblical examples and passages to support the practice of racial discrimination, Mays refuted these, then carefully built a counter-case for Biblical support of racial equality. Segregation, Mays argued, is "tantamount to penalizing one for being what God made him and tantamount to saying to God, 'You made a mistake, God, when you made people of different races and colors." His speech, he later recalled, was interrupted ten times by applause and the audience "stood and applauded me for several minutes at the end."[59]

The debates between Mays and Marais were face-to-face meetings, but Mays also engaged in other forms of debate. Debates are not always oral exchanges and their participants are not always proximate. In his nearly forty years as a columnist for the *Norfolk Journal and Guide* and the *Pittsburgh Courier*, Mays framed many of his writings as debates in which he clashed with opinions advanced elsewhere by others.

Following the international Christian Youth Conference held in Amsterdam in July and August, 1939, Mays wrote a series of columns in the *Journal and Guide* taking up various issues that had proven divisive at the meeting. In his column of 30 September 1939, Mays defends the negative on the question for debate posed in the column's title: "Will Christian Fellowship in the Church and Home Lead to Intermarriage?" Mays explained that this was the proposition "plainly expressed" by a white South African delegate but not subjected to adequate discussion or debate at the conference itself. Mays's column provides the debate the

---

[59]Mays, *Born to Rebel*, 260-261; "The Church Amidst Ethnic and Racial Tensions," address to the World Council of Churches (1954), reprinted in *Born to Rebel*, 351.

conference did not permit. He poses ten arguments and issues raised on the question of intermarriage and answers each in turn.[60]

Mays sometimes constructed his columns as debates with prominent opponents whose contested statements he assumed his audience to have heard or read before. In his "My View" column in the Pittsburgh *Courier* of 19 October 1963, for example, Mays joined a long-distance debate with the famous evangelist Billy Graham, who had recently claimed in a widely publicized report that "race relations in the South are far better than in the North." Mays refutes this proposition. He suggests that Graham is simply ignorant rather than dishonest and sets about dismantling the case and evidence advanced by the evangelist.

Graham relied heavily on isolated anecdotes from his own travels and limited encounters with black people. Mays argues that the data offered by Graham represents far too small a sample to merit the generalization the evangelist has drawn from it. Mays casts Graham's principal anecdote in devastating light: "Even if two waiters from Little Rock did tell Mr. Graham that they prefer Little Rock to Minneapolis," Mays insists, "and even if a white person in Little Rock went across the street to shake hands with one of the waiters, this incident doesn't prove that 'there is love between races down South.'"[61] Unlike Graham, Mays is able to draw upon a lifetime of personal experience and scholarly analysis in his consideration of the relative racial climate of North and South. "Mr. Graham, who has had the protection of a white skin all his life, should be ashamed to say that," Mays admonishes; "Having been born in South Carolina and being unmistakably a Negro and having traveled widely from one end of this country to the other, I am in a better position to speak to this point than Mr. Graham":

> It was in the South where I was slapped momentarily blind because I was a "black rascal trying to look too good."

---

[60]Benjamin E. Mays, "Fear of Intermarriage," *Norfolk Journal and Guide*, 30 September 1939.

[61]Benjamin E. Mays, "My View: Evangelist Doesn't Know the Score," *Pittsburgh Courier*, 19 October 1963.

It was in the South where I barely escaped being lynched as I was driven out of a Pullman car.

It was in the South where I had to step backward out of a dining car to keep from being beat up from the rear.

It is in the South where most hotels, motels and restaurants are closed to Negroes.

It is in the South where millions of dollars have been spent to break down segregation of the public schools.

"The evangelist just doesn't know," Mays concludes.[62] In his personal columns and in individual speeches, Mays frequently framed his remarks as debates against absent interlocutors, whose views provided him with a foil for the more effective expression of his own opinions. Mays drew the formal statement of a debate proposition, such as [Be it resolved that] "Race relations are far better in the South than in the North" or "Christian interrelationship in the church and home will lead to intermarriage," from the words of his opponent and established himself in opposition to the chosen statement. This proposition provided a clear standard of judgment for the exchange and the interactional frame encouraged response and continued discussion.

A formal debate affords equal speaking opportunity and equal standing to its participants. As a figure of immense stature for his audiences and readers, Mays could credibly situate his ideas within the context of a debate with America's best-known evangelist or with the President of the United States. Whether debating against distant opponents or those with whom he shared the stage, Mays employed a powerful rhetoric of resistance which challenged the official rationalizations of racism and challenged white ignorance.

CONCLUSION

Benjamin Mays was committed to the practice of discussion and debate as a prerequisite for social progress. He also believed that

---

[62]Ibid.

providing students with the ability and inclination to advance, support and defend their beliefs was a fundamental responsibility of the educator. These two missions of debate—educational and social—were inextricably linked for Mays. The purpose of Morehouse College, he explained in a radio address, is not "to produce clever graduates, fluent in speech and able to argue their way through; but rather honest [people], who can be trusted in public and in private—who are sensitive to the wrongs, the sufferings, and the injustices of society and who are willing to accept responsibility for correcting them."[63] Debate, Mays believed, was not primarily a contest of individuals, but of ideas; not a diversion, but a goad to action; not simply an expression of differences, but a means to their resolution.

Mays was himself a superb debater, but perhaps his greatest accomplishment in debate was the creation of an environment at Morehouse College and other institutions in which debate was encouraged. "Nobody on the faculty was afraid to think and speak out" at Mays's Morehouse, writes L. D. Reddick, and these teachers in turn encouraged "their students to explore and search for solutions to campus and world problems." As president, Mays sought to give students greater voice in college affairs by permitting them to join the standing committees of the faculty, by expanding the role of student government and by personally engaging students in debate on matters of college governance. "Whenever President Mays wanted to raise tuition," Charles Willie recalls, "he would go before the students, make his case, and ask them to respond."[64] While Mays invited student arguments on matters of college policy, he insisted that they be clearly stated and well-supported. If he offered no rebuttal to a student's argument, he might still be counted on to offer advice as to how the student might make his presentation more effective.

---

[63]Quoted in Charles V. Willie, *Effective Education: A Minority Policy Perspective* (New York: Greenwood, 1987), 4.

[64]L. D. Reddick, *Crusader Without Violence: A Biography of Martin Luther King, Jr.* (New York: Harper, 1959), 67-68; Charles Willie, interview with the author, 29 October 1994.

Debate and the competitive success he achieved in it as an undergraduate helped Mays emancipate himself from prevailing notions of racial
inferiority. He wrote:

> The central questions confronting every black man are what can he
> do to enlarge his freedom, to create in himself a sense of his
> inherent worth and dignity, and to develop economic and political
> security. . . . There is no easy way; there are no easy answers.[65]

In later life, Mays employed debate to advance the difficult deliberations
over how best to achieve economic and political security and to help
liberate others from misconception and misinformation. The notion of
debate as an emancipatory activity is one that informed Mays's early
training in debate and his use of it throughout his public life and career
as college president. Debate, Baird taught Mays and others, should be
employed to "clear the atmosphere, scatter error, and hasten progress."[66]
Few public figures in this century have so exemplified this approach to
the discussion of social issues as did Benjamin Mays.

---

[65] Mays, *Born to Rebel*, 308-309.
[66] Baird, *Public Discussion and Debate*, 14.

4

MAYS'S ACADEMIC FORMATION, 1917-1936

Randal M. Jelks

Understanding the role of Benjamin E. Mays in the modern religious history of African Americans is critical. He was a prominent clergyman, educator, and writer whose commitments left an indelible mark on the African-American Church and the modern civil rights movement. His life was shaped by the African-American community of South Carolina, the political struggles of the Jim Crow era, and the intellectual ideas of Protestant Liberalism. As a clergyman and academic professional Mays belonged to a small generation of well-trained African Americans who used their education as weapons in the struggle against legal segregation. This chapter will explore Mays's intellectual formation by analyzing the influence of Protestant Liberalism in his thought.

In recent scholarship the study of Protestant Liberalism and African-American Christianity has been primarily focused on Mays's most famous student, Martin Luther King Jr.. However, both Mays and King were a part of a tradition of social Christianity which actively heralded racial reform as one of the foremost goals.[1] In fact, Mays's career provides an excellent example of the tradition between the 1920s and 1950s while in the institutional settings of the National Urban League, the YMCA, Howard University Divinity School, Morehouse College, and the Atlanta School Board.

Mays was a modern representative of the historical and symbiotic relationship between African and Euro-American Protestants. The symbiosis taking place between black and white Protestants within his

---

[1]Ralph E. Luker, *The Social Gospel in Black and White: American Racial Reform, 1885-1912* (Chapel Hill: University of North Carolina Press, 1992); Wilson Jeremiah Moses, *Black Messiahs and Uncle Toms: Social and Literary Manipulations of a Religious Myth* (University Park, PA: Pennsylvania State University Press, 1982), esp. chapter 5.

generation was the reformulation of African-American theological concerns in the academic discourse of Protestant Liberalism. Mays's relationship to Protestant Liberalism began at Bates College and evolved more fully in his graduate studies at the University of Chicago Divinity School. His role as one of America's leading religious spokespersons on race relations was derived out of his ability to translate African-American concerns for racial equity in terms fully understandable to educated white Protestants. The vernacular of white mainline Protestants was Protestant Liberalism.[2]

Therefore it is surprising that scholars, with few exceptions, should persist in studying King and his relationship to Protestant Liberalism and not his mentor. Mays was firmly rooted in the theology of Protestant Liberalism and used it as a critical intellectual framework to examine the religious and social conditions of African Americans—conditions which he believed the African-American Church could significantly enhance. Like King, the theological liberalism advanced by Mays was mediated by his life experience within a southern Afro-Baptist religious culture—a religious culture that matured him and gave constant support for all his endeavors. Therefore, Mays's Protestant Liberalism must be placed in the setting of his

---

[2]For a discussion of the symbiosis of American Protestantism during the antebellum years, see Albert Raboteau, *Slave Religion: The "Invisible Institution" in the Antebellum South* (New York: Oxford University Press, 1978); Mechal Sobel, *The World They Made Together: Black and White Values in Eighteenth-Century Virginia* (Princeton: Princeton University Press, 1987). Joseph R. Washington Jr., *Black Religion, the Negro and Christianity in the United States* (Boston: Beacon Press, 1964), 104-5. Washington concludes that Mays is a more sophisticated version of Negro folk religion. I would argue that Mays is a part of larger symbiotic tradition of American Christianity in which African Americans have consistently reshaped for their own purposes. For recent studies including Mays are now pointing to his crucial role in the linkage of Protestant Liberalism and African-American Christianity. See David W. Wills, "An Enduring Distance: Black Americans and the Establishment," in *Between the Times: The Travail of the Protestant Establishment in America, 1900-1960*, ed. William R. Hutchinson (New York: Cambridge University Press, 1989); Thomas Mikelson, "The Negro's God in the Theology of Martin Luther King, Jr.: Social Community and Theological Discourse" (Th.D. diss., Harvard University, 1988), esp. Chapter 2, "The Negro's God Before 1940." For works on the African-American Christianity see also Cornel West, *Prophesy Deliverance! An Afro-American Revolutionary Christianity* (Philadelphia: Westminster Press, 1982); Gayraud Wilmore, *Black Religion and Black Radicalism: An Interpretation of the Religious History of Afro-American People*, 2nd ed. (Maryknoll, NY: Orbis Books, 1983); Peter J. Paris, *The Social Teachings of the Black Churches* (Philadelphia: Fortress Press, 1985).

lifelong membership, ministry and activism as an Afro-Baptist.[3]

It is my contention that the connection between racial reform and social Christianity will be better understood if we understand the role Mays played in the "quiet days of the Negro Revolution." In understanding his role we will gain a clearer picture of how the coalition between white Protestant mainline churches and African-American churches emerged and galvanized into the struggle for civil rights. The story of Christian Churches and the Civil Rights Movement is a rich one, yet it will not be fully understood until Mays's role is made clearer.[4]

THE EMERGENCE OF PROTESTANT LIBERALISM

Protestant Liberalism emerged in the United States in the late nineteenth century as a theological effort to bridge a chasm between Christianity and the modern world. It was an attempt by theologians and clergy to cope with the cultural, political, industrial, and scientific changes occurring in the United States. Protestant Liberal Theology, otherwise known as Protestant Liberalism, espoused that Christianity was an

---

[3]Benjamin E. Mays and Joseph Nicholson, *The Negro's Church* (New York: Arno Press, 1969) and Mays, *The Negro's God: As Reflected in His Literature* (New York: Atheneum, 1968); for examples of Afro-Southern religious mediation in theological formation of Martin Luther King, Jr. see: James H. Cone's discussion in *Martin and Malcolm in America: A Dream or a Nightmare* (Maryknoll, N.Y.: Orbis Books, 1991) and Lewis V. Baldwin, *There is a Balm in Gilead: The Cultural Roots of Martin Luther King, Jr.* (Minneapolis: Fortress Press, 1991). These arguments regarding the religious and cultural heritage of King are also applicable to Benjamin Mays.

[4]See Aldon D. Morris, *The Origins of the Civil Rights Movement: Black Communities Organizing for Change* (New York: Free Press, 1984), 8; and Sudarshan Kapur, "Gandhi and the Afro-American Community, 1919-1955: (Ph.D. diss., Iliff School of Theology/University of Denver, 1990), 130-37; Luker, *The Social Gospel in Black and White*, 320-21. Luker has shown the connections between the Social Gospel and the African-American community. He rightly corrects previous historiography which criticizes proponents of Social Gospel for not addressing the problem of race. However, he does not discuss the Social Gospel's influence on Mays, although, he notes that King is much indebted to him and other African-American religious intellectuals such as George Kelsey and Samuel Williams at Morehouse College. To Luker's credit, he notes that Mays compiled and edited an anthology of Walter Rauschenbusch (the defining theologian of the Social Gospel Movement) thirty years after his death. These factors in Mays's life and work warrant in-depth study.

immanent religion as opposed to a religion focused on heavenly or other worldly concerns. It emphasized practical human experience rather than divine revelation, and it interpreted religion as dynamic phenomena as opposed to a set of doctrinally static tenets.[5]

Protestant Liberalism also emerged out of a mid-nineteenth-century Calvinism that emphasized biblical revelation as the chief source of Christian faith. The Calvinist perspective on revelation was that the Bible was the literal pronouncement of God. On the other hand, Protestant Liberalism viewed Christianity not as revelatory, but as experiential. Some late nineteenth-century theologians began to regard religious faith as a vital psychological need of human beings. Using the insights of German intellectuals and American Pragmatists, Protestant theologians responded to the new sensibilities within American culture by addressing the issues of Darwinism, urbanization, and the emerging social sciences within the universities. In this setting some clergymen and theologians attempted to address the intellectual challenges to Christian dogma with novel social theories and radical biblical hermeneutics; concurrently other theologians attempted to address the socioeconomic-economic crisis of late nineteenth-century American society and its erosion of a Christian America. This confluence of the theological efforts led the more traditionalist interpreters of church teachings and the Bible to unflatteringly label their colleagues as liberals. In 1916, the year Mays entered college, Protestant Liberalism began to dominate in many mainline churches, colleges, and theological seminaries.[6]

BATES COLLEGE

Neither religious curiosity nor intellectual longing motivated Mays to venture out of the South to attend Bates College. It was solely his desire to find approval as an African American in the wider society that drove him to

---

[5]Kenneth Cauthen, *The Impact of American Religious Liberalism*, 2nd ed. (Washington D.C.: University Press of America, 1983), 3-6, 27.

[6]William R. Hutchinson, *The Modernist Impulse in American Protestantism* (Cambridge, MA.: Harvard University Press, 1976), 74-118; see also, George M. Marsden, *Fundamentalism and American Culture: The Shaping of Twentieth-Century Evangelicalism, 1870-1925* (New York: Oxford University Press, 1980).

compete in a prestigious white college. In the 1966 Bates College bulletin he wrote:

> After graduating from high school as valedictorian of my class . . .
> I thought I would go north for college where I could compete with
> whites. Then, I had the erroneous belief that the "Yankee" was
> superior to the southern white man. So, I said to myself, "I will go
> to New England and compete with 'Yankee.' If I do well there that
> would be convincing proof that Negroes are not inferior to white
> men.

Like many African Americans of his generation, Mays wanted to prove his intellectual prowess and command the respect of the white academic community, the first and foremost arena where Jim Crow would be contested was the classroom. Consequently, it should come as no surprise that Mays strongly desired a New England academy. Therefore it was providential that while a student at Virginia Union University in 1916 he met Charles Hadley and Roland Wakefield, graduates of Bates College. Through their assistance Mays was admitted to the college.[7]

New England colleges such as Bates were initially organized to educate the clergy. Yet by World War I the school had evolved into a coed college that trained men and women as cultural Christians. The college therefore continued to have vestiges of its history as a Baptist seminary by offering regular chapel, YMCA, YWCA, and a strong religion department. By the time Mays entered Bates, the college was an elite four-year liberal arts college that instructed students in the languages (Greek, Latin and modern European), Ancient and European History, Rhetoric, Literature, Religion, Philosophy, Mathematics and the physical sciences. While a classical orientation dominated the college curriculum, the social sciences were increasingly important areas of study. Although Christianity played a vital role in Bates campus life the schools' emphasis had shifted towards non-

---

[7]Benjamin E. Mays, "Why I Went to Bates," *Bates College Bulletin Alumnus Issue*, January 1966; *Lord*, 18-19; Mays, *Rebel*, 53; Mays, *Lord*, 18; "Why I Went to Bates"; Hadley and Wakefield respectively went on to have long distinguished careers in higher education. See *Bates Alumnus* (Summer 1945) on Wakefield, and *Bates Alumnus* (July 1975), 28, on Hadley.

sectarianism.[8]

Mays had come to Bates contemplating a career in the Baptist clergy, a profession he believed would give him status to exercise leadership in the African-American community. He was also aware that other professional opportunities were limited to African Americans of his day. Yet, more importantly to him than the availability of professional opportunities was his need to answer an inner vocational calling in Christian ministry, a calling that had been with him from his childhood. Mays grew up in an Afro-Baptist tradition which strictly adhered to a crude Calvinism in its biblical understanding. His home minister, whom he greatly admired, held that the biblical accounts were literal and that it was unfaithful to question any part of the Bible.[9]

However, in the Bates academic community Mays was exposed to a critical examination of the Christian faith in the Department of Biblical Literature and Religion headed by Professor Herbert Purinton, a professor of Biblical Literature and Religion at Bates for thirty-eight years. His field of study was the Hebrew Scriptures, a subject on which he authored two books, *Literature of the Old Testament* and *The Achievement of Israel*. Purinton's department offered courses such as the literary interpretation of the Bible, comparative history of ancient religions, and textual biblical criticism. These courses put Bates in the mainstream of academic Protestant Liberalism.[10]

Mays was introduced to the Social Gospel writings of Walter Rauschenbusch and the socio-historical studies of Shirley Jackson Case through the Religion Department curriculum at Bates. Rauschenbusch promoted the

---

[8]William *Anthony, Bates College and its Background, A Review of Origins and Causes* (Philadelphia: Judson Press, 1936); Laurence Veysey, *The Emergence of the American University* (Chicago: University of Chicago Press, 1965), 203-12; Bates College, Faculty Minutes (16 March 1920), 277; Mays, *Rebel*, 59; Mays, *Lord*, 23-24; Bates College, *Bates College Bulletin Annual Catalogue, 1919-1920*, 112-15.

[9]Mays, *Lord*, 34; *Rebel*, 14, 61.

[10]Biographical sketches of Purinton are found in the *General Catalogue of Bates College and Cobb Divinity School, 1864-1930* (Lewiston, ME: Bates College, 1931), 486; Bates College, "Beloved Bates Professor Dies at Lewiston Home," *The Bates Student*, 17 November 1934, 1; Fred A. Knapp, "In Memoriam: A Neighbor's Tribute," *The Bates Alumnus* (November 1934), 9; Bates College, *Bates College Bulletin Annual Catalogue, 1919-1920*, 39-41, and *Bates College Bulletin Annual Catalogue, 1916-1917*, 46-47.

idea that the Christian could not be a passive agent in the social order, but should promote the teachings of Jesus to individuals as well as the collective society. Rauschenbusch believed that the social order should be Christianized, whereas Case, a New Testament scholar, promoted a critical examination of the environmental factors that shaped Christian writings and Christianity as a religion. Of particular interest for Case and other scholars of this generation was the locating of the historical Jesus.[11]

The critical academic methodology that the Bates Religion Department used must be seen in the wider context of discussion among American Protestants regarding what it meant to be a Christian in the modern world. Kenneth Cauthen suggested that Protestant Liberalism diverged into two camps in the way they related "Biblical faith to modern culture"; one modernist and the other evangelical. Evangelical liberals were those Christian believers "who were searching for a theology which could be believed by 'intelligent moderns.' " Evangelical Liberalism thought itself to be in continuity with historical faith in placing emphasis on the person and work of Jesus as the Christ, whereas, "modernistic liberals can best be thought of as 'intelligent moderns' who nevertheless wished to be thought of as 'serious Christians." The modernist held no continuity with the historic faith, but "believed that there were elements in the Christian tradition which ought to be retained. However, the standard by which the abiding values of Christianity of the past were to be measured was derived from the presuppositions of modern science, philosophy, psychology and social thought. Nothing was to be believed simply because it was to be found in the Bible or Christian tradition." The Bates Religion Department was squarely evangelical in its view of Protestant Liberalism.[12]

---

[11]H.R. Purinton, "Some Recent Books on Religion," *The Bates Alumnus*, (May 1928), 11; Works by Rauschenbusch see, *Christianity and the Social Crisis* (New York: The Macmillan Co., 1907); *For God and the People: Prayers of the Social Awakening* (Boston: Pilgrim Press, 1910); *Christianizing the Social Order* (New York: The Macmillan Co., 1913); *The Social Principles of Jesus* (New York: Association Press, 1916); and *A Theology for the Social Gospel* (New York: The Macmillan Co., 1917). For a biography of Rauschenbusch see Paul M. Minus, *Walter Rauschenbusch: American Reformer* (New York: Macmillan Publishing Co., 1988). For an excellent interpretation of Rauschenbusch's thought see Gary Scott Smith, "To Reconstruct the World: Walter Rauschenbusch and Social Change," *Fides et Historia: Journal of the Conference on Faith and History* 23 (Summer 1991): 40-63.

[12]Cauthen, *The Impact of American Religious Liberalism*, 27-30.

The greatest impact that Bates's evangelical orientation to Protestant Liberalism had on Mays came though the Social Gospel of Rauschenbusch. Rauschenbusch's view was that the Christian had an obligation to Christianize the social order. He believed that essential teachings of Jesus were not simply for the good of individual piety, but the good of society as a whole. To Mays this no doubt was like food to a starving man! In the first instance, it corrected Mays's formative church teaching which sought accommodation with the segregated society of rural South Carolina. Second, the ethics of the Social Gospel squared completely with the non-racial ethics of the Afro-Baptist tradition which he learned both at church and home. Mays's formative religious ethics held that everyone was equal in the eyes of God. Thirdly, Rauschenbusch's critique stood as corrective to the singular emphasis in Baptist theology of individualist's piety and conversion as the most important act of Christian life. Finally, his adoption of Protestant Liberalism in the form of the Social Gospel into his Christian framework serves as continual evidence of a symbiosis of African and European sources in the creation of an Afro-American Christian tradition.[13]

In Mays's mind adopting the theological perspectives of the Social Gospel was not unusual. He certainly did not view them as a form of heterodoxy and unfaithfulness, as in the case of white southern Baptist and other American fundamentalists. What the Social Gospel provided for Mays was an intellectual and ethical framework for his Christian activism against Jim Crow. Years later as the president of Morehouse College, Mays would demonstrate his gratitude to Rauschenbusch by editing the first anthology of his writings thirty years after Rauschenbusch's death. At Bates, Mays solidified his belief in the social character of Christianity and the positive impact that a social faith and sound biblical interpretation could have on the prevailing social order. It was there he constructed his formal intellectual

---

[13]Peter Paris, *The Social Teaching of the Black Church* contends that the "The fundamental principle of the Black Christian tradition is depicted adequately in the biblical doctrine of the parenthood of God and the kinship of all peoples. . . . It was out of the crucible of racial oppression, then, that black Christian tradition emerged as a nonracist appropriation of the Christian faith. (10-11); Mays, *Rebel*, 11; Albert Raboteau, *Slave Religion*, chapter 5.

critique of Jim Crow.[14]

During Mays's senior year at Bates he affirmed his calling as a Baptist minister. To further his quest for both societal acceptance and professional status, he decided to pursue graduate studies in New Testament. Through the assistance of Purinton and the dean of the University of Chicago Divinity School, Shailer Matthews, Mays was admitted to the Divinity School after having been refused admittance to the Newton Theological Seminary solely on the basis of race.

Mays had been persuaded by the numerous virtues of Protestant Liberalism. First, he believed that Christianity was socially relevant rather than an opiate. Second, he left Bates believing that Christian experience was intelligible to the modern mind. The biblical teachings in particular could be studied and explained historically. And third, Christianity was a religion that affirmed the individual and upheld democratic social order. This explains why Mays, having grown up in a conservative southern Afro-Baptist tradition was not shocked at the critical teaching of the University of Chicago. Chicago was an extension of the teaching he received at Bates. In 1982 Mays explained to an interviewer,

> I never set out to be an educator. I went to the University of Chicago, not because I was going to learn how to preach. I went to the University of Chicago because I like their philosophy, that if you can interpret anything in the Bible you need to know the political, social and economic conditions of what was written. That made sense to me. Even coming from an orthodox faith. I set out to, I mean at Chicago, to learn how to understand how each of the 66 books in the Bible were produced.[15]

For Mays the Bible would never again be a tool to justify African Americans as the children of Ham.

---

[14]Benjamin E. Mays, *A Gospel for the Social Awakening: Selections, Edited and Compiled from the Writings of Walter Rauschenbusch* (New York: Association Press, 1950). See also Luker, *The Social Gospel*, 321.

[15]Mays, *Rebel*, 65; Mays, Oral interview by J. Oscar McCloud, January 1982, Atlanta, GA.

BENJAMIN MAYS AND THE "CHICAGO SCHOOL"

The University of Chicago was reorganized in 1890 through the philanthropy of John D. Rockefeller and the firm presidential leadership of William Rainey Harper. The university in the 1880s was a failing and little regarded Baptist institution. By the turn of the century though, under the guidance of Harper, Chicago became a leading research university. One of the chief areas in which Chicago would achieve acclaim was in its research and instruction in the field of religion. Harper, a Baptist clergyman himself and a scholar of the Hebrew Scriptures, desired that the university's Divinity School would advance the "scientific" study of religion as well as be an institution which would actively train leaders for the Church. By the time Mays reached Chicago the Divinity School was an established bastion of Protestant Liberal thought. Its reputation was so cemented that for many religious intellectuals it was simply known as the "Chicago School."[16]

The Chicago School in 1921 was evangelical in its liberalism, but soon shifted to a modernist emphasis. It was known for its efforts to advance the study of Christianity and biblical literature through a "socio-historical methodology." This methodological approach studied religions in the context of the broader environment within which a particular faith developed. It eschewed looking at religion in terms of supernaturalism and evaluated faith claims from the perspective of their particular historical milieu. In addition, Chicago promoted the ideas of the Social Gospel. Shailer Matthews, the Dean of the Divinity School believed that Christianity offered democracy invaluable ethical norms. A properly interpreted Bible could help to make the civilization more humane.[17]

Although Chicago was a great place for Mays to advance his career, the

---

[16]For example see the discussions in the following regarding the "Chicago School." Charles H. Arnold, *Near the Edge of Battle: A Short History of the Divinity School and the "Chicago School of Theology" 1866-1966* (Chicago: Divinity School Association, 1966); William J. Hynes, *Shirley Jackson Case and the Chicago School: The Socio-Historical Method* (Chico, CA: Scholars Press, 1981) and Creighton Peden, *The Chicago School: The Voices in Liberal Religious Thought* (Bristol, IN: Wyndham Hall Press, 1987); Richard J. Storr, Harper's University: The Beginnings; A History of the University of Chicago (Chicago: University of Chicago Press, 1966; Ron Chernow, *Titan: The Life of John D. Rockefeller, Sr.* (New York: Random House, 1998).

[17]Arnold, *Near the Edge of Battle*, 38-40.

environment of the university and the city itself left a great deal to be desired. Mays arrived in Chicago in January 1921 just two years after the bloody race riots of 1919. His arrival at the university also paralleled the tremendous influx of African Americans from the South, otherwise known as the Great Migration. While the university itself was open to African Americans, unlike many educational institutions of similar stature, its openness was not shared by the city of Chicago nor the Hyde Park neighborhood where the university is located. In this regard Mays wrote,

> At Bates College [white] teachers spoke to Negro students on campus and downtown, especially if the Negro student was in the professor's class. I knew one or two professors at the University of Chicago in 1921 who never recognized a Negro student when off campus or on.

He noted that "Lewiston restaurants were open to Negro students without discrimination. Not so in Chicago in 1921." Over his years attending the University of Chicago the "Jim Crowism" of Chicago hardly abated.[18]

Mays attended the university over a fourteen-year period, 1921-1935. His education was interrupted on numerous occasions, but he demonstrated an unwavering determination to complete his studies. Mays spent concentrated time at Chicago during the academic years of January-August 1921, September 1924-August 1925, and September 1932-December 17, 1935 when he was awarded the degree of Ph.D.[19]

The first period Mays spent at Chicago was during the time the Divinity School's high period in socio-historical research on the New Testament. One of the leading scholars within this period was Shirley Jackson Case. Case had spent a year teaching at the Cobb Divinity School of Bates College

---

[18] Allan H. Spear, *Black Chicago: The Making of a Negro Ghetto, 1890-1920* (Chicago: University of Chicago Press, 1967), 22-23, 129-46, 150, 210-213; Mays, *Rebel*, 135-37.

[19]Mays, *Rebel*, 134; Mays, *Lord*, 35. Correspondence with Maxine Hunsinger Sullivan, University of Chicago, Registrar and Transcript Office, 14 June 1991 and August 1991. Mays attended the university the summers of 1925, 1926, and 1930. His transcripts show that he took course work with J. N. Wilt, H. N. Weiman, Theodore G. Soares, E. E. Aubrey, Shailer Mathews, S.C. Kincheloe, Edward Schaub, Herbert L. Willet, Albert E. Haydon and A. E. Holt. Much of his work from 1932-1935 was with E.E. Aubrey and HN Weiman.

upon completing his doctoral studies at Yale University. He and Mays's former professor, Purinton, were colleagues at Bates during the academic year 1907-1908 and seemed to have a mutuality that lasted throughout their professional careers. Case's scholarship had a direct influence on Mays's view of the New Testament.[20]

Case's contribution to American New Testament scholarship stressed the environmental factors in the evolutionary growth of Christianity. Between 1914 and 1924 he published two noted studies on early Christianity, *The Evolution of Christianity: A Genetic Study of the First-Century Christianity in Relation to its Religious Environment* (1914) and *The Social Origins of Christianity* (1923). Case thought that textual criticism of the New Testament used by many scholars was important, yet inconclusive without the broader contest of history and culture. Like many liberal scholars of this period he was significantly influenced by philosophical naturalism. Case believed that the biblical scholar had to give due consideration to science because the notions of revelation were not sufficient to interpret early Christianity. He preferred to think that supernaturalism that had shadowed much of the New Testament discussion was an impossibility not being grounded in any immanent reality. The Scriptures did not simply drop out of the sky, but rather were shaped by an evolving interaction between culture, politics, and geographic location. For Case the New Testament as a set of religious writings was important based on the unique moral sensibilities of the Judeo-Christian tradition that Western Civilization inherited.[21]

Under Case's influence, Mays entitled his Masters Thesis, "Pagan Survival in Christianity." His thesis weaves through pagan practices as related to such matters as the Virgin Birth, the deification of Jesus and stoic philosophical influence on the writings of the Apostle Paul. Mays contended in his thesis that six notable factors influenced early Christianity:

1. The existence of a universal empire (which was begun by Alexander and completed by the Romans).

---

[20] Arnold, *Near the Edge of Battle*, 27; Herbert R. Purinton, "Some Recent Books on Religion," *The Bates Alumnus* (1928).
[21] Hynes, *Shirley Jackson Case*, 35-86.

2. The growing spirit of cosmopolitanism and brotherhood which Stoicism had done so much to inculcate.
3. A conception of a spiritual deity taught by philosophers.
4. The doctrine of immortality and other elements contained in the popular Greek and oriental mysteries.
5. The Jewish ideal of a personal God, which succeeded in awakening the religious spirit where abstract notions of metaphysics had failed.
6. Jewish background (Canon of Scripture and Diaspora).[22]

He concluded that Christianity was not destroyed because it was rooted in paganism. "It simply means," he argued, "that Christianity was inevitably bound up with the environmental forces of the Roman world; that it is an evolutionary movement; and must be modified, as all movements are, by its environment."

Mays demonstrated in his thesis that he understood his subject's general literature quite well. It also showed that he could thoroughly articulate a Case-like position. Whether or not he actually believed all of Case's assumptions is a question that cannot totally be determined. What can be said is that Mays adopted Case's ideas and furthered his own interest in the use of the social historical method. While the specific methodology he learned at Chicago was a heuristic element in New Testament scholarship there is little doubt that Case's philosophical naturalism influenced him in his studies on African-American religious life. He developed a reservation for cultural behavior which appeared to him to be other worldly. He viewed many aspects of African-American religious practices as largely compensatory behavior for past sufferings.

Indirectly conjoined with Mays's view regarding compensatory nature of African-American religious behavior was the positivism of Robert Ezra Park a prominent sociologist at the University of Chicago. Mays's period at Chicago overlaps with Park's long tenure at the school. Park had substantial influence on African-American sociology through E. Franklin Frazier, a Mays contemporary and colleague at both Howard University and Morehouse; and Charles Johnson, president and professor at Fisk University and

---

[22]Mays, *Lord*, 45; Mays, "Pagan Survival in Christianity" (M.A. thesis, University of Chicago, 1925), 5.

researcher of Afro-American southern life. Additionally, Park's work with Booker T. Washington prior to his tenure at Chicago gave him influence with the African-American educated elite that few other Euro-American intellectuals of this generation can claim. Park believed that dominated people, such as African Americans were at that time, possessed little substantial organizational structure to overcome their oppression and relied too heavily on emotionalism and spontaneity as a strategy for modern social change. His analysis sustained Mays's belief that if African Americans were to assimilate more fully into American society as equal citizens that their institutions, particular the church, would have to construct a more sophisticated strategy of social change not so dependent on "pie sky religion."[23]

In the next phase of Mays's study at Chicago, 1932-1935, he was already an accomplished author and social researcher. He and Joseph Nicholson had spent approximately two years surveying and writing a study for the Institute of Social and Religious Research entitled, *The Negro's Church* (1933). The book painted a portrait of the Church as being a forceful element in African-American life, but not one necessarily attuned to its historical context. As Case, Mays came to believe that it was necessary for religious communities to adapt to their environment if they were going to be vital to their religious adherents. He criticized the black church for failing to creatively meet modern circumstances, leaving its believers at times mired in irrelevant institutions.[24] This failure was not caused by some

---

[23]Dorothy Ross, *The Origins of American Social Science* (Cambridge: Cambridge University Press, 1991), 357-361, 438-440; Ralph Ellison, "An American Dilemma: A Review," *Shadow and the Act* (New York: Vintage Books, 1972), 305-8; Booker T. Washington and Robert E. Park, *The Man Farthest Down: A Record of Observation in Europe* (Doubleday, Page & Company, 1912; reprint, New Brunswick, N.J.: Transaction, Inc., 1984), see St. Clair Drake, introduction; Robert E. Park and Ernest W. Burgess, *Introduction to the Science of Sociology* (Chicago: University of Chicago Press, 192`), 872-952. For a critique of Park's theory see Aldon D. Morris, *Origins of the Civil Rights Movement: Black Communities Organizing for Change* (New York: Free Press, 1984), esp. chapter 11.

[24]Benjamin Mays and Joseph Nicholson, *The Negro's Church* (New York: Arno Press & The New York Times, 1969), 278. Mays and Nicholson received short polite reviews except from Walter White, Secretary of The National Association for the Advancement of Colored People, in the *New York Herald Tribune Books Review* (1933). White wrote, "Few American institutions have had greater influence in shaping the destiny and thought of a race

inherent deficit of Negro churches, but reflected the greater failure of racism within American Christianity. Despite the behavioral critiques found in the Negro Church both Mays and Nicholson remained hopeful that the church would be a vital source of social change for the African-American community. They believed that genius of the black church lay in its spiritual vitality as a nurturing institution for African Americans.

Mays continued this line of reasoning in the next phase of his study. Although E. A. Aubrey directed his dissertation, the greater influence on his thought came from Henry Weiman. As one of America's leading theologians, comparable to the legendary Reinhold Niebuhr, Weiman "whetted [Mays's] appetite further for exploration into philosophy." As a leader within the Chicago School, Weiman emphasized the need for a science of God. He was fond of saying that "man is hell bent for God." According to Weiman, to understand how human beings experienced God, one must analytically evaluate their conception of God. This analysis must be based on science. Science, Weiman contended, lifted the veil of sentimentality from Christianity and removed any obscurantist tendencies which religious traditions used to protect their exact notions about God. Weiman considered science crucial because the methodology not only "enables us to get knowledge [about God]; it also transforms the character of experiences because it transforms the habit of response." The knowledge gained about God through scientific analyses allowed "people to commit themselves to the true God and not to some figment of their distorted needs." Mays attempted to wrestle with similar theological concerns as Weiman in his own dissertation.[25]

---

and, in turn, influencing for better or for worse American thought upon a major problem than the Negro Church. At the same time no institution has received as little critical examinations from either white or Negro students of social science. *The Negro's Church*, by Mays and Nicholson, is one of the few examinations of this sort and it is an important achievement in its understanding of all forces which have made it what it is."

[25]While no letter between Mays and Martin Luther King Jr. has been discovered on the subject of Henry Weiman, it is my belief that King wrote on his now controversial dissertation on Weiman and Tillich at the influence of Mays. King himself noted that Mays was his spiritual mentor, and no doubt King's study of Weiman was intended as being complementary to Mays. See the *Journal of American History* (Spring 1991) for more information on King's alleged plagiarism while a student. One interesting note is that E. A. Aubrey would serve as president of Crozer Theological Seminary where King began his

He entitled his dissertation, "The Idea of God in Contemporary Negro Literature," published in 1938 as *The Negro's God: As Reflected in His Literature*. In this study, Mays sought to clarify how African Americans understood God as they faced their struggle in America. In the books' introduction Mays wrote:

> Some people approach God through the sense of moral struggle against sin and evil in which case God reveals himself in the struggle with man. Some approach God through the intellect as did Hegel; in which case God becomes absolute truth. . . .There is still another approach which is akin to the ethical approach. It may be expressed as follows: one may approach God by accepting the traditional views of God, taking for granted as Jesus and the prophets did, but in an effort to achieve fullness of life, emphasizing those ideas of God that support one's desires and struggles to achieve for existence. It is highly possible that the man who is suppressed and feels the injustices of society would emphasize the justice of God.[26]

Consistently throughout this study Mays attempted to clarify how African Americans viewed God under varying social circumstances. He maintained that God for the African American stemmed from the desire for social justice and not the fine points of theology. He saw African-American concerns as centered on practical concerns of basic survival in a "Jim Crow" society. Unfortunately, Mays did not give his reader an alternative conceptualization of God. This, of course, is a by-product of his extensive use of a purely descriptive methodology. Mays's *The Negro God* served as an excellent source of the historical, intellectual and theological formulations of African Americans, however, as reformulation of the theology of African

---

seminary training upon recommendation from Mays; Peden *The Chicago School*, 87; Mays, *Lord*, 44; Arnold, *Near the Edge of Battle*, 66, 88-89.
    [26]Mays, *The Negro's God*, 18. Thomas J. Mikelson, *The Negro's God in the Theology of Martin Luther King, Jr.*, 51-92; Mikelson offers an excellent analysis of Mays's, *The Negro's God* as it influenced the work of Martin Luther King Jr. Mikelson's chapter is very good as theological analysis of Mays's book. However, the historical context of Mays's study in Mikelson's analysis leaves a lot to be desired.

Americans, it was inadequate. Sadly, he never returned to the seminal scholarship begun in this study. To his credit, however, the subject of his dissertation and subsequent book was an unabashed affirmation that African-American religious life was worthy of serious academic study.[27]

Although Mays's training at Chicago was theologically "liberal," it should be noted that all throughout his career at the Divinity School he remained a committed member in the Afro-Baptist Church. While in Chicago he served as the assistant pastor to L. K. Williams, the pastor of the Olivet Baptist Church. No doubt Mays had occasion to preach and teach within his congregation. In these and other opportunities he synthesized his formal academic training with the folk ways and Christian understanding of Olivet's parishioners. Throughout his formal education he was creating a new symbiosis of Protestant liberalism to the African-American Christian tradition.[28]

Mays's education, race, class and church affiliation gave him standing in two communities, one white, the other black. His status within both Protestant establishment and African-American Protestant churches allowed him to critically speak out against the role of Christianity in the support of American racism. This led him to engage white and black Christians alike in relentless attack on the cultural and legal practices of segregation. In every religious or social arena where Mays found himself—the World Council of Churches, Federal Council of Churches, the YMCA, the National Baptist Convention U.S.A., Inc., the Atlanta School Board, and UNESCO—he sought to challenge the pernicious ideology of white superiority.

CONCLUSION

Like all intellectuals and activists, Mays was shaped by contemporary scholarly theories of his day. He employed the theories he discovered at Chicago and Bates in his struggle to understand and overcome the profound dislocation Jim Crow forced on African Americans. He attached himself to the evangelical stream of Protestant Liberalism as expressed in the Social

---

[27]Mays, *The Negro's God*, 255.
[28]Howard University School of Religion, *The News*, no. 2, 12 (January 1936): 2.

Gospel of Walter Rauschenbusch. Within this theological viewpoint, Mays found a profound connection to his own theological heritage of nonracialism. From the Shirley Jackson Case New Testament studies, Mays derived his own use of the socio-historical method to study African-American religious life. Using the formulations derived from Henry Weiman, he studied the variety of African-American conceptualizations of God. The theology of Protestant Liberalism provided Mays a theoretical framework to evaluate the conditions of the African-American community and advocate for its social enhancement.

The Protestant Liberalism that Mays acquired from his studies at Bates and Chicago must be put in one further context. Mays himself, as has already been demonstrated, belonged to an Afro-Baptist tradition. Both schools he attended had as their denomination affiliation roots within the Baptist tradition. Each school reflected the long history of Baptist in the United States, particularly, the freedom to express one's individual conscience. To understand the modern symbiosis between black and white Protestantism is to take seriously the denominational affiliation that gave them connections. The Protestant Liberalism of Mays must be seen in wider discussion of Baptists in America. It was as a Baptist that Mays acquired status in the larger white Protestant establishment.

Being a Baptist Protestant Liberal gave him standing. Until the advent of Martin Luther King Jr., (another Afro-Baptist), Mays was arguably one of the most important African Americans in the white Protestant establishment. This unique position afforded him the opportunity to address America's racial problems to the leading theologians and church leaders of his day in forums which otherwise were closed to African Americans.[29]

Mays used the intellectual sources of Protestant Liberalism to help plant the seeds for an oppositional theology to American racism derived out of African-American culture.[30] His study *The Negro's God* was seminal in drawing attention to the variety of ways African Americans reflected on God. This study allowed for the possibility of distinct theological points of view held by African Americans. In drawing attention to the theological

---

[29]"Biographical Sketch of Dr. Benjamin E. Mays," *The Journal of Religious Thought*, 132-35; Wills, 172-75.

[30]Dwight G. Billings, "Religion as Opposition: A Gramscian Analysis," *American Journal of Sociology* 96 (July 1990): 1, 4.

thought of African Americans, Mays gave legitimacy to theological and ethical sources developed outside the varied theologies of traditional white American Protestantism. In this way, Mays should be seen as a forerunner to the Black Theology Movement which began in the United States in the mid-1960s.[31]

Finally, Protestant Liberalism helped Mays to express an intellectualized evangelicalism with a vision of social change. In his sermons and writings he consistently called for a changed society and chided African-American churches for their failure to incorporate social vision into their faith communities. Mays's theological understandings inspired him to educationally nurture critically thinking men and women to lead African-American churches into direct social action against Jim Crow. Fortunately for him, he was both a participant and a mentor to a social revolution in American history.

---

[31]Cornel West, *Prophesy Deliverance!: An Afro-American Revolutionary Christianity*, 103; for more information on the Black Theology Movement see Gayraud S. Wilmore and James H. Cone, *Black Theology: A Documentary History, 1966-1979* (Maryknoll, NY: Orbis Books, 1979).

5

THE HOWARD YEARS

Miles Mark Fisher IV

This essay discusses Mays's years as Dean of the Howard University School of Religion, Washington, D.C., from 1934-1940. Mays's personal, professional, national, and international accomplishments while at Howard began a great legacy at that institution. During his tenure at Howard he brought the School to national attention and a Class A rating by the American Association of Theological Schools. He also brought himself to national and international attention by promoting the School of Religion and his own work. The two were synonymous in the minds of many people.

In 1934, Howard University was the "capstone" of Negro education in American. Mordecai Wyatt Johnson, the first African-American president of Howard, in the eighth year of his administration, sought to build the best university with the best people that he could employ. As the "capstone" of historically black schools, many Negro scholars wanted to be at Howard. Racial segregation had enhanced Howard's faculty because there were limited opportunities elsewhere for many of them. The University created to serve the newly freed slaves and others was continuing its task under a "separate but equal" federal policy.

Many of the African-American faculty at Howard had continued their education at the major universities of the North because the Southern institutions were closed to them. Though Howard was south of the Mason-Dixon line, it was located in a city that as the nation's capital was more tolerable than many cities of the deep South. In retrospect, Mays made the following statement about Washington, D.C., in his autobiography:

Certainly, Washington is a Southern City, but I felt more secure in Washington in the 1930's when I lived there, than I did in Atlanta when I came here in 1940.[1]

While at Howard, Mays was a member of the greatest community of African-American scholars of that day and possibly of all time. Numbered among these scholars were many nationally known persons of academic renown, namely: Dwight W. O. Holmes, Alain LeRoy Locke, Charles H. Thompson, Charles H. Wesley, E. Franklin Frazier, Ralph J. Bunche, Abram L. Harris, Ernest E. Just, Francis C. Sumner, Sterling A. Brown, John H. Burr, Felton G. Clark, Kenneth B. Clark, William Montague Cobb, Walter G. Daniel, Charles R. Drew, Eva B. Dykes, Walter Dyson, Susie A. Elliott, Howard N. Fitzhugh, Charles W. Florence, Luther H. Foster, Jason C. Grant, William Leo Hansberry, George E. C. Hayes, William H. Hastie, Charles Hamilton Houston, Martin D. Jenkins, Lois Mailou Jones, Ellis O. Knox, Hylan G. Lewis, Rayford W. Logan, John Lovell Jr., Carroll L. Miller, James N. Nabrit Jr., Hildrus Poindexter, Dorothy B. Porter, Emmett Jay Scott, Georgiana R. Simpson, Frank M. Snowden Jr., Howard Thurman, and Stanton L. Wormley.[2] This was the milieu that Mays found when he accepted the Deanship of the School of Religion. This intellectual environment sharpened his mind through the exchange of ideas and stimulating discussions.

Mays had to choose between an offer to go to Fisk University and the offer to go to Howard. He was more inclined to go to Howard because of his friendship with Mordecai Johnson. Moreover, he later wrote:

I was eager to go to Howard for several reasons. I felt the challenge to make the School of Religion outstanding, to lift it, if possible,

---

[1] Benjamin E. Mays, *Born to Rebel: An Autobiography* (New York, NY: Charles Scribners Sons, 1971), 286.

[2] Walter Dyson, *Howard University the Capstone of Negro Education -- A History 1867-1940* (Washington, D.C.: The Graduate School Howard University, 1941), 172-177; Thomas C. Battle and Clifford L. Muse Jr., *Howard in Retrospect: Images of the Capstone* (Washington, DC: Moorland-Spingarn Research Center, Howard University, 1995; Harry G. Robinson III and Hazel Ruth Edwards, *The Long Walk: The Pacemaking Legacy of Howard University* (Washington, DC: Moorland-Spingarn Research Center, Howard University, 1996).

from its stepchild role to a place of respectability in the institution. Moreover, I had great admiration for Mordecai Johnson. I had more than a casual interest in Mordecai Johnson's success at Howa   I am basically a 'race' man. I believe in the black man's ability, and my heart leaps with joy when a Negro performs well in any field. For me it was imperative that the first 'Negro' President of Howard University be an unqualified and triumphant success. I was eager to help him build a great University by making the School of Religion a first-rate institution.[3]

Howard Thurman, a contemporary of Mays at Howard and one of his best students at Morehouse College, best expressed Johnson's vision for Howard University, noting: "I was caught up in Mordecai Johnson's vision to create the first real community of black scholars, to build an authentic university in America dedicated primarily to the education of black youth."[4]

Mordecai Wyatt Johnson, president of Howard University, had a great influence upon the life of Mays. Mays had heard Johnson speak when he was teaching at Morehouse in the early 1920s and had been greatly impressed. There were a number of parallels in their lives: Both were graduates of the University of Chicago, both were Baptists, both were former pastors, both were role models in academic leadership, both were debaters, both had an international perspective, both believed in the Social Gospel, and both believed in nonviolence as a means of ending American segregation.[5]

PERSONAL ACCOMPLISHMENTS

Mays's personal accomplishments were related to his own academic achievement, his wife, and his family. The year 1935 saw three of his hopes achieved, three of his dreams fulfilled. That year, Mays received his Ph.D. from the Divinity School of the University of Chicago at the age of 41. He was also elected a member of Phi Beta Kappa by the Bates College Chapter some fifteen years after his graduation from that institution in 1920. He

---

[3]*Born to Rebel*, 141.

[4]Howard Thurman, *With Head and Heart: The Autobiography of Howard Thurman* (New York, NY: Harcourt Brace Jovanovich, 1979), 87.

[5]Rayford W. Logan, *Howard University: The First Hundred Years, 1867-1967*, 583.

was elected in 1935 a member of Delta Sigma Rho by the Bates College Chapter. He was the first African American admitted to Delta Sigma Rho. He had been excluded on the basis of race from this National Honorary Society for International Debate and Oratory.[6] Because of his race both of these latter honors had been withheld from him while he was a student at Bates. With the terminal degree from the University of Chicago and the Phi Beta Kappa Key and Delta Sigma Rho Key from Bates, Mays was at the top of the class.

Accompanying Mays to Howard was his wife Sadie, a professional in her own right. Mrs. Mays was an educated spouse and the holder of a M.A. Degree from the University of Chicago's School of Social Service. While the Mayses were at Howard, Mrs. Mays worked as a social worker for the District of Columbia during 1934-1935 and taught at the Howard University School of Social Work as an Instructor and Lecturer from 1935 to 1940. She was also in the Juvenile Correction Department of the Community Chest and Assistant Director of the N.Y.A. of the District of Columbia.[7] Mrs. Mays encouraged Mays to maximize his potential. In his book, *The Negro's God*, Mays acknowledged his wife, Sadie G. Mays, who was helpful in discussions and who encouraged him to publish this volume. Mrs. Mays was the originator of the title, *Born to Rebel*.[8]

In 1938 both of Mays's parents, Mrs. Louvenia Carter Mays and Mr. Hezekiah Mays died. They lived to see him transcend his humble beginnings and rise to the position of Dean at Howard. His father was living with him at the time of his death. During this time, both father and son were able to reconcile past differences. Mays dedicated his book *The Negro's God* in memory of his parents.[9]

---

[6]Mays, *Born to Rebel*, 137.

[7]Walter Dyson, *Howard University, The Capstone of Negro Education—A History 1867-1940*, 368; "17 Positions Held by Howard University Professors' Wives," *Washington Tribune*, September 22, 1936.

[8]*The Negro's God*, vii; *Born to Rebel*, iv.

[9]*The Negro's God*, viii, 37.

PROFESSIONAL ACCOMPLISHMENTS

Mays began his years as Dean with a broad base of experience. He had taught at Morehouse College and the State College at Orangeburg, South Carolina; served as the Executive Secretary of the Tampa Urban League; served as National Student Secretary of the YMCA; directed a study of Negro Churches USA; coauthored a book titled *The Negro Church*; written three magazine articles; and had completed all of his work for the Doctor of Philosophy Degree at the University of Chicago. Mays was a University of Chicago man in the tradition of the social gospel movement. He was to broaden this base of experience at Howard.

Mays's professional accomplishments were related to the six goals that he had set for his tenure at the Howard School of Religion, namely: 1) to increase the enrollment; 2) to improve the faculty; 3) to refurbish the physical plant; 4) to enlarge and improve the library; 5) to establish an endowment; and, 6) to seek accreditation by the American Association of Theological Schools.[10] Over the next six years, his efforts were geared toward realizing these goals.

Mays's professional accomplishments must also be understood in light of the Committee on Basic Salaries Report of 1934 which recommended that advances in rank and salary beyond the minimum be considered individually after conference with deans and department heads on the basis of the following factors: (1) competence in teaching and in research; (2) more publications in better journals; (3) value as a counselor and guide of students; (4) increasing administrative ability; (5) standing among one's professional peers as evidenced by their demand for his services as speaker, counselor, committeeman, and leader.[11] Mays's professional achievements epitomized the criteria described in this report.

At Howard University, a major policy change had been implemented in 1932 when the Theological College was abolished by vote of the Board of Trustees. After 1936, only students holding a college degree from an accredited institution were admitted to the School of Religion. Mays astutely assessed that "perhaps the most important factor in building a

---

[10]*Born to Rebel, 145.*
[11]Logan, 272-273.

theological school restricted to college graduates was the number of Negro teachers who were well known nationally in the Negro community."[12]

Mays worked to broaden the range of offerings for the School of Religion. Postgraduate work in the professional departments had been conducted informally for a number of years. The Dean of the School of Religion had been a member of the Committee on Graduate Studies from its first appointment. On October 13, 1936, the Graduate Council voted to approve Mays's request that the Department of Religious Education be permitted to offer a major in this field, leading to the degree of Master of Arts under the Graduate Council. In 1937, the first Master of Arts Degrees in Religious Education were awarded to Anita Turpeau Anderson and Alfonso J. Edwards.[13] In the 1935-1936 Howard University School of Religion Bulletin, Departments appeared under the names: Church History, Christian Theology, New Testament, Old Testament Interpretation, and Practical Theology.[14]

At Howard, Mays was a leader, teacher, preacher, writer, social activist, evangelist, scholar, educator, and advocate. He was involved in the University, the School of Religion, the local, national, and international communities. As a Baptist preacher, he was in demand by the local churches, as well as churches across the nation, and National Baptist and other Conventions. As a speaker, the great "silver tongued" orator and debater was in great demand by organizations of all suasions, schools, colleges, universities, and national groups.

As Dean of the School of Religion, he was involved in the University Council, which addressed the ongoing work of the University. In addition, he was working to realize his six objectives which he held for the School of Religion.

ACADEMIC YEAR 1938-1939

Mays's Annual Reports at the School of Religion for academic years 1934-1935, 1935-1936, 1936-1937, 1937-1938, and 1939-1940 were not available for review for this writing. The only annual report available for

---

[12]*Born to Rebel*, 144-145.
[13]*Howard University Bulletin, 1935-1936*, 45.
[14]Dyson, 186.

review was "Academic Year 1938-1939." These reports provide the best perspective on the activities of the School of Religion and the Dean's activities. "Academic Year 1938-1939" provides the only insight from the School of Religion's Annual Report regarding Mays's work at the Howard University School of Religion. This was Mays's fifth year as Dean.[15]

The Faculty at the School of Religion included: Mordecai Wyatt Johnson, President; Benjamin Elijah Mays, Professor of Christian Theology and Church History, Dean of the School of Religion; Howard W. Thurman, Professor of Christian Theology and Dean of the Chapel; Rev. William E. Carrington, Assistant Professor of Religious Education; John Edward Bentley, Instructor in Religious Education; Rev. Robert William Brooks, Instructor in Church History and Public Speaking; Mr. Campbell Carrington Johnson, Instructor in Social Service; Ernest C. Smith, Instructor in Religious Education; Rev. J. Leonard Farmer, Associate Professor of Biblical Interpretation; Mr. Paul J. Lutov, Assistant Professor of Biblical Interpretation; and Mr. James D. Tyms, Instructor in Christian Theology.[16]

Forty-three students were enrolled with five B.D. and four M.A. graduates in 1939. Two members of the previous year's class were blind. Long before participation of the handicapped was legislated, Howard included the handicapped. As to faculty, there were four full-time professors, one halftime professor, one special lecturer and four part-time faculty. The four full-time professors were the minimum number required by the American Association of Theological Schools for accreditation. The School spent $1,033 for books. Seven hundred dollars came from the budget, and $333 came from a gift. Regarding scholarships, the School had $3,000 for scholarships. Scholarships for students ranged from $40 to $140.

During this year, Howard positioned itself as the leading institution providing graduate seminary work for Negroes. Gammon Seminary had 67 students with only 34 Graduate Students, and Oberlin had 13 Graduate Students. Howard's 43 Graduate Students made it the leader in numbers. The B.D. work was of a high quality, requiring a comprehensive examination and a thesis before one could graduate. The comprehensive examination

---

[15]Benjamin Mays, *Annual Report, 1938-1939, The School of Religion, Howard University*, Washington, D.C., 1939.
[16]Ibid., 8.

was taken only after the student's thesis had been approved and ready for binding. This placed the responsibility for graduation on each individual student.

During the 1938-1939 academic year, Howard Thurman was on sabbatical. Two students replaced him: one student, James Tyms taught his courses, and the other, Leonard Terrell, served as the Acting Dean of the Chapel. This was also the year that the University's Board of Trustees voted on the Carnegie Library Building for use by the School of Religion.

The Twenty-Second Annual Convocation held on November 8-10, 1938, had as its theme: "As I See Religion." The subject was approached from four angles: Protestant, by the Reverend Vernon Johns and Mordecai W. Johnson; Eastern Orthodox, by Paul T. Lutov; Roman Catholic, by the Reverend Maurice S. Sheehy; and, Jewish, by Rabbi Edmund L. Israel.

A proposal was set forth to have a full-time Professor in Church History, New Testament, Old Testament, Theology, Religious Education, Practical Theology, Homiletics, and Social Ethics. The curriculum followed the pattern of the best theological seminaries of the country and appeared on the whole to be sound.[17]

Rayford Logan stated that "perhaps the most valuable contribution of the School of Religion was the Annual Convocation." During his tenure at Howard, Mays invited a number of the outstanding speakers to the Annual Convocation. Year after year, some of the most noted leaders in various spheres of Christian activity brought to the local ministers and church workers a rich store of practical suggestions and a vital quickening of the Christian life. The Convocation served as a clearing house for the exchange of ideas and as a power house for the generation of ideals.[18]

The Convocation Speakers for the years 1934-1939 were as follows: President Albert W. Palmer, Chicago Theological Seminary; Rabbi Edward L. Israel, Har Sinai Congregation; Julius Hecker, Lecturer on Anglo-American Civilization in the First University of Moscow, Moscow, Russia; Ralph Bunche, Department of Political Science, Howard University; William Lloyd Imes, St. James Presbyterian Church, New York, New York;

---

[17] Ibid., 3-17.
[18] Logan, 380; *Howard University Bulletin, 1939*, 12.

J. A. Martin, General Secretary, Colored Methodist Episcopal Church, Atlanta, Georgia; Reverend Marshall She, Mt. Olivet Baptist Church, W. Philadelphia, Pennsylvania; Robert C. Weaver, Advisor on the Economic Status of Negroes, U.S. Department of the Interior; Mordecai W. Johnson, President, Howard University; Jerome Davis, Yale University; Mr. Francis E. Miller, Chairman, World's Student Christian Federation, Geneva, Switzerland; Richard H. Bowling, First Baptist Church, Norfolk, Virginia; Joseph R. Sizoo, Presbyterian Church, Washington, D.C.; Reverend Miles Mark Fisher, White Rock Baptist Church, Durham, North Carolina; Rufus M. Jones, Haverford, Pennsylvania; Rabbi Efraim M. Rosenzweig, Madison Avenue Temple, Scranton, Pennsylvania; Professor Paul T. Lutov, Paris, France; Maurice S. Sheehy, Catholic University, Washington, D.C.; Reverend Vernon Johns, First Baptist Church, Charleston, West Virginia; Paul Lehmann, Elmhurst College, Elmhurst, Illinois; and, Frank T. Wilson, Lincoln University, Lincoln, Pennsylvania.[19]

As Professor of Christian Theology and Church History, Mays taught courses each semester. During 1938-1939, Mays was listed to teach the following courses: First Semester: Church History 201—Christianity in Roman Empire, (3 hours); Theology 211—Theology in the Modern World, (3 hours); Theology 215—History of Dogma I, (2 hours); and, Theology 221—Science and Religion, (2 hours); Second Semester: Church History 202—Christianity in the Middle Ages, (3 hours); Church History 224—History of the Negro Church, (2 hours); Theology 212—Sin and Salvation, (3 hours); Theology 216—History of Dogma II, (2 hours); Theology 218—Christian Ethics, (3 hours); and Theology 222—Modern Philosophy and Science, (2 hours).[20]

Long before the Women's Movement, there were women in attendance and graduates of the School of Religion. During the Mays's years, three women were graduated: Leticia Octavia Jones, Th.B. (1936); Anita Anderson, M.A. (1937); and Reva A. Brannon, M.A. (1940).35 Women who attended the School of Religion during the Mays's years but who did

---

[19]*Howard University Bulletin, 1939*, 10.
[20]*Howard University Bulletin, 1938*, 21-29.

not receive a degree were: Valerie Justin (1932-1935), Lu Sybil Taylor (1936-1937), and Martha H. Eells (1939-1940).[21]

The 1939-1940 academic year was Mays's last year as Dean of the School of Religion. This was the year of good news. On October 20, 1939, the School of Religion moved into the Carnegie Library Building. On December 15, 1939, the School was placed on the accredited list of the American Association of Theological Schools, becoming the second Negro Seminary to be accredited; and, the purchase of the 39,000 volumes of the Auburn Theological Seminary of Auburn, New York, for $10,000 was a real coup when one considers that the annual appropriation for books at the School of Religion was $100 in 1934-1935; $600 in 1935-1936; $798 in 1936-1937; $800 in 1937-1938; $800 in 1938-1939; and $800 in 1939-1940.37 At that rate, it would have taken the School of Religion seventy-five years to purchase thirty-nine thousand volumes.[22]

The move to the Carnegie Library building and the purchase of the 39,000 volumes of the Auburn Theological Seminary of Auburn, New York, were the result of Mays's persuasive discussion with Johnson on these matters. The *Washington Tribune* stated that: "The School of Religion possesses one of the finest library collections for a Seminary of its size to be found in the United States, having purchased recently from the Auburn Seminary thirty-nine thousand volumes."[23]

The placing of the School of Religion on the accredited list by the American Association of Theological Schools took place a little more than two years after the Association began accrediting seminaries. The number of students who enrolled during Mays six years as Dean are set forth in the following table:

STUDENTS ENROLLED, 1934-1940

Academic Year	Graduate	Theological College	Auditors	Total
1934-35	14	14	0	28

---

[21]Dyson, 210.
[22]*Born to Rebel*, 147.
[23]*Washington Tribune*, February 3, 1940.

1935-36	22	10	0	32
1936-37	24	0	2	26
1937-38	30	0	2	32
1938-39	39	0	4	43
1939-40	42	0	2	44
Totals	171	24	10	205

The number of students who graduated during Mays's six years as Dean are set forth in the following table:

STUDENTS GRADUATED, 1934-1940

Academic Year	B.D. Degree	M.A. Degree	Total
1934-35	4	0	4
1935-36	3	0	3
1936-37	7	2	9
1937-38	6	3	9
1938-39	4	4	8
1939-40	4	4	8
Totals	28	13	37

It is significant that the midpoint of Mays's physical life coincided with the height of his achievement at Howard during 1939. This was the apex of his life.

NATIONAL ACCOMPLISHMENTS

Mays's national accomplishments were related to his high visibility as the Dean of the Howard University School of Religion. Being at the Howard very much worked in Mays's favor, providing him the opportunity to speak to audiences across this nation, broaden his involvement, and thereby gain national visibility and prominence. Howard provided the opportunity for Mays to write his articles in the African-American newspapers, magazines, and other publications, and publish and promote his books. Johnson, Thurman and Mays were all in great demand as speakers during this time.

Mays was sensitive to the national and international issues surrounding race relations. He articulated these to colleges and universities; churches and conventions; groups such as the Young Men's Christian Association (YMCA), National Association for the Advancement of Colored People (NAACP), National Urban League (NUL), Association for the Study of Negro Life and History (ASNLH), and the National Business League (NBL). His articles addressed these issues, and the newspapers reached a national audience.

Mays was very active outside of the University. During 1938-1939, he delivered addresses and sermons including commencement speeches and baccalaureate sermons in the following universities, colleges and institutions: State College of Delaware, Morgan State College, Howard University, Lynchburg College, North Carolina College for Negroes, Morehouse College, Tuskegee Institute, Knoxville College, Kansas State College, University of Idaho, Lincoln University, University of Pennsylvania, Princess Anne College, Virginia Union University, Palmer Memorial Institute, South Carolina State College, Alabama State Teachers College, Florida Agricultural and Mechanical College, University of Nebraska, Washington State College, and Mather Academy.[24]

In addition to the universities, colleges, and other institutions, Mays spoke at churches in the District of Columbia, New Jersey, Virginia, and New York. He sponsored University Christian Missions in various colleges and universities throughout the United States under the auspices of the Federal Council of Churches and served on the Board of Management of the 12th Street Branch of the YMCA, in Washington, D.C. This broad range of public exposure during the Howard Years placed Mays in great demand as a speaker across this nation and the world.[25]

Mays was writing columns in the African-American newspapers beginning in the 1930s. *The Norfolk Journal and Guide* ran a weekly column written by Mays. Some of his articles included: "Brotherhood Key to

---

[24]*Annual Report, 1938-1939, The School of Religion, Howard University*, 14.
[25]Ibid., 15-16.

Oxford Conference" (November 6, 1937); "Segregated Churches" (September 23, 1939); " 'Hitler Would Be 'God' to Germans Asserted Mays" (November 13, 1937); and "Fear of Intermarriage" (September 30, 1939) gave Mays a national readership. These articles reflected Mays's international statements, national statements, and race related statements.[26] The periodical and magazine articles which Mays wrote during the Howard Years included:

"Education of the Negro Ministry"
"The Color Line Around the World"
"World Churchmen Score Prejudice"
"The Church Surveys World Problems"
"Christianity in a Changing World"
"Oxford"
"The Most Neglected Areas in Negro Education"
"Benjamin Griffith Brawley"
"The American Negro and the Christian Religion"
"Christian Youth and Race"
"Yesterday and Tomorrow in Negro Leadership"
"The Religious Life and Needs of Negro Students"
"The Negro Church in American Life"
"Amsterdam on the Church and Race Relations"

Of these articles, seven had an international focus, six had a national focus, while one was biographical.[27]

The introduction to Mays's book, *The Negro's God*, reflected how deeply involved he was in articulating the six leading themes then current in the Negro community. These were: 1) The Booker T. Washington Philosophy of self-help, which had been the basis for the founding of Tuskegee Institute; 2) The National Association for the Advancement of Colored People, which was civic and political in nature as it sought to foster human rights under the 13th, 14th and 15th Amendments to the United States

---

[26]"Benjamin Elijah Mays, Vertical File, Moorland-Spingarn Collection, Howard University.
[27]27"Benjamin Elijah Mays," *Sketches of Negro Life and History* (Washington: A. H. Gordon, W. B. Conkey, and Company, 1929), n.p.

Constitution; 3) The National Urban League, with its focus on the advancement of Negroes in industry as well as the urban conditions related to health, recreation, delinquency, and crime; 4) The Negro Business League, which was concerned with economic security of the race through the development and expansion of Negro businesses; 5) The Association for the Study of Negro Life and History, which focused on greater esteem and self respect through the study of history and the teaching of history in the schools; and, 6) Communism, which sought to be the hope of the Negro because of racism and inequitable treatment in America. These were the major themes for the period 1914 to 1937.[28]

INTERNATIONAL ACCOMPLISHMENTS

Mays's international accomplishments were related to his attendance at four World Conferences while at Howard. Mays was encouraged in his international involvements by Mordecai Johnson. Mays's first trip abroad was to attend the World Conference of the YMCA in Mysore, India, held in January 1937. Mays left New York aboard the Queen Mary on November 18, 1936, and returned in March 1937. He was on leave of absence in Academic Year 1936-1937 from November 15, 1936, to February 28, 1937.[29] Mays spent time in London and Paris before going to Port Said, Egypt, Palestine, Jerusalem, and Bombay. One of the highlights of this trip was his meeting with Mahatma Gandhi, on December 31, 1936. He also met with Mr. Nehru and Madam Pandit.[30]

Mays was elected to membership on the World Committee of the YMCA. He left this conference feeling that the pronouncements were too mild and would not impact South Africa, Arabs and Jews, untouchables in India, and segregation and racial discrimination in America. On his return trip, Mays stopped at Shanghai, China; Kobe, Tokyo, Yokohama, Japan; and Honolulu en route to San Francisco, California. Mays literally went around the world on this trip leaving from New York's east coast and returning by San Francisco on the west coast. As a result of this trip, he stated there was no discrimination among the colored peoples of the world.

[28] *The Negro's God*, 10-14.
[29] *Howard University Bulletin, 1936-1937*, 8.
[30] *Born to Rebel*, 55.

Also, Mays was offered a position on the staff of the World's Committee of the YMCA, which he did not accept.[31]

Mays's second trip abroad was to the Church Conference on Church Community and State held at Oxford, England, during the summer of 1937. He was a co-opted delegate, representing no particular denomination. One of the sections of this conference focused on the problem of race outside the United States. Objections were made to the position of the conference by South Africa. Mays's wife Sadie and her sister, Emma C. W. Gray, accompanied Mays on this trip. They traveled in England, Scotland, Holland, Germany, Switzerland and France. In London and Germany, they met with discrimination. Germany's Hitler Youth Groups were beginning to appear throughout the land. The Jews were considered the German's misfortune. The Mays group traveled to southern Germany with Tracy Strong, General Secretary of the YMCA with Headquarters at Geneva, Switzerland.[32]

Mays's third trip abroad was to the meeting of the Central Committee of the World YMCA, held in Stockholm, Sweden, in the summer of 1938. Mays represented the YMCA's of America at the Plenary Session. During this trip, Mays also visited Edinburgh, Scotland. Mays's fourth trip abroad was to attend the Conference of Christian Youth held at Amsterdam, Holland, in the summer of 1939. He was a leader in that conference. He saw the problem of race in greater dimensions on issues related to "Christian Youth and Race." Every race and race problem throughout the world was represented: Black, White, Brown, and Yellow.[33]

The Commission on Race focused on South Africa, the United States, and the Jewish "problem" across the world. The Conference was conservative on race with the Dutch Reformed Church defending segregation. Thus, segregation and Christianity were compatible. The lesson Mays learned was that "Nowhere can a black man escape. On sea and on land, at home and abroad, the same stupid and cruel discrimination spreads its tentacles."[34]

For Mays, the four World Conferences moved the international dialogue to another level. Mohandas K. Gandhi, Madam Pandit and

---

[31]Ibid., 157, 159.
[32]Ibid., 162, 164.
[33]Ibid., 165-166.
[34]Ibid., 166.

Jawaharlal Nehru were influences upon Mays's future direction. This involvement was a part of the ongoing Howard tradition. Thurman had visited with Mohandas Gandhi earlier in February of 1936. Mays summed up the meaning of his trips abroad when he stated:

> These conferences enabled me to learn from experience, from observation, and from wide contact with people across the world that the black-white problem was a major problem [as it still is] and that our Christian people, Negro and White, have their work cut out for them if Christianity is to play a decisive role in solving the problems of race, war, and poverty and thus avoid world catastrophe.[35]

The black newspapers publicized Mays's trips and giving to Mays a kind of celebrity status. His writings addressed the issues by which he was moved and the problems which needed resolution. Race was the pervasive concern at all levels. About race he said: "It is omnipresent, it creates a physical and spiritual climate from which there is no escape. There is no eluding the race problem anywhere on this earth."[36]

At the international level, Mays was aware of the tensions between democracy and totalitarianism, war and peace, colored peoples versus non-colored peoples, the rise of world leaders and the preparation for World War II, and the pervasive nature of race at all levels of mankind's endeavors. Such was Mays's concern for international affairs that in his memorandum attached to his letter accepting the presidency of Morehouse College, he had already committed his sabbatical year, to which he was entitled, to South Africa. Mays stated:

> In accepting the presidency of Morehouse College, I am by that fact violating an agreement which I made sometime ago with the World Committee of the YMCA through its president, John R. Mott, whereby I agreed, Mrs. Mays and I, to give my sabbatical year, September 1, 1940, to September 1, 1941, to the World's

---

[35]Ibid., 167.
[36]Ibid.

Committee by serving the Bantu people of South Africa. I am therefore accepting the presidency as of July 1, 1940, knowing full well that I am obligated to carry out my contract with the World Committee of the YMCA. . . .[37]

The Howard University School of Religion had visibility and participation in world meetings through Mays's presence. Mays made many new friends. He crystallized his thinking on the major issues of the day. He shared these experiences with the American Negro and the broader society through the various media and kept his audiences abreast of the changes in the international community as well as the national community.

TRANSITION FROM HOWARD TO MOREHOUSE

On June 21, 1940, the Executive Committee at Howard University accepted Mays's resignation as dean of the School of Religion. He had realized five of his immediate objectives at the School of Religion: an enlarged graduate enrollment, a strengthened faculty, an adequate library, accreditation by the American Association of Theological Schools; and, an improved physical plant. The physical plant was to have been a temporary arrangement. The establishment of an endowment was the only unrealized immediate objective. Mays's leadership during the Howard Years prepared him for his life's work as president of Morehouse College.[38]

Upon completion of his work at Howard, Mays received a "Proclamation from the Howard University Council in recognition of his distinctive service. The Proclamation read:

Benjamin Elijah Mays

For six years, you have served with honor and distinction as Dean of the School of Religion of Howard University and as a member of the University Council. You have faithfully performed your arduous duties with unflagging zeal and unusual scholastic power.

---

[37]Ibid., 171.
[38]Ibid., 148.

Your earnestness, your sincerity, your love for your fellow councilmen, and your calm and dispassionate manner in treating the problems of the Council have all implanted in our hearts a respect, admiration and deep affection for you.

On behalf of the Council, we present to you this token of our esteem and good wishes for the future as you leave the University to become President of Morehouse College.[39]

Mays had left the new dean of the School of Religion a solid foundation upon which to build. Mays had a special relationship with Mordecai Wyatt Johnson. His own employment as dean, his wife's employment at the university, his trips abroad to four World Conferences, his travel for speaking engagements, his acquiring the Carnegie Library Building for the School of Religion, and his acquisition of the 39,000 volume library collection of Auburn Seminary, speak to this relationship.

THE LEGACY

Mays's personal, professional, national, and international accomplishments laid the foundation for Mays's ongoing legacy at Howard University. His spirit never left Howard. He had an ongoing relationship with Mordecai Wyatt Johnson, who was an alumnus of Morehouse College, class of 1911. James M. Nabrit Jr., who was Johnson's successor in the 1960s, was one of Mays's students and a member of the Morehouse Debating Team along with Howard Thurman when Mays taught at Morehouse in the early 1920s. Mays attended Nabrit's Inauguration. James Cheek, who followed Nabrit as President, always had Mays involved at Howard. He presented him the University Citation in 1974. Up until his death, Mays and Howard University had an ongoing personal relationship. Since his death, Howard University and its School of Divinity have continued his legacy.

Students are a teacher's greatest legacy. During the Howard Years, Mays encouraged his students to aim high. Some of Mays's students at the School of Religion were inspired to make notable contributions in their

---

[39]Benjamin E. Mays papers, Moorland-Spingarn Collection, Howard University.

endeavors. John Bunyan Eubanks (1935) became President of Jarvis Christian College and later Professor at the School of Religion. He was also a Ph.D. from the University of Chicago. James D. Tyms (1937) became a member of the faculty of the Howard University School of Religion. The late Samuel L. Gandy (1938) went to the University of Chicago, received the Ph.D. Degree, and returned as Dean of the School of Religion from 1965 to 1974. The Reverend Andrew Fowler ('39) is presently president of the Washington Bible College and pastor of Capital View Baptist Church, Washington, D.C. James Farmer ('40) was the founder and former National Director of the Congress of Racial Equality (CORE). Samuel W. Williams ('40) went tot he University of Chicago, whence Mays invited him to teach philosophy at Morehouse in 1945. The next year he taught Thoreau's "Civil Disobedience" to Martin Luther King Jr. The late Charles M. Black ('42) was the first black on a City Council in Hawaii. Walter Raphael Hazzard was president of Philander Smith College in Little Rock Arkansas. The late John Albert Middleton was president of Morris Brown College in Atlanta. These students were greatly influenced by Mays's leadership while at Howard, along with other men and women who attended the School of Religion. They carried on the Mays tradition. Over the years, Howard University has supported and remembered the work of Benjamin Elijah Mays.

In 1933, 1937, 1939, 1940, 1942, 1945, 1950, 1952, 1959, 1960 and 1967, the Howard University *Journal of Negro Education* carried articles written by Mays. In 1945, Howard University conferred upon Mays the Doctor of Divinity degree. In 1945, the Howard University Bulletin carried an article written by Mays. In 1945 and 1953, the *Journal of Religious Thought* carried articles written by Mays, and in 1975 the Spring/Summer issue was dedicated to Mays as the Reverend Benjamin E. Mays Honorary Volume Bicentennial Issue.

In 1961, Mays made a brief address for the delegates at a luncheon during the Inauguration of President James N. Nabrit Jr. as the Fourteenth President of Howard University. In 1967, Mays was the Centennial Commencement Speaker at Howard University. In 1974, Howard University presented Mays with the Howard University Citation. In 1977, Mays delivered the 107th Charter Day Speech.

In 1977, Mays sent his private papers and memorabilia to the Moorland-Spingarn Library. This act was indicative of the esteem he had for Howard University. Approximately 230 boxes and 29 scrapbooks were included in the preliminary inventory. In addition, thirty-one boxes of books were packed to be delivered to the Howard University School of Religion.

On April 22, 1987, the School of Divinity held its service of dedication for the Benjamin Elijah Mays Hall which houses the Howard Thurman Chapel. The North Hall in the Benjamin E. Mays Building presently contains an exhibit enclosed in four panels which chronicles highlights from Mays's life. The Spingarn Medal presented to Mays by the NAACP in 1982 and the Religious Leaders Award presented by the National Conference of Christians and Jews in 1970 are included in this display. The School of Divinity's Library has a special section dedicated to Mays. Mays's books are included in the African Collection.

The bronze plaque on the wall in the foyer of the Howard University School of Divinity's Benjamin E. Mays Hall, in part, sums up the contribution of Mays during his Howard years. It reads:

Benjamin E. Mays, Ph.D.
August 1, 1894 - March 28, 1984

Clergyman, educator, world churchman, author, civil rights statesman and counselor to Presidents. Benjamin E. Mays was Dean of the School of Religion 1934-1940. During his tenure he laid the foundations for the present School of Divinity by facilitating the purchase of the Auburn Seminary Library; by negotiating the location of the School of Religion in the Carnegie Building and by leading the school successfully through its initial accreditation by the American Association of Theological Schools in 1940.

"It is not a disgrace not to reach the stars, but it is a disgrace to have no stars to reach for. Not failure, but low aim is sin".

CONCLUSION

A summary of the Morehouse years in his chapter on "Retrospect and Prospect" puts in perspective the Howard years, when Mays stated:

At Morehouse, I had tried to develop an academic community that was supra culture, supra race, supra religion, and supra nation. I tried to build this kind of college because I believed then, as I do now, that unless we succeed in building this same kind of world, mankind's existence on earth is indeed precarious. I knew I could make little impact on the larger society, but I did what I could in the small area over which I presided for more than a quarter of a century.[40]

This statement echoes what Mordecai Wyatt Johnson was striving to do at Howard University when Mays served as Dean of the School of Religion. This statement implied a world view that transcended the many contradictions of our society. As dean, Mays's personal, professional, national and international accomplishments contributed to a great legacy at Howard.

---

[40]*Born to Rebel,* 310.

6

MAYS, KING, AND
THE NEGRO'S GOD

Thomas I. S. Mikelson

It is especially illuminating to examine King's understanding of God in light of Mays's perception of "the Negro's God"—those images of God found in the discourse of black religious and intellectual leaders. Mays was a friend of King's parents and a colleague of King's father in education, community, and civil rights work. Mays represented an impressive synthesis of traditional black piety and theological learning that King admired as a youth and later personally achieved. In his moving eulogy of the civil rights leader Mays spoke of King as like "a deceased son—so close and so precious was he to me."[1]

Like Mays, his mentor, King was deeply religious and highly educated, a minister and an intellectual, an educator and a highly visible public leader. Both were born and raised in the deep South, educated in northern institutions of higher learning, and returned to lives of leadership in the South. King followed the educational path of his mentor to a Ph.D. in theological studies. As a young theologian, in 1938 Mays wrote a book about understandings of God among African Americans. That book, in which Mays examined "the Negro's God" from 1760 to 1938, is invaluable for the light it throws on thinking about God in black churches, and thus on the religious environment that influenced King during his earliest years.

There are two levels of interest in the essay that follows: the influence of Benjamin Mays as an adult role model on the young Martin Luther King Jr. and the light that Mays's scholarly writing throws on the religious milieu that shaped King during his early formative years. Understanding the latter, requires a close look at Mays's interpretation of "the Negro's God" as a source for understanding King's conception of God.

---

[1]*Born to Rebel*, 357.

The social, religious, and educational contexts in which King grew up, contexts that had been influenced significantly by Benjamin Mays, were uniquely suited to inspire his interests in advanced theological education. From early in his life, the youthful King was surrounded by a network of persons who were shaping higher education and theological education for African Americans, not only in Atlanta but also throughout the nation. Mays was in the center of a circle that included Charles Dubois Hubert, Howard Thurman, Mordecai Johnson, Melvin Watson, and George Kelsey. All of those outstanding figures had confronted personally the challenge of religious and theological changes that were moving through many theological faculties, becoming pioneers in a new kind of black theology and theological education. They were educated theologically in a way that African Americans had not been educated earlier. They constituted a first wave of highly trained African-American teachers of theology, and they achieved positions of professional leadership from which they brought lasting changes in higher education and theological education for younger generations of African Americans. All of them, in addition, were persons of reputed religious quality. They represented for younger students a melding of traditional faith and high educational attainment. Their lives and careers moved gracefully in the public worlds of black churches and liberal theological education.

Those profound changes influenced King's spiritual, intellectual, and vocational development. By virtue of his social position and upbringing, King was able, as a child and young man, to witness those changes, and to know personally several of the principal leaders in that process of change. His own family was instrumental in introducing him to traditional black Baptist piety and academic theology. King's grandfather, the Reverend A. D. Williams (1863-1931) had graduated from Morehouse and received an honorary degree from president John Hope in 1906. Both Williams and Hope were strong leaders in the NAACP.[2] King's father, Martin Luther King Sr. (1897-1984), graduated from Morehouse College, became a trustee, and drew even closer to the faculty members who were shaping religious studies there. Primarily through his father's connections, Martin

---

[2]Clayborne Carson, Senior Editor, *The Papers of Martin Luther King Jr: Called to Serve, January 1929-June 1951,* Vol. 1, (Los Angeles: University of California Press, 1992), 36.

Luther King Jr. became acquainted with persons such as C. D. Hubert, Howard Thurman, Benjamin Mays, Melvin Watson, George Kelsey and William Holmes Borders.

Those leaders were shaping African-American higher education and study of religion in their time and for future generations. The educational paths they had taken and that they were opening for the younger King's generation, were paths to leadership within African-American life and paths to recognition in the wider American society. The social location of King's birth and upbringing opened those paths for him, paths that were among the most attractive ones open to him and his contemporaries.

Many have noted the unique and influential spirit of Morehouse College. Benjamin Mays, writing in 1971 about his first extended stay at Morehouse College as a young instructor, fifty years earlier, observed

I found a special, intangible something at Morehouse in 1921 which sent men out into life with a sense of mission, believing that they could accomplish whatever they set out to do. This priceless quality was still alive when I returned in 1940.

Brailsford Brazeal, a Dean at Morehouse when King was an undergraduate there, commented upon that spirit among students and faculty at Morehouse College: "A spirit at Morehouse led our men to believe they could excel in any situation."[3]

That was the "intangible . . . priceless quality" that at age fifteen King discovered for himself as an entering student in 1944. Many persons associated with Morehouse surrounded him for the remainder of his life. He became a "Morehouse Man." His friend and biographer, L. D. Reddick, has observed,

It was inevitable that Martin Luther King Jr., would attend Morehouse College. His grandfather had been a Morehouse man and his father never tired of talking about the transformation that Morehouse had wrought in him.[4]

---

[3]*Born to Rebel*, 172; Interview of Brailsford Brazeal by Judy Barton, April 17, 1972.
[4]Reddick, *Crusader Without Violence*, 62.

The Morehouse network would become a key factor in King's later life. During his student days, the College was in an expansive period; the faculty was growing both in quantity and quality, in the teaching of religion as well as in other disciplines. President Mays's new leadership, beginning in 1940, was forceful and invigorating. King had personal access to President Mays and to other faculty members and alumni such as George Kelsey, Brailsford Brazeal, Howard Thurman, Walter Chivers, Samuel Williams, and, later, Melvin Watson. King's personal world grew to include these and other Morehouse graduates and faculty persons throughout his life. Through that community, King met many of the people who influenced the direction of his life and thought

THEOLOGY, CULTURE, AND SOCIAL LOCATION

An image of God is a construct of imagination, and theology as a whole is a cultural phenomenon, reflecting the social and cultural situations in which it rises to disciplined expression. Images of God are constructed, as Gordon Kaufman wrote in 1972, out of some "long cultural history." Those images belong not to any person but to a people. Benjamin Mays had observed something similar much earlier, in 1938, when he wrote, "The Negro's ideas of God grew out of the social situation in which he finds himself." Both Kaufman and Mays, writing decades apart and from very different social settings, recognize the influence of corporate, forces in the shaping of theological images; such images belong to a people, not to an individual.[5]

Mays's notion of "social situation" and Kaufman's understanding of "culture" are notably different. By culture Kaufman has in mind something more like the whole of a culture than he does some discrete subculture such as African-American culture. He writes: "Theological terms and concepts

---

[5]Gordon D. Kaufman, *God the Problem* (Cambridge: Harvard University Press, 1972), 166; *An Essay on Theological Method* (Missoula, Montana: Scholars Press, 1975,1979), especially Chapter One; Mays, *The Negro's God,* vii. See also Preston N. Williams, "Toward a Sociological Understanding of the Black Religious Community," *Soundings,* (Fall, 1971), 265. Williams argues that "creativity" in the black churches has been "seldom the work of one individual. The community must participate in the creative act and legitimate the product."

are rooted in wide experience and history of a whole culture, or a mixture of cultures. . . ." The "wide" cultural background of theological concepts on which Kaufman's view depends does not take into account the finely nuanced differences within and among subcultures. Mays, on the other hand, did not build his argument on the "wide experience and history of a whole culture." He focused instead on the particular social/historical experiences of African Americans—distinct cultural roots as well as specific victimizations by slavery, segregation, and discrimination in the American experience. Out of that long "hardness of life" has grown a unique understanding of God.[6]

Theology, as David Tracy has argued, is public discourse and theologians must in some fashion acknowledge and address a plurality of "publics."

> The fact is that theologians do not only recognize a plurality of "publics" to whom they intend to speak, but also more and more the theologians are internalizing this plurality in their own discourse.

Tracy holds that theologians possess self understandings in relation to those publics of which they are a part and to which they speak. I treat King's understanding of God as public discourse, generated and shaped in black church culture and addressed to various public audiences in the course of his changing career.

Every theologian, argues Tracy, addresses three large publics—the society, the academy, and the church, and every theologian internalizes something of their demands and "plausibility structures."[7] King, like Mays, spoke from within the culture of the black church and with the tools of America's finest academic training in theology. He spent his life addressing African Americans and the society at large. The church public in which King grew up, by which he was nurtured, and in which he worked through-

---

[6]Kaufman, *An Essay on Theological Method*, 3. See also footnote 7, 18-19 where he discusses the basis in Western civilization for doing theology; the term, "hardness of life," comes from Charles Long, *Significations: Signs, Symbols, and Images in the Interpretation of Religion* (Philadelphia: Fortress, 1986), 197.

[7]David C. Tracy, *The Analogical Imagination: Christian Theology and the Culture of Pluralism* (New York: Crossroad, 1981), 3, 28-31.

out his life was the black church. His father, grandfather, and great grandfather were ministers. He grew up in church, attended college in a black Baptist college, and spent his entire professional life as a minister of black Baptist churches and as a leader of the civil rights movement in America. The movement, while interracial in its outlook and goals, and somewhat in its constituency, was comprised predominantly of African-American people. His colleagues in leadership circles most often were African-American ministers.[8]

At the beginning of the civil rights movement in the South, the "larger society" that King addressed was made up primarily of African Americans, many of whom shared the experience of black churches. Later, as the movement widened, King appealed to the larger American society, but he continued to speak in the discourse of black church culture. Thus, King addressed two public audiences—the African-American religious community (people of the black churches) and the larger society.

Throughout his career, King also addressed the academic public, though not in the usual fashion of most theologians. He spoke on many college and university campuses and many academics joined the movement that he headed. His address to academic audiences, unlike that of most other theologians, was not concerned so much with the customary issues or style of academic discourse as with the implications of theological discourse for the transformation of American society to which the academy belongs. King rarely addressed the academy—that audience to which many theologians address themselves much of the time—in its own familiar academic discourse. That is significant because the issue of race, as Charles Long has pointed out, "is raised within academic theology," not so much by what theologians say about race as by the "historical, religious, and philosophical" structures within which academic theology takes place.[9] When King spoke to the academy, he spoke primarily in the discourse of black church culture, rather than the "historic, religious, and philosophical" structures of academic theology, though he knew the latter very well.

---

[8]Aldon D. Morris, *The Origins of the Civil Rights Movement: Black Communities Organizing for Change* (New York: Free Press, 1984), Chapter One. Morris describes the strong presence of black church leaders in the civil rights movement.

[9]Long, *Significations*, 189.

Since African-American religious communities are indebted to some of the same wider cultural influences as others, they also draw on some of the same God language and imagery. Gordon Kaufman's position emphasizes that wider cultural matrix of shared imagery. That shared God imagery is certainly apparent in King's thought where themes of African-American discourse about God are mingled with themes of academic theology. In spite of that overlap, images of God from the African-American religious tradition that shaped King's thinking possessed a recognizable character, a distinctive "otherness."[10]

Aldon Morris has argued that the "view of religion as a dynamic force for social change was a cornerstone in black churches." The concept that God seeks social change already was central in black church culture long before King articulated it.[11] King addressed the wider public from within that specific black culture. Power, moral goodness, universal love, personal character, and active presence in historical struggles for justice were common attributes of God in African-American literature and in the pulpits of black churches. These themes became central in King's understanding of God. The social experiences of slavery, legalized segregation, and discrimina-

---

[10]Charles Long, *Significations*, Chapter 12, 185 ff. By "otherness," Long means "radical internal criticisms of themselves, their situation, and the situation of the majority culture." See 9.

[11]Morris, *Origins*, See also Preston N. Williams, "Black Church: Origin, History, Present Dilemma," *McCormick Quarterly*, Volume 22(May, 1969): 223-237;"The Black Experience and Black Religion,"*Theology Today* (October, 1969): 255. Williams argues that, "Black religion has throughout its history sought to make the victimized black man capable of carrying his burden. At its best it faced life realistically, enabled men to seek to *overcome their handicaps*, and positively related men to ultimate truth, the true and living God." (Italics mine.) I agree with Morris's assertion that something like the "social gospel" was already in black church culture. King and his colleagues were not creating it or imposing it. I am in some disagreement, however, with Morris's assertion that King and his colleagues were shifting the focus of black church culture from a more passive attitude of "containment" to a more militant one of "social change." His choice of the word "containment" somewhat misrepresents the culture of black churches in the period of the 1920's and 1930's. King, for example, grew up in a context in Atlanta where the churches and clergy, specifically his own father, already were engaged in social change activity based in churches. King grew up in a socially active church and with close ties to N.A.A.C.P. There were passive ideas of God and religion among African Americans in the period before 1940, but the mainline emphases were on social change. On these questions, see also Gayraud S. Wilmore, *Black Religion and Black Radicalism* (Maryknoll, New York: Orbis Press, 1983), especially Chapter 6, 135 ff.

tion had produced distinctive emphases in African-American God language and imagery. Black church culture was the institutional bearer of that imagery. The distinctive attributes of God in King's theology belong preeminently to his people, to Americans of African descent.

Black religious thought existed before the rise of modern Black Theology, and King's thought must be studied in the context of that earlier black religious discourse. I seek to identify "images and meanings" that "lie behind the religious experiences of the black communities in America," and to examine King's concept of God in that context of otherness. It is not my intent to analyze the ways in which King's concept of God was influenced by the intellectual traditions in which he was trained in graduate schools. Such studies already exist.[12]

The images of God in King's thought are remarkably similar, in their central themes and even in some of their nuanced expressions, to images of God in earlier African-American religious thought. Many examples suggest that King's conception of God cannot be understood apart from the context of African-American religious discourse.

The earliest study of African-American thinking about God that spans the generation before King's birth and the years of his youth was Benjamin

---

[12]Charles H. Long, *Significations*, 174. Long is an historian of religions. As such, he separates himself from both a purely social science and also from a purely theological approach to the study of African-American religion. He wishes to create a new method, one more appropriate for the African-American experience. He focuses on three principles: "Africa as a historical reality and religious image; the involuntary presence of the black community in America; and the experience and symbol of God in the religious experience of blacks." (see 174) With Long, I look at "images and meanings" that lie within the religious discourse of African Americans. Also, with Long, I examine the "symbol of God" in black discourse. Unlike Long, I focus more explicitly upon God imagery in religious and theological literature, and not upon prototypical images behind that literature or parallel with it in secular literature such as folk tales, spirituals, and blues. I am, however, like Long, attempting to identify a "structure of the deity" in African-American discourse and in King's thought. For discussions of the non-African-American influences on King, see Kenneth Smith and Ira Zepp Jr., *Search for Beloved Community: The Thinking of Martin Luther King Jr.* (Valley Forge: Judson, 1974), and Ansbro, *Martin Luther King Jr: The Making of a Mind;* John H. Cartwright, "Foundations of the Beloved Community"; Walter G. Muelder, "Philosophical and Theological Influences in the Thought and Action of Martin Luther King Jr."; James P. Harigan, "Martin Luther King Jr.: The Shaping of a Mind," and Lois R. Wasserman, "Martin Luther King Jr.: The Molding of Nonviolence as a Philosophy," in *Debate and Understanding* 1 (1977): 1-216.

E. Mays's book, *The Negro's God*. Mays's book serves well the purpose of this study for several reasons. (1) A significant portion of Mays's study is devoted to the period from 1914 to 1937, the period just prior to King's birth in 1929 and during his early life. (2) Mays used material gathered from "urban Negro Churches" in twelve major American cities: Atlanta, Baltimore, Birmingham, Charleston, Chicago, Cincinnati, Detroit, Houston, Memphis, New Orleans, Philadelphia, and Richmond.[13] *The Negro's God*, at that time, was the more recent of two books that Mays had published. Because King and Mays became acquaintances and then friends, because Mays was a prominent Baptist leader and King was headed toward the Baptist ministry like his father and grandfather, and because King very early showed an interest in thought about God, it is highly likely that King was familiar with Mays's book before he graduated from Morehouse in 1948.

TRADITIONAL RELIGION AND LIBERAL THEOLOGICAL EDUCATION IN AFRICAN-AMERICAN CHURCH LIFE, 1920 TO 1950.

Religious thinking in most African-American churches before 1920 was "traditional," i.e., while it manifested a considerable diversity of expression, it was not influenced to any large degree by academic theological education, liberal or conservative. King's grandfather Williams, in spite of being an alumnus of Morehouse College, represented traditional African-American religious thinking in his preaching.[14] King's father, though he earned a Bachelor of Theology degree from Morehouse College and encountered liberal theological ideas from teachers such as C. D. Hubert and Howard Thurman, continued to think along conservative, traditional religious lines throughout most of his life.

Beginning in the 1920's, a few African Americans earned graduate degrees in theological education from Northern liberal seminaries—schools like Rochester Seminary, Oberlin Seminary, The University of Chicago Divinity School, Andover Seminary, Boston University School of Theology, and a few others. Though only a small number of African-

---

[13]Mays, *The Negro's God*; Mays and Joseph W. Nicholson, *The Negro's Church* (New York: The Institute of Social and Religious Research, 1933), 298.

[14]Interviews with Melvin Watson, Atlanta, 26 February 1982 and 8 October 1986.

American students earned advanced degrees in theological education during that period, many of those who did went on to hold key positions of influence in African-American theological education.

For those pioneering African-American theologians, advanced degrees in liberal theological education often created a tension with traditional religious beliefs. Benjamin Mays, Howard Thurman, Melvin Watson, and George Kelsey, grew up in homes and churches where theology had been traditional. Mays referred often to his own "conservative background and orthodox religious upbringing." Melvin Watson grew up in Ebenezer Baptist Church under the traditional preaching of A. D. Williams and subsequently earned advanced degrees in theological studies at Oberlin Seminary and Pacific School of Religion. The story of George Kelsey is much the same. He grew up in Griffin, Georgia, a son of high school teachers, and then earned advanced theological degrees at Andover Seminary and Yale University, later teaching at Morehouse College and Drew Seminary.[15]

The group of highly trained teachers of religion and theology in King's early social circle were all persons who had faced the tensions between traditional African-American religious thinking and the thinking of liberal theological education. Benjamin Mays had studied with Henry Nelson Wieman at the University of Chicago. H. Richard Niebuhr had been George Kelsey's mentor at Yale University. Howard Thurman claimed a significant influence upon his thought from George Cross at Rochester Seminary, a Canadian who had trained in systematic theology at the University of Chicago; from Edwin A. Burtt, a young philosopher then at Columbia University; and from Rufus Jones, the Quaker mystic who taught at Haverford.[16] Each of the teachers was white, each one a master of Euro-American theology. It is improbable that any of them possessed much understanding of African-American religion. In spite of that, each of the students mentioned achieved an integration of faith and learning, drawing on the religion of black churches and the theology of liberal academic institutions.

For these and others who grew up in traditional African-American churches and then attended liberal theological seminaries and graduate

---

[15]Mays, *Born to Rebel*, 65; Author's interview with George Kelsey, 10 October 1986.
[16]Howard Thurman, *With Head and Heart* (New York: Harcourt, Brace, Jovanovich, 1979), 44,54,75.

schools of religion, there was some tension between the two theological
worlds. Mays, in his biography, writes that even though his religious
upbringing had been conservative and orthodox, the "ultra-modern views"
of his graduate education at the University of Chicago "did not upset my
faith."[17] Even though he disavows any inner tension from those two
different worlds of discourse, his remark, nonetheless, indicates a contrast
between them. Those who observed Mays as a speaker and preacher over
many years saw two sides to his powerful oratory, wide learning and deep,
emotional spirituality. As Professor Reddick put it,

> In the eyes of a young boy, Dr. Mays was a wonderful combination
> of the intellectual and the spiritual. . . . in Dr. Mays, Martin saw a
> man who could speak with force and effectiveness and then leave
> one with something to think about after he had finished talking.[18]

That combination of traits in Mays reflects his synthesis of African-
American religiousness with liberal higher education.

The trend among some African Americans toward higher theological
education placed African-American religious thinking in a new critical light.
For example, Mays distinguished between "mass" and "classical" African-
American religious thought and referred to otherworldly notions of God in
the mass literature of African-American religion as "naive," "ideas of God
that are being rapidly discarded in an age of science." Traditional African-
American ministers were quick to see the danger in Mays's mixing of
traditional liberal religious thought. They reminded Mays of his dangerous
theological ideas, claiming that the Divinity School at the University of
Chicago was "a hotbed of heresy." In spite of criticism, Mays achieved a wide
recognition, as a leading educator and also as a trusted religious leader.[19]

---

[17]Mays, *Born to Rebel*, 65.

[18]Reddick, *Crusader Without Violence*, 62.

[19]Mays, *The Negro's God*, 14, 68; *Born to Rebel*, 65. Mays's book, *The Negro's God*, was
republished in a second edition in 1968, with a new preface by Vincent Harding. Benjamin
E. Mays, *The Negro's God* (2nd edition; New York: Atheneum, 1968). Harding praises Mays
for having assembled a vast amount of original material not available elsewhere from
sermons, poems, prayers, spirituals, and speeches; and for showing that the God reflected in

It will be important to keep this tension in mind during the remainder of this essay. Martin Luther King Jr. grew up in the midst of similar religious and intellectual tensions and in the midst of adult figures whose liberal thought was contributing to those tensions. The religious traditions of his church and family were largely traditional, but from early in his life, he came into contact with liberal theological learning. Such exposure, which began before his college career, increased rapidly after he entered college. The interchange of these religious and theological perspectives was ever-after present in King's experience and thought.

Mays's study of the "Negro's God" is predominantly a study of traditional thinking about God in African-American churches. By 1931 when Mays gathered many of the sermons upon which his analysis is based, some African-American preachers were trained in liberal seminaries and others had been trained in African-American schools by teachers with some liberal, theological training. Mays's study, therefore, reflects a world that was in transition socially, educationally, religiously, and theologically. "The Negro's God" revealed in Mays's study should reflect these transitions. Finally, like others of his contemporaries with advanced theological education, Mays attempted to exercise a reflective distance from his African-American religious tradition in his work as a scholar of religion. In his introduction, he wrote, "The object of the writer is to achieve a high degree of objectivity in the presentation and analysis of data."[20] If either side of

---

the literature of Black people rarely had been an otherworldly God who made them detached from the world. Those two points, wrote Harding, are the strongest aspects of Mays's book. On the other hand, Harding also raised three pointed criticisms of the book--that Mays's methodology is loose and does not hold up, that Mays's own analytic commentary on the literature is disappointing, and that Mays failed repeatedly to provide adequate citations of sources for the literature he quoted. All three criticisms are well taken; the methodology especially is quite puzzling and frustrating. Still, as Harding acknowledged, Mays did gather a large number of "magnificent sources" which are valuable for looking at the African-American understanding of God. The strongest section of Mays's book is the long section in which Mays discussed the period, 1914-37, the period which is most closely related to the present investigation. See Harding's preface in the 2nd Edition, cited above.

[20]Mays, *The Negro's God*, 1st Edition, viii. Vincent Harding has criticized Mays's "mechanistic, sociocultural-psychological mode of analysis" for being loose, overly academic, and inappropriate to the subject matter of religion. Harding is right in criticizing Mays for his poor use of method, but he is wrong in labeling as inappropriate Mays's attempt to use methods of analysis that since Mays's time have proven fruitful in the study of religion.

Mays's religious and scholarly writing is ignored, then his significance—as an educator, scholar, and religious leader—will be misunderstood.

MAYS'S METHODS OF ANALYSIS

Mays's earlier book, *The Negro's Church*, written with Joseph W. Nicholson and published in 1933, was a broad analysis of many aspects of African-American churches, while the later book focused specifically on thinking about God in African-American literature. *The Negro's God* covers the period from 1760 to 1937, which he subdivides into three periods: from 1760 to 1860, from 1860 to 1914, and from 1914 to 1937. The rationale for those subdivisions was straightforward. The earliest published African-American writing dates from around 1760.[21] The period from 1860 to 1914 was marked by segregation, first *de facto* segregation and then, after *Plessy v. Ferguson* (1896), *de jure* segregation. The year 1914 marked the commencement of World War I that changed life in fundamental ways for many African Americans. The experiences of the period were not confined to African Americans; as Mays notes, the entire society was shaken and disillusioned. The impact upon African Americans, nonetheless, was great. The decade from 1915 to 1925 was a period of extensive migration of African Americans from southern rural areas to southern and northern urban areas, bringing into being a new urban reality for African Americans that, in many ways, was socially and religiously destructive. African Americans in large numbers took part in the war effort with pride and with a sense of optimism based on promises of a transformed postwar society, but they were disillusioned by the rapid reassertion of racism following the war. "Spiritual depression and skepticism" followed the War.[22] Mays cited an

---

Mays's premier notion, that religious imagery is rooted in and reflects a social situation, pointed toward later uses of social and cultural analysis in the study of religion. See Harding's "Preface" in Mays, *The Negro's God*, 2nd Edition, pages unnumbered. The words in quotation marks are found on the fourth page of the preface.

[21] Mays began his study of classical literature with Jupiter Hammon, "who is the author of the first poem published by a Negro in the United States. His poem, 'An Evening Thought: Salvation by Christ,' appeared in 1761." *The Negro's God*, 97.

[22] Ibid., 6.

address by Mordecai Johnson at Harvard in 1922 that caught the meaning of the period for African Americans:

> At the close of the war, however, the Negro's hopes were suddenly dashed to the ground. Southern newspapers began at once to tell the Negro soldiers that the War was over and the sooner they forgot it the better. "Pull off your uniform," they said, "find the place you had before the War and stay in it." "Act like a Negro should act," said one newspaper, "work like a Negro should work, talk like a Negro should talk, study like a Negro should study. Dismiss all ideas of independence or of being lifted up to the plane of the white man. Understand the necessity of keeping a Negro's place."[23]

African-American organizations, such as the National Association for the Advancement of Colored People (1909), the National Urban League (1910) the Universal Negro Improvement Association and African Communities League (1914), and the Association for the Study of Negro Life and History (1915), were founded and/or experienced their first substantial growth during this period. Finally, during this period communism began to have an appeal for some African Americans. These factors all represented changes in African-American life. It is important to keep in mind the full sweep of Mays's methodology as it applies to the entire period of his study from 1760 to 1937, but, for the purpose of this essay, I am interested mainly in Mays's findings for the most recent period, from 1914 to 1937.

"MASS" AND "CLASSICAL" TYPES OF LITERATURE

Mays's book moves from period to period, distinguishing two types of literature, "mass" literature and "classical literature. African-American classical literature, in his analysis, includes "the chief productions of Negroes...slave narratives, biography, autobiography, addresses, novels, poetry, and the writings of social scientists." On the other hand, "Mass literature" includes:

---

[23]Ibid., 241.

Sunday school productions, prayers, sermons, and Negro spirituals.
. . . They contain the ideas of God that reach the masses primarily
through the church and through the minister in public utterances.[24]

Mays's categorical distinctions suggest that he was attempting to
interpret his material with the help of a method. The terms, "mass" and
"classical," though loosely defined by Mays, point to other distinctions such
as appeal to the trained or untrained mind, more and less artistic merit,
more and less of the writer's craft. There is no suggestion, however, of more
or less "religious" or "spiritual." He was aware that much of the material
cited in his study came from speakers and writers with little formal training,
especially in the churches. He is deliberate about introducing academic or
"scientific" analysis into his interpretation. Mays identified himself with the
classical approach; mass ideas were too often "naive," containing "ideas of
God that are being rapidly discarded in an age of science." Among divinity
schools of that time, Chicago had become famous for its scientific approach
to the study of religion, called the "scientific study of religion" (or
Religionswissenschaft, the science of religion). Mays was likely attempting to
introduce an empirical method in the manner of his mentors at the Divinity
School of the University of Chicago. Mays's approach is more sociocultural-
historical than evangelical or apologetic, though his own theological
preferences are visible in the work. His method of interpretation reflects
Mays's own educational journey from one of the masses to one of the
classical elite in the discernment of religious matters. It was that journey
that made some of his associates in ministry suspicious of his learning.
Likewise, Martin Luther King Jr. was occasionally the object of similar
suspicion.

"COMPENSATORY" AND "CONSTRUCTIVE" VIEWS OF GOD

From both "mass" and "classical" literature Mays discovered that most
African Americans thought about God in one of two main ways, ways that
he described as "compensation" or "constructive development." Constructive
development, Mays believed, meant that God somehow was interested in and

---

[24]*The Negro's God*, 1.

involved in "needed social adjustment." Compensatory thinking about God was "traditional" in the sense that it was "set forth in the Bible, with primary emphasis upon the magical, spectacular, partial, revengeful, and anthropomorphic nature of God as revealed in the Old Testament."

> Ideas are compensatory when used or developed to support a shallow pragmatism. That is a belief or idea may be accredited as true if it satisfies our desire, "if it uplifts and consoles;" or if it makes us "happier to believe it" even though the belief or idea does not fit observed facts.[25]

Compensatory thinking about God encourages one to think of God as "in his heaven" and to think that "all is right with the world." This idea, writes Mays, "That God will bring his own out victoriously in the end, has had a profound influence upon Negro life." A compensatory understanding of God did not motivate people to be engaged in social transformation because God was in control. It was Mays's belief in general that other-worldly compensatory ideas of God become more attractive when times are hard and less attractive when times improve.[26]

Mays detected in African-American literature a second way of thinking about God that seemed to grow directly from the African-American historical experience of slavery and legalized segregation. They looked for a God who could redeem their historical situation. Mays called that understanding of God a "constructive" view, based on the notion that some "social adjustment" was needed. Mays found throughout the literature references to God's active participation in struggles against slavery, segregation, and discrimination. That understanding of God did not advise leaving events in the hands of God. It found in God values that needed to be infused into the human situation, and human beings were expected to participate in that transformation. Sometimes that meant transforming the lives of individual persons and sometimes it meant changing the larger social, political, and economic structures that order human life.

---

[25]Ibid., 14.
[26]Ibid., 14-15, 25.

Within "constructive" thinking about God, Mays found three different emphases. Some social transformation was envisioned as "universal in scope but . . . is inclusive of the needs of the Negro"; some was "confined primarily to the needs of the Negro"; and a third type was primarily psychological, intended to nurture a "growing conviction that the Negro is not an inferior people."[27] Mays's own theological preferences were on the side of the "constructive" approach. His constructive view was primarily universal, but also addressed the needs of African Americans, including the issue of internalized feelings of inferiority. The constructive approach, as Mays described it, was not so different from the values of liberal, social gospel theology of the 1920s and 1930s. That affinity between African-American thought and liberal theology is instructive for our understanding of Mays and why he found the University of Chicago conducive to his own theological development. It is equally important for any understanding of King's later affirmation of themes from the social gospel.

"SOCIAL SITUATION" AND UNDERSTANDINGS OF GOD

Mays introduced one more principle of analysis into his study by arguing that the ideas of God in the literature of a people reflect the social situation of that people. He wrote: "The Negro's ideas of God grow out of the social situation in which he finds himself."[28] Mays proposed that oppressed groups have thought about God differently from dominant groups. For African Americans, that meant different ways of thinking in each of the three periods that he examined, as social situations changed. Before 1860 African Americans saw God in their struggle for emancipation. From 1860 to 1914, following the end of slavery and the re-legalization of segregation in the 1896 *Plessy* decision, God was understood in the context of a continuing struggle against segregation. After 1914 African Americans asked how God was related to their postwar disillusionment and to the destructive features of urban social experience.

Of course, Mays's own social situation was complex. He was not just an African American. Socially, he was on a boundary between traditional

---

[27]Ibid., 15.
[28]Ibid., vii.

African-American religion and liberal theological education, between the life
of black churches and black college life. Mays's own social situation shows
in his analysis, just as the social situations of African Americans show in
their understandings of God.

Before looking at the findings in Mays's book directly, it is necessary to
comment on Mays's method. The method, as Vincent Harding has written,
has some weaknesses.[29] The distinction between "mass" and "classical"
literature is vague and difficult to follow throughout his book, as is his
distinction between "compensatory" and "constructive" approaches to God.
There are two great strengths of the book that make it quite usable, however.
First, Mays assembled an impressive amount of quoted material that
provided the only accessible printed collection of material on the subject.
Further, his periodization was helpful for discerning a progression of
thought. Finally, Mays had struck upon something important with his idea
that God imagery was influenced by the social situation of African
Americans. His method was vague and lacked the sophisticated argumentation of later theological writing, but his overall argument was and remains
persuasive. He was using an early sociology-of-knowledge methodology
without full mastery. Although others after him used the argument with
greater finesse, Mays was pioneer, pointing the way with a methodology that
later writers have employed effectively as an instrument of liberation.

THE NEGRO'S GOD IN THE SPIRITUALS

African-American spirituals, which "grew out of slave experiences and
subsequent conditions similar to slavery," according to Mays, were a special
kind of mass literature. Spirituals, he argued, were found in all three periods
under consideration and the thinking about God found in them usually was
compensatory. Therefore, rather than study spirituals in each of the three
periods, Mays analyzed them once separately at the beginning of his study
as representative of his findings about mass literature in all three periods. In
the spirituals, God was omnipotent, omnipresent, and omniscient. He was
sovereign and just to the point of cruelty. He vindicated the just and

---

[29]Vincent Harding, "Preface to the Atheneum Edition," in Benjamin E. Mays, *The
Negro's God*, 2nd Edition(New York: Atheneum, 1968), pages unnumbered.

punished the unjust. God was near, especially in times of distress, and there was a feeling of dependence upon him. Those beliefs were compensatory because they enabled "Negroes to endure hardship, suffer pain, and withstand maladjustment, but they do not necessarily motivate them to strive to eliminate the source of ills they suffer."[30] He added:

> In the midst of the most stifling circumstances, this belief in God has given the Negro masses emotional poise and balance; it has enabled them to cling on to life though poor, miserable, and dying, looking to God and expecting Him, through miraculous and spectacular means, to deliver them from this plight. The idea has made Negroes feel good; it has made life endurable for them.[31]

This idea of God, said Mays, "enabled [Negro masses] to keep on keeping on. And it's still effective in 1937."[32] Mays's last sentence, "and it's still effective in 1937," would appear to have at least two possible readings. First, Mays could have been claiming that, according to his study, spirituals possessed an enabling force for "Negro masses" right up to 1937. On the other hand, the sentence suggests, intentionally or not, that spirituals continued to hold authority even for Mays.

I suspect that both of these readings are correct. If so, however, it introduces a problem or an instructive inconsistency. If, as Mays holds, spirituals are generally compensatory according to his definitions, and if Mays's own views were constructive, then in what power was their ongoing religious "effectiveness" grounded, if not in their theology? This reading of Mays, if accurate, is instructive inasmuch as his thought illustrates a synthesis between traditional African-American religious thinking and academic theological thought that was then being taught in seminaries and graduate schools of religion where he and other African Americans were doing their graduate theological training. This reading makes clearer what Mays meant years later in his autobiography when he said that the ideas at Chicago did not "upset" his faith but "made sense" to him.[33]

---

[30]Ibid., 19, 21-24.
[31]Ibid., 25.
[32]Ibid., 26.
[33]*Born to Rebel*, 65.

MASS LITERATURE FROM 1914 TO 1937

In his analysis of mass literature in the period from 1914 to 1937, Mays discovered that, as in the previous periods, the majority of sermons reflected compensatory and traditional conceptions of God. God was seen by most as the one who ultimately assured the welfare of the righteous. However, in sharp contrast with earlier mass literature, slightly over half of the sermons were not only compensatory, but were also otherworldly in emphasis, and some contained what might be called "naive conceptions of God." Mays offered the following illustration of "naive" thinking about God:

> When I shall look over that mystic river and see my Savior on the shore I want to wait until I hear His voice and see the print of the nails in His hands. I am going to shout and sing and pray until I get to glory.[34]

Here is a clear illustration of Mays's awareness of the co-existence of different types of thinking about God. One type, in his judgment, was naive. Opposed to that was a kind of thinking about God that accorded more with modern modes of thinking, a kind of thinking about God that would not be discarded so quickly in an age of scientific thinking. Mays identified himself with the latter type of thinking, orthodox but yet modern at the same time.

In many sermons of this period, the dominant emphasis was upon God as the guarantor of otherworldly, rather than worldly, salvation. That represented a distinctive turn in African-American thinking about God in comparison with the thinking of earlier periods. God was viewed as the source of salvation for individual souls and a force for social transformation. There seemed to be, however, a somewhat surprising lack of connection between these two activities of God. The idea of God as a source of racial uplift was not developed into a coherent social gospel. That brings to mind Melvin Watson's observation about Reverend A. D. Williams, that he was

---

[34]Ibid.,68-69. This quotation is a good example of Mays's inadequate citation of sources. He gives no author for this quotation. He refers to his earlier book on page 75. When that source is checked, the reader discovers that Mays quoted there from a sermon and gives no citation for the source. Thus, the author and the date of authorship are unknown.

a dedicated worker for the good of his people but that he had not developed a social gospel in his preaching; that his preaching was, in fact, even rather otherworldly.[35] According to Mays's study, that pattern of thinking about God was widespread in the period from 1914 to 1937.

Another new note was sounded in the mass literature of this period. In a significant number of sermons, Mays found a universal God who was interested in the welfare of all human beings, regardless of nation, class, or race. All persons deserve to be liberated. Furthermore, liberated personality is God's "most successful force" for revolutionizing the social order. That literature expressed a strong desire for the uplift of African Americans, but their welfare was linked with the welfare of all. Whatever elevates African Americans, elevates others as well since the longings of all peoples are much the same.

> The desires sought are equally obvious. There is the desire for peace; the desire for political and civic security; the desire and yearning for the physical, mental, and spiritual growth of every child; and the desire that each person should enjoy economic security.[36]

This theme of God's universality had appeared in the mass literature of earlier periods but not as a major emphasis. In the earlier literature, Mays found that God's interest had been linked more frequently with the welfare of African Americans. In the period after 1914, God more frequently was viewed as universal, interested in the welfare of all persons, races, and nations.

SUMMARY OF MAYS'S FINDINGS IN THE MASS LITERATURE

In the mass literature of all three periods, Mays found both compensatory and constructive ideas of God side by side. For the most part, even the compensatory understandings of God were worldly rather than otherworldly, suggesting that God ultimately would vindicate those who were oppressed and topple their oppressors. Only in the last period, 1914 to 1937, did

---

[35] Watson interviews.
[36] *Born to Rebel*, 79-80.

Mays discover a significant shift toward otherworldly thinking about God in mass literature. Quite often, that went right along with continued emphasis upon responsibility for social transformation, but the two ideas apparently seemed theologically unrelated. Mays interpreted this as an understandable response to the jarring disillusionments of post-World War I, urban realities for African Americans. It confirmed his belief that otherworldly understandings of God tended, as a rule, to emerge in hard times.

Not all mass literature from 1914 to 1937 was compensatory. There were constructive understandings of God as well but the emphases of those constructive approaches were different in some ways than in the constructive approaches of earlier periods. There was a new emphasis upon God's desire for universal harmony as a solution to social problems, rather than emphasis upon a narrow solution to the difficulties of African Americans. God was seen as a universal God of social righteousness who desired community beyond the boundaries of race or nation. Mays quoted one such sermon to illustrate his point.

> If this kind of Kingdom should come down to earth, no race would want to keep another race down. Our military forces would not be in Nicaragua; they would not be in Haiti. We would gladly help the Philippines to independence and without condescension and without patronage. India would be free and Africa would not be exploited. All forms of segregation and discrimination such as those that exist in the United States in the expenditure of public funds, in travel, in politics, and those that operate against us in social and economic areas would all disappear if the Kingdom of God should come.[37]

We are struck by the international awareness of the preacher, and also by the sense of contemporaneity of concerns in that sermon with preaching during the latter years of this century. It is important also to keep in mind that, by the time Mays was writing his book on God in 1938, he too was keenly interested in international events; for example, he had been to India and conversed with Gandhi. African-American mass literature in the period

---

[37]*The Negro's God,* 79.

contained a growing emphasis upon God's universality. The understanding of God was "developed along social lines that were universal in character, transcending the narrow confines of race."[38]

CLASSICAL LITERATURE FROM 1914 TO 1937

In classical literature of the third period, from 1914 to 1937, thinking about God began to diversify. There was some otherworldly emphasis, though not as much as in the mass literature of this period. According to Mays, that otherworldly theme was a minor one in the classical literature of the period. It was important to note it because it was out of keeping with most of the classical African-American literature in all three of the periods Mays examined.

More common in the classical literature of the period was an understanding of God that was worldly and constructive. Many writers still emphasized that God was the source of welfare for African Americans, but there was a growing emphasis upon God's concern for all persons, races, and nations. That emphasis, which had been only occasional in the literature of earlier periods, took on new importance in this period. In this literature, God came to be understood as "wholly impartial," a God who "from one blood created all races and nations." God set no geographical boundaries or racial limitations, the rights of humanity were divinely given, and all were considered as God's creatures. God was universal and the welfare of African Americans was seen in the context of God's universal activity. Poet Walter Everett Hawkins, extended that reasoning even farther, and relativized Christ, a striking theological innovation, by placing him on a par with the founding figures of other world religions. "Islam and Buddha and Christ," he wrote, "all but tend toward the same goal—these but means toward an end."[39] Most classical literature of the period stressed God's universal character by universalizing, not by relativizing Christianity and the Christian understanding of God. Hawkins relativized Christianity but universalized the concern of God for all persons.

---

[38]Ibid.

[39]Walter Everett Hawkins, *Chords and Discords* (Boston: The Gorham Press, 1920), 45.

In the classical literature of this period, several writers emphasized the link between God and the sacredness of personality, sometimes corporate personality and sometimes individual personality. This is especially fruitful for understanding the later Martin Luther King Jr. That emphasis was not totally new in this period. It could be found, for instance, in the thought of an earlier figure such as Henry Highland Garnet. What was new in the classical literature of this period was the frequency with which the emphasis appeared. Robert Russa Moton, successor of Booker T. Washington at Tuskegee Institute, called African Americans "creatures of God's most perfect handiwork." Affirmation of that work of the Creator was the challenge of work to uplift the race. Failure to appreciate one's race was an insult to God. Kelly Miller based human rights upon the image of God in every person. If the image of God was in each, then full development of personality was "true benevolence." That was the path of racial uplift. Every African-American had to be educated to believe that he or she was " created in the image of God" and that "nothing clothed in human guise is a more faithful likeness of that original." Marcus Garvey argued, similarly, that since all humans were created in God's image, "the Negro race is equal to other races" and the highest tribute the Negro can pay to God is to recognize and appreciate the fact that he is God's masterpiece."[40]

The concept that African Americans are created, like all humans, in the image of God, was often cited in the classical literature of this period as the foundation of the idea that an African American is "somebody," and not "nobody." The idea of somebodiness, Mays wrote in 1938, was taught widely by ministers and parents throughout African-American life.[41] Of course, it eventually became a central theme in King's theology.

Even more noteworthy in the classical literature of the period, according to Mays, was that some writers doubted God, or viewed the ideas of God as socially useless, or abandoned altogether the idea of God as a fiction or even a white man's trick. Traces of those trends, which were not found in the literature of earlier periods, were discovered by Mays in the writings of Countee Cullen, Langston Hughes, W. E. B. DuBois, Walter White, Jessie Richmond, and Nella Larsen. DuBois, in *Dark Water*, expressed a spirit of

---

[40]*The Negro's God*, 166-167, 169, 188.
[41]Ibid.,188.

doubt coupled with suspicion that the traditional idea of God was a white ideology.

> Keep not Thou Silent, O God!
> Sit not longer blind, Lord God, deaf to our prayer
> And dumb to our dumb suffering.
> Surely Thou, Too, are not white,
> O Lord, a pale, bloodless, Heartless thing.[42]

Countee Cullen, in even fewer lines, conveyed a sense of betrayal and an abandonment by that God who is no help to African Americans: "A man was lynched last night; God, if He was, kept to his skies, and left us to our enemies."[43]

In this literature, there was not an out-and-out atheism. More often there was a sense of puzzlement, a belief in God coupled with an inability to comprehend the meaning of God, given the day-to-day experience of African Americans. Such an attitude was reflected in DuBois's piece, "A Litany at Atlanta":

> O Silent God, Thou whose voice afar in mist and mystery hath left our ears ahungered in these fearful days—Hear us, good lord! Wherefore do we pray? Is not the god of the Fathers dead? Thou art not dead, but flown afar, up hills of endless light. Bewildered we are and passion-tossed, mad with madness of a mobbed and mocked and murdered people; We raise our shackled hands and charge Thee, God, by the bones of our stolen fathers, by the tears of our dead mothers, by the very blood of Thy crucified Christ: What meaneth this? Tell us the plan; give us the sign![44]

Langston Hughes abandoned the idea of a God and the religion of Christianity, turning his hopes instead to communism. In 1932, these lines from Hughes appeared in a German communist magazine, *Negro Worker*:

---

[42]W. E. B. DuBois, *Dark Water*(New York: Harcourt, Brace, and Howe, 1920), 275-76.

[43]Countee Cullen, quoted by Mays, *Negro's God,* 229.

[44]DuBois, 231-232.

Listen Christ,
You did all right in your day I reckon
But that day's gone now.
You ain't no good no more
They've pawned you
Till you've done wore out
Goodbye.
Make way for a new guy with no religion at all.
A real guy named
Marx Communist Lenin Peasant Stalin,
Worker Me—
I said, Me
Go ahead on now.[45]

There is anger and impatience in these lines, feelings of betrayal and abandonment by God. Hughes and others did not excise God altogether from their writing but their thinking about God became markedly different from early African-American thought about God. As they lost confidence that traditional belief in God would bring events to their proper conclusion, skepticism, anger, and frustration about that concept of God began to appear in their writings.

In the mass literature from 1914 to 1937, Mays discovered a new incidence of otherworldly, compensatory thinking about God. In spite of the fact that educational standards for African-American ministers were beginning to rise in this period, there was widespread emphasis in preaching about personal, otherworldly salvation. That emphasis contrasted with the dominant emphasis on the idea of God as active in the world, an idea that prevailed in African-American literature from the earlier periods. The God of African-American history never had been predominantly a God of personal and otherworldly salvation, not in mass literature and not in classical literature.

Some mass literature from the period, according to Mays, contained a more constructive view of God. Among those thinkers, God was viewed in

---

[45]Langston Hughes, in *Negro Worker*(November-December 1932). Quoted in *Negro's God,* 238-39.

universal terms more often than in the mass literature of earlier periods. The two new elements, then, in the understanding of God in mass literature in the period were God's otherworldly orientation and God's universality. Both themes had been present in earlier literature but they were not as frequent there.

In the classical literature from 1914 to 1937, Mays discovered predominantly constructive, world-oriented thinking about God. The concept of God in that literature was more frequently universal than in earlier periods and was identified with more radical, systemic social transformations. There was also a more frequent emphasis upon the "image of God" in human nature, a concept that was used to claim the inalienability of the rights of persons and to support the positive self regard of persons and groups of persons, regardless of race, class, creed, or national identity. Finally, in the classical literature of the period, there was a pronounced questioning and even a rejection, of God's relevance for social transformation and the uplift of African Americans.

These are the outstanding features of African-American thinking about God in the period from 1914 to 1937, according to Mays. It will be useful to keep them in mind in any examination of Martin Luther King's understanding of God up to the time when he assumed leadership of the Montgomery boycott in December of 1955.

MARTIN LUTHER KING JR.: GETTING TO KNOW THE NEGRO'S GOD

King's understanding of God reflects many of the qualities of God found in the imagery of the black churches as outlined in 1938 by Benjamin Mays; and also that King's concept of God remained remarkably consistent, in its broad outline, throughout his adult life. King envisioned God as a force for social change on the side of justice; those who walked with God in the struggle for justice could expect a "cosmic companionship." The change in King's concept of God over his lifetime, which many have attempted to explain, resulted from King's deepening vision of the ethical implications of his people's God.[46]

---

[46]Thomas Mikelson, "The Negro's God in the Theology of Martin Luther King Jr.: Social Community and Theological Discourse," (unpublished doctoral dissertation, Harvard University, 1988).

King reminded his followers that God was with them in the struggle. During the year of the Montgomery Boycott (1955-1956), King spoke many times about cosmic companionship as their pre-eminent source of hope. In his 1956 address to the NAACP annual convention, King proclaimed: "We have the strong feeling that in our struggle we have cosmic companionship. That is why our movement is often referred to as a spiritual movement. We feel that the universe is on the side of right."[47] In his address to the Montgomery Improvement Association, in early December 1956, King said to his colleagues:

> . . . the fact that this new age is emerging reveals something basic about the universe. It tells us something about the core and heartbeat of the universe. . . . It says to those who struggle for justice, "You do not struggle alone, but God struggles with you."[48]

On December 20, 1956, King wrote, in his announcement of the successful end of the Montgomery Boycott:

> There have been moments when roaring waters of disappointment poured upon us in staggering torrents. We can remember...deep and confused waters of despair. But amid all of this we have kept going with the faith...that the arc of the moral universe, although long, is bending toward justice...Now our faith seems to be vindicated.[49]

These brief statements sprang from King's conviction that God actively had sided with those who were struggling for justice. This understanding of God places King theologically in the mainline of African-American religious thought and partly explains why his theologically-based leadership carried such strong appeal.

As Mays had shown, most African Americans believed their God to be active in their struggles for freedom and justice. That was true of King's understanding of God from his earliest to his latest writings. King's

---

[47]King, Speech, 27 June 1956, 8-9. All manuscript speeches are housed at the Martin Luther King Jr. Center for Nonviolent Social Change, Atlanta, Georgia.

[48]King, Speech, 3 December 1956, 14.

[49]King, Speech, 20 December 1956, 1.

understanding of God rallied people to take their places in struggles for justice; God never, at any point, legitimated withdrawal from those struggles.

The image of God found in African-American churches, according to Mays, was nearly always personal, and, specifically, human personality was the mark of God's image in human nature. That theme can be found in King's speaking and writing throughout his life. In his first book, *Stride Toward Freedom*, King wrote:

This personal idealism remains today my basic philosophical position. Personalism's insistence that only personality—finite and infinite—is ultimately real strengthened me in two convictions: It gave me metaphysical and philosophical grounding for the idea of a personal God, and it gave me a metaphysical basis for the dignity and worth of all human personality.[50]

Late in 1962, King addressed a group in Nashville, eloquently describing the basis of human worth in personality:

So long as the Negro . . . is seen as anything less than a person of sacred worth, the image of God is abused. . . . Only by establishing a truly integrated society can we return to the Negro the quality of "thou-ness" which is his due because of the nature of his being.[51]

In the last year of his life, King frequently returned to this theme. In a sermon at Ebenezer Church, he said, "There is a power in the universe....And we are here because that power was here first. Our personalities are here because that power was here first."[52]

There are many more examples that illustrate how King's understanding of God follows the themes that Mays found in his research. Throughout the thirteen years of his leadership in civil rights, King interpreted the move-

---

[50]King, *Stride Toward Freedom* (New York: Harper and Row, 1958), 100.

[51]King, Nashville address, 27 December 1962 (transcript in the Martin Luther King Jr. Center for Nonviolent Social Change, Atlanta), 11-12.

[52]King, "Ingratitude," sermon preached at Ebenezer Baptist Church, Atlanta, GA, 18 June 1967 (manuscript at King Center), 7-8.

ment and the issues in theological terms. Over and over again, King spoke or wrote about God's power, God's love, God's moral nature, God's goodness, God's universality, God's personal nature, and God's accompaniment of those who struggle for justice. His words drew on generations of African-American religious thought.

But King also was a formally trained theologian. He attended graduate schools of theology whose professors' views generally were compatible with many of the emphases in African-American religious thought. King's formal education, therefore, gave him philosophical and theological ways of thinking and talking about the God of his early training. King's basic understanding of God changed very little from the earliest written records of his ideas through the end of his life. His background in African-American religion must have predisposed him, for example, toward the theological outlook of Boston University's personalism. His professors at Boston University where he earned his Ph.D., especially L. Harold DeWolf, tutored King in formal categories for expressing his understandings of a personal, powerful, and moral God. The result was a theology more rigorously crafted than much of the theology in black preaching, but sharing many of the same broad themes.

The understanding of God in King's speeches, sermons, and writings, was public discourse, i.e. speech having its formative origins in a particular social world of discourse and speech. King's concept of God was an imaginative construct, most elements of which were close to God imagery in African-American religious discourse. The cultural realm from which King spoke, and from which he drew the essential elements of his God imagery, was the black church.

Throughout his career, King interpreted social problems in light of his understanding of God. Segregation was wrong, he argued, because it violated the image of God in human personality. Civil disobedience was acceptable, even obligatory, when it represented a refusal to obey laws that were undermining human personality. The Vietnam War was wrong because the image of God was in every human personality, Asian and American alike; the war was violating the sacred personhood of Asians as well as Americans, especially black Americans who constituted an unnaturally high percentage of American combat troops in Vietnam. Thus, in the light of his understanding of God, King saw a tie between racism in the United States and racism in American foreign policy. The themes and images in King's understanding of God remained consistent throughout his career.

The last years of King's life deserve special attention because of changes in King's social vision that many have noted. From the end of the Birmingham campaign in mid-1963 to the last year of King's life, though a period of only five years, was a long journey in many respects. The racial situation had changed, theoretically at least, with the Civil Rights Act of 1964 and the Voting Rights Act of 1965. The American situation changed with the assassination of President Kennedy and the involvement of the United States in the Vietnam War. The civil rights movement was torn between the ideals of nonviolence and Black Power. King's leadership had broadened from the single issue of race to include comprehensive issues of economics and world peace. King had become unquestionably a world figure. He spoke more openly about "bearing the cross" of Jesus, no matter what the consequence. He seemed impelled, in a more determined way, to be true to the ethical vision that, through the years of the civil rights movement, had come into clear and disturbing focus.

King's radicalism became more obvious after 1965, after the passage of the 1965 Voting Rights Act, after the violent confrontations with mounted police at the Edmund Pettus Bridge in Selma, after the bombing of a church in Birmingham that killed four young girls, and after police dogs and firehoses were used against children in Birmingham. As King had said to colleagues in his speech at Frogmore, South Carolina, in May 1967: "After Selma and the Voting Rights Bill, we moved into a new era, which must be an era of revolution. I think we must see the great distinction between a reform movement and a revolutionary movement."[53]

What others saw as King's growing radicalness, he saw as faithfulness to the God of his people, as his understanding of that God, and the social implications of that understanding deepened. The ethical implications of that God had escalated in ways that were frightening to himself and others. That certainly must have been one reason why his mentor, Benjamin Mays, at the memorial service at Morehouse that marked King's death, referred to his student and friend as a prophet:

---

[53]King, Speech at Frogmore, South Carolina, May, 1967, 8.

Surely this man was called of God to do this work. If Amos and Micah were prophets in the eighth century, B.C., Martin Luther King Jr., was a prophet in the twentieth century. If Isaiah was called of God to prophesy in his day, Martin Luther was called of God to prophesy in his time. If Hosea was sent to preach love and forgiveness centuries ago, Martin Luther was sent to expound the doctrine of nonviolence and forgiveness in the third quarter of the twentieth century. If Jesus was called to preach the Gospel to the poor, Martin Luther King Jr., fits that designation. If a prophet is one who does not seek popular causes to espouse, but rather the causes he thinks are right, Martin Luther qualified on that score.[54]

These were the summary words of a teacher who had watched his student perceptively and lovingly through the course of an eventful life. Both teacher and student knew that the student's life could best be understood in light of "the Negro's God."

---

[54]*Born to Rebel*, 359.

7

MAYS'S SPIRITUAL REBELLION

Illya E. Davis

As a young boy of five growing up in Greenwood County, South Carolina in 1899, Benjamin E. Mays witnessed a crowd of white men forcing his father to salute, take off his hat, and bow down to them several times as they cursed him and aimed their guns at him.[1] This profound experience led Mays to commit his life to combating psychological, socio-political, and theological injustices. Mays credits his parents as having given him the ethical tools necessary for this life-long battle:

> I am intolerant of dishonesty, particularly intellectual dishonesty, wherein men [and women] ignore or distort truth and plot to take advantage of others for their own indulgence. My parents did little or no ethical philosophizing, but they lived their ideals of industry and honesty. I am indebted to them for their example, and I am grateful.[2]

Mays followed the example set by his parents and from their teachings framed constructive methods of rebellion. This proclivity to rebel against the unjust treatment of human beings was one of Mays's most respected and admired qualities. Mays's autobiography, appropriately entitled *Born to Rebel*, best explicates his concept of rebellion. Throughout this and his other writings motifs of psychological, spiritual, and socio-political rebellion served as Mays's modus operandi as he struggled to humanize an inhumane world.

The first dimension under investigation is what may be called psychological rebellion, defined as rebellion against the false ideals of inferiority and the assumed inadequacies of African Americans. Mays believed that African

---

[1] *Born to Rebel*, 6.
[2] Ibid.

Americans must combat the "chains and images of psychological slavery" through clear pronouncements of the divinity that lay within all humanity, black or white. Mays strongly admonished African Americans and other oppressed groups to realize that God had given to whites no special talents or intellect that gave them the right to subjugate all others who differed from them phenotypically or culturally. Mays believed strongly that God created all humanity without bias towards or against any particular group. The downtrodden of society, particularly African Americans, should reject any psychological concepts of inferiority. Mays further asserts that humanity began as one unit endowed with equal access to all of society's rights and privileges. He wrote:

> The most outstanding light which Christianity throws upon human relationships is the Christian doctrine that human life began in God. . . . Christian light asserts that the human family began in unity. If God is the creator of human life, it is clear that man has status, standing, or uniqueness because God gave it to him. . . . For this reason, it is a foolish notion to think that man is great himself or that he has uniqueness because he belongs to a special group, class, caste, or nation.[3]

Mays realized that one must first become aware of the destructive psychological images of racial inferiority and actively work to free oneself and others from embodying and perpetuating them. To accept such images is to destroy true self-actualization for African Americans and to "choose the low road in life." Living and working out of external definitions of oneself, he argued, is detrimental to the development of one's selfhood: "Nobody is wise enough, nobody is good enough, and nobody cares enough about you for you to turn over to them your future or your destiny."[4] Mays refers to individuals who follow the perceptions and ideals of others as those who traverse the low road in life.

---

[3] *Disturbed About Man*, 18.
[4] Benjamin E. Mays, *Quotable Quotes of Benjamin E. Mays* (New York: Vantage Press, 1983), 6.

Those who walk the low road are slaves to bad habits or to some habit-forming drugs from which they cannot extricate themselves. They are slaves to environment and associations that so condition them that they seldom have the will to aspire for better ways of living. All too often it happens to those who walk the middle way are also slaves. They want to be socially accepted. They want to succeed politically and achieve economically. They seek position and prestige. They are the cautious ones. Adherence to custom and tradition is important to them."[5]

Mays clearly understood that public notoriety and prestige were things of little significance to the betterment of the human condition. He states, "Material things, power and prestige, houses and land, stocks and bonds, may keep breath in our bodies, give us economic and social security, but only our ideals will keep us alive."[6] Mays called upon persons to travel the "high road," the metaphorical expression for speaking out without fear against pejorative images imposed upon African Americans. Mays believed that victory over racism, sexism, and bigotry could be achieved only if they were confronted forthrightly and straightforwardly. "No man is really free," Mays explains, "who is afraid to speak the truth as he knows it, or is too fearful to take a stand for that which he knows is right."[7]

Mays practiced what he preached. Discrimination and inequity were pervasive elements in Mays's childhood home of Ninety Six, South Carolina. Propaganda that dismissed the African American was published frequently saying: "The Negro is a different breed. He is inferior to the white man. At any cost he must be kept down." Mays wrote that such statements, "certainly 'put the rabbit' " in many African Americans who heard them.[8] Mays viewed such perspectives as mere vicissitudes of life that should be conquered. Realizing God's mission for one's life, Mays believed, would empower the disfranchised with a sense of worth:

---

[5]*Disturbed About Man*, 38.
[6]*Quotable Quotes*, 7.
[7]*Disturbed About Man*, 38.
[8]*Born to Rebel*, 22, 25.

To be able to stand the troubles of life, one must have a sense of mission and the belief that God sent him or her into the world for a purpose, to do something unique and distinctive; and that if he does not do it, life will be worse off because it was not done.

Mays rebelled against the restricted horizons of his father and pursued the education he saw as his mission in life. Long after Mays had completed high school and had begun his college matriculation, his father insisted that he return home and work the old farming schedule which had only allowed Mays to attend school for four months out of the year. He later wrote:

I disobeyed him without regret and with no pangs of conscience. It was now crystal clear to me that I must take my education into my own hands and that I could not and must not permit my father to dictate or determine my future.[9]

Mays advocated coping with racism by gaining control of oneself. Rebellion must have the tone of reason: "The man who out thinks you, rules you."[10] Mays also believed in nonviolent resistance as the primary weapon against violent segregationists. In essence, the primary agents in this form of rebellion are psychological and spiritual recalcitrance. "Non-violence is three-fourths invisible, and the results are spiritual and largely invisible."[11] He later speculated that

Negroes in my county fought among themselves because they were taking out on other Negroes what they really wanted but feared to take out on whites. . . . It was difficult, virtually impossible, to combine manhood and blackness under one skin in the days of my youth. To exercise manhood, as white men displayed it, was to invite disaster.[12]

In order to offset this psychological bondage, Mays suggested that

---

[9]Ibid., 38.
[10]*Quotable Quotes*, 5.
[11]Mays, "Non-Violence," an editorial in the *Pittsburgh Courier*, 28 February 1948.
[12]*Born to Rebel*, 26.

reason and intellect should be used against these pernicious conditions. On one of many occasions, Mays was tested. As a high school student he applied for a job that had been vacated by his friend Isaiah Kearse. Arriving at the employer's home, Mays was reprimanded for appearing at the front door. The man called Mays a "black s. o. b." and warned him never to come to the front door again. When Mays referred to his friend as "Mr. Kearse," the employer huffed that "Isaiah" worked for him, but no Mr. Kearse. Looking back on the incident, Mays commented:

> It is degrading enough to deny a man a title of civility because he is black; but to deny him the right to give titles to members of his own race is just going too damn far! I left that man's house in a hurry, no more fearful of what he might do to me than of what I might do to him. Once I realized that Negroes were frequently expected to go to the white man's back door, I never went to see anyone if the back door was a requirement. One has to rebel against indignities in some fashion in order to maintain the integrity of his soul.[13]

Mays imbued many Morehouse men, including Martin Luther King Jr., with his philosophy of psychological rebellion:

> I would not let my environment destroy me, beat me down, or make me accept what it said: that my family and my people were inferior to the white man. When a man accepts that designation of inferiority, he might as well die. He has nothing to live for. When he denies his inherent worth and denies that he is a person of infinite worth and value, he is dead even if he lives to be four score years and ten, or even a hundred.[14]

Mays preached this idea his entire adult life; that rebellion against the psychological oppression comes first from within. Fundamental to Mays approach to psychological rebellion is to counter negative self-images with self love and faith in oneself.

---

[13]Ibid, 47.
[14]*Quotable Quotes*, 11.

A child must learn early to believe that he is somebody worthwhile and he can do many praiseworthy things . . . Furthermore, man could not live hopefully without believing he counts for something in this world. The greatest damage that the white man did to the black man through slavery and segregation was to beat him down so much that millions of Negroes believed that they were nobody. The hopelessness and despair of so many black youths today lie in the fact that they never believe that they have dignity and worth as a human being.[15]

Mays suggests that positive declarations and celebrations of African American ethos and identity are crucial to overcoming years of psychological oppression. He argued:

If the emphasis on blackness and black awareness today means that black people are beginning to be proud of their heritage and proud of being what they are—black—apologizing to no one—not even to God—for what they are, it is a good thing. Man lives best by a belief that he is somebody, God's creature, and that he has status not given to him by man but given to him by God.

Mays understood the necessity for the African American to reconstruct a viable self-image through love of self without conceit, through faith in oneself without presumptuousness.

Mays's concept of rebellion was firmly grounded in his theology. Mays provides options for spiritual rebellion against the evil circumstances of life. Persons must learn to live not only by physical sustenance but by love and affection, the forgiveness of God, faith in God's divine plan, the goals one strives to reach, and the ideals one chooses and chases.[16] For Mays, all persons ought to aspire to a love akin to the love God expresses for humanity. This love ethic is fundamental to Mays's entire concept of rebellion. Mays understood love as a defense mechanism or as a "weapon" against evil and oppression. The biblical concept of *agape* is pivotal to

---

[15]See Mays's sermon, "What Man Lives By," in William M. Philpot, ed., *Best Black Sermons* (Valley Forge, PA: Judson Press, 1972), 34.

[16]*Disturbed About Man*, passim.

Mays's idea of spiritual rebellion. He argued that "we live by the forgiveness of God. No man is perfect enough, no man is good enough not to need the forgiveness of God." It is imperative, according to Mays, that humanity combat hate, malice, or deceitfulness with the forgiveness and love of God. Forgiveness is where spiritual rebellion germinates:

> Man needs forgiveness for the dirty, vicious things that some do to others. How often have we in some little or big way trespassed against a brother? We live by forgiveness of those friends who love us and stick with us though we sin against them. . . . We live by the forgiveness of God.[17]

Humanity must also live by faith—faith in itself and faith in others. Mays writes, "However beastly man may be, we must believe in him and rely on him." The faith one has in oneself serves both a psychological and spiritual purpose. In Mays's view "man could not live hopefully without believing that he counts for something in this world."[18] Mays believed the greatest tragedy of enslavement was its assumption of Africans' worthlessness. Mays believed that the hopelessness and despair of the African American community was grounded in the countless horrific psychological and spiritual browbeatings experienced during slavery.

Mays abhorred the notion that man is in and of himself great. What eventually evolves from such a philosophy is a belief that there may even be gradations of human greatness or goodness: man is greater than woman; peoples of European decent are greater than peoples of African decent; the rich are better than the poor; heterosexuals are more moral than homosexuals. Not only did Mays deem these unnecessary distinctions, but he also viewed these distinctions as erroneous. The human spirit must strive to soar beyond the finite classifications and seek to reside within God's spirit. Mays cites an example of a high spirit, which he recommends, and a low spirit, which he abhors:

---

[17]Ibid.
[18]Ibid.

Stretch your imagination and you will see two men coming down the aisle of a church to pray—a Pharisee and a tax collector. On the right is the Pharisee. He prays thus: "O God, I do thank thee that I am not like the rest of mankind, greedy, dishonest, impure, or even like that tax collector over there. I fast twice every week: I give away a tenth part of all my income" (Luke 18:11-12, Phillips). On the left, in a distant corner, stands the tax collector, head bowed, and with a gesture of despair he cries out, "God, have mercy on a sinner like me" (Luke 18:13, Phillips). The Pharisee is unacceptable, condemned. The tax collector is justified and praised. I like the Phillips' translation: "For everyone who sets himself up as somebody will become a nobody, and the man who makes himself nobody will become somebody" (Luke 18:14).[19]

Mays condemned the self-imposed grandeur of the Pharisee. The Pharisee lifted himself above the people and went to God with the arrogance of a fool. The tax collector, on the other hand, had a disturbed conscience.

I would send him [the tax collector] to my imaginary heaven because he had a disturbed conscience. I see him with my mental eyes agonizing on his bed, unable to sleep; every time he dozes he dreams of the poor widow and her starving children from whom he extracted too much tax money. His conscience [spirit] pricks him, beating him down, because he has robbed the rich. So he stands in the church and cries out in despair, "God, have mercy on a sinner like me!" This man was not far from the Kingdom of God."[20]

The human spirit must thwart the alluring attractions of the material world and strive, through earnest prayer and supplication, to empower the human soul. Mays hoped to liberate the whole being from social despair, narcissism, egocentric hedonism, and oppression through the expression of love, faith, humility, and obedience to God's divine will.

In addition to psychological and spiritual rebellion, Mays advocated a

---

[19]*The Negro's God*, 67.
[20]*The Negro's God*, 68.

form of socio-political rebellion. For Mays socio-political rebellion emanates from his dialectical understanding of the Christian religion as the primary moral and ethical standard in American society and to the Federal Constitution's supposition of the human equity of all citizens of the Untied States of America. Mays was committed to eradicating social oppression and political deprivation. Toward this end, Mays argued for civil disobedience against any laws denying equal protection and privileges to any citizen. Mays was convinced that human laws are ancillary to the laws of God. Consistent with this, one should strive to actualize the teaching of the Christian religion which clearly, according to Mays, teaches the equality of all peoples. He noted:

> A person who does not believe in segregation of races but lives in a community where segregation is prescribed by law must find ways to have fellowship with those of other racial groups despite the law.

Mays's sought to evoke ethical integrity and challenge the segregator to live up to the egalitarianism of the Christian religion and the Federal Constitution. The onus of eradicating discrimination rested with the discriminated as well as the discriminator. In essence, behavior modification of the former and the latter must be imminent if social and political injustices are to be corrected. The oppressed must have faith in God to deliver justice and must never allow violence to seek out justice in God's stead. "When a people fight for freedom with spiritual weapons and not physical weapons—with love and not hate—good will and not ill will—the whole wide world stands up and applauds." [21] He added:

> To the Christian, the time is always ripe to take a stand for, and act on the side of that which is right. He needs to be certain in his own mind that the situation has been thoroughly canvassed and his methods, techniques, motives, aims, attitudes and objectives are truly Christian. Once convinced on these points, he has a mandate from God to take a firm stand and act. . . . What the consequences of his actions will be he [the Christian] cannot always know. He can

---

[21] See editorial by William A. Fowlkes, *Atlanta Daily World*, 20 April 1961.

never know the ultimate outcome of what he does, (whether favorable or unfavorable) for he will probably die before all the results are in. It does not necessarily follow that the cause is set back because immediate reactions are unpleasant, nor that the cause is advanced because immediate reactions are satisfactory. Only time can determine the final outcome. The Christian will leave the consequences of his actions in the hands of God"[22]

Mays believed that being Christian in one's rebelliousness required the courage of Jesus. All Christians, black or white, are bound by the paradigm of Jesus' life to have the courage to create a more amiable and ethical society constructed on the foundation of social equality and love.

By 1968 Mays argued that African Americans were divided, noting that by fighting among themselves they were playing into the hands of whites:

I am sure the white racists must be having a good time while Negroes war against themselves. Maybe this is the time for Negro leadership from the right, left and the middle to get together and see if Negroes could arrive at more unanimity in our efforts to improve our conditions. . . . As long as black people are divided, as we are now, each pursuing his own worse, we will be bogged down in our own divisiveness.[23]

As a united force, African Americans can improve their conditions. Towards this end African Americans who seek to use their education for the social empowerment of the community must specialize in the various academic disciplines:

[we must] not be in too big a hurry to get out to make a few dollars at starvation wages: or if it's medicine, the doctor must not be swept off his feet by the money he is making so that he can't take time out to specialize in some particular brand of medicine . . . Not all

---

[22]Mays, "The Time is Always Ripe," in *The Women's Press* 39 (March 1945): n.p.
[23]"Negroes are Divided," *The Voice*, 1 December 1968.

much prejudice can and will be abolished when more Negroes become first rate in many fields.[24]

Mays spent forty-five years in education and taught his students at Morehouse College during legalized segregation never to patronize establishments that embraced discriminatory practices:

> The Morehouse philosophy was and is that a man doesn't have to accept the view that because he is a Negro certain things were not meant for him. He can be free in a highly segregated society. Long before demonstrations and Supreme Court decisions abolished segregation, the Morehouse students were taught to accept no segregated situation except that which was absolutely necessary, and that though their bodies were segregated their minds could be free. Students who broke faith with this principle and went to segregated theaters, restaurants, and churches went there without administration sanction.[25]

Mays was deeply concerned with the ubiquitous nature of social inequality propagated against African Americans. He would not allow social conformity to dictate his public demeanor. He earnestly taught and practiced a social rebellion that never negotiated his humanity. While attending a banquet for President Truman given by the Federal Council of the Churches, Mays was denied a seat on the rostrum even though he was an executive officer. Moreover, he was asked to sit in the audience with other dignitaries and the president's secret service agents. "Several persons came to request me to move," he later recalled, "saying that the place where I was sitting was reserved for special people. I didn't move."[26]

Mays unwaveringly rejected intimations of inferiority and subjugation. Belligerence was never the goal of Mays's concept of rebellion, whether in psychological, spiritual, or social form. The maintenance of one's integrity was the primary concern of his philosophy of rebellion. Circumstances and

---

[24]"Are We Getting Ready?" *Pittsburgh Courier*, 20 March 1948.

[25]Mays, "Twenty-seven Years of Success and Failure at Morehouse, graduation address, 1967, Program, Centennial Commencement.

[26]*Born to Rebel*, 253.

powers may have sought to make his mind acquiesce and his soul bow, but he never moved.

8

MAYS AS MENTOR TO KING

Freddie C. Colston

Generations of young men and women have expanded their intellectual horizons under the tutelage of Benjamin E. Mays. Many of them have gone forth to serve their communities, states, and nation and have imparted to others the teachings they received. Mays once said that, "there is not a state in the nation where I visit that someone doesn't come up to me and suggest something I said that had an impact on their life."[1] Among the individuals he influenced are: Lerone Bennett, Samuel D. Cook, Charles V. Willie, Mayor Maynard Jackson, Benjamin Payton, Leroy Keith, Charles Merideth, the late William E. Gardner, Hanes Walton Jr., Tobe Johnson, Abraham L. Davis, Alton Hornsby Jr., Michael L. Lomax, Lonnie King, Julian Bond, Judge Horace Ward, Andrew Young, James M. Nabrit, Samuel Nabrit, Louis Sullivan, Walter Massey, the late Howard Thurman, Herschelle Challenor, Marion Wright Edelman, Hamilton Holmes, Charlayne Hunter-Gault and many others who have left their mark on American society. The most famous of his former students was Martin Luther King Jr., the greatest civil rights leader in American history and winner of the 1964 Nobel Peace Prize for his leadership against racial oppression and injustice. This essay examines the influence Mays exerted on the spiritual and intellectual development of Martin Luther King Jr.

While serving as dean of the Howard University School of Religion, Mays became fascinated by India. He eventually visited the country three times: in late 1936 (Martin Luther King Jr. was then only seven years old), early 1937 and again, with his wife Sadie, in 1950. On his visits he observed first-hand how the Indian people used nonviolent resistance to win

---

[1]"Benjamin E. Mays: A Great Georgian," Video, Media Services Center, University of Georgia, 1974.

independence from the British.[2] He met Nehru when he was leader of the Congress Party and conferred with Mahatma Gandhi. But, in addition to first-hand observance of Gandhi's leadership, Mays also "saw the depth of poverty, people sleeping on the streets of Bombay by the hundred thousands because they had nowhere else to sleep."[3]

Mays had a personal conference with Gandhi at his ashram in Wordha on 31 December 1946 while attending the World Conference of the YMCA: Concerning this conference with Gandhi he stated:

I had to choose between making a trip to see and talk with Gandhi and a trip to New Delhi and North India where I could see the Taj Mahal. When I told the great leader I chose to visit him rather than go to New Delhi, he said, "You made a wise choice. When you visit India again, the Taj Mahal will still be here, I may not." He was right. He was emphatic in stating that nonviolence is an active force. Nonviolence is three-fourths invisible, and the results are spiritual and largely invisible. Nonviolence, he made clear, is not a technique or strategy that one uses because he is too weak to use force. It is a way of life. It must be practiced in absolute love and without hate. In a nonviolent campaign, the welfare of your opponent must be taken into consideration. If the campaign destroys your opponent, it must be called off. . . .[4]

Mays was one of several black leaders who traveled to India to discuss with Gandhi the application of the technique of non-violence and feasibility of its use by African Americans. Mays experienced Gandhi's teachings from his own lips and after that inculcated the dimensions of this doctrine in his own teachings, writings and speeches.[5]

---

[2]Edward A. Jones, *A Candle in the Dark* (Valley Forge: Judson, 1967), 133.

[3]*Pittsburgh Courier*, February 28, 1948.

[4]Ibid.

[5]Hanes Walton Jr., *The Political Philosophy of Martin Luther King Jr.* (Westport: Greenwood Publishing Co., 1971), 24. Walton indicates that in 1929 a group of blacks led by Mordecai Johnson heard Gandhi tell them that not only through his technique, but "perhaps" it will be through the Negro the unadulterated message of nonviolence will be delivered to the world.

However, Mays had experienced racial indignities that strengthened his commitment against racism, poverty and oppression. In 1923, with a pistol pressed in his back, he was forced out of a pullman car. Again, in 1942 he was forced out of a dining car on the Southern Railroad between Atlanta and Washington because he refused to take a seat at the segregated table designated for blacks. Instead, he sat at a table with a group of white men. He was approached by three angry white men (the steward and two others). He stepped backward out of the door facing them and thus avoided being thrown off the train. Mays later sued the Southern Railroad because of the practice of segregated dining and won his case on 8 April 1947. Thus long before accepting the presidency of Morehouse College, Mays was in the forefront in the fight of black Americans against racial oppression.[6]

Benjamin E. Mays became the sixth president of Morehouse on 1 August 1940. On 10 May 1940, Trevor Arnett, a former board member and a former president of the General Education Board, called Mays in Washington to inform him that he had been elected to the presidency of Morehouse College. He informed Arnett that he would talk to Mordecai Johnson and think about the offer. He made up his mind in three weeks. However, before accepting the presidency of Morehouse, Mays made clear to the trustees that he must be given a free hand to function as the institution's chief executive. The job was offered to him on these terms. According to Mays, three things had to be done immediately: (1) secure more money: (2) increase the faculty size; and (3) improve the quality of the faculty by hiring better trained teachers.[7] He set out to accomplish these goals. In assessing his intimate reasons for returning to Morehouse as president, he remarked:

I came to Morehouse because it is a great institution. Great in hope; great in ambition; great in ideas, great in aspiration. The men who taught here led Morehouse men to believe that whatever was possible under the sun, a Morehouse man could do it. The teachers were men like John Hope, Samuel Howard Archer, Benjamin Brawley, John B. Watson, C. D. Hubert and others. There were stimulating students like

---

[6]*Pittsburgh Courier*, September, 1966; *Atlanta Constitution*, 29 March 1984.
[7]*Born to Rebel*, 170, 176; Jones, *A Candle in the Dark*, 136.

Samuel Nabrit, James Nabrit, Howard Thurman and others. So I thought of the students and the stimulating things that happened to me while I was a teacher at Morehouse in making my decision to return as president.[8]

When he assumed the presidency of Morehouse Mays was very much in favor of change in the Atlanta community. Therefore, he called for broader discussion between blacks and whites in Atlanta. A small coalition was organized. Mays joined this group along with prominent members of Atlanta's black community, including John Wesley Dobbs, A. T. Walden, C. A. Scott, and the Reverend Martin Luther King Sr. In 1944, along with the heads of the institutions in the Atlanta University Center, Mays organized the Southern Regional Council to improve race relations and eliminate vestiges of discrimination. The group later became integrated and still exists today.[9]

Martin Luther King Jr. entered Morehouse in fall 1944 (following his father who graduated from Morehouse in 1927). The 15-year-old King was a product of two generations of Baptist ministers, but "M.L." as he was called had not yet decided on his career path. For a long time he had wanted to engage in some profession that would help black people. He considered becoming a doctor or lawyer. His choice of professions was to be transformed during the early stages of his career at Morehouse. His studies at Morehouse increased his intellectual awareness and heightened his social and world view.[10]

For most of the years of the Mays presidency at Morehouse, chapel attendance was required of all students every day except Saturday. Many national personalities appeared before the students on these occasions: Mordecai Johnson, Howard Thurman, W. E. B. DuBois, Mary McCleod Bethune and several others. It was here that the image of the "Morehouse

---

[8]*Born to Rebel*, 176.

[9]"Benjamin E. Mays: A Great Georgian"; Martin Luther King Sr., *Daddy King: An Autobiography* (New York: William Morrow and Co., Inc., 1980), 110.

[10]Christine King Farris, "The Young Martin: From Childhood Through College," *Ebony* 41 (January, 1986), 58; Hugh M. Gloster, "Martin Luther King Jr. and Morehouse College: A Committed Student at a Committed College," *Morehouse College Bulletin*, Vol. 48 (Winter, 1986), 6.

Family" was cultivated and intellectual horizons expanded. Tuesday was President Mays's day to speak to the student body. Mays assessed the importance of these chapel sessions in the following remarks:

> Here students can learn firsthand what the basic thinking or philosophy of the president is. I know I made many uninspiring speeches in chapel over the years, but as a rule I prepared for them carefully as I did for engagements away from Morehouse, and usually the students came when I spoke. I must admit it is gratifying now when I meet Morehouse men who were graduated many years ago, men successful in their chosen professions, to have them voluntarily tell me how much a particular speech helped them. If a man can quote in substance something I had said 20 or 30 years before, I feel that I have done something good.[11]

Morehouse College has a long standing tradition of developing men who are committed to social change and academic excellence. At Morehouse, the pursuit of excellence in the classroom was supplemented by daily chapel periods mentioned above and a vigorous and free campus life. Two things were drilled into Morehouse students from their first day on campus to their last: 1) that they were Morehouse men and 2) that they were expected to succeed in life. Young Martin felt a sense of freedom at Morehouse College. King noted, "There was a freer atmosphere at Morehouse and it was there that I had my first frank discussions on race. "M.L." soon fell under the influence of Mays and his chapel addresses. It was in these chapel sessions that he constantly reminded them: "They could be poor; they could be black; their ancestors may have been slaves; they may be segregated and discriminated against, but still be free in their minds and soul. No man is a slave until he accepts it in his mind. . . ."[12] Another dimension of his philosophy that he imparted to the Morehouse student body was stated as follows:

> It is not sufficient for Morehouse College to produce clever graduates, men fluent in speech and able to argue their way

---

[11]*Born to Rebel*, 191-92.

[12]Lerone Bennett Jr., *What Manner of Man: A Biography of Martin Luther King Jr.* (Chicago: Johnson Publishing Co.,Inc. 1968), 26; "Benjamin E. Mays: A Great Georgian."

through; but rather honest men who can be trusted in public and private life—men who are sensitive to the wrongs, the sufferings, and the injustices of society and who are willing to accept responsibility for correcting these ills.[13]

President Mays spoke and young "M.L." listened—remarks transmitted from mentor to pupil, generating a lasting friendship that extended throughout their lives. Martin Luther King heard and digested what Mays said in chapel. He often took notes.

Mays provided insight on his friendship with King as it began during his student days at Morehouse when he asserted:

One never knows what it is that triggers a response, but I am convinced that it was my contact with [him] in Chapel at Morehouse that brought us closer together. There we began a real friendship which was strengthened by visits to home and by fairly frequent informal chats on campus and in my office. Many times during his four years at Morehouse, he would linger after my Tuesday morning address to discuss some point I had made—usually with approval, but sometimes questioning or disagreeing. I was not aware how deeply he was impressed by what I said until he wrote, *Stride Toward Freedom*, in which he indicated that I had influenced his life to a marked degree. "In public addresses, he often referred to me as his "spiritual mentor."[14]

Mays often visited the King family at their Atlanta home and he was a friend of "Daddy King" a member of the Morehouse Board of Trustees. The elder King valued Mays's counsel to Martin and the family throughout his professional career.

While a student at Morehouse "M.L." was a sociology major under the direction of Professor Walter Chivers. Young King was president of the sociology club, sang in the glee club, was a member of the debating team, and began participating in the annual college oratorical contest during his

---

[13]"Martin Luther King Jr. and Morehouse College," 6-7.
[14]*Born to Rebel*, 265.

sophomore year. During this period he wrestled with the choice of a vocation. He apparently desired to become a minister emulating his father and maternal grandfather both of whom he admired greatly. However, he was somewhat reluctant because of his disapproval of the emotionalism of the black church (e.g., shouting, hand-clapping, moaning and amen-ing). But Morehouse widened King's perception of himself and the contribution he could make to humanity.[15]

Morehouse had on its faculty two outstanding seminary trained and scholarly ministers in George P. Kelsey, Chairman of the Department of Religion, and Benjamin Mays. In Mays and Kelsey he visualized his ideal of what a minister could be and came to see that the ministry could be intellectually respectable as well as emotionally satisfying. His acceptance of this possibility paved the way for his entry into the church. These two reputable and scholarly ministers exerted an important impact on Martin's decision to become a minister. Martin had been clearly impressed and motivated during his first three years at Morehouse and told his mother one evening that he had decided to become a minister. After sharing the good news with his father, he agreed to preach a sermon at Ebenezer, his father's pastorate. The sermon was a resounding success. Afterwards, his father felt that his son had found himself, and he thanked God for his son's decision.[16]

Martin was ordained 25 February 1947., Serving on the ordination council were: Benjamin E. Mays, Reverends Samuel Williams and L. M. Tobin of Morehouse, and L. A. Pinkston, president of the State Baptist Convention of Georgia.[17] He became assistant pastor at his father's church when only eighteen years old. In 1948 King was selected to deliver the Senior Sermon during Morehouse's Senior Week. Samuel D. Cook, a classmate of King and then president of the student body recalled:

---

[15]Lerone Bennett, *What Manner of Man*, 27; David J. Garrow, *Bearing the Cross: Martin Luther King Jr. and the Southern Christian Leadership Conference* (New York: William Morrow and Co., Inc. 1986), 36.

[16]Coretta Scott King, *My Life with Martin Luther King Jr.* (New York: Holt, Rinehart and Winston, 1969), 85.

[17]Clayborne Carson, (Senior Editor), *The Papers of Martin Luther King Jr. Volume I: Called to Serve, January 1929 - June 1951*, Berkeley: University of California Press, 1992), 153.

I remember, as if it were yesterday, "M. L.'s" great oratorical flourish. He asserted that there are moral laws in the universe that we cannot violate with impunity. I can see him now in the Chapel in Sale Hall delivering that speech. He electrified us. "M.L.'s" words have stuck with me down through the grinding years.

Cook indicated further that there was no evidence then to predict that King would later become a national, international and historical leader. But, in his estimation, there was compelling evidence that he was destined to become a great orator and preacher for he had a way with words and tremendous communicative powers.[18]

When King graduated from Morehouse in June 1948 he had been accepted for graduate study at Crozer Seminary in Chester, Pennsylvania, along with his best friend from Morehouse, Walter R. McCall. Mays had written a letter of recommendation to Crozer on behalf of both graduates. He endorsed their applications stating that "they are both men of integrity. They both have good minds and in my opinion they could do B work and may do better.[19]

During King's tenure at Crozer the school was headed by Edwin E. Aubrey, who had taught Mays at the University of Chicago. In his three years at Crozer, King began to read in depth the great social philosophers—Aristotle, Plato, Rousseau, Hegel, Locke, Ricardo, Brightman, and Adam Smith. While at Crozer, Mordecai Johnson, president of Howard University, came to lecture on his recent trip to India and discussed how Gandhi had used passive resistance in the struggle against the British. After that lecture, King bought several books on the Indian leader and read them thoroughly. King graduated from Crozer in 1951 as first in his class after having also won other academic honors. He was president of the student body and won the J. Lewis Crozer Fellowship that enabled him to enter

---

[18]Renee D. Turner, "Remembering the Young King," *Ebony*, 43 (January, 1988): .40-46. Contained in the same article are reminiscences of King's classmates: Judge Horace To Ward, Robert E. Johnson, editor of the 1948 Maroon Tiger, George D. Kelsey, late professor of religion and philosophy at Drew University, and William G. Pickens, professor of English at Morehouse College.

[19]37. Carson, 153. See the same also for the letter of recommendation written by "Daddy King" on behalf of his son, Martin.

Boston University to study toward his Pd.D. in the philosophy of religion. Later, after the death of professor Edgar S. Brightman, he switched to systematic theology.[20]

He entered Boston University in September 1951. After having been at Boston University for a short while, King was introduced to Coretta Scott by Mary Powell, a student at the New England Conservatory of Music who was married to a nephew of Mays. Powell played the role of matchmaker.[21] Coretta Scott, also a student at the Conservatory, became his wife in June 1953. Near the completion of his doctoral studies at Boston University in August, 1954 Martin was confronted with the crucial decision whether to enter university teaching or the ministry. He and Coretta decided to return South where it was felt he could make the greatest contribution to those who needed him most: the poor, the downtrodden, the dispossessed, and the disenfranchised.

His father was pleased with the decision to return South and attempted to persuade his son to join him as co-pastor at Ebenezer. "Daddy King" prevailed upon his friend, Mays, who offered Martin a position on the Morehouse faculty where he could jointly occupy the Ebenezer position. But when the pulpit of Dexter Avenue Baptist Church in Montgomery became vacant (with the dismissal of its minister, the Reverend Vernon Johns), Martin accepted the pastorate there in April 1954, and agreed to start in September.[22]

Martin was thrust into the annals of history when he became president of the Montgomery Improvement Association and leader of the Montgomery Bus Boycott that unfolded in December 1955. King began to utilize the Gandhian technique of nonviolent resistance. In February 1956 as the Montgomery Boycott intensified, Mays played a significant role in his support of Martin's commitment to the leadership of the struggle. During this period, in retaliation against the boycott leaders, the grand jury issued indictments against most members of the Montgomery Improvement

---

[20]Ted Poston, "Fighting Pastor: Martin Luther King Jr.," *New York Post*, April 10, 1957.

[21]Coretta Scott King, 52.

[22]Taylor Branch, *Parting the Waters: America in the King Years: 1954-63* (New York: Simon and Schuster, 1988), 489.

Association under the State of Alabama's anti-boycott law.[23] Martin was out of the city at the time on a speaking engagement in Nashville, Tennessee. Afterwards he traveled to Atlanta to visit his family and was informed of the pending indictments. His mother and father feared for his life if he returned to Montgomery where his home had been bombed. (His wife and young daughter escaped injury and were staying with his parents in Atlanta.)

In an effort to persuade Martin not to return to Montgomery, his father summoned to his home some of Atlanta's most influential black leaders: Mays, C. R. Yates, Vice President of Citizens Bank; T. M. Alexander, an insurance broker; Bishop S. L. Green of the A.M.E. Church; a white Atlanta attorney, Dan Duke, and Rufus Clement, president of Atlanta University.[24] Martin's father wanted these men to endorse his desire to persuade his son not to return to Montgomery. At first the group expressed support for the elder King's position. But Martin was adamant in informing them that he could not abandon his friends in Montgomery:

> I must go back to Montgomery. . . . My friends and associates are being arrested. It would be the height of cowardice for me to stay away. I would rather be in jail ten years than desert my people. I had begun the struggle and I can't turn back. I have reached the point of no return. In the moment of silence, I heard my father break into tears. I looked at Mays, one of the great influences in my life. Perhaps he heard my unspoken plea. At any rate he was soon defending my position. The others joined him in supporting me.[25]

Mays came to Martin's defense in his typical direct, honest and convincing style. This represented the kind of moral-ethical decision-making Mays advocated in his chapel assemblies, writings and speeches. Mays even offered to pay for legal counsel if needed. This support of his friend and former student temporarily lifted a heavy burden from "Daddy King's" shoulders. His father decided to drive Martin and his family back to

---

[23]Garrow, 48.

[24]Martin Luther King Sr., *Daddy King*, 171.

[25]King, *Stride Toward Freedom* (New York: Harper and Row, 1958), 144. See also Stephen B. Oates, *Let the Trumpet Sound: The Life of Martin Luther King Jr.* (New York: Harper and Row, 1982), 92.

Montgomery the next morning.

Later, at the height of the Montgomery Bus Boycott, city authorities accused King of perjury for failure to pay state income taxes in 1956 and 1958. Mays appeared as a character witness in Martin's behalf. Concerning the charges Mays stated: "I believe that if Reverend Martin Luther King had never been a leader of the Montgomery Bus Movement and if he had not been a crusader for civil rights, he never would have been indicted by the state of Alabama and charged with perjury."[26]

Because of his emerging stature and effective leadership of the bus boycott, King received national and international recognition. In May, 1957 he received the Spingarn Medal for making the most significant contribution in the field of race relations that year. In June 1957 Morehouse College bestowed an honorary degree (the first from an institution of higher learning). In bestowing the degree, Mays said:

> You are mature beyond your years, wiser at twenty-eight than most men at sixty; more courageous in the righteous struggle than most men can ever be; living faith that most men preach about but never experience. Significant indeed is the fact that you did not seek the leadership in the Montgomery controversy. It was thrust upon you by the people. You did not betray the trust of leadership. You lead the people with great dignity, Christian grace, and determined purpose. While you were away, your colleagues in the battle for freedom were being hounded and arrested like criminals. When it was suggested by legal counsel that you might stay away and avoid arrest, I heard you say with my own ears: "I would rather spend ten years in jail rather than desert the people in crisis." At that moment, my heart, my mind and my soul stood erect and saluted you. I knew then that you were called to leadership for just such a time as this . . . On this our 90th anniversary, your Alma Mater is happy to be the first college or university to honor you this way.[27]

In June 1959, Reverend King delivered the commencement address at

---

[26] *Pittsburgh Courier*, 5 March 1960.
[27] Bennett, 79.

Morehouse. The address was entitled, "Remaining Awake Through A Great Revolution." He said to the Class of 1959: "You are graduating at a time when the world is experiencing one of the greatest revolutions ever known, a world-wide revolution." He urged the class to be active and alert and not sleep through the changes taking place in the world around them. He predicted that in the next ten years the majority of the people of Africa would have their independence and colonialism would be eliminated. He concluded urging the graduates that if they are content with mediocrity they are sleeping through a revolution, and he exhorted them to be ready to face opportunities as they arise.[28]

Mays prevailed upon King to deliver speeches at Morehouse whenever he was available and his schedule permitted. Accordingly, he made several speeches at the request of Mays. There were additional instances where the Mays-King friendship blossomed during the leadership of the civil rights movement.

In his writings and speeches Mays supported the right of a Catholic to become President of the United States. President Kennedy later had Mays under consideration for appointment to the U. S. Commission on Civil Rights and to become Ambassador to Israel. That triggered opposition from Georgia's two senators, Russell and Talmadge. Learning of this predicament, King sent a telegram to President Kennedy and urged him to appoint Mays to the Commission. He maintained:

> It would be a tragedy if such a distinguished American were deprived of the opportunity to serve his country in a unique position merely because of unwarranted and false accusations made by two senators from Georgia. It seems obvious that [one of] the objections the senators have to Mays is that he has not been an accommodating ultraconservative leader.[29]

Mays did not receive the appointment to the Civil Rights Commission. However, he was appointed as a member of the Advisory Council of the Peace Corps in 1961. He also was among the delegation that represented

---

[28] *Morehouse College Bulletin*, July, 1959, 3.
[29] *Atlanta Constitution*, 2 March 1961; see also Branch, 380.

the United States at the State Funeral of Pope John XXIII, in Rome in 1963.

President Mays prevailed upon King to teach a seminar at Morehouse after he returned to Atlanta to co-pastor Ebenezer Baptist Church with his father. The seminar in Social Philosophy was taught during the 1961-1962 academic year. King later had to give up this teaching duties because of heavy responsibilities as leader of the civil rights movement.

After King's immortal, "I Have A Dream" speech delivered at the March on Washington in August 1963, his mentor gave the benediction. Mays planned to participate in the 1965 Selma March but could not because his wife was undergoing treatment at Mayo Clinic.[30] In a 1963 letter to King after the assassination of President Kennedy, Mays issued a warning to be careful. In this letter he stated:

President Kennedy's death was almost more than I could take. If they hated him, you know they love you less. I hope that you will take every precaution as you move around.[31]

After King received the 1964 Nobel Peace Prize, Mays led the move to honor King both at Morehouse and in the Atlanta Community. The Morehouse Convocation recognizing King for receiving the coveted award was held in Archer Hall on 7 January 1965, with 2,700 persons in attendance, and 1,300 people from the Atlanta community honored King in the Dinkler Plaza Hotel on 27 January 1965. When King spoke out against the war in Viet Nam in 1967, his friend and mentor gave his wholehearted support for his position, although King's position was generally not popular among the American establishment.

Throughout the course of the civil rights movement, King and Mays were in frequent contact when crucial decisions were to be made. King contributed generously to his beloved Alma Mater, and his mentor contributed financial support to the civil rights cause. The two friends were

---

[30]*Born to Rebel*, 270.

[31]Letter to Martin Luther King, 29 November 1963. Archives, Martin Luther King Center for Social Change, Atlanta, Georgia.

in constant contact.[32]

After King's assassination it was Mays who delivered the eulogy for his beloved friend. The funeral was held on the college campus where Martin had been guided under the tutelage of Mays into the ministry.[33] Approximately 150,000 people assembled on the Morehouse campus for the funeral honoring the slain leader. With the world watching via television, Mays delivered one of his finest speeches in his captivating, direct, and classical style. His remarks on this historic day have been repeated many times and some excerpts are stated here again. In his eulogy to King he remarked:

To be honored by being requested to give the Eulogy at the funeral of Martin Luther King Jr. is like asking one to eulogize his deceased son—so close and so dear was he to me. Our friendship goes back to his student days at Morehouse. It is not an easy task; nevertheless, I accept it with heavy heart and with full knowledge of my inadequacy to do justice to this man; he would pay tribute to me on my final day. It was his wish that if he predeceased me, I would do the homily at his funeral. Fate has decreed that I eulogize him. I wish it might have been otherwise, for, after all, I am three score and ten and Martin is dead at thirty-nine. . . .

Too bad, you say, that Martin Luther King died, so young. I feel that way too. But as I have said so many times before, it isn't how long one lives, but how well. It's what one accomplishes for mankind that

---

[32]Mays, *Born to Rebel*, p.271. See also *Pittsburgh Courier*, January 23, 1965. The Mays -King letters are on file at Mugar Memorial Library at Boston University (which had been involved in litigation with the King estate concerning ownership) and with Clayborne Carson King Papers Project at Stanford University. None of the letters are found in the Mays Collection at Moorland-Spingarn Research Center at Howard University. Dr. Mays recognized the historical value and significance of this correspondence for future reference and possibly turned over his copies to the King Collection. The only other correspondence between the two men was mentioned previously from the Archives at the King Center for Social Change. Mays's presidential papers are at Morehouse College, though they are not yet available to the public.

[33]Coretta Scott King, 331; Leonard Ray Teal, "Benjamin E. Mays, Teaching by Example, Leading Through Will," *Equal Opportunity* (Spring 1983), 14-22. See also *Pittsburgh Courier*, April 27, 1968.

matters. No! He was not ahead of his time. Every man is within his own star, each in his own time.

I close by saying to you that Martin Luther King Jr. believed: If physical death was the price he had to pay to rid America of injustice, nothing could be more redemptive.

Mays continued to write and speak about Martin Luther King Jr., and his accomplishments long after his assassination. On one occasion, Mays stated: "The man had great ability. He was brilliant. He was articulate. He was honest. He was sincere. And he dealt with the issues of life; the problems of racial economic justice; war and peace and the problems of the poor. King spoke to the common people who need a spokesman because they cannot speak for themselves."[34]

Again, in 1975 assessing King's significance as a leader, Mays gave the following four reasons for King's greatness:

1. He had the ability to articulate convincingly the cause he espoused. He had a gift of speech that few men have. . . .

2. He was a leader in the true sense of the word. A real leader is one who leads and the people follow. He was in front in the Marches in Montgomery, Birmingham, Selma and Chicago. This makes King stand out among leaders.

3. He was committed in the doctrine of nonviolence. He did not merely preach nonviolence but he lived it and he walked it.

4. All this shows that King had unusual courage. I can conceive of one leading the masses but lacking the courage to attack our "sacred cow," the Viet Nam War from the prestigious pulpit of Riverside Church in New York.[35]

---

[34]*Pittsburgh Courier*, 27 April 1968.

[35]Benjamin E. Mays, "Martin Luther King Jr.," a sermon delivered in Duke University Chapel, 11 January 1976.

Speaking in 1976, Mays presented a rather thorough analysis of his evaluation of the contributions of Martin Luther King Jr., and their relationship. He noted:

> Martin Luther King Jr., was a powerful man and I was, and still am, so inspired by his integrity, his courage, and his commitment that I can never be completely objective about him. I was wholeheartedly in accord with most things he did. Even when I had reservations about a course of action I hesitated to criticize him, both because I thought his judgment might well be better than mine, and because I could never doubt the sincerity of purpose. It angered me to hear him accused of not being sincere, or of things for the plaudits of the crowd . . . In conversations, on public platforms, in my weekly articles in the *Pittsburgh Courier*, I found myself in the happy position of defending his . . . stand on many issues.[36]

In writing about King in 1978 he espoused the position that Martin Luther King Jr., is a martyr because he literally turned American around in its thinking about the black man in American life. In celebrating King's forty-ninth birthday, he took the time to tell the nation that we must fulfill the commitments that we made to God in founding the Republic.[37]

In 1980 in observance of King's fifty-first birthday, Mays indicated that he had participated in all of the birthday celebrations since his assassination at the age of 39. He also acknowledged that he had written and spoken about King more than any other individual. He considered the fifty-first observance of his birth to be one of the best celebrations. About this celebration he stated:

> Nobody knows why Rosa Parks chose not to get up and give her seat to a white man. Maybe she was too tired to get up. . . . She just sat. And she was arrested. Thank God for Rosa Parks. She made it possible for Martin Luther King Jr. to prove in action his belief in

---

[36]*Pittsburgh Courier*, 11 January 1975.
[37]*Pittsburgh Courier*, 4 February 1978.

nonviolence, as he had learned it from his teachers at Boston University, writings of Reinhold Niebuhr, Mahatma Gandhi, Jawaharlal Nehru, Jesus, Tolstoy and others. He tried it out, of all places in Montgomery, the capital of the Confederacy, and Birmingham, one of the evil cities at that time, the homeplace of Eugene "Bull" Conner and Selma.[38]

Outside of the close-knit King family, Mays exerted the greatest influence on Martin's spiritual and intellectual development. Martin Luther King Sr., once remarked "that Mays had as much to do with Martin's upbringing as the family." The family valued his counsel and held Mays, the great educator, in high esteem. The relationship between Benjamin E. Mays and Martin L. King Jr., developed from mentor-student into a prodigious friendship that lasted throughout both their lives and the model they established still endures as an example for the mentor-student relationship with implications for institutions of higher learning, churches, civic, and other organizational structures in the 1990s and beyond.

Mays himself expressed high regard for the teacher in the one-room Brick House School in rural Epworth, South Carolina where his formal education began. He further expressed admiration for his teachers at South Carolina State College, Virginia Union University, Bates College, and the University of Chicago. He considered his former teachers his dear friends because they helped to challenge, cultivate and motivate him and open his mind. Mays was, above all, a great teacher who demonstrated clearly by example the important influence a teacher can exert in helping to shape youthful minds. Mays possessed a uniqueness of character, wisdom, intellect, vision, and oratorical style that no one could ever forget. Once one heard him speak, one craved the opportunity to hear him again, and some of the words of wisdom he spoke remained with his audiences for many years.

During his tenure as president of Morehouse College, Mays knew what his students needed to hear. He told them "that no one is a slave until he accepts that condition in his mind and soul." "Even when one rides in the back of the bus, his mind should be up front," he often advised. Mays, like

---

[38]*Pittsburgh Courier*, 2 February 1980.

most African Americans of his day, had been victimized by racial indignities and injustices. He understood the social forces affecting youth. And he used his chapel talks to counsel self esteem, racial pride, social responsibility and the pursuit of academic excellence. Young King absorbed what President Mays advised, and they cultivated a unique mentor-student relationship.

Benjamin E. Mays, circa 1965

(L-R) Kendall Weisiger, Chairman of the Morehouse College Board of Trustees, Mordecai Wyatt Johnson, president of Howard University, and Benjamin E. Mays, at the Morehouse commencement exercises, 1950.

One of the many times Mays and his wife, Sadie Gray Mays, hosted Morehouse students for dinner at the President's Residence on campus, circa 1965.

In Archer Hall on the Morehouse campus in January 1965, after Martin Luther King Jr. won the Nobel Peace Prize. Twenty-seven hundred persons packed the school gymnasium to honor King.

1957 post-Commencement dinner for honorary degree recipients in Robert Hall on the Morehouse campus. King is the main speaker for the occasion. Coretta Scott King is seated to her husband's left, with Mays to her left.

Mays greets an unidentified graduate and his mother at a lawn party after commencement exercises in 1951.

King speaking at a 1966 convocation in Archer Hall. Mays is seated second from the left.

State funeral of Pope John XXIII, 16 June 1963. Mays is pictured
with Vice President Lyndon B. Johnson.

Mays at the 1969 memorial service honoring Martin Luther King
Jr. at Ebenezer Baptist Church in Atlanta.

Mays pictured with Joseph H. Jackson, president of the National
Baptist Convention, USA, Inc., August 1963.

Mays and his wife Sadie in 1966.

Mays addressing a Founder's Day Banquet at Morehouse, c. 1965.
Albert Manley, president of Spelman College is seated to Mays's
right.

Mays at the author's installation as the first Dean
of the Martin Luther King Jr. International
Chapel, 7 October 1979. Mays delivered the
invocation at the ceremony.

(L-R) The author, Theodore J. Jemison (president of the National Baptist Convention USA, Inc.), Mays's successor Hugh M. Gloster, Mays, and Thomas Kilgore Jr. at Jemison Day at Morehouse, 18 November 1982.

Mays with the King Chapel assistants (preseminarians) after delivering his final sermon to the college, entitled "You Shall Reap What You Sow." (L-R, beginning with the third from the left: Mays, Hugh M. Gloster, and the author.)

9

MAYS'S EDUCATIONAL PHILOSOPHY

Barbara Sue K. Lewinson

The educational philosophy of Benjamin Mays has a religious base that began early in his youth. It is from a particular conception of what it is to be a Christian that his thinking evolves. In this chapter the religious basis of his educational philosophy will be described first since it is from this base that his other ideas evolve.

THE RELIGIOUS BASIS OF MAYS'S CONVICTIONS

One of the most fundamental bases for Benjamin Mays's educational thinking is his religious convictions. During Mays's childhood religion was, for the majority of Negroes, a major focus in their lives. The church provided not only religious instruction but was the center of Negro social life. It was a social center for Mays and the Christian religion was the most fundamental influence on his life and educational thinking.

Mays held that to believe in man from the Christian point of view one must accept the view, both scientific and biblical, that humanity began in unity rather than in multiplicity. Man's status is to be found "because he is a kin of God," not in race or geography or economics. Mays noted further:

> If the statements above are true, it must also be true, as the Christian faith affirms, that the life of each individual is of intrinsic worth and that the life of each person is sacred. This conviction must cover the entire human family. It must include members of every race and nation, the high and the low, the rich and poor, the learned and the untutored. If this is what one believes intellectually

about man, such a belief must be completed in his behavior three hundred and sixty-five days out of the year.[1]

What does Mays think of an atheist's point of view? Can an atheist accomplish the same types of things in education as one who accepts the tenets of the Judeo-Christian religion? The basis of his reply would be that it depends on the actions of the person. What mattered for Mays was ethics rather than theology:

> The man who denies the existence of God but spends much time fighting for justice for the poor has a lot of God in him. I knew a man in my childhood who was a great shouter: from the way he behaved, he had good religion and he talked about God. But he was quite a thief. . . . God was dead in that man's life. . . . If God does not make men love more, hate less and do justice toward men, he is not there. God is truly dead. . . . Bob Ingersoll was called an agnostic, infidel, and an atheist. But when he found Fred Douglass out in the cold in a Chicago park, took him home and gave him a bed, warmth, and food, he showed that God was alive in him.[2]

Using the belief of the unity of man and the worth of each individual Mays fought to end segregation and to raise African Americans to higher intellectual levels. One belief that stems from his religious convictions is that one can become better by raising oneself above his environment.

> The Christian cannot excuse himself by saying, "I cannot go against tradition; I cannot buck the mores; I cannot jeopardize my political, social, or economic future." The true Christian is a citizen of two worlds. Not only must he answer to the mores, but he must give an account to God. And with God's help he can be loyal to the highest and to the best he knows.[3]

---

[1] Mays, "When Do I Believe in Man," *International Journal of Religious Education* 21 (September 1944), 3.

[2] Mays, "Is God Dead?", *Pittsburgh Courier*, 1 April 1967, 13.

[3] Mays, "The Obligations of the Individual Christian," *The Christian Way in Race Relations*, ed., by William Stuart Nelson, (New York: Harper, 1943), 225.

Thus, one cannot indefinitely act at variance with one's beliefs. Ultimately, action and belief must coincide in the individual who feels he is ultimately responsible not to human beings but to God. Mays believed that if Christianity floundered on the issue of race it would never survive as a universal religion. Christianity, not the Negro, is at stake. Democracy, he argued, was also at stake. If educational opportunities were limited to only one race, then American democracy is conditional, rather than universal. Mays, therefore, sought an America where Democracy and Christianity do not break down in the face of racial differences. He wrote that the fight was not only for African Americans alone, but more importantly a fight to protect Christianity and Democracy: "Looking back on our century historians will point out that one of the greatest contributions the Negro made to America was his patient but unrelenting demand that America make good on its dreams of 'justice to all.'"[4]

Within the framework of Christianity as an all-encompassing basis for the activities of life, Mays sees religion as a working force and the church as an institution that should lead rather than follow in developing the rights of African Americans. Mays did not believe that religion should be totally other-worldly-oriented. At the same time, the sole function of the church is not only to change the social order. He saw the function of the church changing by desire and necessity. Yet, the core should remain the concern for and belief in God. This relation between function and belief is brought forth when he discusses the religious needs of current college students.

While here agreeing with much that black students criticize in the black church, among them poor ministers, a lack of relevance, and the like, Mays remained positive in his approach to the church, saying that it is one of the only institutions where the African American's word is not challenged by whites. Since emancipation, the church has provided one of the only places where the black man was told he was as good as any other human being. Following emancipation the church came to the rescue of the Negro educationally and religiously. The African-American heritage, said Mays, is therefore very much a religious one. It is through faith coupled with intelligence that African Americans will find security in the midst of

---

[4]Mays, "Race in America: The Negro Prospective," *The Search for America*, ed., by Huston Smith, (Englewood, NJ: Prentice-Hall, 1959), 72.

insecurity. A belief in God and the justice of God will enable students to fight other injustices. Mays thought that the more clearly one understands religion the more likely he will be to have faith. Part of the students' lack of faith, according to Mays, is due to lack of knowledge about God. He noted that "unless liberal prophetic religion moves more progressively to the left in the effort to achieve complete citizenship rights for the Negro, he will become more irreligious and he will become more militant and communistic, in his efforts to attain full manhood in American life."[5]

Again and again, as Mays's desire for educational development evolved, one sees the religious tie. A good Christian cannot in conscience accept segregated schooling. A racially unified society is the only kind that is in accordance with Christianity and everything that delays development of such a society is a sin not only against humankind, but against God. He has berated the churches, for example, for not taking the lead after the Supreme Court decision in 1954. He has criticized the church for its timidity in civil rights, but this does not alter his beliefs or his hope for the future of the church. He argued that human beings cannot live by knowledge or intellect alone. To assume otherwise, he maintained, was one of the chief sins of our time. Intellect and knowledge do not insure goodness. Two possible ways to insure goodness are through education both formal and informal, and through religion. He acts on the belief that one will complement and develop the other.

THE THREEFOLD PURPOSE OF EDUCATION

As Mays's religious and educational ideas matured he developed what he considered to be the threefold purpose of education. From this threefold purpose of education stems all his educational ideas. Education is designed (1) to train the mind to think clearly, logically and constructively; (2) to train the heart to understand and sympathize with the aspirations, the sufferings and injustices of humankind; and (3) to strengthen the will to act in the interest of the common good. To summarize and state the purpose in Christian perspective, Mays argued that education was designed to glorify

---

[5]*The Negro's God*, 244.

God and serve humankind.[6] Education without moral commitment means the purpose of education has not been accomplished. Education does not insure goodness. Education is an indispensable weapon if the mind is to be developed, the welfare of the people advanced, and the nation to survive. When poverty is abolished, trained minds will abolish it. However, for education to do what it should, there must be a commitment to God in the sense that one uses one's education for purposes other than to just fulfill one's own desires and needs. More education will not weaken but strengthen an individual's belief in God. Mays's statement about the plan of science in human affairs points out education's dual purpose. According to Mays, nothing can stop the development of science, but also nothing can eradicate the need of vital religion in human life:

> The social sciences have had their influence upon man's religion. Medical science has made man less dependent upon prayer for extending the life span, and psychology and psychiatry have done a good bit to improve man's behavior. These insights have been good for the health of religion, but they have no negative effect upon the moral and ethical truths of the Christian faith. . . . Just as man cannot live well without science, so he cannot live fully without religion. Every man who accomplishes anything significant in life must live by faith, dreams, and ideals.[7]

Mays has learned from science that man has an infinite mind and although much will be discovered he feels the unexplainable is inexhaustible. "Science can't ever explain everything."[8] However, to say that there are certain things which are not explainable is not saying that God is the only explanation. There may be other explanations of which society is not yet aware. Therefore, the reasons behind things unexplained by science at the

---

[6]Mays, "Desegregate and Integrate to What End?" *Livingston Founder's Day Address*, (February, 1964), 5.

[7]Mays, "The Challenge to Religion as it Ponders Science," in *Religion Ponders Science*, ed., by Edwin P. Booth, (New York: Appleton Century, 1964), 142-145.

[8]Author's personal conversation with Mays, 30 May 1972.

present time are intellectually open. For example to Mays, the theory of evolution has not proved or disproved the existence of a God. His statement in *Why I Believe There Is A God*, exemplifies his total concept of life, and how he ties other areas to religion:

> Man is a discoverer and not a creator. Man can be creative but not the creator. God is the creator. The scientist can do his work because the universe is dependable. The laws of evolution are discovered by man. They were put there by God. The formula for water was discovered by man and it gives water throughout the universe. The universality belong to God. If the universe were not orderly, the scientist could not function. The scientist did not make the universe orderly. The order came from God.[9]

Specifically speaking, education should be sought for its own sake. This means that it should be sought for the enrichment of life, for the sheer enjoyment of knowing how to distinguish between truth and error, between good and evil, and between that which is first rate and that which is second rate. It is good also for that which follows from it. The trained mind develops leadership, enabling a leader to deal with others from a position of strength rather than weakness. Respect comes for oneself and from others.

Education is not for the purpose of lifting one above one's fellows but to enable one to help one's fellows. One's destiny cannot be fulfilled unless one uses his knowledge not only to benefit himself but to benefit others. This is a prime obligation since a brilliant mind is not independent, but is a gift of God.

THE ROLE OF SCHOOLS IN DESEGREGATION

The purpose of education cannot be achieved in a segregated school system because it denies the basic Judeo-Christian idea of the worth of each person. Segregation branded as inferior the person who is being segregated. Mays thus criticized the schools as well as the churches for the role they

---

[9]Mays, "Why I Believe There Is A God," in *Why I Believe There Is A God*, introduction by Howard Thurman, (Chicago: Johnson Publishing Company, Inc., 1965), 7.

have played since the 1954 Supreme Court decision.

> It is clear that all too many schools provide no leadership to insure
> peaceful desegregation, either educationally or in the larger society.
> The proper role of the schools up to now, should have been what it
> was not—the provision of a more positive and constructive
> leadership to insure peaceful change and acceptance of change."[10]

The schools have been in the background instead of the foreground in
the work of desegregation. Schools were desegregated as a result of court
orders, Mays complained, rather than as a result of a moral or ethical
commitment.

> I think the great need is an education with a social conscience, a social
> concern; Science has made the world a neighborhood. It is left for all
> of us—leaders in education and religion—to make it a brotherhood.
> There is no guarantee that education alone can do this job. It may be
> that religion and education cannot do it. But it must be done if
> mankind is to survive.[11]

He also calls for schools to provide a platform for the free airing of ideas and
should be a place to debate attitudes formed in a responsible academic
setting, attitudes which will be fed back into the locales from which students
come.

THE ROLE OF BLACKS IN ACHIEVING
DESIRABLE EDUCATIONAL LEVELS

To Mays, it is not only blacks, but also whites who are responsible for
raising the educational level of black children and fulfilling the purpose of
education. Whites have the responsibility, in dealing with black children
from the lowest levels, to develop in the children a positive perception.
Whites must believe that children can and will learn, and deal with them in

---

[10]Mays, "The Role of the Schools in a Social Revolution," *Teachers College Record* 65,
(May 1964), 685.
[11]Mays, "My Views," *Pittsburgh Courier*, 7 May 1966, 13.

this manner. They must deal with children as individuals coming to school with special abilities, talents and unique conceptions. Whites need to develop a commitment to every child reaching a desirable education level. Mays believed there also was necessary a commitment, largely lacking in the past, to the idea of full-fledged citizenship.

Still, if African Americans are to achieve what they are capable of achieving as human beings, no longer circumscribed by color, they must play the major role. Their role is important at all ages and in all situations. For example, Mays believed that parents must:

> assume more responsibility for the education of their children. The future cannot be left to chance, and certain habits and ideas must be instilled in the child while it is very, very young. . . . New opportunities, hitherto unknown, are opening to Negroes, the message must be gotten through to Negro parents everywhere that the future is brighter for the Negro child than at any time since emancipation. At this point Negro parents must do their job or their children will suffer the consequences.[12]

> Educators and parents must do something about the small number of Negroes in colleges and universities. Poverty accounts for the small collegiate enrollment, home background explains a part of it, and there is a lack of motivation in the Negro environment and in so many of the Negro homes. Now that segregation is being abolished, the Negro youth must be made to understand that new doors are opening everywhere and more doors will open in proportion as he becomes skilled in the arts and sciences and in proportion as he applies himself and his ability to compete in every area of American life. Before too long, the competent Negro will never be denied a place in industry and it is getting that way now. And we must see to it that every able Negro mind gets a change to be trained and go to college and university.

---

[12]Mays, "My View: The Home Is The Foundation," *Pittsburgh Courier*, 1 May 1965, 13.

We must look for the exceptional student. If the parents are unable to assist him to go to college and university, we must find a way. This must be the concern of every Negro educator and it must be the concern of every church. We cannot afford to neglect any boy or girl with real ability.[13]

He considers the white and black leaders' role as important, yet it is not only the leaders but all African Americans to whom he said:

Deprived of the best schools, reared in homes economically below standard, denied the opportunity to read good books in elementary and high schools, robbed of the opportunity to qualify for the best jobs, you are, almost overnight challenged to meet the toughest competition in the modern world.[14]

And the role of Blacks is important for there is no substitute for academic excellence. Thus, Mays argued:

Whether we like it or not, we must read more and socialize less, study more and frolic less, do more research and play less, write books and articles and become recognized in our respective fields. It is better by far to be known by the articles we write than by the bridge we play; by the books we publish than by the house we live in. It is better to have our students rave about our great teaching than about our beautiful cars. It is better to have our colleagues envious of our scholarship and research than of our houses and land.[15]

If blacks are to meet the increased opportunities that may be available to them in the last part of the century, they must be willing and able to meet the competition of blacks and whites at the highest levels. They must be willing to accept the responsibility that goes with it. Mays puts much of the responsibility for what will happen to African Americans and to the

---

[13]Mays, "Too Few in College and University," *Pittsburgh Courier*, 4 April 1959, 13.

[14]Mays, "Desegregate and Integrate to What End?, *Livingston College Founder's Day Address*, February 1964, 5.

[15]Ibid., 5.

traditionally black college upon blacks themselves. First the student. The student cannot excuse himself by saying he has been discriminated against. He has to work twice as hard to overcome his disabilities because it is only through true and real academic achievement at the highest levels in competition with all people, black and white, that he will have a real claim on the better positions that will be given to him because he is the best. He will be able to force more than token integration and the statement, "no qualified Negro could be found for the job," will not be true. He sees the professional world opening up in much bigger ways to black students, but he emphasizes again and again the fact that with greater opportunity will come greater competition. And blacks must be ready for the opportunities or they will be meaningless for them.[16]

Although there must be even greater striving for academic excellence in the future, Mays did feel that blacks have achieved much in spite of great odds and it is through a school such as Howard University that the impetus for desegregation in schools came about:

> It is conceivable that if there had been no Howard University that we would not have had the May 17, 1954, decision of the United States Supreme Court, declaring segregation in the public schools unconstitutional. That decision was and is one of the most historic documents in the annals of American law. It is most significant that the decision was argued and won by a Howard University Law School graduate, Thurgood Marshall.[17]

However, from children through black leaders, intellectual competence must be much further developed and on a broader scale. The leadership should not be afraid or most concerned with being well thought of by white friends and white people in general. They should be most concerned with developing a diversified leadership and with becoming competent and unselfish in every area of life. Leaders should strive to become leaders of people, not just leaders of Negroes.

Mays shows a genuine and sincere compassion for all humankind and

---

[16]Mays, "What's Ahead for Negro Schools," *Together* 6 (June 1962), 29.

[17]Mays, "Higher Education and the American Negro, *"What Black Educators are Saying,* ed., by Nathan Wright, (New York: Hawthorn Books, Inc., 1970), 107.

thus, becomes a humanist. In relation to education,

> White teachers should serve in black colleges, just as black scholars
> should be able to serve in white colleges. The emphasis on blackness
> must not mean that Negroes should not qualify to fill high positions in
> education and in all other areas of American life, whether integrated or
> desegregated.[18]

To achieve leadership among all men, not just blacks, one needs academic
excellence and skills that the community needs.

Is there a real solution from a humanistic point of view? Mays did not
know, but stated:

> It seems to me, however, that we have no choice but to continue
> our efforts to make this country a decent place for all Americans.
> As Henry van Dyke says, in *The Other Wise Man*, "It is better to
> follow even the shadow of the best than to remain content with the
> worst." I have the faith to believe that whites and blacks can
> improve their relationship to the extent that they can live together
> in peace, each respecting the other. Whether we like it or not, we
> can neither elude nor escape each other.[19]

Pride and dignity must be developed and upheld. It is only through
individual striving for the very best, Mays felt, that this would happen.
Satisfaction with mediocrity will not bring about development of the tools
within oneself to work for a world integrated in all areas. Mays wrote:

> When competence is needed in science, whether in Government,
> industry or education, no allowance will be made for the inferior
> schools Negroes have had to attend for decades upon decades. The
> only comment you will hear: "Negroes are not qualified. They failed
> the test." When a man of experience is needed to fill a certain post,
> no allowance will be made for the fact that the Negro has never

---

[18]*Born to Rebel*, 318.
[19]"Higher Education and the American Negro," 111.

been given a chance to get the kind of experience needed for the job. He will be passed by and the only comment—"No Negro could be found with the proper qualifications."[20]

Thus, black children must not only go to school but strive twice as hard to overcome their deficiencies. Black private universities play a major role in helping black children to do this.

In conjunction with this idea of the role of Blacks in achieving higher educational levels, is the idea of the expansion of the role of black professors. Not only must there be many more black students in the previously all-white universities, but there must be more black professors as well. They show two things to the black student., They show him that the university is really trying to integrate at all levels; and they act as models. There is also the possibility that they can deal with some of the special circumstances from which black students might come. Lastly, they can act as a motivating force.

The Negro teacher from elementary school through the university, has a new weapon of motivation. He can give the Negro student a new incentive such as he has never had before. These new developments must be impressed upon the minds of Negro youth. I am convinced that a lack of incentive to strive for excellence on the part of so many Negro youths can be traced in part to a feeling that even if he strove for excellence it would end in futility. The future for the competent Negro is not wholly rosy, but it is much rosier than it has been.[21]

He wrote of the various Black Studies Programs that were developing and in which a large proportion of the professors are black. Their value is in helping black students achieve a sense of pride in his background and heritage. If such programs become exclusionary—that is, "for African Americans only—they do not fulfill their total purpose. Part of this purpose is to make all, including whites, aware of the rich diverse heritage that African Americans bring to this country.

---

[20]Mays, "Desegregate and Integrate to What End?", *Livingston College Founder';s Day Address*, February 1964, 5.

[21]Mays, "My View, Reward for Excellence," *Pittsburgh Courier*, 17 May 1959, 13.

Mays, in stressing the role of Blacks in raising their own academic level always considered academics a top priority in his work. A student cannot expect to compete successfully if after going to an inferior high school he then goes to an inferior college. As Dean of the Howard University School of Religion he stressed academic excellence. When he arrived, he found twenty-eight students, fourteen with college degrees, and fourteen who were combining two years of college and two years of theological work. When he left not only had he enlarged the enrollment, but improved the academic level of its students, increased drastically the size of the library, and succeeded in getting the seminary accredited. It was only the second black seminary to qualify for membership in the American Theological Association.

In his final commencement address at Morehouse, he touched on what had always been his primary goal for the College:

Perhaps the greatest success the College has achieved in twenty-seven years is the high academic quality of teachers who comprise the faculty. This was our choice despite pressures from many sources to direct our meager funds to other useful and interesting but non-academic pursuits. Not to provide the students with the ablest faculty available is criminal and irresponsible. . . . The number of doctorates on the faculty is seventeen times greater than it was in the year 1940-1941. Excepting one or two, the rest hold master's degrees; and many have studies from one to four years beyond. Three hold the B.D. Degree. . . . In academic training, this places Morehouse above all predominantly undergraduate Negro colleges. . . . It has taken twenty-seven years of constant planning to build and maintain a faculty of this strength. . . .

Morehouse is small in numbers. However, the quality of the work done speaks for itself. (e.g., Morehouse with a Ford Foundation Grant recruited bright young scholars who had not finished high school. Among those recruited was Martin Luther King Jr., class of 1948.) By 1967 more than three hundred Morehouse men had earned M.D.s and D.D.S.s (forty of these achieved distinctions as specialists—diplomats in medicine.) A high percentage of Negro physicians are graduates of Morehouse. Combining the degrees in medicine and the Ph.D.s in education, one out of every nine

Morehouse graduates has earned an academic or professional doctorate.[22]

THE ROLE OF BLACK UNIVERSITIES

In the interim between what Mays called desegregation and integration the role of blacks in universities such as Howard is vital. The role of black universities is consistent with Mays's basic educational premises. He has been connected with what were basically black colleges for most of his professional life, and his concepts concerning their past, present, and future role merely broaden the base of action. As he conceived it, the role would not disappear with desegregation, but would be greatly expanded.

Mays saw the role of historically black colleges as having been exceedingly important since they have provided virtually the only opportunity for a black child to attain a college education. Accepting many students who would not have been admitted into white universities, they have raised their academic level to the point that they were able to pursue graduate work at the finest schools. Many of the black colleges have been criticized for the level of the academic work they attain. In some black colleges, there were departments which offered high school work and within the four year academic program some of them offered what is virtually high school level work in their first year. This practice has enabled black students to make up academic deficiencies. In some ways, this practice is the equivalent of the compensatory programs which the previously all-white universities are now attempting.

To say that black colleges are no longer needed is to accept two false assumptions, according to Mays. First, it assumes that black students will desert black colleges as white colleges open up to them, and further, it assumes white students will not attend formerly all-Negro schools. African-American colleges have become integrated faster than have formerly all-white colleges and universities. Mays observed:

This development points the way to a unique opportunity for the Negro schools: they can become the country's first truly interracial,

---

[22]Commencement, Morehouse College, June, 1967.

intercultural, and international centers of education. . . . Negro colleges have no prejudices to overcome, or fears to subdue. They have been "segregated"—but not "segregating"—institutions. Unhindered by the traditional customs of the past, they are free to become ongoing experiments in democratic education. Confronted as we are with classroom and teacher shortages, plus predictions that college enrollments will double in 10 years, it would be folly not to utilize the educational facilities and trained faculties of the Negro schools. They meet the special needs resulting from three centuries of disability and they are demonstrating their ability to serve all society.[23]

Mays believed that the formerly all-black schools cannot be justified just because they fill a special need. They must be willing to strive for academic excellence while at the same time remaining aware of the disabilities peculiar to deprived students. They must prepare their graduates to compete successfully in every area of life at the same time that they are developing a larger role. These black colleges are changing and, according to Mays, will very definitely survive but in a different form. The form of these schools will change as will the former primarily white university.

I believe in Negro colleges. For twenty-seven years I was president of one where the student body was almost one hundred percent black and where the faculty and board of trustees were racially mixed. But I do not believe in a Negro college or university if this means that all students, all faculty and staff members, the student body, and all financial support must be black. Even if the idea were a practical one, I could not embrace it, for setting people apart fosters segregation which Negroes have fought against for a century. I do not believe that exclusively Negro colleges are necessary to engender race pride in Negro students, or that the salvation of Negro colleges lies in driving out white trustees, white faculty, and white students.

---

[23]Mays, "What's Ahead for Negro Schools," *Together*, 6 (June 1962), 32-33.

Nor do I believe that the black man's educational salvation lies in weakening black colleges by draining black scholars and students away from them to attend white colleges—colleges which for the most part are not free of racism. Colleges and universities that are deserving should be supported by state and philanthropic funds; racial identification should not determine the amount of support they receive. If race is a determining factor, this means there is racism in high places; and racism belongs nowhere in American education. White teachers should serve in black colleges, just as black scholars should be able to serve in white colleges. The emphasis on blackness must not mean that Blacks should not qualify to fill high positions in education and in all other areas of American life, whether integrated or desegregated.[24]

Throughout his career Mays dealt primarily with traditionally oriented private colleges. The black private colleges were established by various religious groups and although many are now private, they are still church-related. Mays states that a black church-related private college

will be freer to emphasize quality in education. Whereas a tax-supported Black college must accept any graduate of any accredited high school, the private and church-related college will be free to select its student from among the high school seniors best qualified to do college work. . . . The significance therefore of the Black private and church related colleges lie in their freedom to experiment, to explore, to inquire unrestricted, to develop a leadership of spiritual power, to overcome the dangers that permeate a secular society and to become centers of interracial, intercultural, interfaith and international living.[25]

As Mays put it, as the white world has needed a Harvard or Yale, so has the

---

[24]*Born to Rebel*, 317-318.
[25]Mays, "The Significance of the Negro Private and Church Related College," *The Journal of Negro Education* (Washington, D.C.: 1960), 248-251.

black world needed a Morehouse or a Howard. As Mays saw it, the role of the black private college would not disappear, but rather expand with the advent of desegregation.

FUTURE OF EDUCATION FOR BLACKS

Mays's views of the development of education for blacks in the future were positive. At the elementary level he foresaw the eventual end of segregation not only as a result of the schools' actions, but as a result of legal action followed eventually by other social changes, such as changes in the housing pattern. For Mays education plays a great role in developing the full potential of the black man. He did not see that role as a circumscribed and limited one. Nor does he see the type of education which should be offered to the black student as one which should be limited in any way intellectually or professionally. The role of education will be expanded. But, in addition to numbers, Mays is most concerned that high quality at the college level be maintained where it exists and created where it does not.

The improvement of the academic conditions, for Mays, always superseded every other consideration. His central vocation was to achieve for African Americans the highest academic achievement equal to the best education available for whites in order that blacks might compete at the highest levels. He always believed that this sort of achievement is possible within the traditional college atmosphere.

10

"OF ONE BLOOD": MAYS AND THE THEOLOGY OF RACE RELATIONS

Mark Chapman

No issue placed a greater strain on the faith of African-American Christians than the problem of racial segregation and the support it received from white churches. How could white Christians bar black people from their churches and yet claim to read the same Bible and worship the same Jesus as African-American Christians? For some blacks, the contradiction between basic Christian faith claims and the racist practices of white churches was too powerful to overcome. Consequently, these persons renounced Christianity as an impotent religion incapable of solving the nation's race problem. Indeed, Elijah Muhammad's denunciation of Christianity as "the white man's religion" came to characterize the mood of a new generation influenced more by the spirit of Black Power than the desire for interracial harmony.

Pre-Black Power religious intellectuals in the 1930s and 1940s were also painfully aware of the wide gulf between the gospel of Jesus and white American Christianity. When they traveled overseas and encountered Muslims and Hindus, they were frequently put in the awkward position of having to explain their allegiance to a religion that discriminated against them. Benjamin Mays was confronted by Muslims in Egypt who told him that Islam, unlike Christianity, had no racial barriers, while Hindus in India accused Howard Thurman of being a "tool of the Europeans."[1] Indeed, the sharp criticism Thurman received from one Hindu educator poignantly

---

[1] See *Born To Rebel*, 155; and Howard Thurman, *With Head and Heart* (New York: Harcourt Brace Jovanovich, 1979), 124. Thurman was reluctant to go to India in 1936 for fear that he would looked upon as an apologist for Western Christianity. He was right. See p. 125 where he writes, "Everywhere we went, we were asked, 'Why are you here, if you are not tools of the Europeans, the white people?'... I felt the heat in the question 'If Christianity is not powerless, why is it not changing life in your country and the rest of the world? If it is powerless, why are you here representing it to us?'"

captures the dilemma of Negro Christian leaders who visited parts of Africa and Asia: "I think that an intelligent young Negro such as yourself, here in our country on behalf of a Christian enterprise, is a traitor to all darker peoples of the earth. How can you account for yourself being in this unfortunate and humiliating position?"[2]

Despite such interrogation, Negro Christian thinkers before and after World War II insisted that the genuine application of Christian principles to the problem of race offered the most promising solution to America's greatest moral dilemma.[3] As African Americans during this period intensified their struggle for civil rights, religious scholars sharpened their critique of white Christianity and developed a theology of race relations based on the community's desire for freedom. The major architect of the new theology of race relations was Benjamin E. Mays, the renowned scholar, ecumenical church leader, and educator.

Before the rise of Martin Luther King Jr. to international prominence in the wake of the 1955 Montgomery bus boycott, Benjamin Mays was America's most assertive public spokesman for the theology of race relations. His active participation in ecumenical conferences throughout the world made him one of the most visible Negro churchmen of his time. No pre-Black Power religious thinker in the 1940s and 1950s had a greater impact on discussions of Christianity and race than Benjamin E. Mays. Throughout his long and distinguished career, Mays summoned the national and international Christian community to implement the demands of the gospel by eradicating racism in its own fellowship and leading the fight against it in the world at large.[4]

The theology and educational philosophy of Benjamin Mays challenged generations of young people to join the struggle for racial and social justice

---

[2]Thurman, *With Head and Heart*, 114.

[3]Negro Christian intellectuals met at the Institute of Religion at the Howard University School of Religion from 1944 to 1948 to discuss "what role should the Christian life play in the solution of the race problem in America." Several important essays presented at the Institute (including ones written by Benjamin Mays and George Kelsey) were published under the title, *The Christian Way In Race Relations* edited by William Stuart Nelson (New York: Harper and Brothers, 1948).

[4]For a thorough resume and complete listing of publications, degrees, and honors received by Mays, see "Biographical Sketch," in *Journal of Religious Thought* 32(Spring-Summer, 1975), 132-137.

The theology and educational philosophy of Benjamin Mays challenged · generations of young people to join the struggle for racial and social justice in America. Mays was an instructor at Morehouse College during Howard Thurman's student days in the early 1920s, and was president when Martin Luther King Jr. matriculated there in the mid 1940s. As Lerone Bennett has shown, he had a profound impact on Thurman, King, and countless other students who went on to make significant contributions to the civil rights movement. Indeed, the observation of historian Orville Vernon Burton is worth emphasizing: "King's fame overshadows Mays's, but I believe there could not have been a Martin Luther King Jr. if there had been no Benjamin Elijah Mays. From their days together at Morehouse, through the years of the civil rights struggle, and until King's death, the pair shared the same philosophy and goals."[5]

Keith D. Miller makes a similar point in his recent study of King's language and its sources. Miller noted that, "What Mays had been to liberal black (and to a lesser degree white) religious and academic circles King—with the benefit of a huge social movement and the medium of television—would be to America."[6] Therefore, because of his far reaching impact, an understanding of Mays's theology is essential for any discussion of twentieth century African-American religious thought. What did he have to say about the Christian gospel and its relationship to American racism and imperialism?

CHRISTIANITY, AMERICA, AND THE WORLD

Mays's life and thought epitomized black people's enduring faith in Christianity and America. Despite the painful awareness that their religion (as interpreted by many whites) and country considered them inferior, Negro Christians continued to believe in the noble principles of Christianity and

---

[5]For an excellent interpretation of Mays's role as an educator whose philosophy molded Martin King, Julian Bond, and other civil rights leaders, see Lerone Bennett, "Benjamin Elijah Mays: The Last of The Great Schoolmasters," in *Ebony* 32(December, 1977), 72-80; See Orville Vernon Burton's Foreword to the 1987 edition of Benjamin Mays's autobiography *Born To Rebel* (Athens: University of Georgia Press, 1987), xli.

[6]Keith D. Miller, *Voice of Deliverance: The Language of Martin Luther King Jr. and Its Sources* (New York: The Free Press, 1992), 44.

democracy. In fact, they maintained that the actual implementation of Christian and democratic principles offered the only viable solution to America's race problem. Accordingly, Benjamin Mays and other integrationist thinkers articulated a theology of race relations that they believed would lead to the redemption of the church and nation they so deeply loved.

The Experiential Roots of Mays's Theology of Race Relations

When Mays graduated from high school in 1916 at the age of twenty-two, he was determined to matriculate at a prestigious New England college. He desperately wanted to prove to himself and the world that blacks could compete on the same intellectual level as whites. Mays was particularly disturbed about the "myth of Negro inferiority," and the manner in which blacks "accepted their denigration." As he saw it, their lackluster response "tended to make each new generation believe that they were indeed inferior." Therefore, in September 1917, after spending his freshman year at Virginia Union University, the budding scholar set out for Bates College in Lewiston, Maine in order to "prove my worth, my ability." It is significant to note that while Mays rejected the myth of Negro inferiority, he wanted to compete academically against Northern whites (whom he considered at the time the measuring rod of intellectual ability), so that he might have "prima facie evidence that Negroes were not inferior."[7]

The three years Mays spent at Bates College had a decisive impact on his thinking. For the first time in his life, he met white people who treated him as a human being. No doubt, this positive experience with Northern whites helped to shape his conviction that there was, in fact, a "Christian way in race relations" capable of producing justice and harmony between blacks and whites. Mays described his encounters with white students and faculty at Bates in this fashion:

We met and mingled as peers, not as "superior" and "inferior." This was a new experience for me. I was getting another view of the white

---

[7]Because of his responsibilities on the farm, Mays never spent more than four months of the academic year in school until he was nineteen years old—when he finally mustered the courage to disobey his father's command to return home at the end of February. See *Born To Rebel*, 38, 50.

man—a radically different view. They were not all my enemies. For the first time, whether on campus or in the town of Lewiston, whether alone or in a group, I felt at home in the universe.[8]

Mays would continue to feel "at home in the universe" throughout the rest of his educational and professional career. Having completed all his course requirements for his Ph.D. at the University of Chicago by the summer of 1934, Mays accepted the deanship of the School of Religion at Howard University in Washington, D.C. Thereafter, his reputation as an educator and churchman spread rapidly throughout the nation and the world. In 1936 Mays was one of thirteen Americans selected to attend the 1937 YMCA World Conference in Mysore, India, where he was also elected to the organization's World Committee.[9] By the end of 1939 he had attended three more ecumenical meetings in England, Stockholm, and Amsterdam. In *Born To Rebel*, Mays described the significant impact these international gatherings had on his thinking:

> These conferences enabled me to learn from experience, from observation, and from wide contact with people across the world that the black-white problem was a major problem . . . and that our Christian people, Negro and white, have their work cut out for them if Christianity is to play the decisive role in solving the problem of race, war, and poverty and thus avoid world catastrophe.[10]

Indeed, these trips abroad while dean at Howard strengthened Mays's resolve to relate the gospel to the pressing social and political realities facing America and the world.

After a successful six year term at Howard University, Mays accepted the presidency of Morehouse College, where he began his teaching career nineteen years earlier. In addition to strengthening the college financially

---

[8]Ibid., 55.

[9]Note, it was on this trip to India that Mays first met and talked with Gandhi. For a detailed account of Mays's first trip overseas, see his article, "The Color Line Around The World," in *Journal of Negro Education* 6(January, 1937), 134-143.

[10]*Born To Rebel*, 167.

and academically, Mays also found time to continue his participation in national and international ecumenical organizations. In 1944, he became the first African-American to be elected vice president of the Federal Council of Churches of Christ in America, which was organized in 1912 (now the National Council of Churches). Four years later, he attended the organizing meeting of the World Council of Churches in Amsterdam, Holland, and was chosen to represent the National Baptist Convention, Inc. on the Council's Central Committee (the official voice of the organization between Assemblies). Between 1948 and the Second World Assembly in 1954, Mays, one of two blacks on the ninety person committee, attended meetings in Switzerland, England, Canada, and India.[11]

In many respects, Mays's participation in the ecumenical movement epitomized the dilemma of Negro Christians in the post World War II years. On the one hand, he experienced moments of spiritual exultation and renewal upon witnessing the embodiment of Christian universalism in the World Council of Churches. Noting the lack of segregation at international meetings, Mays argued that "one would have to be in an Assembly of the World Church to really know what Christian fellowship is." Even more significant was his description of a communion service at the 1948 Amsterdam meeting, where he "noted a Methodist sitting next to a Baptist, an Anglican sitting next to a Presbyterian, a Chinese communing beside a Japanese, an American white man seated with an American Negro, and an African communing with a Dutchman."[12]

But despite feelings of optimism produced by the achievement of integration and ecumenicity at world meetings, Mays knew that the realities of segregation and discrimination awaited him when he returned to the United States—as it did African-American soldiers who experienced social equality in Europe during World War II. Yet another important reality that tempered Mays's idealism was his recognition that even "in world gatherings, as elsewhere, the Negro is likely to be the forgotten man." Mays was referring to his belief that if it were not for the persistence of African-American delegates, the World Council's pronouncements on race would be weak and blacks would be overlooked for positions of influence and

---

[11]See Mays's report of his accomplishments as dean of the School of Religion in *Born To Rebel*, 145-148, 256.
[12]Ibid., 254.

leadership.[13] Mays also knew that church resolutions and pronouncements at international conferences (no matter how strong) would not, in and of themselves, solve the race problem in America. Indeed, the reality of racism at home and abroad kept Mays from an exclusive commitment to theological liberalism.

Having worked and prayed his way through high school, college, and graduate school; received significant appointments in the Federal and World Council of Churches; and succeeded in the academy far beyond many of his white peers, Mays had demonstrated that education, religion, and positive race relations were effective means by which the poorest black child could transcend the limitations of his or her environment.[14] As president of Morehouse College from 1940 to 1967, and a frequent public speaker at church conferences, colleges, and universities across the country, Mays repeated this message to thousands of students, preachers, and educators. In similar fashion, he told the American community at large that its credibility as a world leader depended on it being a nation where all people—regardless of race, sex or creed—could rise above their limitations to achieve their goals and dreams.

America and World Leadership

More than any other African-American religious scholar in the post war years, Mays consistently emphasized the global implications of the American race problem. From his extensive travels, he knew that "the eyes of the world are upon America." Whether in Asia, Africa, or Europe, Mays was constantly asked about the status of race relations in the United States. He used these opportunities to put the racist, un-Christian, and undemocratic practices of America and its churches before the scrutiny of world opinion. Like other pre-Black Power thinkers, Mays reminded the American public that the news of segregation and discrimination was known throughout the world:

---

[13]Ibid., 255.
[14]*Lord The People*, 65.

For good or for ill, we can no longer live in isolation. Whether we like it or not, what happens in one corner of the earth resounds around the world. In attitudes and ideas, we may be thousands of miles apart; but in time and space we are very near. The press, the radio, the airplane, and sheer economic necessity now make isolation impossible.[15]

America could no longer hide. Advances in technology meant that the nation's race problem was now a global issue, discussed in the most remote corners of the earth. Ironically, America had invited this close international scrutiny because it presented itself as the leader of the democratic world. Therefore, Mays reminded the nation that:

Today the eyes of the world are upon America to see how she treats today and will treat tomorrow the minorities within her borders such as Jews, Mexicans, American Indians, Negroes, and Japanese who are loyal American citizens. Our moral leadership in the post-war world will be greatly advanced or retarded on this point.[16]

Like other Negro leaders, Mays argued that America's international influence depended on its treatment of the poor and oppressed in its own backyard. Clearly, if America was to claim moral leadership on the international level, it would first have to practice democracy at the domestic level. Pre-Black Power religious thinkers made this point unmistakably clear as they reminded the nation of its moral obligation to practice the democracy it so eloquently preached.

Yet it was precisely America's wartime propaganda that fueled black people's historic quest for freedom. Having fought in World War I to "make the world safe for democracy," African-American soldiers returned to the states expecting to share in the fruits of democracy; certainly, their disappointment was still fresh in their minds when they fought again in World War II. Convinced that World War II pronouncements "helped India, made the Africans restless, and stimulated Negroes in the United

---

[15]"World Aspects of Race and Culture," in *Missions* 40(February 1949), 83.
[16]"The Eyes of the World Are Upon America," *Missions* 35 (February 1944), 75.

States," Mays described the impact of these experiences on the black freedom struggle:

> Each time, we fought for a way of life for all peoples. . . . As a result of what we claimed we were fighting for, the race crisis has become global in character. We intensified the aspiration for equality of treatment and equality of opportunity on the part of American Negroes and the colored races throughout the world. The race problem can no longer be localized. It is now global.[17]

Just as W. E. B. DuBois prophesied in 1903 that "the problem of the twentieth century is the problem of the color line," Mays predicted in 1946 that the postwar years would be full of global racial tension. Mays stated his position forthrightly: "Either the colored races will obtain more than they have now, or there will be increasing tension in the years ahead."[18]

Having traveled to Africa and Asia as early as 1937, Mays knew firsthand that "the colored races of the earth do not share in world control." But even worse, Mays observed that "they do not have the decisive word even in their own native lands." European imperialism meant that "the 992 million colored peoples in Asia are not free to shape and mold their own lives," and "the 142 million Africans neither own nor control Africa." Mays also noted, "the 13 million Negroes in the United States live only on the periphery of American democracy."[19]

However depressing the plight of colored peoples around the world, Mays argued that there was reason for hope. As he saw it, this hope was to be found in the people's determination to be free, which is why "the pressure from below will increase rather than diminish in the postwar years." He added:

> The colored races of the world will never be less submissive than they are now; they will never want less than they want now; they will never be less vocal in their assertion of their desire for equal

---

[17]"The Colored Races in the Postwar World," in *Missions* 37(February 1946), 77.

[18]W. E. B. DuBois, *The Souls of Black Folks* (Chicago: A.C. McClurg and Co., 1903), 27; Mays, "The Colored Races in the Postwar World," 76.

[19]"The Colored Races . . . , 76.

opportunity than they are today. Increasingly and more vigorously they will oppose exploitation, segregation, and discrimination based on color and race.[20]

But Mays also knew that in their struggle for justice, the oppressed would encounter unyielding white resistance. Predicting that "the way of the colored races in the postwar world is going to be exceedingly difficult," Mays paraphrased the oft-repeated maxim of Frederick Douglass that "power concedes nothing without a demand." Mays put it like this:

. . . those who occupy vantage points are seldom willing to share their privileges with the less privileged. Persons in control usually do all they can to keep persons not in control from rising to their level. They may help them a bit but rarely to the point of equality.[21]

As Mays viewed it, colored peoples around the world shared the same fate; they will experience agony and frustration as the white nations continually "close the doors of opportunity" in their faces. But Mays urged the world's struggling people not to lose heart. His firm belief in Christianity led him to the conviction that "in the final analysis, the forces of evil and reaction cannot win." Like other pre-Black Power religious thinkers, he argued that there was a "moral order in the universe" that leaned in the direction of justice. Consequently, he urged the American churches to muster "the Christian courage to solve the color problem within its own borders" by becoming "Christian in their daily lives, private and public," and demanding that the government treat the oppressed in light of the Christian principles of love, justice and equality. Mays firmly believed that American Christians had all "the tools with which to work" (the teachings of Christ, the Declaration of Independence, and the U.S. Constitution); all they needed now was the *will* to "practice what the church has been teaching for 1900 years."[22]

Ultimately, Mays remained hopeful because he believed that the world climate in the postwar years meant that "the number of people who believe

---

[20]Ibid.
[21]Ibid., 77.
[22]Ibid., 79-80.

in justice and equality for all races will never be fewer than they are today." Therefore, he concluded that the struggle for racial justice around the world must be waged with courage and determination:

> The battle will not be easy but those who believe in Jesus, in God, in justice, and in equality cannot and will not retreat. Upon complete victory in this area, hangs the welfare of all mankind.[23]

All Life Is Interrelated

In addition to calling on America to fulfill its claim to moral world leadership, pre-Black Power religious thinkers waged a theological battle against white racist interpretations of Christianity that undergirded segregation. These racist distortions of the faith were based on the false notion that black humanity is defective, and therefore not worthy of fellowship with whites. As George Kelsey (a Morehouse graduate, professor, and Director of Morehouse School of Religion from 1945 to 1948) noted in his classic text *Racism and the Christian Understanding of Man*, segregation developed as a plan of political action to separate "inferior," "defective" black being (the out-race) from "superior," "god-like" white being (the in-race).[24] In light of this gross distortion of the Christian doctrine of humanity, pre-Black Power theologians articulated a theological anthropology that emphasized "the oneness of humanity," and the "interrelatedness of all life."

Perhaps the most important element that shaped Negro theologians' views on Christianity, America, and the world, was their firm conviction that God is the creator of all human life and thus, all men and women, regardless of race or nationality, are brothers and sisters. Benjamin Mays, George Kelsey, Howard Thurman and others pointed to the Genesis creation story to demonstrate their claim that "the human family began in unity." In a speech delivered at the Eighth Congress of the Baptist World Alliance in Cleveland, Ohio, Mays underscored this view by clarifying the

---

[23]Ibid., 80.

[24]See George D. Kelsey, *Racism and the Christian Understanding of Man* (New York: Charles Scribner's Sons, 1965), 24, 27, and 33.

Christian doctrine of creation. As Mays saw it, Christianity does not speak of:

> one origin for the French and another for the German; not one for the English and another for the Irish; not one for the Chinese and another for the Japanese; not one for the Bantus and another for the Dutch of South Africa; and not one for the Russian and another for the American.[25]

No, for Mays and other pre-Black Power religious thinkers, Christianity declares that "the various races and nations of the earth have a common ancestry and that ancestry is God, for God 'has made of one blood all nations of men to dwell on all the face of the earth.' "[26]

Secondly, Mays contended that modern scientific research supported the Christian claim that "all life is interrelated." In his sermons and addresses he frequently referred to the work of anthropologists Ruth Benedict and Margaret Mead to reinforce his belief in the oneness of humanity. Furthermore, Mays argued, "we could quote scientist after scientist on the question as to whether there is or is not an inherent superiority which one race possesses over another."[27] On the contrary, Mays proclaimed that "the structure of the body proves kinship." Here again, he emphasized the obvious in his attempt to demonstrate the absurdity of racist conceptions of humanity:

> In all normal human beings, we find the same number of toes, fingers, teeth, muscles, and bones. There are tall people and short people in all parts of the world. There are long heads and round heads among all races. There are brilliant people and stupid people in every race of mankind.[28]

---

[25]"Christian Light On Human Relationships," in *The Eighth Congress of the Baptist World Alliance* (Philadelphia: Judson Press, 1950), 149.

[26]Ibid.

[27]"Of One Blood: Scripture and Science Make No Race Distinctions," in *Presbyterian Life* (February 5, 1955), 29.

[28]*Seeking To Be Christian in Race Relations* (New York: Friendship Press, 1957), 20-21.

In addition, Mays contended that science repudiates the notion that there is such a thing as "Negro blood" or "white blood;" in reality, there are four blood types (A, B, O, and AB) that are found in all peoples throughout the world. Therefore, citing John Donne's poem "No man is an Island," Mays concluded that "whether we like it or not," all nationalities "must inhabit the globe together."[29] Indeed, Martin Luther King Jr. also frequently quoted John Donne to emphasize "the interrelated structure of reality" that makes all people "links in the great chain of humanity."[30] Howard Thurman used similar language to express his belief in the interrelated structure of human life. In his essay "God and the Race Question," Thurman stressed that:

> The human lungs, heart, liver, and so forth, are all the same. The blood types are the same. The air we breathe and the food we eat serves the purpose in every human body. Physical death and birth are the same for all mankind. For better or for worse we must live together on this planet.[31]

Finally, Mays and others argued that the unity of the human family compelled Christians to be concerned about the welfare of *every* human being. Since "we are tied together with an inescapable destiny," Mays told the 1945 graduating class of Howard University, "what affects one, affects all. What affects the sharecropper in Mississippi, affects the millionaire on Park Avenue. What hurts the poor Negro hurts the poor whites." Indeed, Mays's famous protégé, Martin King used similar metaphors in the early 1960s to articulate his vision of the American dream and its role in the creation of the beloved community.[32]

---

[29]"Christian Light on Human Relationships," 152. See also *Seeking To Be Christian in Race Relations*, 21.

[30]Martin Luther King Jr., "Facing The Challenge of a New Age," in James M. Washington (ed.) *A Testament of Hope* (San Francisco: Harper Collins, 1986), 138. See also "The American Dream" in Ibid., 210.

[31]Howard Thurman, "God and the Race Question," in *Together*, edited by Glenn Clark. (Nashville: Abingdon-Cokesbury Press, 1946), 120.

[32]Howard Thurman, "God and the Race Question," in *Together*, edited by Glenn Clark. (Nashville: Abingdon-Cokesbury Press, 1946), 120; Benjamin E. Mays, "Democratizing and Christianizing America in This Generation," in the *Journal of Negro Education* 14 (Fall

CHRISTIANITY AND RACE RELATIONS

Pre-Black Power Critique of American Christianity

Negro religious scholars exposed the sins of American Christianity just as they revealed America's hypocritical claim to be the moral leader of the democratic world. They attacked American Christianity for failing to take bold action against racism and segregation, proclaiming that the church functioned as "a taillight instead of a headlight." As they saw it, the overwhelming majority of white churches shunned their responsibility to "the least of these" and made "a mockery of the gospel" by condoning racism in the church and society. Accordingly, Negro theologians in the 1940s and 1950s constantly reminded the American churches that they must use their spiritual and material resources to help solve the race problem in the nation. They insisted that the institutional church could "break the back of segregation" and racial discrimination if it only applied its efforts toward that end. Pre-Black Power religious intellectuals understood their role as that of prophets sent by God to prick the conscience of American Christianity with the message, "Struggle with the oppressed to eliminate racial segregation and discrimination, or renounce your claims to Christianity and democracy."

Negro theologians consistently challenged the church to live out the demands of the gospel in the area of race relations. Indeed, Benjamin Mays took full advantage of every opportunity to urge white Christians to apply the basic principles of their faith to the problematic area of race relations. Likewise, William Stuart Nelson (who succeeded Mays as dean of the Howard University School of Religion) warned the white church that "the increasing tension between White and Negro Americans is of the deepest and most immediate concerns to the religious community, for it poses a serious threat to America's internal peace and conceivably to our social and religious structure." Like Mays and other Negro theologians, Nelson challenged the American churches to re-order their priorities by making the

---

1945), 533.

race problem more important than fundraising, passing resolutions, holding theological debates, and building new structures.[33]

The important issue pre-Black Power theologians wanted to underscore was that the institutional church failed to take the problem of racism and segregation seriously. As veteran churchmen, they knew from experience that even when denominations and other national church bodies passed resolutions condemning racism, local white ministers and their parishioners continued to shun their moral responsibility and refused to challenge segregation in their churches and communities. However, the realism of Negro theologians did not lead them to conclude that Christianity was impotent in the fight against racism. On the contrary, they reminded Americans that "the religious impulse" fueled the anti-slavery movement, and was responsible for efforts to provide an education for blacks after emancipation.[34] Evaluating the contemporary church in light of these historical moments, Nelson captured the essence of pre-Black Power theologians' critique of American Christianity:

> Except for philanthropy, the period since the Civil War has proved almost completely barren of any determined effort initiated and sustained by the religious community to solve the problem of Negro-White relations in America.[35]

Segregation: "The Greatest Scandal Within The Church"

For Mays, the failure of the American religious community effectively to challenge racial segregation in the church and society was a source of deep anguish. While Mays encountered less discrimination abroad, he nevertheless lamented that, "Nowhere can a black man escape. On sea and on land, at home and abroad, the same stupid and cruel discrimination spreads its

---

[33]William S. Nelson, "Religion and Racial Tension in America Today," in *Journal of Religious Thought* 2 (Spring-Summer 1945): 164; William S. Nelson, "The Influence of Institutional Christianity Upon Secular Power," in *The Journal of Religious Thought* 4(Winter 1946-47), 49.

[34]See Mays, "The American Religion and the Christian Religion," 533.

[35]Nelson, "Religion and Racial Tension in America Today," 169.

tentacles."[36] Mays understood segregation to be "the greatest curse that can be imposed upon any one" because it denies individuals respect as a full human being, restricts their opportunities, and leads to a climate of violence against the segregated group. But more importantly, Mays interpreted racial segregation as a sin against God. In a 1952 address at Yale Divinity School, he made this point crystal clear:

> Segregation on the basis of color or race is a wicked thing because it penalizes a person for being what God has made him and for conditions over which he has no control. If one were segregated because of ignorance, he could learn and change the situation. If one were segregated because of poverty, he could work and improve his economic status. If he were segregated because of uncleanliness, he could bathe and become acceptable. But if one is segregated and stigmatized because of his race, he is penalized for something which he cannot change. And to do this is tantamount to saying to God you made a mistake in making a man like this. Of all the sins, this is the greatest.[37]

Clearly, Mays hated racial segregation with every fiber of his being, and he dedicated his life to eradicating it. But he especially despised segregation in the church, calling it "a great strain on my religion." Unlike secular organizations that made no pronouncements about the sacredness of human life and the meaning of reconciliation, the church is blatantly hypocritical. In fact, Mays argued that "hypocrisy" is the mildest term one can apply to a church that "maintains a segregated house, and simultaneously preaches the fatherhood of God and the brotherhood of man."[38] Mays lamented the fact that the local churches lag far behind secular bodies such as professional boxing, major league baseball, theaters, universities, and the public schools in advocating social change in the area of race. Accordingly, in an address

---

[36]*Born To Rebel*, 167.

[37]"The Christian In Race Relations." Delivered as The Second Address in the Henry B. Wright Lecture Series, Yale University Divinity School on April 16, 1952. In this lecture, Mays also wrote, "Segregation based on race, therefore, is without Christian foundation and is the greatest scandal within the church."

[38]*Born To Rebel*, 241-243.

before the Second Assembly of the World Council Of Churches in 1954, he cautioned the body that, "It will be a sad commentary on our life and time if future historians can write that the last bulwark of segregation based on race and color in the United States and South Africa was God's church."[39]

Although Mays criticized the white church for its failure to eliminate racial segregation in the church, he was careful to add, "I certainly do not want to give the impression that the blame is all on the side of white churches." As he saw it, "the exclusively racial church" (black or white) is an inadequate expression of Christian community; therefore, Negro congregations that opposed the *full* integration of the churches (for whatever reasons) "may be just as un-Christian at this point as the white church."[40] Indeed, Mays and other pre-Black Power theologians reminded the Negro church and community that it had a pivotal role to play in the creation of better race relations in America. Yet, like black theologians in the late 1960s and 1970s, Negro theologians insisted that self-love is a prerequisite for better race relations.

"The Moral Obligations of Negro Christians"

Having lived in the South for most of his life, Mays knew first-hand segregation's devastating effect on the Negro community. On countless occasions, he suffered the indignities of discrimination, and several times feared for his life. As an educator, Mays also knew the impact that segregation had on the minds of black youth; therefore, he dedicated his career to instilling character and pride in young people as he encouraged them to fight segregation and oppression. The first thing Mays sought to do was to combat the inferiority complex that accompanied legalized segregation. The simple message he proclaimed to thousands of young Negroes year after year was, "You are as good as anybody. And you have the right to aim at the stars and make your mark in the world." Mays knew that legalized segregation, along with the prejudice and violence that accompanied it, placed a "badge of inferiority" on every black child. The system of segrega-

---

[39]"The Church Amidst Ethnic and Racial Tension." (Appendix B) in Ibid. 355.
[40]"The Christian in Race Relations," 4.

tion meant that blacks had inferior schools, jobs, and accommodations. As a result, Mays observed that many Negroes grew up believing that they were inferior to whites, and that their subordinate role was ordained by God. Segregation meant that for many youth, "the nerve of aspiration was cut, ambitions dulled, hopes shattered, and dreams killed." Mays elaborated like this:

> The segregated system with its inevitable consequences of inequality has warped the minds and spirits of thousands of Negro youths. They either grow to manhood accepting the system, in which case they aspire to limited racial standards; or they grow up with bitterness in their minds. It is the rare Negro child who comes through perfectly normal and poised under the segregated system.[41]

However, Mays consistently preached that Negroes could throw off the "badge of inferiority," even as they fought to end racial segregation and discrimination. He noted the impact of the two World Wars on the black freedom struggle, claiming that they helped to intensify agitation for justice on the homefront. Suggesting that "morale is caught more than taught," Mays argued that as children associated "with parents, teachers and adults who were cringing and kowtowing, less and less," they too would gain self-esteem and pride.[42]

In his effort to combat the effect of segregation on the black community, Mays consistently referred to the achievements of famous Negroes who succeeded under the most adverse circumstances. Recalling the impact Booker T. Washington, Frederick Douglass, and Paul Lawrence Dunbar had on his life, Mays noted that "Every Negro who achieves significantly is a builder of morale for the Negro child." Indeed, Mays frequently cited the accomplishments of figures such as Jackie Robinson, Joe Louis, Marian Anderson, Paul Robeson, Richard Wright, Charles Drew, and Ralph Bunche, to let young people know that they too could achieve if they put their minds to it. As Mays understood it, parents, teachers, and ministers must continually tell children the same things that were told to him as a

---

[41]"Improving The Morale Of Negro Children And Youth," in *The Journal of Negro Education* 19 (Summer 1950), 423.
[42]Ibid., 421.

child growing up on a farm in South Carolina: "Character and ability are the important things. You are as good as anybody."[43]

While Mays emphasized the importance of building pride and self-esteem, as a minister of the gospel he also knew the dangers of self-righteousness and hatred. He cautioned Negroes not to think that they were more virtuous than whites simply because they were oppressed. Accordingly, Mays told Negroes that, "no one race has a monopoly on virtue and no one race has a monopoly on things that are evil. We are potentially no worse and potentially no better than other races." As he viewed it, Negroes must not only criticize the un-Christian behavior of whites, they must also be critical of un-Christian conduct in their own community, where all too often "Negroes are just as brutal and cruel to each other as the members of the dominant group are to Negroes." Indeed, Mays claimed that if Negro Christians were to avoid the sin of hypocrisy and self-righteousness, they should "earn the right to criticize" whites by practicing democracy and justice in those areas where they have complete control. When this is done, Negroes can criticize white Christians "with cleaner hands," and participate more effectively in improving race relations.[44] Emphasizing the value of self-criticism for interracial fellowship, Mays concluded:

> Criticisms are likely to be more effective and better received when those who give them accept the fact that they themselves are not perfect, and that they are part and parcel of the evil they condemn.[45]

In addition, Mays believed that Negroes participate in the evil of segregation when they are dishonest and evasive when discussing the race problem with whites. He understood that the violence inflicted upon blacks during slavery and Reconstruction made them develop techniques of survival when dealing with the white community. To be sure, these were times when it was safer to tell whites what they wanted to hear if blacks were to exist in

---

[43]Ibid., 424. See also Mays, "Democratizing And Christianizing America In This Generation," 533-34.

[44]"Obligations of Negro Christians in Relation to an Interracial Program," in *The Journal Of Religious Thought* 2(Autumn-Winter 1945), 44-45.

[45]Ibid., 46.

a hostile environment. Mays knew that even in 1945 it required a degree of courage to express one's true feelings about racism to whites. Nevertheless, he noted that now "a critical Negro public is demanding that Negro Christian leadership be straightforward and honest" in their interactions with white leaders. Like other pre-Black Power thinkers, Mays believed that a commitment to honesty and integrity was the only way to achieve genuine progress in race relations.[46]

Not surprisingly, Mays was disturbed by Negro leaders, who out of selfish motivation, were hypocritical and evasive in order to promote themselves to a position of prestige in the eyes of the white community. In fact, in his weekly column for the *Pittsburgh Courier*, he described this type of leader (who had neither the respect of Negroes or whites) in a style that anticipated the scathing critique of Black Power advocates:

"Uncle Thomas" has two outstanding traits. He is afraid and he is extremely selfish. He seeks in his every mode to please the white folk. He is physically afraid. He is also afraid he will not hold his position nor stand well in the eyes of the ruling majority if he says or does something which the white people do not like. He usually finds out their wishes before he puts forth his program. Mingled with fear and awe of and respect for the white man, he idolizes that which is white. He just cannot stand on his feet and strongly express a point of view at variance with white people.[47]

Finally, Mays urged Negro Christians to reject the spirit of hatred and revenge because they too will be under God's judgment if they seek to oppress others. Mays insisted that Negroes must continue to open their church doors to all people, and be free of prejudice against other minority groups such as Jews, Mexican-Americans, Asian-Americans, Native-

---

[46]"Obligations of Negro Christians in Relation To An Interracial Program," 44. Howard Thurman emphasized the same point in the third chapter of his *Jesus and The Disinherited* (Nashville: Abingdon Press, 1949).

[47]Mays wrote a weekly column for the *Pittsburgh Courier* beginning in 1946. Quote taken from January 14, 1950 column entitled, " 'Uncle Thomas' May Hold a College Degree From Morehouse or May Be From Columbia U."

Americans, West Indians and "other minority peoples."[48] But it is important to emphasize that despite the ethical weaknesses of white and black churches, Mays deeply believed that the Christian religion, when practiced with boldness and integrity, could help solve the problem of race relations in America.

"Democratizing and Christianizing America"

Mays combined the social justice theme of the Old Testament prophets with the liberative element of black religion as he reminded America and the church of its obligation to practice democracy and equality. Whether he was speaking to a black or white audience, he emphasized the importance of themes such as justice for the oppressed, individual honesty and integrity, self-help, and Christian service. At colleges, universities, and ecumenical conferences throughout the nation, Benjamin Mays persistently challenged Christians to apply the power of the gospel to the problem of racism in America.

In a 1945 commencement address at Howard University, Mays spoke about these issues in a manner that was characteristic of pre-Black Power religious intellectuals. Mays challenged the graduating class to be "prophets of a new day" by working to democratize and Christianize America in their generation. He argued that if Adolph Hitler could shape German society toward evil purposes in one generation, then committed Christians can make America a truly democratic and Christian society. Reminding his audience that "it does not take a 100 years to perfect social change," Mays reasoned that:

> If Germany through brutal means can build a kingdom of evil in one decade and if Russia, through brutal processes, can construct a new order in two decades, we can democratize and Christianize America in one generation.[49]

---

[48]"Obligations of Negro Christians in Relation To An Interracial Program," 47.

[49]"Democratizing and Christianizing America in This Generation." Commencement Address at Howard University, June 8, 1945. Published in the *Journal of Negro Education* 14 (Fall 1945).

Of course, when Mays spoke of democratizing and Christianizing America, he knew that there was already some level of democracy and Christianity practiced in the United States. However, he emphasized that America never intended for its democracy to function effectively "as Hitler planned his kingdom of evil to function effectively"; nor has America been committed to Christianity in the way Russian leaders were committed to building a new political and economic structure. Mays issued a prophetic challenge to the nation:

> We are what we do and not what we say. We are as democratic as we live and we are as Christian as we act. If we talk brotherhood and segregate human beings, we do not believe in brotherhood. If we talk democracy and deny it to certain groups, we do not believe in democracy. If we preach justice and exploit the weak, we do not believe in justice. If we preach truth and tell lies, we do not believe in truth. We are what we do.[50]

Mays clung to the belief that the Federal Government and the Christian churches of America would ultimately be forced to practice what they preached:

> The United States is *obligated* by virtue of its Federal Constitution and by virtue of its Christian pronouncements to become Christian-ized and democratized. If America is to maintain integrity of soul, and if our Government is to escape the label of hypocrisy and deception, it has no choice but to plan deliberately to bring to full fruition the four freedoms—for which we claim we fought on the battlefields of Europe and Africa; and for which we claim we are fighting in the Pacific.[51]

Clearly, Mays had faith that America would eventually live up to its obligations to treat all of its citizens with justice and equality. Like other pre-Black Power religious thinkers, he appealed to the moral conscience of

---

[50]"Democratizing and Christianizing America in This Generation," 531.
[51]Ibid., 528.

America in an effort to improve the plight of oppressed blacks. Mays referred to the noble ideas contained in the Declaration of Independence and the Bill of Rights to assure Howard University students that America had no choice but to extend the rights of full citizenship to Negroes. He also sought to remind the graduates of their responsibilities to pressure the federal government to take a more active role in solving the basic problems that confront African Americans. For example, Mays contended that the Government could end unemployment "within less than a decade" if it was truly committed to democracy. Concomitantly, he believed that once the problem of unemployment were solved, many other obstacles would also be overcome: friction between the races would be minimized; healthcare could be provided for every citizen (those who could pay and those who could not); delinquency would decrease; slums could be eliminated and decent housing provided for all; and educational facilities (especially in the South) would be enhanced. Speaking in the nation's capital, Mays reminded the graduates and the politicians that it was "the responsibility of the Federal Government to see that these things are done." Anticipating criticism, he added:

> Let those who oppose these measures on the ground of cost, bear in mind that we spend more in one year to prosecute this war than we would spend in twenty-five years in constructive measures such as these.[52]

Most importantly, Mays argued that the Government must abolish segregation in all areas where federal money is spent including: federal Agencies in Washington, the armed forces, employment, education, housing, hospitalization, and wherever else "the people's money is spent." Indeed, Mays spoke as a prophet of social justice as he urged the church to be Christian and the government to be democratic.

Mays concluded his commencement address by emphasizing themes that were hallmarks of his educational pedagogy and oratorical style. He told the graduates to develop strong moral character by practicing honesty and integrity in their personal and professional lives. Whether they became

---

[52]Ibid., 530.

doctors, lawyers, ministers, teachers, or politicians, they should stand for principles and not for that which is expedient:

> Let it be known in your community and in your profession that you are not for sale . . . that you are not putty to be molded and twisted in the pattern of injustice and incorruption. Develop strong, rock-ribbed, steel girded characters so that whoever bumps up against you, will bounce back because they came up against a man or a woman who is not for sale. . . .[53]

Anticipating Black Liberation Theology, Mays told students that if they were to democratize and Christianize America in their generation, they had to stand with the oppressed in their struggle for freedom. He urged the graduates to be in solidarity with disfranchised blacks in the South, poor whites, the untouchables of India, persecuted Jews, and "the millions in Africa who are groping for freedom." By speaking out against injustice wherever they find it, they "will be symbols of the new day," and "express the hopes and aspirations of the suppressed peoples everywhere." As they struggle against injustice in America and around the world, they must never lose hope, because God is on the side of the oppressed:

> You cannot lose. The future is on your side. The moral order of the universe will support your views. The planets, the sun, the moon, and the stars in their courses will fight on your side. Even God will fight on your side. History proves that all injustice defeats its own end.[54]

CHRISTIANITY, THE BIBLE AND NONVIOLENCE

No examination of the theology of race relations espoused by Benjamin Mays and others would be complete without a brief analysis of their understanding of the Bible and its impact on their interpretation of Christianity and nonviolence. Essentially, Mays sought to expose the fallacy

---

[53]Ibid, 532.
[54]Ibid, 533.

of racist interpretations of Scripture, and provide a biblical hermeneutic that would reinforce the Negro community's quest for integration.

"Of One Blood": Biblical Support For Integration

Perhaps the most important aspect of Mays's biblical interpretation is his assertion that *nothing* in the Old and New Testaments supports racial segregation. On the contrary, Mays underscored the biblical affirmation that faith and not race is the standard by which God judges human beings. For example, although the ancient Israelites emphasized the importance of separation, it was always on the basis of religion and not race. In fact, Mays noted, "the nations that surrounded Israel belonged to the same racial stock as Israel," and converts from other nations and races were always welcomed. Indeed, for Mays, a careful study of the Old Testament will show that no support for racial segregation can be found there; when Israelite religion proscribed intermarriage with surrounding cultures, it was done solely on the basis of preserving their distinctive religious tradition, not to maintain racial purity.[55]

Likewise, Mays emphasized that the New Testament advocates universalism and repudiates segregation based on race. First, Mays referred to the teachings of Jesus to support his claim that "To deny the universalism in the teachings of Christ is to deny the very genius of Christianity." Jesus' parable of the Good Samaritan (Lk. 10:25-37); his declaration about finding more faith in a Roman centurion than in all Israel (Lk. 7:1-10); and his teaching about God's concern for the non-Israelite (Lk. 4:23-30) all show that "from the beginning of his career, Jesus proclaimed a religion that was supraracial, supranational, supra-cultural, and supraclass."[56]

Additionally, Mays noted that the early church opened its fellowship to all persons regardless of ethnic background, class, or gender. As he saw it, the descent of the Holy Spirit at Pentecost (Acts 2:1-11); Peter's realization that "God is no respecter of persons" (Acts 10:34-35); Paul's declaration that in Christ Jesus there are no distinctions that divide humanity (Gal. 3:28) and his sermon in Athens proclaiming God as the

---

[55]"Of One Blood: Scripture and Science Make No Race Distinctions," 7.
[56]Ibid.

Creator of all human beings (Acts 17:24-28), all demonstrate that the early Christian church was an integrated community that renounced all forms of segregation and discrimination. Finally, and most importantly, Mays argued that the "universalism in the gospel is climaxed and attested to by the fact that Christ died for all mankind." Therefore, he concluded that those who seek biblical support for racism and segregation will search in vain; instead of supporting racial segregation, it is a manual for integration and universalism.[57]

The Ministry of Jesus: Love For God and Humanity

Like other pre-Black Power religious scholars, Mays believed that genuine Christianity was based on Jesus' teaching that "all the law and the prophets" are based on fervent love for God and humanity (Mt. 22:35-40). For Mays, it was Jesus' profound love for God *and* human beings that brought him into conflict with the religious establishment:

> If Jesus had gone throughout the Palestinian or Greco-Roman world merely talking about God and doing nothing to help man, he would hardly have run into trouble because almost everyone in the world of his day believed in God or in gods. Jesus got into trouble because he believed in man, a belief interlaced and interwoven with his concept of God.[58]

Referring to Jesus' many confrontation with the Pharisees (i.e. Mk. 3, Mt. 23), Mays emphasized Jesus as a defender of the poor. Again, he contended that it was Jesus' "belief in man, which went with his belief in God, that sent Jesus to the cross." Based on Jesus' example and teaching, Mays concluded that genuine Christianity combines an equal love for God, self, and neighbor; in fact, "the religion of Jesus might be thought of as a triangular religion, and an equilateral triangle at that."[59]

Mays also examined the parables to highlight the social aspects of Jesus' ministry and to underscore the responsibilities of contemporary Christians.

---

[57]Ibid., 8. See also, *Seeking To Be Christian in Race Relations*, 56-60.
[58]*Seeking To Be Christian in Race Relations*, 26.
[59]Ibid., 34, 38.

For example, in an address at Bucknell University in 1954, he interpreted the parable of the rich man and Lazarus as a Christian call to social responsibility. Mays argued that Jesus did not condemn the rich man because he was a bad, immoral person who exploited the poor; nor, for that matter, does Jesus praise Lazarus as a man of virtue. For Mays, the rich man went to hell because he had no social conscience, which was indicated by his inability to see the suffering of Lazarus.[60]

Mays also frequently referred to Jesus' teaching on the Judgement (Mt. 25:31-46) to emphasize his belief that God is concerned about how we treat "the least of these." For Mays, the test of true Christianity is "not how I treat the educated, but how I treat the man who can't write his name." For Mays the New Testament emphasizes the love of God *and* humanity. "And yet how strange it is," he lamented, "that this aspect of the life and teachings of Jesus has become such a neglected area in our daily practices."[61]

Love, Reconciliation and Nonviolence

Negro theologians understood nonviolence to be the only Christian means of struggle validated in scripture. Indeed, for Mays, Thurman, and others in their generation, the praxis of Jesus was the authoritative source for Christian living in the area of race, and therefore, they rejected hatred, bitterness, and violence as acceptable Christian behavior. For them, nonviolence was the *only* way Negro Christians could be true to the love ethic of Jesus. Mays expressed this view in his sermons and speeches, but it is also found in the writings of Howard Thurman, George Kelsey, and Martin Luther King Jr.

Underlying Negro theologians' thinking on love, reconciliation, and nonviolence is a firm belief in the power of Christianity to transform lives. In fact, Mays referred to the Apostle Paul's Damascus Road experience and the conversion of St. Augustine to illustrate his claim that "as pessimistic as any Christian may be about man, he can never deny the power of the

---

[60]Doris L. Gavins, "The Ceremonial Speaking of Benjamin Elijah Mays: Spokesman For Social Change , 1954-1975" (Unpublished Pd.D. dissertation, Louisiana State University, 1978), 203.

[61]*Seeking To Be Christian in Race Relations*, 44.

Christian religion to make men better."[62] Therefore, Mays interpreted Jesus' teaching on forgiveness, reconciliation, and love for the enemy quite literally, stating that "there is no limit to what the religious man must do to perfect reconciliation or right relationship with his fellowman." Accordingly, Mays argued that *Christian* nonviolence (not all who participated in nonviolent demonstrations embraced it as a philosophy based on religious conviction) is thus rooted in a profound love that seeks to redeem oppressors, not to humiliate or destroy them.[63]

In addition to the teachings of the New Testament, Mays noted that nonviolence was rooted in the history of the black experience of protest and resistance. He contended that the spirituals are not songs of hate, revenge, or conquest, but rather songs of the soul that helped slaves survive and protest without bitterness and violence. He also cited the leadership of Frederick Douglass, Harriet Tubman, Booker T. Washington, W. E. B. DuBois and the NAACP to show that a tradition of nonviolence has shaped black peoples' drive for full citizenship.[64]

Finally, Mays's December 1936 conversation with Gandhi helped to shape his understanding of the philosophy of nonviolence as "an active force" requiring spiritual and moral courage. Indeed, as Sudarshan Kapur has demonstrated in his recent landmark book, *Raising Up A Prophet*, the encounter of Negro intellectuals with Gandhi in the 1930s and 1940s (including Benjamin Mays, Howard Thurman, and William Stuart Nelson) laid the theological foundation which Martin L. King Jr. later built upon in the 1950s and 1960s.[65]

By the early 1960s, Benjamin Mays had seen great progress in race relations in America. He was encouraged by the early successes of the civil rights movement, and interpreted the National Conference on Religion and Race held in Chicago from January 14-17, 1963 as an historic moment for the American religious community.[66] Chaired by Mays, this interfaith

---

[62]Ibid., 109.

[63]Ibid., 38, 85.

[64]Ibid., 81.

[65]*Born To Rebel*, 156; Sudarshan Kapur, *Raising Up A Prophet: The African-American Encounter With Gandhi* (Boston: Beacon Press, 1992). See especially 81-100. For a discussion of Thurman's encounter with Gandhi, see *With Head and Heart*, 130-135.

[66]*Born To Rebel*, 261-263.

meeting (conceived as a religious commemoration of the one hundredth anniversary of the Emancipation Proclamation) brought together for the first time leaders from the Jewish, Roman Catholic, Orthodox, and Protestant faiths to "speak to the nation with a united voice" about the problem of racism in American society.

In his opening address to the delegates, Mays expressed an optimism that was characteristic of pre-Black Power Christian integrationists:

> We come this week to think together, to work together, to pray together and to dedicate ourselves to the task of completing the job which Lincoln began 100 years ago. . . . We believe that this conference will create in us a new sense of urgency to do in the next ten years what we failed to do in the past 100 years—abolish from among us racial discrimination and prejudice.[67]

Seven months later, the American religious community gathered again to reaffirm its commitment to the ideal of racial equality. The celebrated March on Washington that culminated in King "I Have A Dream" speech gave Mays and his contemporaries a profound hope that under the leadership of their young, dynamic colleague, "the Christian way in race relations" was beginning to change the nation. At this historic moment, Mays was called upon to pronounce the benediction.

---

[67]See Mays's Introduction to *Race: Challenge To Religion*, edited by Matthew Ahmann (Chicago: Henry Regnery Co., 1963), 5.

11

MAYS AND RACIAL JUSTICE

Verner Randolph Matthews

In presenting the development of Mays's concept of racial justice revealed in his literary works, it is necessary to look at those works using various categories which the process of selection and synthesizing of relevant data indicate are appropriate. Such categories are: the theological-philosophical basis, the political factor, the economic factor, the social factor, and the educational factor. Appropriate questions will be addressed to each category and to the works as a whole.

THE THEOLOGICAL-PHILOSOPHICAL BASIS

Theology shaped Benjamin Mays in all areas of his life. His views on race, religion, and society were strongly influenced by the Bible, and his concept of racial justice reflects this influence. As a Christian and a theologian-educator, Mays's racial views are theological and find expression in the following manner. First, God is sovereign. Second, human beings are the creation of God. Third, to be just and practice justice in a social setting, human beings must experience the new birth in Christ. Finally, with this new spiritual orientation, the love ethic of Jesus will become the guiding principle in human behavior, social ethics, and in all human relations.

Mays often quoted Micah 6:8 to express his view on racial justice: "He has showed you, O man, what is gold, and what does the Lord require of you but to do justice, and to love mercy, and to walk humbly with your God." May's concept of racial justice is expressed most clearly in his book, *Seeking to Be Christian in Race Relations*. In an attempt to show how a practicing Christian can act positively in achieving creative race relations within the social setting of today's world, Mays wrote *The Christian in Race Relations*.[1] Both of these works, along with others, suggest the importance of theology in Mays's thinking as the basis for his concept of racial justice.

The Nature of Human Beings

Mays's view of the nature of human beings is basically theological. All of Mays's presuppositions begin with God who is transcendent yet eminent, sovereign and Creator, based upon his reading of Genesis 1:28-29; 2:7; and Romans 2:21. God created human beings as physical beings with the potential to interact socially with other human beings in creative, productive, and loving ways. In addition, human beings are spiritual-moral beings, created in the image of God, whose nature is spiritual and moral. As spiritual beings, human beings are aware of God, they can experience God's presence, and they can have meaningful fellowship with their Creator. As moral beings, human beings can make decisions affecting their lives and others, and they are responsible for the decisions they make. Human beings have an innate sense of God's moral law incorporated in their nature by the Creator as His creation.

Mays was uneasy about human beings in their creation and in the far-reaching implications of their being made in the image of God. On the one hand, he stated:

> God in creating human beings, faced the awful dilemma of making them free in personality with the potential for good and evil, or making them a machine without power of choice, without personality. So in making human beings free to choose he had to make them free to choose right or wrong, truth or falsehood, war or peace, the high road or the low road.[2]

In this Mays finds agreement from Paul Tillich, who stated, "It is the image of God in man which gives the possibility of the Fall. Only he who is the

---

[1]*Seeking to be Christian in Race Relations* (New York: Friendship Press, 1957); "The Christian in Race Relations," in *Rhetoric of Racial Revolt*, by Roy L. Hill (Denver, Col.: Golden Bell Press, 1964), 120-139.

[2]*Disturbed About Man*, 91.

image of God has the power of separating himself from God."[3] On the other hand, regarding the "image of God," Mays points out that:

The nature of man is paradoxical, diabolical, and contradictory. Here he is made in the image of God, made also it seems, in the image of the devil. Potentially honest, potentially dishonest; potentially forgiving, potentially revengeful; potentially truthful, potentially a liar; potentially capable of rising to the divinity of God, capable also of descending to the level of the devil; potentially capable of building a kingdom of heaven on earth. This is man. And this is why Jesus spoke to Nicodemus in John 3:3, "Unless one is born anew he cannot see the kingdom of God."[4]

The Christian faith as revealed in the Bible makes clear that human beings are unique among the creatures of the earth. This uniqueness can be seen, first, in what God did for human beings in the creative process; he breathed into human nostrils his own breath, and the human being became a living soul (Gen. 2:7). God did this for humans only and not for any other creature. Second, human beings are unique in that they are somebody, not in their own right, but because God conferred dignity and value upon them. Finally, human beings are unique by having been created in God's own image, and thus being free moral agents without physical and moral restraints.

Mays found a common brotherhood of human beings who belong to the human family. That family relationship traces its origin to God who is a common creator-father. This common brotherhood of all persons is foundational for Mays's concept of racial justice. Further, the life and happiness of every human being is to be respected by all other human beings.

Freedom is a vital aspect of every person's nature and uniqueness. Human beings are never wholly slaves to the conditions in which they find themselves. Mays makes this point when he says:

---

[3]Paul Tillich, *Systematic Theology,* vol. 2, *Existence About the Christ* (Chicago: The University of Chicago Press, 1957), 33.

[4]*Disturbed About Man,* 92.

. . . so man or woman, boy or girl, can live in a community of hatred and ill will without hating. No person is bound to be prejudiced against Jews, Negroes, or Gentiles, just because prejudice against them is deep-seated in his community. Any person with God's help and grace, can rise above prejudice against a religious or racial group. It is this freedom in persons to think, to choose, to see values and to pursue them, and his power to create a better community that helps to distinguish human beings from animals.[5]

Human beings, Mays affirmed, finally are dependent upon God for the kind of world that they can build. The Christian faith declares that the universe is essentially ethical and essentially moral. God must be in the plans of human beings in building the right kind of world for all persons to live in harmony and peace with one another: first, because God and not human beings created the laws that will bring peace among nations. Second, God and not human beings has created the kind of justice that will enable one race to live in harmony with another race. Finally, the Christian faith affirms that righteousness and not armaments, justice and not economic power, ultimately sustain a nation, and the spiritual laws that make this so are as real and as unchangeable as the laws of science. Human beings are dependent upon God in sustaining their lives on earth, and they need to discover God's law, so that their choices can be spiritually rewarding and beneficial to all human beings.

The Nature of Justice

To Mays justice was more than an abstract or theoretical idea. Underlying his concept was a philosophical-theological notion of justice as a right and a responsibility and as a principle and a practice. Justice is something one does. It is pragmatic and is defined in terms of relationships: Persons' relation to God and to their fellow human beings form the basis for justice and determines its out-working in human relationships.

Justice is the ability of human beings to live in harmony with one another, recognizing each other's uniqueness, dignity, and right to function

---

[5]*Seeking to be Christian*, 154.

and develop their potential to the maximum. It finds its basis in God; therefore, it is theologically oriented. Justice as expressed in human relationships is reflected in people seeing each other first as human beings, children of one God, and second, as members of a particular nation or race. The true Christian, Mays argued, would deal justly with people in this fashion. Mays felt the right to equal opportunity in a democratic society, regardless of race, creed, or color, is also a vital and necessary part of his definition of justice.[6]

Racial Justice

Racial justice for Mays is the fair and equal treatment practiced by one race toward another living in community (whether it be on a local, national, or international level), based on the right of persons of every race to have equal opportunities to grow, learn and live to the best of their native abilities. Mays's concept of racial justice is biblically based and focuses on these four principles. First, God is sovereign and is above all things. Second, God created human beings and they are unique and each individual is of supreme worth because of divine origin. Third, human beings, in order to be just and practice justice to their neighbors socially, must be born again (John 3:3). Finally, in dealing justly with human relationships, the inner motivation for accomplishing justice with one's neighbor will be Jesus' love ethic.[7]

Mays argued that because we use the adjective "racial" before justice, we do not have racial justice in American contemporary society:

> If we had racial justice, you wouldn't need the adjective. The fact that you had to say racial justice, it means that justice breaks down when it comes to the black man. You talk about racial justice, you are not talking about racial justice for the white man, you are talking about racial justice for the Negro. That means that somebody out there is discriminating against you. That's the white man and sometimes the Negro, too. . . . Justice belongs to God and

---

[6]Ibid., 50, 8; Mays, "The Negroes and the Will to Justice," *The Christian Century* 28 (October 1942): 1317.

[7]Author's interview with Mays; *Seeking to Be Christian in Race Relations*, 107.

doesn't belong to man. And any man who tries to administer justice
to his fellow man on the basis of superiority and inferiority is taking
unto himself the role of God.[8]

The origin of justice is in God who is both universal and sovereign. God
is impartial and good, accepting human beings as they are and dealing justly
with all persons.. Mays believed that justice can come from no other source
but God, who as Creator made the world and human beings both dependent
upon Him. Racial justice is practiced between racial groups in society,
wherein each group recognizing the uniqueness of the other as persons and
exercises neighborliness.[9] This binds them in a common humanity looking
beyond race. Human beings cannot create or practice the kind of justice
that creates an atmosphere of harmony and mutual respect because they are
sinful and have a paradoxical nature. Therefore, Mays attributed the origin
of racial justice to God:

God and not man has created the kind of justice that will enable
one race to live in harmony with another race. This is not the kind
of justice or law that the strong and mighty usually impose upon
the weak. It is God's justice, man's task to discover God's laws and
base his choices and actions upon them.[10]

Achieving Racial Justice in Contemporary Society

To achieve racial justice in contemporary society, Mays taught that
human beings must seriously consider certain basic factors necessary for
bringing about positive and creative relationships among human beings.
First, God is the source of life; human beings are unique, having common
ancestry with other human beings; and, therefore, human beings cannot
consider themselves superior to other human beings in the society. In
Mays's thinking, the notion that a race, class, or natural groups are great of
themselves or endowed with special gifts that make them better than others

---

[8]Mays interview.
[9]*Seeking to Be Christian,* 11; *Disturbed About Man,* 108.
[10]*Seeking to Be Christian,* 15.

is a foolish one.[11]

Second, there must be a basis apart from human beings for achieving racial justice and establishing good race relations. The basis for good relations, Mays postulated, is found in the Christian doctrines of human beings, Christ, and God, and the application of Christian insights and convictions to everyday living.

Third, racial justice can be an achievable goal in contemporary society if human beings recognize that God is the father of all human beings (in his role as creator and human accountability as such).

Fourth, they must recognize that all human beings are brothers because they belong to the human family and that family is one, world-wide, irrespective of race, geographical location, and class. This common relationship should lead human beings to be neighborly toward each other. Neighborliness translated into meaningful human relationships leading to the attaining of lasting racial justice in contemporary society, Mays concluded, is seen in the helpful and sympathetic response of humans to human need. He argued:

> If God is common father and if all men are brothers, then it follows that the human family is one. It belongs together even to those who hold that God is the father of believers only and that only believers must also hold that nationality and race are not prerequisites for brotherhood.[12]

Mays uses the story of the Good Samaritan (Luke 10:29-37) to illustrate the idea of neighborliness, extending beyond race, religion, or class and responding helpfully and sympathetically to human need. Racial justice would become a reality with the practice of this principle in human affairs and in social, political, and economic relations.

---

[11]*Disturbed About Man*, 17.
[12]*Seeking to Be Christian*, 15.

THE POLITICAL FACTOR

Human beings live in community within which there is social, political, economic and educational interaction. There are also differences with the community which must be recognized. For a community to function properly, where human and civil rights of all persons must be considered, there must be government. Those persons who live in community together must have a vital part in the formation of that government, so that it can be representative of the community as a whole. Government must enact laws that protect the rights of all citizens without bias or favoritism. Every person is a citizen in the community and must be given the right to participate in the political process of selecting persons for positions in government and, if necessary, removing them from office.

The political process must be concerned with the just and equal treatment of all citizens and the political well-being of the total community. If there are documents formulated for the proper governing of the community (the Constitution or Declaration of Independence), then every effort by the elected is to be made to insure justice for the electorate. Any other approach does not serve in the best interests of the community as a whole.

Human Rights and the Role of Government

The pronouncements of the United Nations on human rights are expressed in a document entitled *The Universal Declaration of Human Rights*. Broad in scope, embracing the world community of nations setting forth how human rights ought to be respected, protected, and guaranteed by member nations. Though there was no claim to be a Christian document, Mays nonetheless accepted it as a Christian theological basis for a declaration of human rights.[13]

Human rights and citizens' rights to be free are basic to American democracy. These rights are clearly set forth in the Constitution and the Declaration of Independence. Mays believed that the founding fathers made the religious concept of the individual's equality before God and other human beings one of the foundations of democracy. Persons are equal in

---

[13]*Seeking to Be Christian in Race Relations*, 10.

the sense that they brought nothing into this world and they take nothing out. Further, every person is equal before God, and no person is to be denied an opportunity of trying to become the best possible person he can become.

Government is responsible for seeing to it that the proper environment is created where these human rights can be pursued in an objective and creative manner. Further, in guaranteeing human rights to all citizens, just and fair laws must be enacted, enforced, and incorporated into the political life of the nation.[14]

Laws and Ordinances Mandated by Government

Any laws or ordinances mandated by the government, whether on a national, state or local level, that are designed to deny due process to citizens whether black or white, are unjust. Such laws are enacted by legislators who act with a deliberate disregard for the Constitution and the Declaration of Independence and they also violate the rights of the individual. In Mays's view, the state has no right in a democracy to enact laws that deny citizens due process under the law. Laws aimed at segregating and discriminating against blacks are aimed at circumventing the Constitution and are designed to brand certain people as inherently inferior, unfit to function as normal human beings. Further, these laws stigmatize them as being less than children of God. By any standard of justice, Mays concluded, the laws of segregation are undemocratic since they are imposed by the strong upon the weak without the latter's participation in the making of these laws.[15]

After Reconstruction, every Southern state without exception passed laws designed to strip blacks of their rights under the Constitution and return them to a former state of slavery under a new umbrella called the "Jim Crow laws." With emancipation in 1865, new opportunities were opened to blacks to receive an education, to vote, to own property, and to become self-sufficient. Several blacks were elected to both the U. S. House of Representatives and the Senate. Threatened by blacks' accession to power, whites took steps to reverse that progress. They enacted grandfather

---

[14]"The Christian in Race Relations"; Mays, "Democratizing and Christianizing America in This Generation," *Journal of Negro Education* 14 (Fall 1945): 531.

[15]*Seeking to Be Christian in Race Relations*, 126.

clauses, literacy tests, and other local laws and ordinances intended to disenfranchise blacks through pseudo-legal means. Together with the more blatant use of fear and intimidation, these strategies eventually relegated African Americans once again to a powerless and subservient state. On the federal level, the Supreme Court's 1896 *Plessy v. Ferguson* decision, which set forth the "separate but equal" doctrine, was interpreted by Southern politicians and legislators as supporting their enactments denying blacks due process under the law based on race.[16]

The Responsibility of Citizens to Obey the Laws

Laws are made to protect the rights of citizens living together in a community, whether it be on a national, state, or local level. When laws are enacted and enforced impartially and take into consideration the humanity of all citizens, such laws are just. It thus becomes the citizen's responsibility to obey the law. When each citizen assumes this responsibility, an atmosphere of mutual respect for each other will have been created.

However, human nature being what it is, some laws seek to segregate and discriminate against a segment of the community. Such laws subjugate and dehumanize specific peoples based on race. Mays believed that any law that discriminates against or segregates people in general and blacks in particular deserved to be disobeyed. The Christian cannot support segregation laws in any form and Mays believed it was a matter of Christian responsibility to work diligently to change unjust laws.[17]

Basis for Just Government

Mays suggested five principles that provide the underlying basis for a just government. First, a just government would be one that in all of its basic institutions represents all the people, regardless of race, creed, or color

---

[16]C. Vann Woodward, *The Strange Career of Jim Crow* (New York: Oxford University Press, 1959), 59, 102.

[17]*Seeking to Be Christian in Race Relations*, 87, 90; *Born to Rebel*, 180.

and will not allow the practice of segregation or discrimination toward any of its citizens. A second principle would call for a government that acknowledges the worth and integrity of every individual in the community. Mays's third principle called for a just government to acknowledges God. Mays expresses his fourth principle as one in which people respect, practice, and adhere to America's founding documents, the Constitution, the Bill of Rights, and the Declaration of Independence. Finally, in summarizing these principles, Mays felt that the will, the objectives, and the purposes are far more basic to achieving a just and equal government than the methods used to accomplish it.[18]

THE ECONOMIC FACTOR

Economic opportunity as well as economic equality are essential to the well being of the citizens in the community. A person should be able to be employed in a job commensurate with his skills regardless of race, religion, or national origin. To establish economic restrictions based on race or any other criteria by any persons in the society is discriminatory and prevents human beings from realizing their talents in creative employment. Access to the economic institutions of the society must be made available to all people, and there must be no relegating of certain types of employment to one segment of the community because of race. This is unjust, unfair, and in Mays's opinion, ungodly, as it affects the ability of persons to support their families or have the opportunity toward better employment.[19]

Economic Equality

Mays held that in a democracy every able-bodied person is entitled to an opportunity to work and to advance on the job. There is the necessary economic mechanism to provide a job for every person who is willing and able to work, regardless of race. Full employment and economic equality are objectives that both the federal government and private industry should establish as priorities. Both public and private sectors should devise plans

---

[18]"The Christian in Race Relations; "Democratizing and Christianizing America," 529-530.

[19]"Democratizing and Christianizing America," 530.

utilizing the best minds and talents to make full employment possible for every able-bodied man and woman. We are able because we have the resources; America needed only the character to propose and the will to execute, concluded Mays.[20]

Economic equality could be achieved as opportunities for blacks are provided so that blacks may be able to realize their potential, exploiting their skills on a competitive basis as any other member of society. Further, economic equality could be realized when equal opportunities are provided for all segments of the society so that the potential and talents of the individual may be utilized for the betterment of society. There can be no economic equality, Mays argued, when any segment of the society is denied access to equal opportunity to maximize its potential.[21]

The Right to Provide for One's Family

All able-bodied individuals in a democratic society are entitled to an opportunity to work, so that they may provide from productive labor the means to support a family. Such a right is guaranteed by the Constitution and the Bill of Rights. As the protector and preserver of human rights, the state is obligated to insure and protect the economic right of all persons to support their families. Mays contended that blacks who have always been loyal to this country are entitled to an equal opportunity to earn a living and an equal opportunity to be permitted to advance on the job so their families may be adequately provided for.

The Kinds of Jobs Open to Blacks

The history of black people in America has determined the kinds of job opportunities available to blacks. Blacks were brought to America as slaves in order to provide cheap labor for the cotton industry. Slavery was one of several ways by which the white man sought to define the status of blacks and assure their subordination. There were no opportunities for self-

---

[20]Ibid., 530-531.
[21]*Born to Rebel*, 95; "Democratizing and Christianizing America . . . ," 532.

realization, use of personal skills, abilities, or talent, or exposure to economic pursuits where these things could be productively utilized. Employment designations were set and prescribed for blacks with the intent of, first, using them as laborers, and second, to keep them in servitude, with humiliation and dehumanization as the end.

In recounting his youth, Mays stated that the only jobs to which black males were relegated were either on a farm or as a common laborer, along with the occasional instances where blacks were carpenters or masons. Black women also assisted the men on the farm. Many worked as domestics in the house of the white plantation owner. Educational opportunities for blacks were few, for there was no need for education to be a farmer. Mays fought whites who tried to prevent him from getting an education to secure a job commensurate with his talents. Because blacks were untrained, dependent upon whites for their economic survival (share cropping), and held in a subservient role, they remained in a state of poverty, experiencing a sense of entrapment. This in turn developed in the black psyche a negative self-image because blacks were at the bottom of the economic and social ladder. Further, they were considered second-class citizens, locked into servitude and dependency, ending finally in psychological slavery.[22]

Inadequate Resources and Their Psychological Effect

Mays's analysis of the effect of inadequate resources emerged from his boyhood family experiences of seeing his father attempt to provide honestly for his family and, later, his growing understanding of the damaging psychological effect of the lack of proper resources. Looking back on those early years as a teenager, Mays saw his father renting forty acres of land to grow cotton. He owned two mules to be used in farming the land, placing him just above a sharecropper. The Mays family lived on the ragged edge of poverty, a condition Mays called "respectable poverty."[23]

The elder Mays paid two five hundred pound bales of cotton for every twenty acres rented. He had to borrow money against the number of bales of cotton he anticipated selling at harvest time. He never cleared enough

---

[22]"Democratizing and Christianizing America," 529-530; Woodward, 87; *Born to Rebel*, 8.
[23]*Born to Rebel*, 20.

from one crop to carry his family from one September to the next. From September through February, the family was on its own; every March a lien had to be placed on the crop so that the family could get money to buy food and other necessities from March through August, when the sale of their cotton brought a glimmer of relief. Mays and his siblings helped with the farming chores. Because of this necessary dependence, when Mays expressed a desire to go to school after March (he was allowed to attend school during the winter months, November through March), his father very strongly objected. He bitterly opposed his son's efforts to get an education, seeing no need for it since all black men would eventually follow in their father's footsteps and become farmers.[24]

Because of their constant indebtedness, Mays's father stifled any aspiration his children had of bettering themselves through education or any other effort unrelated to farming. He saw such vain hopes as irrelevant to their situation and advised his children to dismiss them from their minds. Eventually, to escape this physical and psychological confinement, Mays's siblings left home, assuming the responsibility for their own lives and future. Although the basic necessities were provided by Mays's father, his income could only manage to sustain his family on a subsistence level. He felt tied to the land, indebted to creditors, and locked in by segregation and racial discrimination with no possible opportunity for bettering himself. The family experienced some negative behavior from Mays's father as he sought a way of escaping the heavy responsibility placed upon him which he felt inadequate to meet. Nevertheless, Mays cited some positive things learned and experienced during this period of his life. He learned honesty and industriousness from both his mother and father. Yet through their poverty, Mays concluded, his parents gave the children principles that transcended their poor condition and gave them appreciation for each other.

In his adult years Mays meditated on those experiences. He believed that in order to provide the necessary financial resources for the family every able-bodied person should be given the opportunity to work and advance on the job and to prepare for any job, trade, or profession in keeping with his ability. When the family breadwinner does not provide for such opportunities and unemployment or underemployment results, other avenues must be

---

[24]Ibid., 36.

sought to meet the need. Often this must be in the form of public assistance, which makes a family feel dependent on the government for support, looked down on by the community, and results in a low self-image.[25]

The Lack of Employment

Mays believed that complacency, resignation, hopelessness, and the death of aspiration will prevail wherever employment opportunities are limited to specific vocations offering no possibility of advancement or realization of potential. Farming, domestic work, and menial labor tasks were the areas of employment offered to members of the black community in Mays's early life. Farmers have no need of formal education reasoned Mays's father. This attitude prevailed throughout the community and most parents would only allow their children to go to school during the winter months.[26]

Although some progress has been made in black employment, racial discrimination in employment still exists. Overt job discrimination is one of the important hurdles which must be overcome before color can disappear as a determining factor in the lives and fortunes of human beings.

THE SOCIAL FACTOR

For Mays any attempt to analyze problems within a society must begin with a definition of society and the structure of a particular social unit in which the problems exist. Generally, when Mays spoke of society, he meant the various elements in a community that are essential to human existence. A society must have a government, economic resources, social activities, educational institutions, and civic and recreational facilities. These factors are indispensable to the proper functioning of any society, whether primitive or advanced. Specifically, Mays defined society "as a community, nation or broad grouping of people having common traditions, institutions, and other collective activities and interests." A social order is seen by Mays as "the

---

[25]"Democratizing and Christianizing America," 530; "The Negroes and the Will to Justice," 1318.

[26]*Born to Rebel*, 32, 36.

totality of involving human interrelationships within that social unit or any part of it."[27]

For a society to function and recognize the rights, privileges, and freedoms of the various segments of the society, it must be integrated. An integrated society for Mays must be built in recognition of the fact that God is absolute.[28] The roots of an integrated society must be in spiritual values, whether they are pursued in Judaism, Christianity or in some other religion. Mays is very clear in his view on integrating the social order when he says:

> An integrated social order is one which will recognize that the human family is one. From the standpoint of the Christian faith, man has a common father, God. From the point of view of science, man has a common ancestry. It is implicit in the Christian faith that all men are brothers, sons of one father. Science proves that by blood all men are brothers.[29]

Major Social Problems

Among the many social problems facing humanity, Mays considered the following as major ones needing the immediate attention of the nation as a whole in finding adequate and long-lasting solutions. The first is the problem of black-white relations. The race question continues as one of the most disturbing, baffling, and persistent problems confronting not only Americans but humanity as a whole. W. E. B. DuBois, at the beginning of the century, alluded to the fact that the problem of race or the color line would be the problem of the twentieth century. It continues to vex American society as it nears the beginning of the twenty-first.

The second is the problem of unemployment among blacks (the last hired and the first fired) and akin to that, equal employment for blacks on the same basis and level as whites, based on skills and not color. The third

---

[27]Eli Ginzberg, assisted by James K. Anderson, Douglas W. Bray, and Robert W. Smuts, *The Negro Potential* (New York: Columbia University Press, 1956), 95; Mays, "The New Social Order When Integrated," *Religious Education Journal*, March/April 1963, 155; *Born to Rebel*, 209.

[28]"New Social Order," 156.

[29]Mays interview.

is the problem of poverty among black people, coupled with that of the homeless emerging as one of the far-reaching consequences for our society. Mays considered ministering to the poor to be necessary and vital to the national interests. A fourth major social problem Mays considered as needing attention is what he calls the economic survival facing senior citizens. This is a severe problem facing senior black citizens in contemporary society. As a means of dealing with this issue Mays suggested planning for old age through savings. The fifth problem is the education of black people for meaningful and productive vocations so that they can participate creatively in all facets of American society. Finally, Mays considered important as a social problem what he calls dealing with the basic realities of life, how black people could survive with limited or no resources.[30]

During World War II, Mays listed some of the areas on which America needed to move if the nation had the will to justice. Among these were voting rights for blacks, legal justice, and police brutality. Lerone Bennett, commenting on Mays as an educator, said, "Mays addressed himself to the major problems of oppression and manhood." Mays saw the resolution of these major social problems as vital to the well-being of black people.[31]

Institutional Racism and Harmonious Race Relations

As blacks and whites seek to improve relations between them so that both races can live and work together in an atmosphere of respect, Mays suggested that there must be a serious effort made by both races to work toward achieving such a goal in the social order. Both racial groups must talk straight and communicate with each other in honest dialogue, dealing positively with the issues, problems, and practices that alienate both groups from each other. Mays viewed race prejudice as the pervasive element affecting America and infecting all of its institutions.[32]

---

[30]Ibid; *Seeking to Be Christian in Race Relations*, 9; W. E. B. DuBois, *Souls of Black Folks* (Chicago: A. C. McLurg & Company, 1903), 10; "The Negroes and the Will to Justice," 1318; Mays, "Benjamin E. Mays at 81," *Black Enterprise*, May 1977, 26-29.

[31]"The Negroes and the Will to Justice," 1318; Bennett, "Benjamin E. Mays," 98-101.

[32]*Seeking to Be Christian*, 15; "A Plea for Straight Talk Between the Races," *Atlantic Monthly*, December 1960, 1.

In a perspective largely shared by Mays, Joe R. and Clarice Feagin have defined institutional racism as

> the process where those in the superior position seek to monopolize basic resources. In this process, privileges become institutionalized, that is, it becomes imbedded in the norms (regulations and informal rules) and roles (social positions and their attendant duties and rights) in a variety of social, economic, and political organizations.[33]

For Mays institutional racism affects black-white relations in the following ways. First, it restricts the full development of African Americans as a group. Second, it places power of mobility in the hands of the dominant group. Third, it creates resentment, hatred, and distrust between groups. Fourth, it frustrates ambition and circumscribes the areas of occupation that one group imposes on another. Finally, it seeks to maintain the balance of power so that the system is perpetuated and kept intact. Institutional racism separates races instead of bringing them together into meaningful and creative human relationships that can lead to a growing, developing, and productive society.[34]

Mays, a social activist in the best sense of the word, with a deep commitment to social justice, believed in an integrated society. He believed that a social order will be new when it is integrated. Integration for Mays means the "unification and mutual adjustment of diverse groups or elements into a relatively coordinated and harmonious society or culture." Integration cannot be legislated or court mandated. The Supreme Court decision of May 17, 1954 meant desegregation. Desegregation paves the way for integration, but desegregation is not necessarily integration. An integrated social order, says Mays, would have no segregation and no discrimination based on race, religion or social position.[35]

---

[33]Joe R. Feagin and Clairece B. Feagin, *Discrimination American Style* (Englewood Cliffs, N.J.: Prentice-Hall, Inc., 1978), 92.

[34]Mays, "Moral Aspects of Segregation," 170-175.

[35]*Born to Rebel*, 319; Mays, "The New Social Order When Integrated," 232.

THE EDUCATIONAL FACTOR

As perhaps the best known black educator in America, Mays gave twenty-seven years of faithful and distinguished service as president of Morehouse College. Mays continued his active interest and concern for the education of youth in his position as president of the Atlanta School Board, the first black elected to that position.[36]

Mays's Definition of Education

Education for Mays could no longer be considered as the gaining and acquiring of skills to get ahead in the world. Such a view of education uses it as a means to an end that is self-centered and narrow in outlook. Mays defined education in terms of social responsibility and the educated person as an instrument to bring about positive social change in society. Mays saw education as preparing individuals to be liberated from ignorance and fear, to be able to do something in the world around them to correct some of the problems, and to make it a better place in which to live. Implied in this definition is also the preparing of black students for various occupations so that when the doors of opportunity are open, they will be able to compete favorably in a competitive society.[37]

The Right of Every Citizen to an Education

Mays considered education essential to the well-being of every society. Education should begin in childhood when a child is both impressionable and open to the adventure of learning. He believed that early education gives to the child a sense of personhood and the wholeness necessary for functioning in society. Education can be formal, within the school setting, or it can occur informally within the home. Education is imperative for black people, and in Mays's view, the only way out of bondage for blacks is to develop their minds so that they will be able to hold their own in a

---

[36]Bennett, "Benjamin E. Mays," 101.

[37]"The Negro Liberal Arts College," *Journal of Negro Education; Seeking to Be Christian,* 23; Mays interview; *Born to Rebel,* 92; *Lord, the People Have Driven Me On,* 50.

competitive society.[38]

Every citizen should be given an opportunity to be educated so as to achieve economic independence, which, in turn, creates self-pride. It is the right of every citizen, says Mays, to receive an education that allows the opportunity of discovering one's capabilities and potential and permitting their minds unrestricted development. Segregation creates a feeling of inferiority to the extent that persons can never know what their capabilities really are. Further, segregation and discrimination make human beings slaves in their minds, never permitting growth and development of the mind through creative educational pursuits. It is Mays's view that education, when operating freely and without restrictions in a democratic society, will inspire and motivate persons to grow to full maturity and share the results of their knowledge and skills for the well-being of society.[39]

The Role of Government

In a democratic society, there should be freedom for every citizen to learn without discrimination. It does not make good sense, according to Mays, to provide a better education for one group than for another. If a person has to belong to a particular race to be granted educational opportunities, then the democracy is conditional rather than universal. Those ideals in the Constitution must be implemented so that democracy can function throughout the nation without regard to nationality, race, class, or caste, guaranteeing the whole citizenry free access to the economic, political, educational, and social opportunities in the system.[40]

Mays rejected any efforts by government at any level to restrict access to education to the dominant group in power. He wrote:

Whenever a strong dominant group possesses all the power, political, educational, economic, and wields all the power; makes all the laws; writes all constitutions, municipal, stage, and federal; and

---

[38]*Born to Rebel*, 80, 160; *Lord, the People Have Driven Me On*, 70; Mays interview.

[39]*Lord, the People Have Driven Me On*, 81; *Born to Rebel*, 165; *Seeking to Be Christian*, 90.

[40]"Race in America: The Negro Perspective" in *The Search for America*, ed. Huston Smith (Englewood Cliffs, N.J.: Prentice-Hall, 1959), 190, 158, 125.

contributes all the money, determines all policies—governmental, business, political and educational, when that group plans and places heavy burdens, grievous to be borne, upon the backs of the weak, that act is immoral.[41]

Mays believed that a democratic government is designed to protect the weak and guarantee their rights under the Constitution. Mays always held that federal laws took precedence over state and local laws. Any local laws advocating segregation of the races and preventing the equal education of all citizens should be corrected by the Federal government by withholding funds to that state, county, or municipality and reminding communities of the constitutional provisions involving the right of every American to an education.[42]

Like most African Americans, Mays hailed the Supreme Court's 1954 *Brown* decision as an important "effort to abolish a great evil through orderly process." He continued:

And we are morally obligated to implement the decision or modify the Federal Constitution and say plainly that this Constitution was meant for white people and not for Negroes, and that the Declaration of Independence which says in essence that all men are created equal, that they are endowed by their creator with certain inalienable rights, and that among these are life, liberty, and the pursuit of happiness, was written for whites.[43]

The Effects of the Separate but Equal Doctrine

In the aftermath of the Supreme Court's 1896 *Plessy v. Ferguson* decision, which affirmed the separate but equal doctrine, no serious effort was put forth to equalize educational opportunities for blacks until lawsuits began to be filed in the courts beginning in 1935. Over those years the gulf of inequality in education widened. From his experience as an educator and examining the history of this decision as it affected education among blacks,

---

[41]"Moral Aspects of Segregation," 170-175.

[42]"Realities in Race Relations," *The Christian Century*, 25 March 1931, 404-406.

[43]"Moral Aspects of Segregation," 172.

Mays believed the South would never be able to provide enough funds to maintain separate but equal school systems for the two races.[44] Mays substantiated this conclusion in the following manner:

For example, according to a 1931 issue of *The Christian Century* thirteen Southern States during the school year, 1918-1919, spent $12.91 per capita for each white child of school age, $4.42 for each Negro child—a difference of $8.49. During the school year 1924-25, these thirteen states spent $27.95 per capita for each white child of school age, for the Negro child $9.53—a difference of $28.43. In 1931 these thirteen states were spending per capita for each white child of school age $40.92, for the Negro child $15.78—a difference of $24.14. In other words, from 1919 to 1931, the per capita for the white child increased $28.01, for the Negro child, $11.36.

It is not surprising, therefore, that the various surveys prove that the education Negroes receive in the segregated public schools of the South is, in most instances, inferior to that received by the whites. It will take many decades for the Negro to overcome the handicaps in his education. Commenting on the point of inequality in segregation, Eli Ginzberg in *The Negro Potential* writes: "Because of deficiencies in their home and community environments and in the schools they attend, Negroes have far less opportunity to acquire a solid education than do most white populations among whom they live. A man's education is exceedingly important in determining his eventual position on the economic scale."[45]

Education and Racial Justice

Mays considered education essential to any effort to achieve racial justice in America. He felt a psychological imposition early in life because of this unjust and racially assigned status of inferiority, which he never accepted, and expressed it, first, as robbing him of his God-given dignity as

---

[44]Mays, *Seeking to Be Christian*, 35.
[45]Ibid., 73-74.

a person; and second, of denying him access to an education in which his potential could be realized.[46]

Mays's educational experience gave him a sense of freedom and a strong sense of self-confidence. He had many positive role models at South Carolina State College and Virginia Union University, and he concluded that their educational achievements were a basic resource to be used in achieving racial justice and equality for blacks in the society.[47] Further, education was and is the means by which blacks can successfully compete in an open society on the basis of competence and self-confidence. In an address to a boys conference at Benedict College, Mays pointed out the importance of education:

> We must contend for justice; we must never relinquish our claim until the mind and character become the standard of the man—not race, not color. We must prove our equality by producing great scientists, great artists, great businessmen—in fact whatever man has done, we black men must do if we are to take our place in the world of competition.[48]

Education prepares black men and women to take their places in a highly competitive society and feel confident that they have what it takes to achieve. Further, education can be a means of blacks and whites discussing their problems, their differences, and their attitudes in an attempt to find adequate solutions toward achieving racial understanding and justice.

In answer to the question, "What would I do if I had the option to live my life over again?" Mays answered that question by combining education, religion, and race relations:

> I would indeed follow the same programs I have followed since the turn of the century: education, religion, and race relations. I have always believed that education is imperative for the black man, and his only way out of bondage is to develop his mind so that he will be

---

[46]*Born to Rebel*, 34.

[47]Ibid., 35, 41.

[48]"The Goal," a speech to Negro Older Boys Conference, Benedict College, South Carolina, 26 February 1926.

able to hold his own in a competitive society. I would hold to religion because without religion and a firm belief and faith in God, the black slaves would hardly have survived. I would strive for better racial relations because the black man and the white man are both citizens of the United States.[49]

Education and Black Advancement

Mays believed that education was the only way out of bondage for African Americans. Education has those inherent factors of inspiration and motivation necessary to move blacks to press their claims for full participation in American democracy. Education provides for blacks the opportunity of realizing innate potential, creating a self-awareness so that they can accept with dignity their own worth, and make meaningful contributions to society.[50]

At the completion of his education at Bates College, Mays felt that he was prepared to enter society with self-confidence, self-assurance, and self-awareness gained through competitive experiences in the pursuit of an education. He describes his experience in this manner:

> Through competitive experience, I had finally dismissed from my mind, for all time, the myth of the inherent inferiority of all Negroes and inherent superiority of all whites—articles of faith to so many in my previous environment. I had done better in academic performance, in public speaking, and in argument and debate than the vast majority of my classmates. I concede academic superiority to not more than four in my class. I had displayed more initiative as a student leader than the majority of my classmates. Bates College made these experiences possible.[51]

Early in Mays's life, he considered education essential to his psychological, personal, and mental well-being. Apart from getting an education,

---

[49]*Lord, the People Have Driven Me On*, 56.
[50]*Lord, the People Have Driven Me On*, 70, 89; "The Negroes and the Will to Justice," 522.
[51]*Lord, the People Have Driven Me On*, 125.

Mays would have felt trapped in farming, carpentry, and laboring as a life vocation. For Mays such vocations offered no future. For Mays the desire for an education was both a dream as well as a goal so that he could find himself and make his contribution to the world.

Education and Self-Confidence

Mays saw education as the most important means for black people to develop self-confidence and self-awareness. For Mays, both formal and informal education are important to the development of a positive self-image. Formal education in the school, the college, and the university provides the discipline and order necessary to train the mind and spirit.[52] Informal education in the home, the church, and the community also contributes mightily to black self-confidence. Mays's mother, though unlettered and untutored, taught her children that they were just as good as anybody else in the world. The effect of her teaching gave Mays at a very early age a sense of his own self-worth and pride. This included a pride in his color. Later, referring to the emphasis on blackness during the 1960s, Mays concluded that he did not have to wait seventy years for someone to teach him then to appreciate his blackness. His mother taught that to all of her children. From his father Mays learned to be industrious, to work hard and long for the things one needs and want. From both, he learned honesty and industry. In addition, the people in the church and community recognized his gifts and talents, and encouraged him to believe that his intelligence would help him make something of himself. [53]

As president of Morehouse College, Mays always emphasized the importance of education in achieving vocational skills and instilling self-confidence, which leads to self-awareness. A Morehouse student is taught and learns well that "a man's reach should exceed his grasp," and he should never accept the idea that the ceiling is the limit of his striving. Mays was also conscious of the personal responsibility of educated blacks to awaken in black youth the same sense of self-confidence and self-awareness they experienced in their educations. Mays insisted that the self-worth and self-

---

[52]*Born to Rebel*, 31.
[53]*Born to Rebel*, 2, 12, 290; *Lord, the People Have Driven Me On*, 16.

confidence experienced through education should be translated into social and political action for the betterment of society as a whole.[54]

Mays's concept of racial justice remained the same throughout the course of his writings. Throughout his writings he preached the basic idea of the equality of all men and the universality of man as the creation of God. His concept always had as its ultimate goal the bettering of black-white relations. If human beings are to practice justice in every area of life, they must recognize each other's humanity and respect each other's right to freedom.[55]

---

[54]*Lord, the People Have Driven Me On*, 32; *Seeking to Be Christian*, 86.
[55]*Seeking to Be Christian in Race Relations*, 120.

12

MAYS'S COMMENCEMENT ADDRESSES

Doris Levy Gavins

Commencement addresses are traditional at the closing festivities of a school or college when degrees or diplomas are conferred. Giles Wilkerson Gray and Waldo W. Braden explain that the address is designed "to strengthen or intensify existing attitudes or opinions." This type of speech generally seeks an emotional rather than an intellectual response. They also state that since "the occasion is a most significant aspect of the stimulating speech," the speaker must conform to "the traditions, customs, precedents, and rituals" of the event. They further suggest that the speaker has a duty to "live up to the expectations of the program planners and prepare to meet the listeners in a spirit consistent with the other events on the agenda."[1] Alan Monroe sees the speaker as poised physically, letting his voice suggest his depth of feeling in order to instill in his audience a deep feeling of reverence or devotion.

In her book, *Commencement*, Gertrude Jones describes the commencement generally as the culmination of the inspiration fostered by the school. She regards its purpose as threefold:

1. To recognize the attainment of a level that has been set up by one society's established institutions—recognition;
2. To sum up the experience gained thus far in life's "quest for values"—retrospection;
2. To open the doorway leading to a new and higher level of experience—inspiration.[2]

---

[1]Giles Wilkerson Gray and Waldo W. Braden, *Public Speaking* (2d ed.; New York: Harper and Row Publishers, 1963), 387-92.

[2]Gertrude Jones, *Commencement* (New York: A. S. Barnes, 1929), 10.

The format is usually structured in keeping with the formality of the occasion. While the speaker is expected to inspire the audience, who is likely to be in general agreement with his theme, the subject must be realistic and well within the comprehension and interest of the audience. The speaker must be aware of time limitations, remembering that the major concern is the awarding of degrees.

Benjamin Mays had ample experience with commencement exercises, for he actively officiated as college president until he retired in the Summer of 1967. Aside from his administrative affiliation, he participated in many commencement exercises as well, having received fifty-six honorary degrees. At many of these institutions Mays served as commencement speaker and was cited generally for his devotion to education and commitment to human rights and brotherhood. Regarded as an accomplished preacher early in his career, Mays was also acclaimed as a commencement speaker.

CAMPUS PROTEST IN THE 1960S

The 1960s served as a peak in Mays's career as commencement speaker, but at the same time the turbulent period symbolized the academic protests, which began when the first wave of student dissent swept across the United States with the advent of the Free Speech Movement at Berkeley in 1964. The strong united student front could not be ignored by professors and administrators who were accused of concentrating on irrelevant education. However, few activities escaped the reproach of student criticism. The cloak of reverence was stripped from the stately tradition of commencement as dissident students rejected what they called remote speech topics, thereby, forcing anxious speakers to take another look at their roles.

Speaker reaction varied from disbelief to a disturbed concern. As a result, campus speakers used great caution in their presentations. For example, Vice President Hubert Humphrey spoke on peace, while other speakers defended the policy in Vietnam and attempted to show that there was prospect in the global battles. Some speakers dismissed the dissent and called it a temporary substitute for the panty raids and other pranks. Others noted the increased momentum, but still did not approve the new activism. Sol M. Linowitz warned the students that "true involvement calls for far more than carrying a banner or joining a march." Sargent Shriver reminded students that they must decide not "should I act?" but "which side am I on?" Carl. T. Rowan advised the black student not to concentrate "so exclusively on street demonstrations that he forgets other fields of battle." William Manchester, summarized the situation with words from John Kennedy—"Instead of leadership we have problem solving teams. Instead of judges we have referees . . . and in lieu of grace and style we have the cult of informality, which in some obscure way is regarded as democratic virtue."[3]

Characteristic of most arguments, some speakers agreed with the student stand for relevancy. Concurring, Secretary of Labor, W. Willard Wirtz reprimanded commencement speakers for having "a good deal in common with grandfather clocks: standing usually some six feet tall, typically ponderous in construction, more traditional than functional, relating essentially commonplace information."[4] Others compared them to Polonius, and criticized this type speaker for "speaking only to himself and to his own generation, confessing his own failures or omissions or hopes, and interpreting the world in his own image."

In spite of speaker response, protests escalated by June 1966, and in many instances graduates were joined by sympathizing faculty members. Protesting the presentation of an honorary degree to Robert McNamara, "a dozen N.Y.U. faculty members and 131 graduates . . . walked out of their commencement exercises to protest U. S. military action in Vietnam."[5] Picket signs outside read: "No Honors for War Criminals." In the same year, without incident, Mays received honorary degrees from three universities: Morris College in Sumter, South Carolina; Ricker College in Houlton, Maine; and Raleigh, North Carolina's Shaw University.

June 1967 was considered a tranquil year for major universities. Consequently, universities and colleges and the government used caution. Those members of Lyndon Johnson's cabinet who identified with the president's policies in Vietnam turned down invitations. Universities and colleges used a low-key approach. They invited speakers who would not disturb the campus: The University of Michigan invited Zakir Husain, President of India; Yale awarded an honorary degree to the jazz immortal, Duke Ellington; Hubert Humphrey spoke on peace at four colleges; Roy Wilkins, of the N.A.A.C.P., appeared at Oberlin. At his granddaughter's

[3]"Dissent on Dissent," *Newsweek*, June 21, 1965, 86.
[4]"Commencement 1965: The Generational Conflict," *Time* 85 (June 18, 1965), 32.
[5]"Universities," *Time* 87 (June 17, 1966), 74.

school, Shipley School for Girls, Dwight Eisenhower discussed the "perils of the miniskirt."[6]

The following year, the class of '68 at Columbia University saw two commencements. One took place in the Cathedral of St. John the Divine, normally the substitute location when it rained. The other was staged on the steps of Low Library by the 300 protesting graduates who had walked quietly out of the cathedral when Richard Hofstadter began the commencement address.[7] Most commencement ceremonies that year were quiet and peaceful, as was the situation when Benjamin Mays addressed the 4,191 graduates at Michigan State University.

Neither a businessman nor a politician, Mays utilized his ministerial training and speaking experience to adapt to potentially restless listeners. Speaking on less controversial subjects, he escaped campus protest. As the protest rhetoric escalated in 1964, Mays spoke to a polite audience at a small liberal arts college for men—St. Vincent College, in Latrobe, Pennsylvania. In 1965 while commencement speakers spoke out against the activism at major universities, Mays spoke of values to a predominantly black audience at Lincoln University in Jefferson City, Missouri. Before quiet audiences, during the protest lull of 1967, Mays received honorary degrees from Harvard University, Cambridge, Massachusetts; Morgan State College, Baltimore, Maryland; and Grinnell College, Grinnell, Iowa.

Even though attitudes had changed on his own campus at Morehouse, Mays was not a victim of the academic protests and student discontent. For one thing in 1967 during the heat of national unrest, Mays delivered his final commencement address as President of Morehouse College and retired at age 72. Before a warm cheering audience, he received an honorary degree from the college where he had been President for twenty-seven years.

Mays's customary formality, conservatism, and candor in speaking, along with his non-political allegiance, shielded him from the stigma of academic protests. Considering these qualities, this chapter focuses on commencement speeches that Benjamin Mays delivered at six universities: June 13, 1954, "His Goodness Was Not Enough," Bucknell University, Lewisburg, Pennsylvania; January 8, 1960, "Education—To What End?"

---

[6]"Playing It Safe," *Newsweek* 69 (June 26, 1967), 78.
[7]"The Class of '68," *Newsweek* 71 (June 17, 1968), 101.

University of Liberia, Monrovia, Liberia; June 9, 1968, "The Universities' Unfinished Work," Michigan State University, East Lansing, Michigan; June 8, 1970, "Three Enemies of Mankind: A Challenge to the University," Emory University, Atlanta, Georgia; May 31, 1970, "The Challenge of the Seventies," Centre College, Danville, Kentucky; May 19, 1975, "Abraham or Terah, Which?," Dillard University, New Orleans, Louisiana.

SOCIAL SETTINGS

The setting for Mays's commencement addresses ranged from the 80,000 seat Spartan Stadium of Michigan State University in East Lansing, to the intimate oak tree-lined quadrangle of the Dillard University campus in New Orleans. The audiences also reflected diversity., The Michigan State address was delivered to parents and friends of 4,191 graduates; the Dillard address was delivered to parents and friends of some 200 graduates. As might be expected, the diversity in audience size displayed little difference in the degree of pomp and ceremony, the characteristics of the audience, and the structure of the commencement exercise. In order to get a picture of the schools discussed, a brief current profile of the six institutions will serve to indicate differences in type, location, size, religious affiliation, and finances.

Bucknell University, founded in 1846, is located in a town of 6,000 in Lewisburg, Pennsylvania. This private institution, built on 300 acres of land, had an enrollment of 3,200 graduate and undergraduate students. Sixty percent of these students are Protestant. Bucknell's admission policies are ranked as "highly selective," resulting in eighty-eight percent of the freshmen in the top fifth in their high school graduating classes and ninety-five percent in the top two-fifths. More than two-thirds of the faculty members held doctoral degrees. Tuition was two thousand dollars and fifty percent of the student body received financial aid.

The University of Liberia, the major educational institution of the country is located in Monrovia, Liberia, on the continent of Africa. It was founded as a college in 1862 and became a university in 1951. It incorporates Liberia College, Teacher's College, School of Law, College of Agriculture and Forestry, College of Business and Public Administration, College of Medicine and College of Science and Technology. The University had one hundred and ninety faculty members for an enrollment of 1,980 students. No information was given on the tuition or the admission policies.

Michigan State University, founded in 1855, covers two thousand acres in East Lansing, Michigan, and had an enrollment of 47,796 graduate and undergraduate students. The admission policy is classified as "selective", but the university has "enrolled more national merit scholars than any other institution of higher learning." Eighty percent of the freshmen were in the top fifth of their graduating classes and ninety percent were in the top two-fifths. The tuition was $630 and $1,485 for out-of-state students. Fifty percent of the students received financial aid.

Emory University, private and formerly Methodist related, is located on 500 acres in Atlanta, Georgia. Founded in 1836, it had an enrollment of 7,334 graduate and undergraduate students. The admission policy was considered "highly selective", with eighty percent of the freshmen in the top fourth of their graduating classes. The tuition was twenty-four hundred dollars and only twenty percent of the students received financial aid. Ninety percent of the faculty members above instructor level held doctorates; consequently, the "faculty compensation is above the national average."

Centre College is located on 50 acres in the small town of Danville, Kentucky, four miles from Louisville, Kentucky. Formerly a Presbyterian school, Centre was founded in 1819 and by the time of Mays's speech had an enrollment of 800. The admission policy was "very selective", with seventy percent of the freshman from the top fifth of their graduating classes; ninety percent were in the upper two-fifths. The tuition was two thousand dollars and only thirty-eight percent of the students received financial aid.

Dillard University, with an enrollment of 1,186, is located on sixty-two acres in New Orleans, Louisiana. This university, founded in 1869, is still affiliated with the United Church of Christ and the United Methodist Church. Admission was open to high school graduates with the required fifteen units from a recognized high school. Tuition was thirteen hundred dollars and ninety-five percent of the students received financial aid.

AUDIENCES

At these universities, Mays spoke to four predominantly white audiences and two predominantly black audiences, namely, the University of Liberia and Dillard University. Mays stated that his "philosophy for dealing with the predominantly black and predominantly white audiences is essentially as in one," and that he usually considers "a current topic that would be of interest to the graduates in the senior class and to the faculty and commencement listeners." However, Mays explained that he was aware of existing job discrimination against blacks and, therefore, selected his subject according to the needs of those to whom he was speaking.

The descriptions of the institutions suggest that Mays's audiences differed on economic and educational levels. Traditionally, at these universities, the predominantly white audiences included a larger number of alumni and guests in addition to faculty, family and friends. The amount of tuition, financial aid, and admission policies of the predominantly white universities suggest that their audiences were generally middle to upper middle class with third or fourth generation college graduates. Possibly they would have attended many such occasions and would, therefore, be more demanding of a commencement speaker.

The audience at predominantly black University of Liberia probably was highly selective since the small discriminating student population represented only a limited segment of the people. On the other hand, predominantly black Dillard University had an open door admission policy; students are accepted from all levels of academic preparation. However, they must meet the standards established by the university in order to remain beyond the first semester. Of those who remain, ninety-five percent received financial aid, a fact that indicated the general economic status of attending students. Thus a large number of students come from poor families, a condition that may indicate a smaller number of middle or upper middle class relatives and friends in the commencement audience. In an article Mays explains that investigation of the educational status and the economic background of the majority of the parents and relatives of blacks students prove they cannot "assume a superior air toward the average and less-than-average citizens in the community, for the vast majority of them will be taking that attitude toward their parents, sisters, brothers, uncles, aunts, and near kin."[8] Granted progress has been made in many areas economically

---

[8] Mays, "The Role of the Negro Liberal Arts College in Post-War Reconstruction," *Journal of Negro Education*, 9 (July, 1942), 403.

with the availability of better jobs, but education has moved along at a slower pace. With this fact in mind, the audience at Dillard University may have been less sophisticated and knowledgeable of commencement exercises in general and commencement speakers in particular. The new experience may contribute to a larger interest in the awarding of degrees than in what a speaker had to say. However, since Mays chose a religious theme for this church related institution, he was probably accepted readily as a preacher.

The barely one hundred graduates and their guests at Centre College certainly created an intimacy for the speaker that was impossible to achieve for the guests and friends of the 4,141 graduates at Michigan State University. Bucknell and Emory Universities probably had similar audiences in that they had "highly selective" admission policies, were private with some religious affiliation, and over fifty percent of their faculty members had doctorates. The difference was that Emory, a southern university, had twice as many students, but only twenty percent received financial aid in comparison to fifty percent at northern Bucknell University.

GOALS

Mays utilized the same goals for the commencement addresses as he did generally for his sermons: to inform and stimulate his audience of the need for social change. The commencement listeners, however, were different because they represented varying segments of society. The speaker would have less in common with them than he would as preacher in a church. Therefore, Mays had to make his message relevant for the restless graduate, and stimulating for the disinterested and undecided listener.

Prior to the period of fashionable requests for black speakers, Mays was compelled to argue his convictions from the pulpit in black churches and in articles written for journals and black owned newspapers, for at that time speaking in public involved certain risks for a black man. Originally Mays argued mainly that the church had a role in correcting social ills; but by the late Forties his goal was to attract the attention of society by attacking the racial and economic status of the schools. Believing that "segregation in education restricts and circumscribes the mind," and "puts a limit to free inquiry and investigation," Mays argued that "legalized segregation inevitably resulted in inferior schools, inferior accommodations, and inferior jobs."[9]

Believing effective interchange to be the answer to many problems, Mays contended that "most of the white people . . . have never known the cultured and trained Negro." As a result, "Negroes and white people in the South never had honest communication and if what is communicated is false, it can hardly be called communication." Mays explained that the May 17, 1954 decision of the United States Supreme Court acted as an instrument that paved the way for honesty between the races.[10]

Escalating his speaking by accepting "every invitation to speak for the people," Mays chose the platform from which to reinforce his written arguments. He outlined two simple prerequisites for a successful public speaker: "First, the speaker should be sure that his message has real content, and second, the speaker should say only what he believes." Explaining this pulpit oratory, Marcus Boulware described his theory as an embodiment of "the public speaking of Jesus Christ who spoke his doctrine as utmost truths." In an interview in 1977, Mays agreed, stating that his major goal in any speech was "to tell the truth." He apparently followed the tenets of John Broadus who explains that "the preacher's aim is to convince the judgment, kindle the imagination, move the feelings, and give a power impulse to the will in the direction of truth's requirement."[11]

Since Mays concerned himself with telling the truth, his primary goal was to have his audience believe his assertions. Then technically his immediate goal was to achieve a favorable response. Thonssen, Baird, and Braden contend that "response is a major determinant of rhetorical effectiveness;" and that "by its inherent nature, speech seeks response." Therefore, the main concern of any speaker is mastering the necessary skills needed for gaining an effective response. Using this criterion, the writer assumes that Mays believed his listeners were aware of the existing condi-

---

[9]Mays, "The Color Line Around the World," *Journal of Negro Education*, 6 (April 1937), 141; "Segregation in Higher Education," *Phylon*, 10 (April, 1949), 401.

[10]Mays, "A Plea for Straight Talk Between the Races," *Atlantic Monthly* 206 (December 1960), 85-86.

[11]Marcus H. Boulware, *The Oratory of Negro Leaders 1900-1968* (Westpoint, Connecticut: Negro Universities Press, 1969), 189; John A. Broadus, *The Preparation and Delivery of Sermons* (New York: Harper and Brother, 1944), 11.

tions. Evidently he chose to (1) make the audience believe there was a need for change; (2) reorder systematically their thinking; and (3) as Alan Monroe puts it—"to direct them toward a definite course of action" by making the aroused feelings lasting.[12]

Apparently Mays divided his audience into two groups and devised a strategy to inform those auditors who knew least about the subject while stimulating those who were more knowledgeable. Ultimately most would be on the same level when he presented his recommendations, either implicit or explicit. It is not always clear whether Mays sought only a covert response or whether he opted for an overt response. The subtlety of his approach makes it difficult to determine. His persistent concern for social change compels one to expect an immediate call for action, rather than the optimistic belief in the future action of man. Mays's speeches set out to build "good human relations based on truth, honesty, and sincerity." His heritage instilled the impetus for change within him and apparently his ultimate goal was to create a similar momentum in the hearts of modern society.[13]

THEMES

Mays used the same themes for social change in the commencement addresses that he used in his sermons: war, poverty, racism, and social justice. Striving for a lasting arousal of emotions, Mays addressed himself to the stimulation of man's attitudes in recognizing the need for implementing change. Many of Mays's commencement addresses before 1960 reflected his customary practice of using religious texts to develop his themes. Mays was equally as direct and explicit in his commencement addresses as he was in the sermons, but the themes were not as steeped in scripture as they were in his sermons. In the address at Bucknell University, given on 13 June 1954, he demonstrated his usual reliance on a biblical text. This address was given in the wake of the Supreme Court's *Brown v. Board of Education* decision declaring segregation in the public schools unconstitutional. The

---

[12]Lester Thonssen, A. Craig Baird, and Waldo W. Braden, *Speech Criticism* (New York: The Ronald Press, 1970), 535-36; Alan H. Monroe, *Principles and Types of Speeches* (Chicago: Scott, Foresman, 1962), 391.

[13]Mays, *Atlanta Monthly* (December 1960): 89.

fact that Bucknell is a private institution, in a small northern Pennsylvania town with sixty percent of the student body Protestant, apparently provided Mays with an audience likely to sympathize with the biblical concepts of a black Baptist college president from the South. Being a black speaker before a predominantly white audience probably influenced Mays's strategy very little. Seemingly, Mays was primarily concerned with the economic status of his audience and their subsequent assistance; the fact that his audience was white was incidental.

The address at Bucknell was based on Luke 16:19-31, relating to the fate of the rich man who ignored the beggar at his door. Speaking to an affluent audience, Mays made a strong plea for the development of a social conscience, while explaining two of his social change themes: the existence of poverty and the need for social justice. Revealing his knowledge of world conditions and magnifying the growing destitution at home, Mays spoke of a large number of people dying of slow starvation, specifically referring to the "starving millions in Asia."

Emphasizing the need for social justice in "trying times," Mays stressed that man should begin worrying about his brother, implying that no one can escape involvement because "the destiny of each man is tied up with the destiny of another." To point out the importance of this concept, he explained the importance of good human relationships, stating that "we are so interlaced and interwoven that what affects one touches all."

At the University of Liberia Mays followed the trend of the 1960s, speaking on the practical aspects of gaining an education. The university that consisted of a small enrollment comprised less than one-tenth percent of the million and a half population. These Liberians were probably interested in a realistic outlook to their problems. Consequently, Mays held biblical references to a minimum. Though far removed from the college campuses of the United States, Mays spoke as an interested black man to a black audience, and was concerned with stimulating attitudes toward improving conditions for the less fortunate. Therefore, he addressed himself to the question, "Education—To What End?" Mays listed for the graduates various selfish reasons for obtaining an education. Then he emphasized the tremendous achievements possible for those who pursue education for unselfish reasons, for reasons designed to help "elevate the masses."

Back in the United States, Mays remembered the hostile world of the early twentieth century when he was a poor young man struggling to get an education. Noting present conditions, Mays asserted to his audiences at Michigan State and Emory that the world was no different for the elements of war, poverty, and racism still exist. He did more than guide the youth into the so called "hostile" world; instead he attempted to prepare them for its realities.

The speeches at Michigan State and at Emory Universities addressed the same theme that the "priorities of colleges and universities should be to eliminate war, abolish poverty, and exterminate racism." Mays entitled the earlier speech at Michigan State, "The Universities' Unfinished Work." Two years later, however, with only a few changes, he called his address at Emory University, "The Three Enemies of Mankind." Explicit in the introduction of his first theme, probably because of the anti-war feelings of most college youths, Mays asserted: "When it comes to war, it can be argued with considerable logic that man is not any more civilized today than he was ages ago." Secondly, apparently directed at the typically complacent American, he argued that "poverty is not only in far off South America, Africa, Asia, and the Middle East, but poverty is here in the affluent U.S.A." Mays introduced his theme on racism with a definition by noted anthropologist Ruth Benedict:

> Racism is the dogma that one ethnic group is condemned by nature to hereditary inferiority and another group is destined to hereditary superiority. It is the dogma that the hope of civilization depends upon eliminating some races and keeping others pure. It is the dogma that one race has carried progress throughout human history and alone ensure future progress.

Speaking at Centre College on the topic, "The Challenge of the Seventies," Mays introduced three of his social change themes. Apparently mindful of the turbulent Sixties and describing his feelings, Mays opened with a quotation by Thomas Paine: "These are the times that try men's souls." Reflecting this condition, he discussed the war in Vietnam and the spreading of the war into Cambodia. He questioned the wisdom of the United States in spending more money for expeditions to the moon than for "the 29,900,000 Americans in the United States living in poverty." He pointed out that the racial problem "is the most explosive problem confronting the United States today." Aside from the old problems of war, poverty, and race, Mays reminded these students of the problems of a population explosion, water and air pollution, and the increased drug problem.

Mays attested to the uncordial treatment of an aggressive society, but occasionally he lacked first hand experience. For instance, he was too young for one war and too old for another, yet he maintained a knowledge of the demoralizing effects of war because he lived through a period when blacks agonized over the fact that they were permitted to fight abroad, but they were not permitted to vote at home. Mays was "fifty-two years old when he was permitted to vote for the first time."[14]

In speaking to the predominantly black audience at Dillard University, Mays was strongly concerned with advancement. In an effort to enhance change, Mays commented on the many facets of minority problems. He used the biblical story of the achievements of Abraham and Terah as an basis for the proposition—"satisfaction must never be your lot." The idea was that Terah was complacent because he became satisfied when he attained success in Hanan and remained there even though his goal was to journey on to Canaan. Abraham, on the other hand, was left with the responsibility of going on to Canaan where he not only formed a great nation, but was "immortalized in history and eternity." Mays explained the need to achieve above one's capacities in order to avoid complacency. To this predominantly black group he added the problems of "white flight" which he inferred maintains segregated housing, and the "black on black" crimes that significantly retard black growth. By this he meant that not only is the population of blacks affected by the crimes, but the image presented to the general public is detrimental to the cause of those seeking assistance for the black man in need.

ORGANIZATION

Mays structured his commencement addresses using the classical Aristotelian division for epideictic speeches: the exordium, preparing the way; the exposition, explaining the theme; emotional proof, amplifying the

---

[14]Bennett, "The Last of the Great Schoolmasters," *Ebony* 32 (December 1977), 76.

theme; and the peroration, inspiring the auditors.[15] Similarly, John Broadus describes the formal elements of a sermon as the introduction, discussion, and conclusion. In examining the organization of these speeches the writer will consider the following areas: the development of speech divisions, the proportioning of materials, and the general adaptation to the specific audience.

Opening statements differed from speech to speech because Mays sometimes used varying pleasantries to establish ethical appeal before going into his formal introduction. For example, with the predominantly black audience in Liberia and with the predominantly southern white audience in Atlanta, Mays opened with conventional courtesies. At the University of Liberia he expressed his delight at being honored, extending greetings from Morehouse College. Modestly, Mays acknowledged that sixty nations were represented, and, ". . . yet you have invited me, an American . . . you have conferred upon me a signal honor which I hardly deserve, but which I shall cherish as long as I live. You not only honor me today, but most of all you honor Morehouse College in Atlanta, Georgia, U.S.A." Evidently attempting to create an atmosphere of harmony between the two schools, Mays reminded the audience that, "Morehouse is not in Atlanta, Georgia, alone, but throughout the United States and the world wherever Morehouse men are found. Morehouse is here in Liberia, and we are proud of the work being done by Morehouse men in Liberia."

At Emory University Mays expressed his gratitude for being invited. He admitted good heartedly to the audience that, "Nobody came here this early in the morning just to hear me speak. . . . The trustees, the president and faculties are here in the line of duty. Members of the graduating class . . . to get diplomas. The rest . . . to see . . . graduates." Mays closed his opening remarks by saying, "So whether you like it or not, you are stuck with me for approximately twenty minutes beginning now."

Apparently following the tenets of Cicero "to teach first before using techniques of pathos," Mays revealed his religious proposition early in the introduction of his speech "His Goodness Was Not Enough" at Bucknell University. He first read Luke 16:15-31, a passage on Dives, a rich man, and Lazarus, a beggar, who sat humbly by seeking only crumbs from the

---

[15]Thonssen, Baird, and Braden, 74.

table. Specifically, Mays stated his theme: "To explain why a man, who in the traditional sense was a good man and despite that fact, is condemned and consigned to a place of torture and torment." Mays explained the often misinterpreted version of the parable that Dives was condemned because he was rich and Lazarus was rewarded because he was poor. Instead, Mays viewed Dives as a man lacking social conscience and Lazarus as a victim of social injustice.

Attempting to show similarity between the social injustices of biblical times with that of modern times, Mays described the poor who lack sufficient food, proper health programs, and necessary education. Balancing his materials, he drew a parallel to show the selfishness of modern man with his possessions. To this university audience, at a school where ninety-five percent of the freshmen were in the upper two-fifths of their high school class, Mays argued that social justice is a basic right for all and must not be based on class and selfish existence.

Issuing a warning, Mays closed his Bucknell speech by summarizing the ultimate fate of Dives who because of his lack of social conscience, built "a gulf so fixed and so wide that it was too late for Dives to make amends." Concerned for the prevailing problems of economic growth in Liberia, Mays spoke to the select few who unfortunately represented an insignificant number of the million and a half inhabitants. But Mays knew that he had to reach the intellectuals of the country in order to change the conditions of the masses. Therefore, "Education—To What End?," the address at the University of Liberia, was briefly introduced with a few statements on the virtues of nations spending billions of dollars for education leading to his theme—"Education For What?"

Using the problem-solution-benefit organization, Mays first gave the purpose of education and distinguished between selfish and unselfish reasons for acquiring an education. Second, he emphasized the need for the unselfish application of education in order to help elevate the masses. Finally, he established the role of education in creating a better life in Liberia for everyone. Mays reasoned that education is an indispensable weapon because an educated man, a trained race, or a literate nation is better qualified to defend itself against the strong and the unscrupulous; and the trained mind can be persuaded to incorporate needed change. Mays closed by offering a challenge and by predicting that the University of

Liberia would "play its part in furthering the cause of peace, in abolishing poverty, in eliminating disease, and in extending the reality of freedom."

Speaking at the nation's first land-grant college, Michigan State University and at the prestigious private college, Emory University, Mays gave identical addresses. He introduced the addresses by predicting future accomplishments of man: "Diseases will be conquered . . . a man placed on the moon, . . . the comforts of life will be multiplied, . . . an increase in college graduates." However, he pointed out that man still had not conquered three of the major enemies of mankind: war, poverty, and racism. Mays stated his assertive proposition that the priorities of universities should be to eliminate war, abolish poverty, and exterminate racism.

In "The Universities' Unfinished Work" at Michigan State and "Three Enemies of Mankind" at Emory University, Mays divided the problem into four areas, each based on the proposition that the university should assume the responsibility of educating students how to live in a world without war, poverty, and racism, rather than educating them simply how to get ahead in the world. Mays argued that the resulting benefits would: First, produce a United Nations which will be "made to work so that the behavior of big nations will come under its judgment as well as that of small nations;" Second, insure social justice for the poor in the United States, "where no family of four will get less than $3,300 a year income, where every able-bodied man will be guaranteed a job with a minimum adequate wage, where good schools exist, and where recreational facilities and schools are adequate;" Third, exterminate racism, not only for the good of the United States, but for the good of the world, thereby, laying the foundation for a permanent peace. Lastly, Mays argued that educators should define the kind of world they are trying to build; they should devise ways to measure progress in goodness and in developing right attitudes as is done in measuring progress in intellectual development; and they should develop skills to make students into that kind of citizen.

At Michigan State and at Emory University Mays predicted in his conclusion that most graduates would be successful in their chosen fields. He reminded them of the importance of social justice for all Americans. However, at the Methodist related Emory University Mays added a segment to his conclusion and cautioned the graduates not to doubt their ability to contribute to American society as one individual. He reminded them that, "great ideas are born for the most part in the mind of one man," and that, "every man is called of God . . . to do something worthwhile." At both universities Mays challenged the graduates, "to join in a crusade to eliminate war, abolish poverty, and exterminate racism."

Changing times apparently brought about a shift in focus and attitude for Benjamin Mays. Seemingly in 1970 he was now not as concerned with stimulating an awareness of the need for social change as he was stimulating a dissatisfaction with existing conditions. Speaking to the audience at Centre College, where only thirty-eight percent of the student body received financial aid, Mays evidently felt he could dispense with preliminaries. Pointedly he introduced his speech "The Challenge of the Seventies with a quotation from Thomas Paine—"These are the times that try men's souls." This sentence served as the theme for the speech.

The discussion was divided into two parts: problems and recommendations. In the approximately twenty-five minute speech, Mays again asserted that the problems of war, poverty, and racism are conditions that continue to contribute to the overall twisted values of the United States. He explained how "leaders appropriate money far more freely for expeditions to the moon than for the physical well-being of the nation . . . and would rather outdo Russia in space than provide adequate food for millions of poor Americans."

Mays pointed out the role of the graduates in dealing with the problems of war, poverty, and racism. Probably realizing that those untouched by these problems may lack concern, Mays argued against taking a laissez-faire attitude and cautioned against avoiding involvement by blaming the less fortunate for their conditions. The conclusion of the speech was almost as brief as the introduction. Mays closed by challenging graduates to abolish war, eliminate poverty, and eradicate racism. Additionally, he asked them to "blot out drug addiction, control the increase in population, and save us from air and water pollution."

Opening the speech at Dillard University, a denominational religious college, Mays used the rhetorical question—"Abraham or Terah, Which?" He told the parable of Terah who set out for the land of Canaan, but upon arriving in Haran and becoming successful, settled and many years later died there. However, before Terah's death and in spite of success, it became Abraham's responsibility to leave Haran and go to Canaan where he built a great nation. Following his interpretation of the parable, Mays explained the interpretation of an American preacher who called Terah complacent; Mays disagreed and pointed out that it was Terah's idea to leave Ur in the first place and he was not a failure in Haran, but was a successful man. However, leading to his theme, Mays considered the other view that if Terah did not continue because he was satisfied, ". . . then that is a condition to be deplored." With this condition in mind, Mays stated his recommending proposition: "Satisfaction must never be your lot."

In developing his theme, Mays compared the success of Terah who stayed in Haran with the greatness of Abraham who moved on to Canaan. Obviously, Mays attempted to instill in the graduates that they must not become satisfied with the achievements of their ancestors, but must build and accomplish in order to achieve benefits for themselves and for mankind. Mays insisted that with diligence they could help "erase poverty and crime, war and disease, discrimination and segregation, injustice and man's inhumanity to man." After emphasizing the tragedies of complacency, Mays pointed out two kinds of ideals: personal development and service to the people. Using the parable as a reference for emphasizing the ideals, Mays reminded the graduates not to be satisfied because their elders had brought them from Ur of the Chaldees to Haran, because "we are a long way from Canaan."

As in previous speeches, Mays argued briefly for social change, pointing out that the racial situation is not only a race problem but is also a class problem; that war in Vietnam proved nothing except tremendous deaths and scores of wounded men, and high expenditures; and that poverty, unemployment, and crime are still highly visible.

Mays closed his speech by reminding the predominantly black audience of their courageous ancestors who survived under the most austere conditions. He offered words of encouragement and predicted that they would take up the struggle for human rights where their elders stopped.

FORMS OF SUPPORT

Mays employed illustrations, quotations, statistics, and epigrams to heighten his appeal for social change. Because of tight schedules, he had limited time in which to impress his audiences. Mays typically used explicit forms of amplification to assure speedy understanding and subsequently gain substantial agreement. Gray and Braden describe amplification as the process by which speakers "repeat, enlarge, review, and even exaggerate and dramatize" in order to highlight concepts and ideas. Mays applied this process of amplification to his commencement speeches.

Illustration

In the two speeches based on biblical parables, Mays used numerous illustrations as amplification. For example, at Bucknell he used an illustration to introduce his speech. Apparently hoping to develop interest and create a mental picture of the unjust biblical situation, Mays told the graduates about Dives, a selfish rich man. The illustration was designed to identify similar attitudes encountered in a selfish society. For instance, he explained to the graduates that maybe they did not believe in Hell, but argued that if there is no Hell, God should create one. Using modern examples, Mays magnified his contention:

> There ought to be a Hell for a man like Nero who burned innocent Christians alive; . . .A Hell for Hitler and his associates—who killed 6,000,000 Jews; . . . A Hell for Mussolini; . . . A Hell for Jumbulinganada, a notorious criminal of South India. . . .

Similarly, Mays combined biblical and modern illustrations to dramatize his contention that "God is no respecter of persons":

> . . . God called Abraham, a rich man, and made him the Father of his people; . . . God called Moses, a keeper of the flock and made him the lawgiver and the great emancipator. God called Lincoln from a Kentucky log cabin . . . God called the two Roosevelts, born with silver spoons in their mouths, . . . God called Ramsey McDonald from a two room cabin in Scotland . . . . He called Churchill. . . . He called George Washington, a wealthy Virginian. . . . He called Booker Washington, the slave-born. . . . He made Milton a great poet, but he made Shakespeare greater than Milton.

At Dillard arguing the plight of Terah, Mays tried to instill in the graduates the desire to think "lofty thoughts and to accomplish great things." He listed many who had achieved greatness at early ages.

Coleridge wrote his "Ancient Mariner" at 25. Goethe and Victor Hugo produced works of enduring value at 20. Lord Bacon began to philosophize at 16. Julius Caesar began his career at 17; William the Conqueror before 20 . . . Rembrandt famous at 24. Mozart, Beethoven, Mendelssohn, Schubert and Schumann were real producers at 20, having produced something original by 13. Jesus . . . at 12, Booker T. Washington at 30. Countee Cullen and Langston Hughes . . . in their twenties. Dunbar and Martin Luther King Jr. . . . in their thirties.

To emphasize the role of education at the University of Liberia, Mays used an illustration to defend his position that an educated man or a trained nation is better qualified to defend itself, because "strong nations for the most part exploit weak nations, that strong races usually take advantage of weak races, and that strong individuals are inclined almost always to push weak individuals around." Clarifying his position, Mays admitted that he had never "known a nation, however religious, seen a race, however democratic . . . , known an individual, however Christian . . . who would not take advantage of the ignorant, the weak and the coward."

In protesting the war in Vietnam, Mays reminded the graduates at Michigan State and at Emory University that "man is not any more civilized today than he was ages ago." Using examples to clarify, he noted that centuries ago, "the Persians, the Babylonians, and the Egyptians sought to settle their differences on the battlefield. The Greeks, the Romans, and the Carthaginians resorted to the sword in order to achieve their objectives." He cited the modern experience of learning nothing from wars because two decades after World War I, came World War II, followed by the war with Korea, and then the war in Vietnam.

Dramatizing the plight of the poor in "The Challenge of the Seventies," Mays contended that "We are what we are by luck or the grace of God," that no one can determine whether he will be a genius or a moron. He used an illustration of two babies born at the same time, one from wealthy parents and the other from poverty stricken parents. Explaining, Mays said:

By virtue of the origin of their births, the son of the wealthy parents will experience cultural surroundings . . . and his educational advantages will be unlimited. The poor boy may never go beyond the fifth grade. Why should the wealthy boy think he is better and

look down on his brother in poverty? Neither chose his parents ...
or their places of birth.

Apparently Mays wanted to set the record straight for his small audience
at Centre College who may erroneously have believed the racial situation had
improved greatly in the United States. He told the audience in Kentucky
that "few blacks are better off in 1970 than they were in 1950." Speaking
of the economic inequality between black and white in the United States,
Mays argued that for the masses this condition was hardly any better than
it was twenty-five years ago. He stirred up the unforgettable images of the
riots in Los Angeles, Cleveland, Detroit, Newark, and Washington as
reminders of the still existing racial problem.

Quotation

Mays always recited his quotations from memory and that he was careful
to select quotations easily recognizable to the audience. Mays used
quotations in all parts of his speech, but his chief method was to leave a
lasting impression stirring the emotions of his audience with poetry in his
conclusions.

As might be expected, Mays used biblical quotations at Bucknell and
Dillard Universities. However, these were few in number. At Bucknell, Mays
supported his statement that one man's destiny is tied up with another, by
interpreting a quotation from Jesus, "Inasmuch as ye did it unto the least
of these, ye did it unto me." He used a quotation from Luke 16:36 to
amplify his belief that the man who lacks a social conscience creates a great
gulf between himself and people: "Besides all that, a great gulf yawns
between us and you, to keep back those who want to cross from us to you
and also those who want to pass from you to us."

At Dillard, showing admiration for the enterprising actions of Abraham
and explaining why Abraham left Haran for Canaan, Mays pointed out how
God told Abraham, "Get thee out of my country, and from thy kindred, and
from thy father's house, unto a land that I will show thee and I will make of
thee a great nation, and I will bless thee and make thy name great, and thou
shalt be a blessing."

Mays quoted words of Omar Khayyam in the conclusion of the address at Bucknell University in order to impress the graduates that once history is made, it can never be changed:

The Moving Finger writes; and having writ, Moves on; nor all your piety or Wit Shall lure it back to cancel half a line, Nor all your Tears wash out a Word of it.

At the University of Liberia, Mays recited a poem by John Donne to remind his audience that "we are tied together with an inescapable destiny."

No man is an Island, apart to himself;
Each man is a piece of the Continent, a part of the Mainland;
If a clod of earth be washed away by the sea,
Europe is the less, as though a promontory were.
Every man's death affects me, because I am involved in humanity;
Therefore send not to learn for whom the bell tolls:
It tolls for thee!

Mays used the same quotation at Bucknell University and Centre College.

To the Liberians, Mays magnified his statement that education should make one sensitive to the needs of the world with a quotation from Eugene Debs: "As long as there is a lower class, I am in it. As long as there is a criminal element, I am of it. As long as there is a man in jail, I am not free." At Centre College Mays recited the same quotation to support his statement that "the destiny of each and every person is the destiny of all men."

He used quotations only in the introduction for the speeches at Michigan State and at Emory University. To amplify his statements concerning the potentials of man, Mays called on Shakespeare who makes Hamlet say:

What a piece of work is man! How noble in reason; how infinite in faculty! In form and moving how expressive and admirable; In action how like an angel; In apprehension how like a God!

Still enhancing the future role of man, Mays quoted Alexander Pope who says in his *Essay on Man*: "Go, wondrous creature! Mount where science guides; Go, men sure earth, weigh air, and state the tides; Instruct the planets in what orbs to run; Correct old time, and regulate the sun." Mays quoted the words of Disraeli to express his expectation of the university's role as "a center of light, liberty, and learning." This quotation led to his proposition that "the university's work will never be finished."

Statistics

Mays employed few statistics in his ceremonial speaking to support his statements. However, he did use the statistics as a type of shock treatment to inform and stimulate the thinking of his listeners. Often the audience was aware of the social ill mentioned but they did not know its severity. Therefore, Mays enhanced his message on social change by using overwhelming statistics concerning social injustices. For instance, at Michigan and Emory Universities Mays utilized statistics to amplify his contention that "education is wholly irrelevant when it comes to providing ways to build a war-free world." Quoting statistics to clarify his position against satisfaction to the predominantly black audience at Dillard University, Mays reminded them not to become complacent because integration only appears to be successful. Evidently employing statistics to shock the black audience, Mays argued the growing existence of black on black crime. He explained:

> In 1974 one person was shot to death every minute with a hand gun somewhere in the United States. Only 20% of the killings ... are done by criminals . . . Last year, 1974, 99.6 percent of all blacks murdered in Chicago were killed by blacks. Of the 682 blacks murdered in Chicago in 1974, 675 had blacks as their executioners.

Epigrams

Mays was personally pleased with his skill in the use of epigrammatic statements, of which he was particularly adept in wording. The usually applicable witty sayings were applied to guarantee not only audience acceptance but audience remembrance as well. Taken out of context, the epigrams lose some of their power, but essentially they demonstrate a skill in phrasing complementary to ceremonial speaking. For example, Mays told his audience at Bucknell that, "There is no virtue in poverty per se, and there is no vice in wealth per se." In order to restate the premise that "God is no respecter of persons," Mays said, "He calls the great and the small, the rich and the poor, the lettered and the unlettered to do his work." He reminded the audience that everyone owes a debt of gratitude to God, "no man can lift himself by his own bootstraps." In Monrovia, Mays summed up his argument that the purpose of education is to help mankind with the statement, "to whom much is given, much is required." Emphasizing the university's role at Michigan State and Emory Universities Mays told the audiences that, ". . . the town should come to gown and the gown should go to town so that there will be no unnecessary gap between those who live on the boulevards and those who live in the slums."

Emotional Appeal

Gray and Braden define appeals as "any procedure which will bring about some response, whether it be to impel the listeners to think, to feel, or to act." Motives are "the strivings toward these goals or end results" in an attempt to influence human behavior. As is traditional in ceremonial speaking, "Mays appealed to the emotions of his listeners, but he also used logical appeal. Seeing nothing unusual in this approach, Thonssen, Baird, and Braden contend that emotional expression and logical expression are not exclusive of each other. Consequently, Mays's appeal for social change was directed to the mind and to the heart so that the two played supporting roles in manipulating the audience to obtain his desired response.

The numerous speaking engagements provided Mays with considerable understanding of typical human reactions. The problem Mays faced was the problem of choice of motive to fit the various groups. Apparently dealing with different races amounted to dealing with different socioeconomic classes: those who needed help and encouragement and those who were needed to provide assistance for the less fortunate. The degree of help requested depended on the economic level of the school and its accompanying audience, and not on the predominant race present. Mays contended that the race problem was a class problem. Therefore, accepting the fact that people respond in accordance to their feelings, Mays proceeded to seek agreement by appealing mainly to fair play, altruism, ethnocentrism, self-esteem, and self-actualization.

As might be expected, Mays used mainly an altruistic appeal in his religious speech at Bucknell University. Based on a passage from St. Luke, "His Goodness Was Not Enough" made a strong plea for the development of a social conscience. Using the biblical characters of Dives and Lazarus as a parallel for middle and upper middle class man and the poor of the land, Mays explained that Dives should have done more than give to charity, he should have helped to build a society where no man needed to beg. Implying that outside intervention is necessary for the welfare of hopeless persons trapped within the system, Mays described the poor people of the earth who were starving mentally and physically. He reminded his audience that the strong and healthy "must be concerned about the plight of other peoples." Realizing that racial prejudice was less prevalent in a small northern town, Mays emphasized the dangers of class distinction instead. In explaining how Dives saw Lazarus as only a beggar, not worthy of the crumbs from his table, Mays made his altruistic appeal by requesting that the audience not be guilty of the same attitude. He reasoned:

> The test of good religion is not how we treat our peers and those above us, but how we treat those beneath us; not how we treat the man highest up, but how we treat the man farthest down, . . . but the real test of my religion would be how I treat the man who has nothing to give—no money, no social prestige, no honors. Not how I treat the educated, but how I treat the man who can't write his name.

In Monrovia Mays knew that the graduates before him represented only a small segment of the population of Liberia. Therefore, in appealing to self-actualization, he explained that "the use of education for the common good is mandatory because trained minds are rare," and that only "a small percentage of the total population of the world is college trained." Mays reinforced his appeal to duty by reminding his listeners that "man can fulfill his true destiny in this life only in proportion as his skills are used in the service of mankind." Because education is so vital in this country, Mays did not let up on his appeal to self-actualization, instead he set up a hypothetical situation to amplify his appeal:

For if one has a better mind than his fellows, more wealth than his fellows, is more favorably circumstanced than his fellows, has a better opportunity to develop than his fellows, he is obligated to use his skills in the interest of the common good.

Beyond presenting the practical values of education and arguing for needed social change in his address at the University of Liberia, Mays appealed to the self-esteem of his listeners. Aware of the problems in the country and the need for additional technology, he assured the graduates that trained minds would accomplish the necessary changes among nations, and the "University of Liberia will play its part."

Once Mays explained the intricacies of the "three major enemies" of mankind at Michigan State and Emory Universities, he obviously had to consider the complexity of his two audiences before making his appeals. Before the huge audience in Spartan Stadium at Michigan State University and before the basically southern audience of the much smaller private Emory University, Mays was more general in his appeals. He had the advantage of Michigan State being a northern university in East Lansing and possibly because of education and location would be more liberal toward change. However, even though Emory University was located in the South, it was also located in metropolitan Atlanta, and because of education and upper-class socioeconomic status, the audience might also be more open to change.

For those who accepted his argument that "the destiny of white and Negro America is still one destiny," Mays appealed to fair play. Seeking help by expounding on the proud American heritage for freedom, Mays asked his predominantly white audience at Michigan State and at Emory Universities:

> . . . to strive to desegregate and integrate America to the end that this great nation of ours, born in revolution and blood, conceived in liberty, and dedicated to the proposition that all men are created free and equal, will truly become the lighthouse of freedom where none will be denied because his skin is black, and none favored because his eyes are blue; where the nation is militarily strong but at peace, economically secure, but just; learned, but wise; and where the poorest will have a job and bread enough to spare.

In appealing to self-actualization, he recommended that the graduates solve the conflict between society and change. After reminding them all of their duty to society, Mays asked the graduates at both schools to develop their potentials to the fullest extent by becoming "involved in worthy programs designed to make a better world." Mays requested that they not turn their backs on the poor, but rather do their part "to enable them to rise to positions of respectability and honor."

In defining the role of educators, Mays reminded them of their duties as educated men "to create a world where good men will be free and safe to work to improve society and to make men better." It is interesting to note that Mays omitted the explicit statement to the educators at Emory University, where he presented the same argument but recommended by implication. One explanation is that Mays made an additional appeal to fair play in his address to the southern audience at Emory University which was not given at Michigan State University. Admitting that many in the audience were cynical about him and his motives and considered his statements about war, poverty, and racism to be mere facts of life, Mays disagreed and attempted to stimulate a sense of justice. He explained that "peace is better than war; an adequate standard of living is due every living creature; and black and white can live in the same community in peace and with justice." In a final appeal to a sense of justice, Mays assured his audience that "no man can maintain the integrity of his soul by giving allegiance to a lesser good."

Speaking in Danville, Kentucky, to the small audience at the exclusive Centre College, Mays expressed dissatisfaction with the twisted values of national political leaders in respect to their treatment of war, poverty, and racism. He specifically pointed out the discord and lack of progress in the areas of poverty and race relations. Because of the apparent upper class status of this audience, Mays chose to appeal to a sense of altruism. Obviously attempting to create a philanthropic atmosphere, he reminded them that "poverty will never knock on your door." Turning to the graduates, Mays asked them to accept the problems inherited from an earlier generation. He explained that they must solve the problems because "most . . ., being white, will never know what it is to be black and robbed of opportunities, opportunities which you will have for the sole reason that you were born white." He reminded them of the plight of the poor who were not always too lazy or lacking in mental ability to work. Striking out at excessive pride, Mays argued that "we are largely what we are by luck or the grace of God." Emphasizing this contention, he reconstructed illustrations to defend his position that there are "two things a man cannot choose: his parents and his place of birth."

Clearly appealing to an upper class status at Centre College, Mays commented on the quality of education given to the graduates, and that they were among "the favored few." He urged the graduates to "do something worthwhile which others can do; but by all means do that unique, distinctive thing which if you do not do it, it will never be done." Graduates were cautioned never to take a laissez-faire attitude toward the problems of their generation, but instead become "sensitive souls who hear the call to respond to the needs of our time."

For his predominantly black audience at church related Dillard University, Mays established his case by giving a lengthy discussion contrasting the biblical roles of Abraham and Terah. Acknowledging that some social change had taken place over the previous decade, Mays built an awareness of still existing social problems. Consequently, he warned the audience against a growing satisfaction with present accomplishments. He reminded the graduates that it was their duty to continue their education in some form after graduation. Switching briefly to an appeal to altruism, he urged them not to be "content to move on to Canaan for mere selfish reasons." Apparently using "Haran" to represent a current status in life and "Canaan" to represent a future status, Mays strategically interspersed his appeals with biblical references to either Abraham or Terah to heighten his appeal.

After lengthy biblical and modern illustrations, Mays appealed to self-esteem. He personally identified with the problems of continued discrimination, but explained that if enslaved ancestors had survived and multiplied for 246 years of cruel bondage, and his generation had lived through condoned lynching, political disfranchisement, and state supported segregation, he knew the graduates would not be turned around by anyone. Using a positive approach, Mays shows his confidence in the ability and determination of the graduates by stating, "I know . . . you will continue our struggle to the end."

Style

Often style is mistakenly related to delivery or to speaking mannerisms of a speaker. However, according to Thonssen, Baird, and Braden, rhetorical style is "the way in which a language pattern is used, under a given set of conditions, (1) to make ideas acceptable and (2) to get the response sought by the speaker."[16] Continuing they contend that style or language is important only to the extent that it helps prepare and subsequently open the minds of the hearers to the ideas developed in the speech.

Since commencement addresses are classified as epideictic or ceremonial speaking which appeals to the emotions, language must then serve as a stimulus in order to affect reactions in the listeners. I. A. Richards, in his discussion of emotions and attitudes, states that, "The attitudes evoked are the all-important part of any experience."[17] Richards describes the emotional experience as having two main features: ". . . a diffused reaction in the organ of the body brought about through sympathetic systems. The other is a tendency to action of some kind or groups of kind."[18] The idea behind these principles is that emotive language is used to support emotional attitudes which, subsequently, through stimulation will produce the desired response. Therefore, these principles can be applied to epideictic speaking which attempts to persuade people through their passions. The epideictic speaker is concerned primarily with putting his listeners in a favorable frame of mind.

The attitudes of the listeners are always a speaker's major concern and Mays was no different; he sought approval from all segments of his audience. His concern was reflected in his concentration on directness, correctness, and clearness of style. He rejected the use of charming phrases to project humor, or the use of slang to establish identification with the young. Instead Mays's language was serious throughout. Appropriately, he was constantly aware that his goal was to stimulate his audience and not to entertain them. Consequently, his oral style was simple, direct, and appropriate for the occasion and the listeners.

---

[16]Ibid., 515.

[17]I. A. Richards, *Principles of Literary Criticism* (New York: Harcourt, Brace and Work, 1925), 132.

[18]Ibid., 101.

The imposed time requirement compelled Mays to be brief, placing the burden of audience understanding on his use of language. Therefore, to achieve the desired understanding and subsequent agreement, Mays chose concreteness over abstractness, and favored the explicit applications of words.

An example of concrete language can be best seen in the one contention used in all of the commencement addresses considered. After surveying the problems demanding change, Mays stated simply and clearly: "The destiny of each and every person is the destiny of all men." Even though the wording varies slightly in each address, the conflict between society and change can be understood readily by those listeners in agreement. Complacent listeners are at least made to think about the reluctance of an affluent society to handle the problems of war, poverty, racism, and social injustice.

Most of Mays's emphasis was devoted to stimulating his affluent audience at Bucknell with emotive descriptions of the plush existence of Dives and the inhuman existence of Lazarus. However, he did use emotive words to magnify his quest for social change. Speaking of poverty, Mays described the poor people who had "diseased emaciated bodies" and who were "dying" of "slow starvation." To stir the feelings against war, Mays used names like Nero, Judas, Hitler, Napoleon and Mussolini, whom he referred to as war lords who committed political suicide.

On the other hand, Mays used the names of "Jesus of Nazareth, Gandhi and Nehru of India, Saint Francis of Assisi, Lincoln and Booker T. Washington of America, Schweitzer of France, and Tubman of Liberia," for his audience at the University of Liberia to show great men of history who "identified themselves with the common man."

Mays employed antithesis to impress his listeners when he told the audience in Monrovia that there is a fundamental selfishness or defect in human nature. He explained: "We respect strength and not weakness, courage and not cowardice, knowledge and not ignorance, the man who stands on his feet in a manly way and not the man who cringes and kowtows." Continuing the contrast of ideas to stimulate those of better circumstances, Mays reminded them that "The poor do not have an equal chance to bargain with the rich. The ignorant man starts out handicapped when confronted with the man who knows. The coward is licked as soon as he faces the fearless."

Mays opened his speech at Michigan State and Emory with repetition of the word "will" eleven times. Setting the pace for future accomplishments, Mays said:

> We will do many things, . . . Longevity will be . . . extended. . . . diseases will be conquered. Cancer will be cruel. We will . . . place man on the moon. Passenger planes will fly a thousand miles an hour. We will develop, . . . comforts . . . will be multiplied. We will increase the number of college graduates . . . More brilliant scholars will be born.

Typically, Mays used emotive language and sentences to stimulate the imagination of his listeners. Mays felt confident that most people oppose war and ignorance and perhaps only wanted to stir and not inform his auditors. For instance, in dealing with war and using startling statistics, Mays told the people that in the last 3,500 years there was a war somewhere on the earth "nine out of every ten hours." He told the northern and southern audience that "Goodness is as important as literacy. An honest heart is as important as a brilliant mind." He reminded them of popular leaders of the common man: "Jesus, John Kennedy, Robert Kennedy and Martin Luther King Jr.," explaining that all were men of peace, and all were murdered.

On more controversial ground, at Michigan State Mays protested the attitudes of the "racist" and the "Black Power" advocate who argue for "separatism." He omitted this statement at Emory University in the South. Perhaps he felt the terms would stir negative responses in the southern audience.

However, Mays dramatized the plight of the poor before both audiences, using emotive charged sentences to prod the imagination of affluent listeners. He described the nutritional anemia of pregnant mothers who were so ill-nourished that they were routinely given blood transfusions during childbirth. He discussed the pregnant mothers who were so nutritionally motivated for iron and calcium that they ate clay, and they ate starch for calories to supplement their food. Supplying possibly new information, he told of thousands of babies born each year to these mothers who subsequently develop protein deficiency and later permanent brain damage as a direct result. Mays described the children who went to school without breakfast and were sent home because they were in pain and too hungry to learn. Some mothers, he continued, kept their children home "so that at least they can cry themselves to sleep from hunger in their mother's arms."

To those less familiar with his emphasis on the deplorable urban conditions of the poor, Mays told of the people in cities who "go to the city dump digging for food." He explained that the people go there looking for "cheese, butter, meat, doughnuts, or whatever is edible that has been thrown away." Apparently, Mays felt confident in accomplishing his plea for social change by emphasizing the conditions of the poor before the middle and upper middle class audience at Michigan State and Emory. Using the same strategy at Centre College, Mays attempted to impress his audience with the death rate of the newborn babies of poor mothers, explaining that the infants died mainly because of malnutrition. He told of the irreversible brain damage caused by "protein deprivation," and how "protein and iron deficiency" caused "nutritional anemia."

Indicating that racism caused the widening gulf of economic inequality between black and white, Mays spoke of the slums and ghettoes that were increasing steadily. He reminded them of the riots in the cities of Los Angeles, Detroit, Newark, etc. He described the campus demands of black students that resulted in the wanton killing of six blacks, "shot in the back" by the National Guard in Augusta, Georgia, and the killing of two blacks at Jackson State College in Jackson, Mississippi, Mays evidently assumed these incidents had not been publicized in the small northern community of Danville, Kentucky.

Mays placed most of his emotive language in his scriptural message about Abraham and Terah for his audience at Dillard University. However, he did utilize the device of antithesis to argue against complacency for the youth satisfied with varying segments of change. For example, he said, "The tragedy of life is often not in our failure, but rather in our complacency; not in our doing too much, but rather in our doing too little; not in our living above our ability, but rather in our living below our capacities." As examples of premature achievers, he listed the names of great men from history who achieved at an early age: Coleridge who wrote his "Ancient Mariner" at age twenty-five, Goethe and Victor Hugo who produced works of value at twenty, Julius Caesar who began his career at seventeen, Michelangelo who produced great works by nineteen, among others. Hoping to influence by naming contemporary blacks who had achieved at a young age, Mays cited

Booker T. Washington, W. E. B. DuBois, Countee Cullen, Langston Hughes, and Martin Luther King Jr.

Because of the emphasis Mays placed on the themes for social change, he often duplicated his selection of emotive words. Attempting to mobilize the attitudes of the predominantly black audiences at Monrovia and at New Orleans, Mays attempted to dramatize the plight of the poor with the parable of the rich farmer who heard the "diseased, emaciated bodies" cry out for health, the "starving stomachs" cry out for bread, and the "illiterate minds" cry out for literacy.

Assessment

One may assume that Benjamin E. Mays was a successful commencement speaker because he received numerous speech invitations from many universities and colleges. With a variety of audiences it can be further assumed that Mays's apparent success is attributed to his effective speaking to various levels of people. A speaker must consider the interest levels of all listeners, namely, faculty and guests. One's skill is best demonstrated by making the message relevant to all.

Mays considered the graduates first in his presentation. With years of experience as a teacher and as a college president, Mays was in a position to identify with the graduates who were aware of mass arrests, court injunctions, suspensions, and negotiations of the 1950s and 1960s. It was obviously difficult to speak with the traditional sense of nostalgia, while at the same time remain aware of the radical chants of disenchanted students who opposed the war in Vietnam, who protested the delay in civil rights, and who cried out for an end to poverty and unemployment. Conscious of youth protest, Mays capitalized on the demands for change in the university by appealing for change in the structure of the American system. Young and old alike could relate his argument that the policy of preparing students to live in harmony should take precedence over concern for advancement in an affluent society.

To the general audience, Mays clearly focused on the here and now, often the slogans of the youth. Reflecting on national problems, Mays denounced war, poverty, racism, and social injustices. He contended that man generally avoided the truth concerning these problems because it was convenient to look the other way. Just as Booker T. Washington attempted to disprove the erroneous belief of nineteenth century southern whites that education would make the free black men criminals and antisocial, Mays attempted to prove to twentieth century man that poverty forces the poor into criminal acts and makes their behavior antisocial. Mays went a step further in dealing with the complexities of twentieth century man and argued that war drains the country financially; that racism stifles the growth of the country; and that social injustice destroys the brotherhood in man. Beyond the practical value of appealing for social change, he expounded on the personal benefits gained in providing change for all. His concern for social justice for everyone obviously removed any suspicious of any ulterior selfish motives. His pleas were based on the premise that man must change because "the destiny of each and every person is the destiny of all men."

Mays was unpretentious in his presentation; a simple direct style and contemporary subject matter describe his strength best. The simultaneous technique of explaining scripture while seeking social change, permitted the audience to carefully examine their own motives in response to the subtle attack on their individual weaknesses. Mays never lashed out with verbal assault; consequently, the auditors felt comfortable with the preacher-educator who was flexible enough to speak to everyone. His use of non-religious support blended with religious appeal obviously balanced his amplification, thereby, impeding the alienation of any listener. However, his consistency in the use of varied amplification is reminiscent of the "commonplaces" used by ancient Greek rhetoricians. In *The Art of Persuasion in Greece*, George Kennedy, describes commonplaces as memorized sayings, used again and again, and inserted into a speech like arguments to support some position. These commonplaces served as building blocks from which a speech could be constructed.

Finally, Mays was evidently cognizant of the attention span of most listeners and apparently agreed with the philosophy of James A. Winans who explains in *Speech-Making* that "too many words and phrases . . . make style tiresome. It is better to be brief than to be tedious."[19] Mays followed the timely warning of Winans that "audiences like brevity, that is, they like short speeches." His speeches ranged between twenty-five to thirty-five minutes in duration. Therefore, Mays established a common ground with

---

[19]James A. Winans, *Speech-Making* (New York: D. Appleton-Century, 1938), 196.

his audiences for a careful intermingling of social truths with humane feelings.

13

MAYS AND THE KINGDOM NOT OF THIS WORLD

Samuel DuBois Cook

My subject is "Benjamin E. Mays and the Kingdom Not of this World." By the kingdom not of this world, I mean the Kingdom of God, the kingdom of human service, social righteousness, excellence, social and racial justice, caring, the ethics of concern, brotherhood, the search for ever higher possibilities of achievement, and the Beloved Community of all of God's children, all humankind beyond race, color, creed, gender, nationality, ethnicity, culture, socio-economic and educational status, and other artificial and arbitrary boundaries of human alienation and estrangement. The kingdom not of this world is the kingdom of the ideal, the kingdom out of sight, the kingdom that is always a-coming, dynamic, not static. The kingdom not of this world represents the prophetic tradition and not only ethical idealism and transcendent humanism but also moral perfectionism.

The kingdom of this world and the kingdom not of this world bear a creative and dialectical relationship. They are characterized by unity and continuity, creative interaction, mutuality, interdependence, and complementarity. They are mutually inclusive rather than mutually exclusive. They do not constitute two realms of being but a continuum, a single river of value, essence, and meaning.

Vision of the kingdom not of this world must create moral tension and conflict between the "is" and the "ought," the ideal and the real, promise and fulfillment, potentiality and actuality, what we are and what we ought to be. It should remind us that, whatever our failures and shortcomings, we were made for the highest, the noblest, the best. We were made to walk the high road, not the low road. We were made by God; we were made for God.

Bennie Mays represented the kingdom not of this world—the kingdom that must ultimately redeem the world. Bennie Mays represents the kingdom of higher possibilities, the kingdom out of sight, the kingdom of human excellence, the kingdom not of this world. "The only kingdom which can defy and conquer the world," said Reinhold Niebuhr, "is one which is not of this world."[1]

The kingdom not of this world represents an uneasy conscience, a disturbed conscience, a troubled conscience, an outraged conscience. In *Disturbed About Man*, Mays confessed:

> I am not disturbed about God and I am not disturbed about the Devil. But I am disturbed, I am uneasy, about man. I am uneasy about man because we have no guarantee, no infallible proof, that man is going to make it on the earth, no guarantee that he is going to pull through. I call history to my aid and history's data are disappointing. . . . I am uneasy about man because history gives me no guarantee that man is going to pull through. . . .
>
> . . . When I hear all the explanations given by the social scientists and the theologians, I still do not understand why man cannot take this beautiful world which God has given him, live and help live, settle down and be decent. . . . I am uneasy about man because God, in creating man, faced the awful dilemma of making man a free personality with potentialities for good and evil, or making him a machine without power of choice and without personality. So in making man free to choose, he had to make him free to choose right or wrong, truth or falsehood, peace or war, the high road or the low road.[2]

Steeped in the tradition of the neo-Orthodox school of Karl Barth, Emil Brunner, Reinhold Niebuhr, and Paul Tillich, Mays did not succumb to the romantic illusions about human nature and culture of liberal Protestantism and the secular humanists and idealists. He profoundly understood the limits of human knowledge and the easy optimism of modern culture. He was skeptical of the sufficiency of scientific knowledge, the virtue of technological power, the "disinterested" character of reason, the intrinsic goodness of human nature, and the inevitability of progress.

---

[1] Reinhold Niebuhr, *Beyond Tragedy* (New York: Scribner's Sons, 1937), 284.
[2] *Disturbed About Man*, 90-91

I am uneasy about man because of the paradoxical, diabolical, contradictory nature of man. Here he is, made in the image of God, made also, it seems, in the image of the devil. Potentially honest, potentially dishonest; potentially forgiving, potentially revengeful; potentially truthful, potentially a liar; potentially capable of rising to the divinity of God, capable also of descending to the level of the devil; potentially capable of building a kingdom of heaven on earth, capable also of building a kingdom of hell on earth. This is man. This is you. This is me. . . . I am uneasy about man because we have no guarantee that when we train a man's mind, we will train his heart; no guarantee that when we increase a man's knowledge, we will increase his goodness. There is no necessary correlation between knowledge and goodness.[3]

Mays's theology and anthropology are rooted in the belief in the universality of human sinfulness, an affirmation of human depravity, the bondage of the human will to evil—what is called the doctrine of "original sin." Unlike some theologians, however, Mays did not believe in total human depravity. He was no Karl Barth, who in his commentary on Romans proclaimed the absolute transcendence of God, the "Wholly Other." Barth asserted the radical discontinuity between God and man. On the contrary, Mays allows for more freedom, more moral efficacy, creativity, and choice, more responsibility within the context of a defective will, an inclination to evil, and the centrality of human egoism and pride (*hubris*), both individual and collective.

For Mays, however, the situation is not hopeless. There is no need to despair about the human condition. Human nature contains certain ethical resources, certain constructive powers, an element of the divine as well as the demonic. Deeply embedded in humankind is a conscience, a moral sense, the tension of "right and wrong," a "push" and "pull" of moral impulses and vitalities, an ingredient of moral uneasiness.

It has been well said that man's dignity and misery, creativity and destruction, are rooted in the same source. Mays believed that

---

[3]Ibid., 92.

Hope lies in the very nature of man. Although there is a paradox in man's nature, there is a spark of divinity in him that will not leave him alone. When man is at his worst, down in the gutter, possessed completely by sin, something in him rises up and makes him hate the act which he has committed. He may not always be able to overcome his tendencies to sin but down in his heart he wants to be a decent fellow. . . . There is something in man that will not let him rest satisfied down in the gutter. . . . . Man cannot leave God alone, and God cannot leave man alone . . . .There is hope, then, because man has an uneasy conscience, and since this is so, he is always a candidate for the kingdom of light—there is the great possibility that men will repent, be reborn and be redeemed.[4]

The kingdom not of this world represents an uneasy conscience, a disturbed conscience. The kingdom not of this world should make us profoundly disturbed by the tragedy of racism, anti-Semitism, sexism, poverty, hunger, homelessness, violence, militarism, oppression, illicit drugs, sexual license, homophobia, adult illiteracy, AIDS, teen-age pregnancy, alcoholism, child abuse, neglect, children born to drug-addicted mothers, capital punishment, terrorism, ecological exploitation and indifference, the plight of the handicapped and the disabled, and the illegal drug culture. We should be profoundly disturbed by the insufficient affordable housing, inadequate health insurance, the astronomical school drop-out rate, twisted values and priorities, the pathology of our inner cities, underemployment, unemployment, the terrible plight of the Black underclass, the radical decline in the sense of personal responsibility, and the increasing rush to blame others, "the system," culture, or history for our failures.

The kingdom not of this world should make us profoundly disturbed by the increasing disorganization, disintegration, and breakdown of the family, especially the Black family through illegal drugs. We should be deeply troubled by the agonizing increase in illegitimate births and one-parent, mainly female-headed households. Too many unwanted children are brought into this world. Too many children are born into this world without the slightest chance of experiencing a semi-decent life of development, dignity,

---

[4]Ibid., 94-95, 97-98.

growth, honor, hope, success, self-esteem, and self-realization. Such a tragedy militates against the health, stability, and progress of the civic culture or the social order.

These often unwanted children, lest we forget, are equally God's children and bear the mark and spark of the divine. They reflect the creative and redemptive love of God. And they are not responsible for their being in this world. They deserve genuine opportunities for self-development, productive lives, and responsible citizenship and personhood.

The kingdom not of this world should make us deeply disturbed and uneasy by the fact that we have more young Black males in prison than in college. We should be disturbed by the tyranny of peer pressure, with all of its dreadful consequences. Peer pressure is almost always wrong and destructive. Following the crowd is always dangerous. Mays used to tell his students that he would rather go to hell following his own light than to stumble into heaven following a crowd.

We should be especially disturbed by the continuity and depth of racism in various subtle, covert, insidious, sophisticated, and "respectable" forms as well as by the resurgence of racism in its brutish, vicious, and ugly forms. Like anti-Semitism, racism in all its forms is an infinite evil, a cancer on the body politic, and an insult and an offense to God who created us all.

We should also be concerned by the tragic failures within the Black community. Self-help is a great tradition in the Black community—dating back to slavery. Self-help is a moral imperative and desperate necessity in the Black community today. We must fulfill our responsibilities and solve the problems within our power such as drugs, teen pregnancy, Black-on-Black crime, staggering Black homicides, etc. We must break the searing cycle of violence within the Black community. No heresy is involved in emphasizing the centrality of Black personal and social responsibility for certain thorny problems in the Black community.

The affirmation of self-help involves uniting our African roots and origins with our New World pilgrimage. A heightened sense of responsibility — both individual and collective—are a hallmark of the Black heritage and experience—just as are the great virtues of industry, thrift, self-reliance, the centrality of the family, and the work ethic. Despite racial stereotypes, the work ethic is deeply rooted in the Black historical experience. Hard work is the heritage of Black people. We know the dignity, beauty, and value of honest labor. A profound sense of individual and collective responsibility must be a vital part of the Black future and destiny. Self-help and racial solidarity and pride are prominent features of Black participation in the historical process.

In the cultivation and pursuit of self-help as a key element in the continuity of Black progress and in the salvation of the Black community, we must tap the special ethical, religious, social, and intellectual resources of our historic institutions: churches, the home and family, schools (particularly colleges and universities), and the press.

Of unique significance in coming to grips with the complex problems of the Black community is the tradition of affirming the intrinsic worth of the human person as an autonomous center of meaning because of the creative and redemptive love of God. We are all God's children. Hence we must affirm reverence for all human life. To reclaim this simple belief would effect a revolutionary transformation in the Black community.

This normative conceptual framework and spirit are critical. Belief in the individual's intrinsic value have inspired Black people in their long struggle against the dehumanization of slavery, segregation, discrimination, and other forms of racism, oppression, and injustice. These values nurtured Black life and provided hope and inspiration. Attitudes, beliefs, and behavior based on the genuine and vigorous affirmation of, and commitment to, the imperishable vision of the sanctity of human life and the intrinsic worth of every individual will make a great qualitative difference in the Black community and, of course, the larger community. Significantly, the very same principles and beliefs which inform and inspire the most effective arguments and bulwarks against racism are the very same arguments and bulwarks that can salvage the internal structure and dynamics of the Black community from self-destructive impulses, and patterns of behavior and conduct.

The level of senseless killing and mindless violence has reached intolerable proportions in the black community. Too often, human life is viewed as cheap, expendable, and profane, rather than precious, irreplaceable, and sacred. Increasingly, human life is treated as an "it" rather than a "Thou," a thing instead of a person. Thus we must reclaim human life in all its dignity, sanctity, beauty, and worth.

It is imperative that we develop and implement strategies and programs of self-help. The prophetic message of Mays keeps us disturbed, ethically restless, contemptuous of moral complacency, and constantly driven by an uneasy conscience. "The kingdom not of this world," said Reinhold Niebuhr, "is always in this world in man's uneasy conscience."[5] Time and again Mays said the same thing and in a variety of ways.

To carry on the Mays's legacy, each of us must become voices of the uneasy conscience, the disturbed, the ethically restless, the dissatisfied, the deeply troubled, and the outraged conscience. All of these represent the kingdom not of this world. We must become mortal enemies of moral and social complacency, moral self-conceit, arrogance, false pride, self-deception, moral congratulations, and self-righteousness.

Mays's ultimate meaning and significance is that he represented both dimensions of the uneasy conscience—both the critical and the constructive. Beyond his rebellion against social injustice and dehumanization were his love affair with the world of higher possibilities of achievement and passion for human excellence in its various manifestations. He was morally restless, always dissatisfied with every achievement, every effort. He was always looking for something higher, better, richer, nobler, fuller. He was always looking for new worlds to conquer, new mountains to climb, new rivers to cross, new fields of human endeavor to cultivate and harvest, new challenges to meet, and new joys to create. When he died at the golden age of 89, he was aspiring to complete, among other things, three books.

We must always look up and strive, with all our heart, all our mind, all our strength, all our soul, for something higher and better and to be better than we are; always reaching, aspiring, climbing, improving, morally restless, soaring, in flight.

The kingdom not of this world is always in this world in man's search for higher possibilities. The heart of the ethical consciousness is the anguished cry of the human heart for something better, richer, nobler, higher. We must always look up, whatever our achievements. Higher possibilities always beckon, always prompt and nudge. There is always the sense of incompleteness, of the unfinished task. "Every round goes higher, higher," says that great pilgrim Negro spiritual.

Mays was right when he said the "Man is really what his dreams are. Man is what he aspires to be. Man is the ideals that beckon him on. Man is the integrity that keeps him steadfast, honest, true." He was intolerant of

---

[5]Niebuhr, 279.

mediocrity, complacency, self-satisfaction. He was scornful of low aims, cheap ideals, and indolence. He worshiped at the shrine of excellence. His life was a divine romance with the world of higher possibilities. The deep beauty of the life of Mays is that even at the top, Mays still looked up. Even at the peak of the mountain, he was still climbing, still climbing, still climbing.

He is dissatisfied even in heaven. He is looking for something more divine, more blessed, more perfect. No achievement ever satisfied him. Somehow, he always heard the call of duty to move up higher, to conquer new worlds, to achieve nobler things. A divine voice kept telling him that there are other mountains to climb, the "promised land" has not been reached. Yes, Bennie Mays represents the uneasy conscience—the kingdom not of this world.

If that light in Mays were dark, oh what a darkness. Mays spoke for the creative process, the moral order, the universe, the eternal, and the kingdom not of this world when he uttered these immortal and unforgettable words:

> It must be borne in mind that the tragedy of life doesn't lie in not reaching your goal. The tragedy lies in having no goal to reach. It isn't a calamity to die with dreams unfilled, but it is a calamity not to dream. It is not a disaster to be unable to capture your ideal, but it is a disaster to have no ideal to capture. It is not a disgrace not to reach the stars, but it is a disgrace to have no stars to reach for. Not failure, but low aim is sin.[6]

---

[6]Ibid., 120.

14

THE LAST OF THE
GREAT SCHOOLMASTERS

Lerone Bennett Jr.

Before 500,000 could march on Washington, D.C., before 30,000 could march from Selma, before there could be rebellion in Black America and renewal in the White Church, before SNCC could sit-in, before Stokely Carmichael could talk Black Power, before Martin Luther King Jr. could dream, history had to take the flesh and form of certain black men who were bold enough, wise enough, and selfless enough to assume the awesome responsibility of preparing the ground for a harvest, the fruits of which they would probably never taste themselves.

Of the handful of men called by history to this delicate and dangerous task, none tilled more ground or harvested a more bountiful crop than Benjamin Elijah Mays. A lean, beautifully-black preacher-prophet who served as Schoolmaster of the Movement, Mays's ministry of manhood spanned some fifty-seven years, twenty-seven of them as president of Atlanta's prestigious Morehouse College. During that period, Mays, who later served as president of the Atlanta Board of Education, helped lay the foundation for the new world for black and white Americans.

The world that created Mays and the great Schoolmasters of America, the world of daily chapel and moral exhortations and unlimited horizons and hopes, disappeared with the electronic age. But Samuel DuBois Cook, a former Mays student and the former president of Dillard University, and others believe that the Mays legacy is one of the great possessions of black people and America. And he believes with others, including Hugh Morris Gloster, Mays's successor at Morehouse, that the Mays's legacy is crucial at this juncture in American life.

Far in advance of his time, a rational man in an irrational age, a Christian in a pre-Christian country, a tough black stone in a raging white fire, Mays sounded the premonitory chords of our era, and it is impossible to understand our era or the warning chords pointing to the future without some understanding of what he and the vanguard he represented.

Mays not only anticipated our era; he also risked place and position in unrelenting efforts to push major institutions into the modern world. One observes with interest that he organized his life around the Black Church and the Black School, the two centers of resistance around which the Black man's will to survival was structured. The Black Church in particular was the embodiment of the Black man's will to see and be, the expression of his belief that his suffering had a meaning and would have an issue.

Benjamin Mays came out of that great tradition and he gave new dimensions to the tradition of the Black Church and the Black School, which had lost much of their force and relevance. Many schools and churches had become accommodating instruments of the status quo. By helping to renew the mission of these vital institutions, Mays played a major role in redirecting the historical wave of today.

Mays also sowed seeds of renewal in the White Church. As a speaker and preacher before thousands of influential White groups and as a high official of the Federal Council of Churches and the World Council of Churches, he hammered away at the sins of the Church. Never one to bite his tongue or to gild the truth with polysyllabic placebos, he told the American Baptist Convention in 1951 that the "Christian Church is the most highly segregated institution in the United States." It was during this period that Mays made, for perhaps the first time, the now famous statement that "eleven o'clock on Sunday morning is the most segregated hour in America." Of like tone and texture was his electrifying address to the second General Assembly of the World Council of Churches in Evanston, Illinois, in 1954. "Anyone," he said, "who seeks shelter in the Bible for his defense of racial segregation in the church is living in a glass house which is neither rock-proof nor bullet-proof."

No less important was Mays's role in refurbishing the role of the Black college president. This has always been a difficult role, and it was even more difficult in the 1930s and 1940s, when Black college presidents had to satisfy conservative White public officials and philanthropists and restless and, yes, confused Black students. Finding themselves in an untenable position, in the crossfire of conservative White patrons and increasingly militant students, the best of the conservative college presidents offered themselves as willing sacrifices, making conscious efforts to educate men and women who graduated despising them. The worst became servile supplicants who turned out timid carbon copies of themselves.

It is a measure of Mays's greatness that he entirely transcended these categories. Morehouse students never thought of him in traditional terms because he was not a traditional Black college president. When the NAACP was America's SNCC, Mays was a conspicuously active member. And when the interests of the White power structure clashed with the interest of the Black people, he was found on the side of the mothers and fathers of his students. In the 1940s, when all or almost all public doors in Atlanta were closed to Paul Robeson, he opened the door of Sale Hall Chapel and gave Paul Robeson an honorary degree. In the 1960s, when the sit-in controversy sent most college presidents scurrying for cover, Mays was one of the courageous few who said students were right and deserved the support of their elders.

Against the traditional view of Black education as "accommodation under protest," Mays pressed a new conception of education as the liberation of power through the mastery of the accumulated lore of the ages. He conceived education broadly as an instrument of social and personal renewal, and he anticipated Paulo Freire's conception of education as "the practice of freedom." What Martin Luther King Jr. said about Morehouse College was echoed by almost all of his contemporaries. "There was a freer atmosphere at Morehouse," King said, "and it was there that I had my first frank discussion on race. The professors were not caught up in the clutches of state funds and could teach what they wanted with academic freedom. They encouraged us in a positive quest for solutions to racial ills and *for the first time in my life, I realized that nobody was afraid.* (Emphasis supplied.)"

As an educator, Mays addressed himself to the major problems of oppression-manhood. He did not intend, he said, to make lawyers or doctors or teachers—he intended to make men. And he intended to make them the hard way. "He who starts behind in the race of life," he used to say, time and time again, "Must run faster or forever remain behind."

God was real in the Mays's household. Louvenia Carter Mays was deeply religious and her son caught her spirit and relied heavily on God and prayer. "I needed to rely on something," he said. When Mays was six years old, he started work, cleaning up around the house and making beds. At the age of ten, he was hard at work in the fields, plowing, chopping cotton, spreading guano. Learning the alphabet from his oldest sister, he entered the one-room colored school with a head start on his contemporaries. This made a significant impression on the teacher who told Hezekiah and Louvenia Mays that their son was destined for great things. When Mays followed up this initial triumph by reciting the Beatitudes on a Children's Day program at Mount Zion Church, the elders decided that the Mays boy was "marked" and was going "to be somebody." So impassioned was his recital that old men and women lumbered to their feet, screaming and shouting. Looking back on this early triumph more than half a century later, Mays said, "I can still see them today, waving handkerchiefs, weeping, and shouting."

Buoyed by a climate of expectancy, Mays decided to make the prophecies come true. "Somehow," he said later, "I yearned for an education. Many a day I hitched my mule to a tree and went down deep into the woods to pray, asking God to make it possible for me to get an education. . . . I sometimes say, I prayed myself into an education."

Poor though he was, Mays managed by economics and odd jobs, including cleaning outhouses, to finish high school program at South Carolina State. He then attended Virginia Union where he decided that he wanted to test his mind against the best White minds of the day. He applied for admission to several big Eastern schools and was rejected on racial grounds. (One of the major universities later awarded him an honorary doctorate.) In 1917, he was admitted to Bates College in Maine. Waiting tables, tending furnaces, and running on the road as a Pullman porter, he worked his way through Bates and later received his M.A. and Ph.D. degrees at the University of Chicago. After pastoring a church in Atlanta and teaching mathematics and English at Morehouse and South Carolina State, where he married Sadie Gray, Mays was appointed executive secretary of the Tampa (Florida) Urban League. The rising young teacher-activist spent two years at this post before accepting a position as national student secretary of the YMCA. In 1934, he became dean of the Howard University School of Religion.

In 1940, on the eve of the new era, Mays became president of Morehouse College. He was 46 years old. Although he did not know it at the time, Morehouse, which had an enviable record of producing preachers, teachers, and college presidents, was in danger of losing both its identity and independence. The story of how Mays saved Morehouse, of how he triumphed over internal and external forces and gave the school a new birth of purpose, is beyond the scope of this article; and the point of these observations is to emphasize the spirit of independence that motivated the man. "If Morehouse is not good enough for anybody," he said at the beginning, "it's not good enough for Negroes."

It was this spirit that endeared him to the generations of students who entered Morehouse in the 1940s and 1950s. Although he taught no classes, his spirit permeated the campus, and students made a point of catching his now-famous Tuesday morning Chapel talks. Week after week, Tuesday after Tuesday, for twenty-seven years, he preached engagement, responsibility, and stewardship. Education he said, was an obligation, not a privilege. One was obliged, he said, to put one's theoretical knowledge at the disposal of the people.

In this effort, the man Morehouse students called "Buck Benny" was engaged in a total war against a system of ideas and values that had wormed its way into the neurons of his students and did not cease to destroy them, even while they slept. Mays wanted them to "invent souls," to use Cesaire's beautiful phrase. He wanted to root out the weaknesses and evasions that were the heritage of three hundred years of spiritual and material oppression. "If you are ignorant," he told his students, "the world is going to cheat you. If you are weak, the world is going to kick you. If you are a coward, the world is going to keep you running."

Strong himself, Mays demanded strength from his students. He had developed early in life, he said, "a hard, maybe cruel, certainly an exacting and unrelenting philosophy," which he applied to himself, to his students, and to all mankind. And the philosophy was simply this: "No person deserves to be congratulated unless he has done the best he could with the mental equipment he has under the existing circumstances."

In concrete terms, Mays demanded a sense of mission. Every man, he said, is called of God to do his very best in every situation and to make some unique and distinctive contribution, which only he can make. "Do whatever you do so well," he used to say, "that no man living and no man yet unborn could do it better."

Freedom is hard. Benjamin Mays understood that. There were no excuses and no hiding places in his world. The greatest crime was to give up; the greatest sin was to "aim low."

A witness for freedom, and a model of freedom, Mays created a climate of freedom that bore fruit. Not accidentally, a disproportionately large number of his students went on to make their mark as college presidents, lawyers, doctors, teachers, Ph.D.'s, and hellraisers. It is also no accident that a disproportionately large number of his students and disciples played prominent roles in the Freedom movement.

Throughout this period and into the 1970s, Mays remained on the battle line, preaching the acceptable year of the Lord. He was honored repeatedly in these years. Presidents Kennedy and Johnson appointed him to various commissions and delegations. In 1963, he was appointed by President Kennedy to the official U.S. Delegation to the funeral of Pope John XXIII. On another occasion, he was considered for the position of Ambassador to Israel. Press reports of this said he declined the honor, but Mays said: "I was never offered the position. One could hardly turn down the President of the United States. When people came here to feel me out, I expressed a desire to stay in the field of education, and I never heard any more about it. Much later, when Sadie and I were going to a reception line at the White House, President Kennedy stopped and announced: "I wanted to make an Ambassador out of this man, but he preferred to be an educator."

He always believed, with Kant, that moral worth, not happiness, is the goal of life. "Die young, die middle-aged, die old," he has said, "[but] remember that the most useful life and most abundant life is the one in which one dreams that which will never completely come true, and chooses ideals that forever beckon but forever elude. To seek a goal that is worthy, so all-embracing, so all-consuming, and so challenging that one can never completely attain it, is the life magnificent; it is the only life worth living."

This was the life—hard, demanding, magnificent—that Benjamin E. Mays has lived and is still being lived by others. And in the eighty-third year of that life, he looked back through the haze of the years and said that he was "satisfied but not complacent" about the changes he had witnessed in his days. "There is no doubt," he said,

> that the Negro is a thousand times better off than he was at the turn of the century. There is no doubt that virtually every Black boy has a much better chance to get an education than I did. . . . There is no doubt that we have made some progress in race relations, but you still have to keep your eye on the struggle against racism in the world and the fact that what the Negro has gained he has gained

through the struggle, and through the courts, and through marching and boycotting.

What advice would he have for the young today? His only advice is "the challenge I accepted for myself, to keep tiptoeing and never accept mediocrity as a goal."

15

SEEDS OF REVOLUTION

Noel C. Burtenshaw

Sedition was hatched in chapel. The revolution was sown on Tuesday mornings in the chapel on the Morehouse campus. Benjamin Mays, president of Morehouse, waded into injustice unmercifully in those chapel gatherings. The men of Morehouse would go to the far ends of the South, to the far ends of the nation. They would even be found across new nations of Africa. But always they would remember the Tuesday morning chapel meetings. "I spent half of my life," said Mays," demonstrating to myself I was not inferior. I spent the rest carrying that message to the students at Morehouse ." They learned it well on Tuesday mornings in the chapel.

"They would come up to me after chapel," recalls the famed Atlanta leader, "and want to chat and question. That was all right. They came first in my book. Sadie, my second wife, (his first wife, Ellen, died in 1922) and I often had them over to the house just to sit and chat. That was good too. We all learned a lot."

Sedition was planned at Mays's home also. "Your mind does not have to sit in the back of the bus," he would say. They sat. They hoped. They learned. When the time to march came, they, his men of Morehouse, would be ready. It was in that chapel on the campus that he pounded home the message. "I went into a police station in Tampa one time to get some information. They looked at me and said, 'Nigger take your hat off when you talk to us.' Well, I never wore a hat again. There are ways to rebel. I have spent my life doing it. You can too." They listened. Down the years, they listened.

In the mid-1940s, a bright young man came from the city of Atlanta to Morehouse. He resided on campus but one year. For the remainder of his college years, he lived at home. His father was an Atlanta pastor. Going to the Tuesday chapel assembly was not a necessity for him. But young Martin

Luther King Jr. never missed a morning. And he had questions—many, many questions.

"Often, he followed me to the office," recalls Mays in his home in Southwest Atlanta, "and we would talk for ages. Sometimes faculty members wanted to see me, but if Martin was there first, we talked. He was always there first."

The young King introduced his college president to his family. Sunday dinners together became a regular occasion. The friendship developed. The faith teachings, the life experience, the determination of Mays to be fully free were all deposited for future reference in the mind of the black minister's son, Martin Luther King Jr. "The first crisis between the King family and I came," remembered the former Morehouse president, "when Martin wanted to lead the Montgomery march. His father did not want him to go. "Enough has been done" was his attitude. He called me and I said, "This is his moment; this is God's will. Let him go.'" King went and marched to the strains of the old spiritual: "Ain't gonna let nobody turn me round."

Mays had lived by that spiritual all his glorious days. He is a son of the South. He was born on "Dr. Childs' place" out in the country, in Greenwood, S.C., back in 1894. Both his parents were former slaves. Memories of those South Carolina days are vivid. "I remember meeting my first mob when I was four. They were on their way to Phoenix (S.C.) to lynch Negroes. I remember knowing this is not right. I am a person like them. I remember my father telling us how he fought two white men at one time. He knocked one down and then took on the other. I felt good for him. He later noted:

> I remember there were two things blacks did not do. First was pass a white man on a dusty road. Second was pass a white man on a muddy road. I also remember that my father did both. . . . I remember that I wanted to learn, to go to school, but my father wanted me on the farm to work. So we compromised. I was allowed to go four months of the year. The rest I gave to him.

But it wasn't enough for the young Benjamin. Education was his vocation. He felt it. He knew his destiny lay in fulfilling his own need to know and also the unmet needs of blacks in the South. He armed himself well for that life of academics.

"I got a lot of opposition, it was hard going," remembered Mays. "My father did not want me to go to South Carolina State. My teachers there said I would freeze (I almost did) if I went to Lewiston in Maine and funds almost prevented me from going to the University of Chicago. But I followed my destiny." He obtained his doctorate in Chicago and in 1940 became president of Morehouse in Atlanta.

"I knew I was at home here in Atlanta," says Mays, but like the rest of the nation and especially the rest of the South, life for a black man or woman was not easy." The message of inferiority was constantly being preached and to those willing to accept or believe the message, life could be simple. The president of Morehouse College had no intention of believing or allowing others to believe those heretical preachments.

You handled it in this way," said the untiring revolutionary. "You used segregated facilities only when you had to. I did not ever have to go to a segregated theater, so I didn't go. But I had to use the public bus at times. It was difficult to have to go to the back or maybe not get on at all. If too many whites showed up, you got no seat."

The men of Morehouse looked to their president for leadership, but so did his city and also the nation. "When Pope John died in 1963, I was one of five Americans sent to the funeral by President Kennedy. That was an honor. I asked then-Vice President Johnson on the plane how he felt about civil rights. He told me things were moving too slow. I would meet and speak with him many times (when he was) president on the same matter."

"In Atlanta, Ivan Allen, the mayor, was a friend and a friend of our cause. Also Chief (of Police Herbert) Jenkins was a good man. He was very helpful at times. He called me when Martin was killed and he said he knew that blacks were beginning to gather at Paschal's Restaurant for march on downtown. He asked me if I could stop the march. I told him I could not. 'Okay,' he said, 'give me 20 minutes to get the right officers over there to make sure we can keep it calm.' I knew I could hold them for 20 minutes, I did. There was a peaceful march.

"Of course," remembers the famed educator, "it was Mayor (William B.) Hartsfield who first hired black police in Atlanta, and he will be remembered for it. They had to use the Butler Street 'Y' as their police station and they could not arrest whites. But it was a beginning."

The most exciting time for Benjamin Mays during his long and varied life was the Martin Luther King era. The dream of a lifetime was coming true. Was King the greatest leader of black people? "No, he wasn't the greatest leader," said Mays. "We have had no great leader since Booker T. Washington. And I hope we never need just ONE again. Martin was one of many. He brought them together—the teachers, the doctors, the tradesmen —and inspired them all to rise up. The moment had come."

Was one man responsible for Dr. King's death? "One man shot him," says Benjamin Mays pointedly, "and he's behind bars. But others were involved. The police let him escape. He was arrested in Europe. Of course, there was a conspiracy. They wanted him dead; someone paid to have it done. He disturbed the status quo. And the conspirators are still out there."

Before King left for Memphis and his final march on behalf of the garbage strikers in that city, he came to see his old teacher. "It was another campaign for him. There was always danger. He knew it would be dangerous." King was shot on April 4, 1968. He was 39 years old. Dr. Benjamin Mays, before a crowd of 200,000 people, preached his eulogy.

For twenty-seven years he had served as president of Morehouse College. He had been mentor and spiritual father to Martin Luther King Jr. Presidents and Prime Ministers sought his counsel. Each year this modern day prophet, who saw and helped an entire nation change its legal system to heal injustice, traveled from coast to coast carrying his respected message that all men and women are God's children. My question to this unique man of our generation was this: Now that segregation is dead, what is the next chapter for the minority peoples of this nation? With ice in his clear voice, tempered by the softness in his eyes, he answered, "Who said it is dead?" In that final instant I had the feel of those revolutionary seeds planted over many years in the Morehouse chapel by Benjamin Mays.

16

THE EDUCATION OF BENJAMIN MAYS: AN EXPERIENCE IN EFFECTIVE TEACHING

Charles Vert Willie

Mays began his educational odyssey when he was six, but he was twenty-two years old when he finished high school. He attended school only four months each year until he was nineteen—the age at which he first remained in school the full term. He completed high school at South Carolina State College for Negroes, which had an academy at that time. He was the valedictorian of his class and earned a prize in oratory. He spent a year at the predominantly black Virginia Union University in Richmond, Virginia, and three years at the predominantly white Bates College in Lewiston, Maine.

Mays said his high school teachers encouraged him and helped him plan for future study. The teachers at Virginia Union were competent and had a special interest in their black students. Mays also attributes his desire for an education to his teacher in the one-room school, his church minister, and the church people. He said, "All my teachers were lavish with their praise and encouragement."

Against the advice of friends, Mays enrolled in Bates College in 1917. He said the weather was cold and few blacks were there. He lived in a predominantly white world. He called it a new physical and spiritual environment. In this new setting, he found "the hearts at Bates were warm." There were a few incidents, of course — little manifestations of prejudice — but they were rare.

During the first semester at Bates, he was embarrassed and chagrined to receive the first and only D in his whole academic career. He balanced his near-failure in a course his first year at Bates with superior performance in the declamation contest. He won first prize. Committing the oration "The

Supposed Speech of John Adams" to memory, Mays won the recognition of both faculty and students by his victory. Campus gossip had it that Bennie could not hope to win because of his southern accent. Mays heard that the wife of his biology teacher had studied speech. He asked Professor Pomeroy, his biology teacher, to intercede and to determine if his wife was available for coaching. Mrs. Pomeroy agreed, coached Mays, and he won. He said, "I have always been deeply appreciative when people did things for me that they were in no way obligated to do. I shall never forget Mrs. Pomeroy."

The professor of Greek also helped. Mays said the subject was difficult and troubled him greatly. Some students in the class made him the object of rather unkind amusement because of his pronunciation of the Greek words. Mays asked the professor for a conference. His teacher invited him to this home, analyzed the problem, made some suggestions, and assured him that he had the ability to do the job. With this support, Mays began to improve and by the end of the semester he made an A.

Despite the shaky beginning, by the end of his years at Bates, Mays had served three years on the debating team, was selected Class Day speaker, and graduated with honors.

At Bates, the desegregated educational experience enabled Mays to dismiss from his mind forever the myth of the inherent inferiority of all blacks and the myth of the inherent superiority of all whites. These myths were believed by many in South Carolina where Mays was born. At Bates, Mays said, he liberated himself by accepting himself as a free person with dignity and worth. The self-liberation process resulted from his awareness of his own performance. He had done better in academic performance, in public speaking, and in argumentation and debate than the majority of his white classmates.

The story of Benjamin Elijah Mays is recorded in his autobiography, *Born to Rebel* and in the chapter "The Black College in Higher Education" that he prepared for the book *Black Colleges in America* (1978, 19-28). It is a story about the education of a disadvantaged student and demonstrates the kinds of support from teachers, friends, and significant others that are effective and sustaining. Mays said he has felt his indebtedness to people who were sympathetic with his desire to get an education, including his mother, his older sister and his other brothers and sisters, his pastor, and the teachers in his life. His teachers opened up new vistas of learning, inspired him, called on him to recite and praised his performance, interceded in his behalf, gave him jobs to earn money, made loans to him, trusted him, and encouraged him to plan his future[1]

SUPPORT KINDLY GIVEN

Probably the most important ingredient in the education of a disadvantaged student is the provision of support in a kindly way at the time the student needs it. The support is significant in confirming the student's sense of self, in enabling him to risk new experiences, and in sustaining him in time of trouble. Mays received these supports and benefitted greatly from them.

Support of a student in trouble is no support at all unless it is kindly given. Otherwise, the student does not trust the source of support. Trust is the major component that mediates a learning relationship between teacher and student. Mays trusted the evaluation of his talents that his Sunday school teacher made and he was motivated to seek new experiences because of the praise he received for what he had accomplished.

Because the hearts of the teachers at Bates were warm, Mays could ask for help in a new physical and spiritual environment that was unsettling. Receiving the help that he asked for, when he needed it, and also receiving the assurance from significant others that he could prevail, Mays transcended his difficulties and succeeded.

A student can accept coaching and correction from teachers whom he trusts. A student will risk failure by exploring new experiences if he is admired for being himself. A student will endure difficulty if he does not suffer alone but is sustained by a teacher who suffers with him, who is concerned about the student's capacities as well as the student's circumstances.

As a midterm project, I asked the students in my course "The Teaching of Urban Students to prepare autobiographies of their educational experiences. The students characterized the teachers most influential in their development as kind—not tough, not hard, not unyielding. Kind teachers trust their students, encourage them, treat them with dignity, and affirm

---

[1]*Born to Rebel*, 1-8.

their self-worth. One university student said, "My favorite elementary school teacher taught us science. I loved him because he always asked, 'Why?'and because he was very kind to us. He was a gentle man who liked children."

This experience is contrasted with that of a high-achieving student who learned basic skills but felt "haunted by the fear of punishment and humiliation" from the teachers if she failed to know the right answer. The student got good grades but said the humiliation showered on those who did not answer correctly shrouded her later learning experiences "in fear, tension, and anxiety." To avoid the risk of humiliation, the student said, "I learned to be completely passive—to sit quietly in my seat, speaking only when called upon, and always know the answer." This adaptation of extreme passivity the student described as a "burden" she has carried into adulthood because of years of anxiety-filled experiences in school.

Kind teachers urged Mays to be active, not passive, and provided opportunities for him to speak out. They praised him for his achievements, large and small; encouraged him to accomplish more, but sustained and consoled him when he experienced difficulty.

STUDENT-CENTERED AND POPULATION-SPECIFIC METHODS

Knowledge of the individual's capacities and special circumstances is necessary to student-centered teaching and population-specific instructional approaches. Kind teachers attempt to understand students and tailor learning experiences to the needs and circumstances of the individuals. This can be done by accepting each student as he is before attempting to teach new ways. Students who believe that what they bring to school is rejected will tend to resist new information offered.

By building on capacities already developed, the teacher provides the student with an opportunity to experience success even if he fails initially in the acquisition of new knowledge or the development of other capacities. Success experiences are significant components in the self-concept of students. Although Benjamin Mays had difficulty in Greek and received a near-failing grade in one course during his first year at Bates, he also won first prize in the declamation contest and the respect of faculty and students for his public speaking.

Coming from a culture that emphasized oral communication, Mays's public speaking capacity was well developed before he came to Bates. His teachers provided an opportunity for him to experience success in what he brought to the school despite the difficulties encountered in other areas. Experiencing acceptance of what he brought to the situation, he was able to accept coaching and correction that facilitated his mastery of the new information offered. Bates College started with Mays where he was and took him to where it wanted him to be—an honor student who performed well in both spoken and written forms of communication. He achieved this because he was praised for what he did well, assured that he could master new knowledge, and helped when he needed it in concrete ways that were specific to his circumstances. At Bates College, Benjamin Mays experienced a student-centered education that was specifically oriented to the needs of a person affiliated with the population group in which he was socialized.

With reference to the folk traditions of blacks in the United States, a controversy has erupted concerning the language that they should be taught in school "black English" or standard English. "Blacks knows that their language be's all right" and do not have to be taught to speak that way. Teachers, however, will have difficulty getting blacks or any cultural or language groups to learn new ways of writing and speaking if they do not accept as valid the language patterns that students bring to the school. For example, to reject black English with ridicule is to humiliate those who speak that way. Students who are humiliated and ridiculed tend to resist accepting new knowledge from those who reject them and their way of life.

Thus, the instructional issue is whether students are accepted as they are before the teacher attempts to change them. By accepting students as they are—including their black English or other language—teachers gain students' confidence, which Martin Buber declares is the only access to a person. When confidence has been won, resistance against being educated gives way. According to Buber, a student who has confidence in his teacher accepts the teacher as a person, one who may be trusted. In a confidence-sharing, trustworthy relationship, the teacher also accepts the student before desiring to influence the student.[2]

---

[2]Martin Buber, *Between Man and Man* (Boston: Beacon Press, 1947), 106.

THE TIME DIMENSION IN LEARNING

Finally, the education of Benjamin Mays demonstrated that time is a dimension in learning, that each person must learn what he must learn in the time that is available, and that the temporal learning pattern for one person or group may differ from that of another.

Mays prepared himself as an educator by participating in an unorthodox learning pattern. He never considered himself too old to learn, but he wished he had time to catch up on the reading that he had missed as a child. This he could not do, "for each passing day makes its own new demands."[3]

Although he was twenty-two when he graduated from high school ("a bit retarded because of having only four months of schooling per year in South Carolina"), Mays graduated from college at the age of twenty-six and received a Ph.D. from the University of Chicago as he approached the fortieth anniversary of his birth. The slow beginning did not deter Mays from a spectacular career—election to Phi Beta Kappa, induction in the South Carolina Hall of Fame, dean of the Howard University School of Religion, president of Morehouse College, president of the Atlanta School Board, spiritual mentor of Martin Luther King, Jr., recipient of fifty-six honorary degrees—from Harvard and other colleges and universities in the United States and in Africa, and winner of the Spingarn Medal given by the National Association for the Advancement of Colored People (NAACP). Despite an uncertain start at Bates, where he received his only D, Mays graduated near the top of his class. His progress in time is not unlike that of other black students at predominantly white colleges.

I have been critical of the use of the scholastic aptitude tests of the College Board because their value is limited to predicting performance the first year of college. Scholars connected with the Educational Testing Service, which prepares the tests for the College Board, state that first-year grade averages are appropriate as the criterion measure because studies have found no systematic difference in validity coefficients when test results were compared with first-year, two-year, or four-year averages.[4]

---

[3]*Born to Rebel*, 10.

[4]W. B. Schrader, "The Predictive Validity of College Board Admission Tests." In *The College Board Admission Testing Program*, ed. William H. Angoff (New York: College Entrance Examination Board, 1971), 118.

My study of black students and white students at predominantly white colleges confirmed this finding for white students. The proportion of such students who received grades at A and B levels the freshman and senior years of college varied less than five percentage points. But the proportion of black students who received such grades for these two time periods varied nearly forty percentage points. My study used cross-sectional rather than longitudinal data; also, grade averages were self-reported. These factors temper the certainty with which conclusions may be stated.

The findings suggest, however, a temporal difference among racial populations in adapting to college as a learning environment in terms of the acquisition of good grades. The adaptation of the majority population the first year of college is similar to its adaptation the fourth year, but not so with the minority; from a first year that was almost a disaster, the minority students at predominantly white colleges improved dramatically to the fourth year, in which the proportion who earned good grades was ten percentage points above the proportion of majority students who got such grades.[5]

The experience of minority students in my study was not unlike that of Mays, who received one A and one D his first semester at Bates but one C, two Bs, and eight As his senior year. What a difference a few years make! In *Born to Rebel*, Mays summarizes his academic record: "Until I entered Bates, I had always been a 'straight A' student. During my first semester at Bates, I made only one A, and was embarrassed and chagrined to receive the first and only D in my whole academic career. In the second semester, I made three Bs and three As. In my junior year, my record was ten As, five Bs and three Cs. In my senior year, I received eight As, two Bs and one C. I was one of fifteen to be graduated with honors."[6]

Biblical wisdom reminds us that there is a season and a time to every purpose (KJV, Ecclesiastes 3:1). Timing in the education and achievements of Mays differed from those of his white contemporaries. His life-time career and accomplishments fulfill a biblical thesis: "Better is the end of a thing than the beginning thereof: and the patient in spirit is better than the proud in spirit" (KJV, Ecclesiastes 7:8). Be slow to reject those who appear to be retarded. In the end, they may make a mighty contribution. Teachers are

---

[5]Charles V. Willie, *Black Students at White Colleges* (New York: Praeger, 1972), 68.
[6]*Born to Rebel*, 57.

counseled to be patient with students so that in due season they may be fulfilled. The education of Benjamin Elijah Mays has taught us these things.

17

MAYS'S LEADERSHIP AT MOREHOUSE COLLEGE

Dereck Joseph Rovaris

Morehouse College in the 1930s had been severely hurt by the stock market crash and the subsequent Great Depression. Income from tuition, enrollment, and the endowment all witnessed decreases. Salaries were low, the physical plant was in need of major improvements, and the college was unable to control its own destiny. In addition to all of this, there remained a strong leadership void following the departure of longtime President John Hope. This was the Morehouse that Benjamin Mays inherited in 1940. By the time he retired in 1967, he had turned it around. His successor, Hugh Gloster remarked, "when Mays retired he left a strong and stable institution; a strong base from which I could work. Improvements throughout the college had brought Morehouse to a place of distinction.[1]

This rank of distinction was accomplished through Mays's charismatic leadership, which helped the college to flourish in a number of areas. According to Addie Louise Joyner Butler, author of *The Distinctive Black College: Talladega, Tuskegee, and Morehouse,* "a charismatic leader is needed for the initiation of an organizational legend." Mays provided Morehouse with that kind of leadership enabling it to achieve its distinctive ranking.

---

[1]Hugh M. Gloster, interview by author, 22 February 1988, Atlanta. As Mays's successor, Gloster was most informative and reliable as a source of information. His insight into the history and development of Morehouse was not unlike that of his immediate presidential predecessors, Mays and Hope. In that regard, a complete study of his twenty year tenure would add tremendously to the Morehouse story. His understanding of the College was equaled by his respect for Mays and his accomplishments at Morehouse; Edward A. Jones, *A Candle in the Dark: A History of Morehouse College* (Valley Forge: Judson Press, 1967), 300.

. . . the seeds were planted by John Hope and the saga grew into full fruition during the tenure of Benjamin E. Mays . . . Dr. Mays brought the institution out of a crisis of demoralization and planted it in the fertile grounds of distinction.[2]

Mays did not have to force his ideas on anyone to bring about this change. Those involved with the college simply followed his lead. Butler utilized Burton Clark's, *The Distinctive College* to help define her work. Describing the nature of charisma, she relied on Clark's earlier description: "A charismatic leader is obeyed neither because of the authority derived from his office nor because of a traditionally legitimized status, but because others are attracted by his unusual qualities and devote themselves to his person."[3]

According to Samuel DuBois Cook, "[f]or Bennie Mays, a better life is the thing. For him, we are called by God to human betterment and enrichment. If we fail on those scores, we disappoint God, break His heart, and make Him cry."[4] Improving the lives of the students with whom he came in contact so that they might go out and improve the world in which they lived was what Mays sought to do at Morehouse. The notion of "a better life" constantly motivated Mays as it was an integral component of his strong Christian beliefs. It was his hope that through his efforts, others also might become motivated to make "a better life." As a by-product of this motivation, a small, Southern black institution of higher education was nurtured into adulthood and was moved into the ranks of distinction.

This chapter will examine Mays's administrative style, his personal character and philosophies, and the way in which they affected Morehouse. There will also be a review of how he responded to various questions and issues as they affected the college. It begins with a look at two men in whose

---

[2]Addie Louise Joyner Butler, *The Distinctive Black College: Talladega, Tuskegee, and Morehouse* (Metuchen, NJ: The Scarecrow Press, Inc., 1977), 2, 101. In her book, Butler selected these three distinctive colleges based on their qualifications as identified by Burton R. Clark in *The Distinctive College*. Butler indicated that each of these schools met the outlined criteria for distinction that included unique institutional mission, organizational saga, and dynamic leadership. For the condition of the college prior to 1940, see: Jones, *A Candle in the Dark*, 122-133.

[3]Butler, 2; See also Burton R. Clark, *The Distinctive College: Antioch, Reed, and Swarthmore* (Chicago: Aldine Publishing Co., 1970), 240.

[4]*Quotable Quotes of Benjamin E. Mays*, xiv.

lives he figured prominently: Samuel DuBois Cook and Hugh M. Gloster. Both are Morehouse men, with Cook having been a student and Gloster a faculty member during the Mays's administration. Both became college presidents in their later years.

COOK AND GLOSTER

Samuel DuBois Cook, president of Dillard University and graduate of the Morehouse Class of 1948, came to know and admire Benjamin Mays as a student. Through the years they developed a close personal relationship, as well. As he did for many friends and colleagues, Mays officiated at Cook's wedding in Mays's home on the Morehouse campus. Cook would similarly honor Mays in 1975 by conferring Dillard's first honorary degree on him.

Cook is arguably Mays's most ardent living supporter. Delivering the eulogy at Mays's funeral, Cook said "I am one of Bennie Mays's 'boys'. I have been one of his 'boys' since I was a kid . . . and I will be one of his 'boys' until I die."[5] Cook eventually established himself as a giant in black higher education all the while relying on Mays's influence and wisdom. Cook called on Mays often, and they came to know each other quite well. He intently followed Mays's career and was asked by Mays to assist on a number of projects, including writing introductions for two books and completing a third. His recollections of Mays provide valuable insight to Mays, his style, and his administration.

While working as an Atlanta University professor of political science in 1956, Cook had an office down the hall from Mays's office. From that vantage point he could more closely observe the style and character of his professional mentor. Cook has been accused by some of trying to imitate Mays as he led Dillard University. In some respects, Cook would welcome such a comparison since he held Mays in such high esteem. A visual tour of Cook's office walls revealed countless dozens of photographs and awards. However, two pictures which were quite prominent and much larger than the

---

[5]*Morehouse College Bulletin: Founder's Day Issue* 46 (Winter 1984), 14.

rest stand out—one of Cook's classmates, Martin Luther King Jr. and the other of Bennie Mays.[6]

Like Cook, Hugh Gloster has been accused of trying to imitate and compete with Mays. Gloster did not see himself this way. As mentioned, Mays was a role model for Gloster, but Gloster admired Mays as an example, not as a blueprint. Instead of competing with Mays, Gloster merely accepted the challenge given him to continue to build and develop Morehouse. Prior to Mays's retirement he took many opportunities to meet with Gloster in order to acquaint him with the operation and to facilitate a smooth transition. Gloster said of those meetings,

> . . . he did more than brief me for a new position: he took advantage of every opportunity to motivate and inspire me by challenging me privately and publicly at least to equal and if possible to surpass his record as president.[7]

It was neither imitation nor competition that led to Gloster's successful development of the college; it was admiration and the acceptance of the challenge given him by a mentor and a friend.

According to Gloster, he enjoyed a "long and close personal relationship" with Mays. He first heard Mays speak at a YMCA program and became immediately impressed with his strong beliefs in Christianity and democracy. In Mays's first year as president, he asked Gloster to join the faculty. Gloster accepted the offer in 1941 and taught at Morehouse until 1943 when he took a USO military leave. During his brief time on campus he could recognize the turnaround that Mays had begun at Morehouse. He also received support and encouragement from Mays to help him finish his Ph.D.[8]

---

[6]Samuel DuBois Cook, interview by author, 14 January 1988, New Orleans. Mays canceled several important engagements in order to attend the presidential inauguration of his former pupil. Mays so admired Cook that he asked him to write the Introduction for *Born To Rebel*.

[7]*Morehouse College Bulletin: Founder's Day Issue* 46 (Winter 1984), 10-11; Hugh Gloster interview.

[8]Ibid.

Gloster left Morehouse in 1946, much to the disappointment of Mays, but according to Gloster, "it didn't affect their relationship and they kept in touch." As Mays considered his retirement, he informed Gloster that he would be a candidate for Mays's successor. Once Gloster took office, he received continued support and assistance from Mays.[9]

Performing in the shadow of a "living legend" was difficult, but Gloster accepted the challenge. Although Gloster never admitted to competing with Mays, he could hear the constant comparisons, made more frequently because of Mays's continued presence in Atlanta. Gloster responded by trying to improve on the numbers in enrollment, endowment, and faculty salaries. He also instituted an aggressive effort to improve the school's physical plant. He was very successful in all of these efforts, posting gains far and above what his predecessor had accomplished.[10]

Yet there remained a fundamental difference between these two administrations. Gloster did not possess Mays's charisma and as a result, his leadership style was more collegial. Still, both men sought to build a "Greater Morehouse," and in their own ways, they both did. Alton Hornsby, a member of the Morehouse history faculty since 1968, compared the administrations and direction of Gloster and Mays. He suggested that Gloster's development of the college centered on "building up the physical plant and expanding the college into the areas of business, engineering, and medicine." On the other hand, Hornsby added, Mays "spent a significant amount of time trying to instill confidence and self esteem . . . he was more interested in building men of academic quality and character."[11]

ADMINISTRATIVE STYLE

When asked to describe Mays's administrative style Cook replied, he was democratic with a small 'd'; collegial, to a degree." Mays was a tough

---

[9]Ibid; see also, Jones, *A Candle in the Dark*, 252-253, 258.

[10]*Morehouse College Bulletin: Founder's Day Issue and Twenty-Year Report* 49 (Winter 1987), 1.

[11]Alton B. Hornsby, interview by author, 22 February 1988, Atlanta. Hornsby who serves as editor of *The Journal of Negro History*, has been a faculty member at Morehouse since 1968. He was a student under Mays during the late 1950s. His historical training provided him with a critical perspective of the college and its administration.

administrator who allowed those under him to have significant input on most matters, but he reserved the right to make the final decision. The faculty for the most part determined policy, but only with significant input from Mays. Cook added that although Mays was "very humane, . . . when he made a decision that was it; you couldn't run over him."[12]

Few academic leaders can articulate their position on all of the issues confronting their institutions and its various agents. Just as rare is the administrator who can clearly diagram the administrative chain of command from top to bottom. Like so many of his peers, Mays could not keep up with every issue that arose on his campus. Nevertheless, he was still able to clearly articulate the organizational flow chart for his administration. The following diagram was shared in a 1962 letter from Mays to J. George Harrar of the Rockefeller Foundation:

Board of Trustees

President

Assistant to the President   Administrative Committees

Academic   Registrar   Dir. of   Dir. of Student   Bursar and Asst.
Dean   Placement   Personnel   Treasurer

Department Heads   Faculty and Staff   Superintendent   Accountant
                                         Bldgs & Grnds   Cashier
                                                           Secretary

Dean of Instruction   Auxilliary Enterprises
(plans to add position)

This was how Mays structured his administration. All major decisions were funneled through the president's office. It was a highly centralized organization, with at least seven people reporting directly to Mays: the Academic Dean, the Registrar, the Director of Placement, the Director of Student Personnel (Dean of Students), the Bursar and Assistant Treasurer,

---

[12]Cook interview.

the Administrative Committee, and an Assistant to the President. These seven do not include other members of the Administrative Committee, aside from the chairs and the entire faculty and staff who apparently reported to Mays, not to the Academic Dean or Department Chairs. Omitted from the chart above was the Director of Financial Aid, who was added prior to 1967 and who also answered directly to the president. It also appears that prior to 1967 the Superintendent of Buildings and Grounds became an administrative officer who also answered directly to the president.[13]

There were no vice-presidents and likewise there existed no cumbersome "communications network." With the exception of major construction or changes to the goals and missions of the college which required approval from the Board of Trustees, Mays had the final word. There was little doubt as to who ran Morehouse. This type of organization was not uncommon at the traditionally black institutions. In most cases, the president was clearly in charge.

In assessing the black college president and his leadership role, Earl J. McGrath observed,

> . . . the gap between his training, ability, and strength of personality and the other members of the staff has often been so wide that he has been in fact the only person in the academic body capable of giving the leadership and making the decisions on which the very survival of the institution depended.[14]

This strong, dominating type of presidency was necessary for survival for many traditionally black institutions and many white institutions as well. Until the mid-twentieth century those American colleges that were most successful were often inextricably linked to a very successful and forceful president. The survival of the American colonial and early nineteenth century colleges usually depended on the strength of their presidents. In the late nineteenth century such presidents as Charles Eliot at Harvard, Henry Tappan at Michigan, William Rainey Harper at Chicago, and Daniel Coit

---

[13]*Morehouse College Bulletin: Founder's Day Issue and Twenty-Year Report* 49 (Winter 1987), 6.

[14]Earl J. McGrath, *The Predominantly Negro Colleges and Universities in Transition* (New York: Bureau of Publications, Teachers College, Columbia University, 1965), 124.

Gilman at Johns Hopkins present dramatic examples of strong presidents who shaped, built, and redirected their respective institutions.[15] Traditionally black institutions shared the tradition of strong presidents, as witnessed by Booker T. Washington at Tuskegee, Mordecai Johnson at Howard, and John Hope at Atlanta.

In keeping with this tradition of strong leadership, Mays was in fact a commanding figure on his campus, and he seldom relinquished much control. He operated a "very closely guarded, closed shop;"[16] "a tight ship' that allowed him to be "at the focus of everything."[17] It has been suggested that Academic Dean Brailsford Brazeal (Dean of Men prior to 1940) was Mays's "second-in-command," however that could not be substantiated. According to the organizational chart, Brazeal's position as Academic Dean was apparently the second highest position in the college administration. However, organizational charts do not always reveal how an organization really works. It has been suggested by others that the Mays-Brazeal relationship became strained over the years. Lonnie King, former Morehouse student leader, recalled,"you rarely saw the two of them together."[18] Samuel DuBois Cook suggested that there existed tension between Mays and Brazeal, and "instead of firing Brazeal, Mays simply worked around

---

[15]John S. Brubacher and Willis Rudy, *Higher Education in Transition* (New York: Harper & Row, Publishers, 1976). Brubacher and Rudy present a chronological look at various topics affecting the development of the American college and university. Among other topics, the authors analyze the impact of strong presidents on the college movement and on particular institutions.

[16]Alton Hornsby interview.

[17]Tobe Johnson (Chairman of the Political Science Department), interview by author, 22 February 1988, Atlanta.

[18]Lonnie King, Special Assistant to the President, Coppin State University, interview by author, 28 July 1989, Columbus, Ohio. Lonnie King was the indisputable Morehouse student leader of the 1960 protests to desegregate downtown Atlanta. He convened several preliminary meetings to organize objectives and protestors. King (no relation to Martin Luther King Jr.) became the spokesperson for the demonstrations as he led the protesters in their marches, helped draft statements, and met with officials (including Mays) to plan strategies. The demonstrations were effective, and as a result, a desegregation order was agreed upon in September, 1961. Because of his involvement, King became well acquainted with President Mays and garnered a great deal of Mays's admiration and respect. For more on Lonnie King, see: Jones, *A Candle in the Dark*, 217 and 221 and Mays, *Born To Rebel*, 287-296.

him, trying to make a bad situation palatable, until it was time for Brazeal's retirement. He was very humane about it."[19]

Very little is written or documented about the chain of command under Mays. He worked most closely with his faculty for whom he felt an affinity and to whom he delegated many assignments. Tobe Johnson referred to Mays's administrative style as "very personal, authoritarian, benevolent." Johnson went on to suggest that Mays "never really trusted anyone other than himself, ultimately. But he realized he couldn't do it all himself . . . he sort of micromanaged. . . . he got into all kinds of details."[20]

Mays remained authoritarian throughout his tenure, and he meted out assignments to whomever he felt would be able to do the best job with that particular task. At times Mays appeared obsessive as he personally tended to minute details that should have been delegated to others. His distrust for the satisfactory completion of these tasks by others seemed to consume him. Johnson recalled that Mays would "personally inspect the latrine at commencement to make sure it was clean for the parents."[21] Most would agree that a college president has many more important tasks to which he must attend, especially during commencement. However, Mays's selfish distrust of others and his selfless belief that he was not above checking the restrooms together prompted him to do this task himself. His authoritarian delegation of assignments often began with himself.

PHYSICAL PRESENCE AND CHARACTER

To understand Mays's authoritarian nature, one must also understand his authoritarian presence. Mays's physical stature made it easy to see why he was perceived by so many as having a dominating character. Standing six feet tall with what Tobe Johnson described as "very keen features for a black man," Mays made quite a physical impression.[22] This was enhanced in later years by the striking contrast between his smooth ebony complexion and his closely groomed, grayish white hair.

---

[19]Cook interview.
[20]Tobe Johnson interview.
[21]Ibid.
[22]Ibid.

Johnson described Mays as ". . . a very fit man. He was a vicious volleyball player who loved to play at the net and smash."[23] This statement challenges the belief that Mays was against athletics, a popular criticism levied against Mays while he was president.[24] While he always regarded athletics with respect and appreciation, he would never place it high on the agenda for Morehouse College. Relatively speaking, for Mays there were more important concerns with which to deal. He was not against athletics; he was simply more in favor of academics. Nevertheless, Mays enjoyed participating in sports (he played football at Bates), and he supported the Morehouse teams.[25]

Part of the criticism levied against Mays resulted from the poor showing the athletic teams, especially football, had shown since 1940. Once a dominating powerhouse that had won numerous championships, the football teams of Mays's era lost more games than they won. With rising academic scholarship standards came the downturn of athletics. Critics argued that since the college would not grant athletic scholarships the program could not be competitive. They called for the abandonment of the program or the awarding of grants in aid. Mays held fast to the notion that it was not in the best interests of the college to award aid based solely on athletic ability when there were so many who deserved aid based on need or academic ability.

Tobe Johnson continued in his description of Mays's physical presence. Mays, he said, "was a very graceful man . . . [walking] with an erect carriage with his head back." Mays was a spirited individual whose quick pace and long strides were more than once confused with arrogance or impatience. Yet he was more frequently viewed as, "very sincere, authentic, and unpretentious." Johnson described Mays as proud and perhaps conceited, but possessing just enough "impishness" to let people like him.[26]

---

[23] Ibid.

[24] O. Vernon Burton in the Introduction of, Benjamin E. Mays, *Born To Rebel* (revised edition), 1986, xxxi.

[25] Mays, *Born To Rebel*, 149-150. See Photograph, #7; "Forty-Eighth Annual Maroon and White Day Grid Classic Official Program," 20 November 1948, 2. College and University Files. Morehouse Athletics. Atlanta University Center Woodruff Library Archives.

[26] Tobe Johnson interview; Cook interview.

To some, Mays appeared unapproachable and aloof; to others he appeared larger than life, and yet to many others he seemed warm and inviting. A student under Mays and a faculty member and department head under Gloster, Alton Hornsby stated that the contrast between the two presidents was much more obvious. Hornsby saw Mays as more of an aristocrat, "you held him in awe." He saws Gloster as having a much more familiar style, "he would more often approach you."[27]

In contrast, Ann Barbre, a faculty member at Xavier University of Louisiana, had a quite different experience with Mays. As a visiting high school student at an Atlanta summer program she was engaged in conversation by a gentleman who appeared not only to command a great deal of respect, but who took a great deal of interest in what she had to say. This gentleman, later identified as Benjamin Mays, listened intently and queried her about her future goals, all the while maintaining eye contact and showing interest. "Although he did not know me and I was a mere teenager," said Barbre, "he took the time and spoke to me as if I really was important."[28]

Similar stories could be told, but the physical impression that Mays exhibited was on more than one occasion misinterpreted as cold and disdainful. Among other things, he was also criticized for being old-fashioned and conservative, which were both true. However, there were people involved with Morehouse who did not think those qualities were best for Morehouse. They wanted to see Mays "catch up with the times." They voiced their complaints, but their numbers were usually small and ineffectual. Undaunted, Mays continued to lead the college in the manner in which he was accustomed. By and large, he was viewed as a warm and genuine individual. Tobe Johnson added that in case anyone needed reassurance, "Mays always had a twinkle in his eye" to let them know that they were welcome.[29]

---

[27]Alton Hornsby interview.

[28]Ann Barbre, interview by author, 29 February 1988, New Orleans. Dr. Barbre has served for several years on the College of Pharmacy Faculty at Xavier University of Louisiana.

[29]Gloster interview; Johnson interview.

It was this same physical presence that welcomed so many and allowed Mays to lead an institution in an authoritative and singleminded fashion. An inspiring as well as intimidating appearance helped Mays to direct a black college at a time when dictatorial leadership was the norm. Beyond all of this, in order to understand Mays, one must first understand that central to his leadership, his administration, and his character was a strong and unwavering faith in God.

Ultimately, according to Mays, it was his unabashed faith in God that allowed him to lead Morehouse in the fashion that he did. He truly believed this and made no apologies for his faith. His belief sustained him in everything he did. Christianity was Mays's life work. He did not stop being a Christian in order to be president of a college and likewise he did not stop being president in order to be a Christian. Instead he tried to live out the gospel in his duties as president by utilizing strong Christian principles with a compliment of democratic ideals. That was the way he carried himself, the way he led Morehouse, and the way in which he tried to treat everyone. His strong faith, more than any other single factor, was responsible for the success that he was able to achieve. Mays suggested:

> . . . the quest of the human spirit is a quest for some form of salvation. Man can best be saved...by giving himself to others,...to some great cause,...to some great truth,...to some great institution,... in the obedience to God's will and in the interest of the common good.[30]

When asked about scandals that occurred between Mays and his faculty or his students, nearly everyone contacted replied that they doubted if any major scandals occurred. They allowed that what scandals did occur were usually minor and even those were very rare. Most of these respondents added that those which did happen were closely guarded incidents that very few people ever knew about.

To be sure, there existed several episodes that could fall into such a category, i.e., a physically abusive faculty member and one with a drinking

---

[30]Mays, "The Road to Blessed Immortality", *The Pulpit*, 31. Undated photocopy in Benjamin E. Mays File. South Carolina Library.

problem could qualify. There were also reports of Mays allegedly purging his faculty of suspected homosexuals. No one could substantiate the assertion, or would go on record as having said so, but this allegation was mentioned in two separate interviews. The reasons for having so few scandals attached to Mays, with few people willing to discuss them and even fewer people aware of them, are two-fold. As Gloster proposed when he was asked about scandals connected to his immediate predecessor,

> . . . it would be hard to find out if they occurred. I have no reason to believe that they did, but when working with a figure so admired by most and only recently deceased, his image is still in the minds of many. Nobody is willing to speak ill of a person like that publicly. . . . [31]

After Gloster allowed that "surely things could have happened," he pointed out that "the manner in which information was controlled would not have allowed such information to travel very far, or to too many people.[32]

HIGH EXPECTATIONS

An integral part of Mays's leadership style was his high expectations. He expected great things of himself and he expected great things of others. He often said:

> The tragedy of life is often not in our failure, but rather in our complacency; not in our doing too much, but rather in our doing too little, not in our living above our ability, but rather in living below our capacities.[33]

To Mays, failure resulted from not having done a job to its fullest. Mere completion, or even satisfactory completion of a task was not enough; the task had to be done to the best of one's ability. Accordingly, this required stretching one's ability to its uppermost limits, towards the higher expecta-

---

[31]Hugh Gloster interview.
[32]Ibid.
[33]*Quotable Quotes*, 4.

tions. With high expectations as his goal for everyone, especially his students and faculty, Mays fully recognized that on many occasions they would fall short of their goal. Mays then reminded them of one of his more popular sayings: "The tragedy in life doesn't lie in not reaching your goal. The tragedy lies in having no goal to reach. . . . Not failure, but low aim is sin."[34]

Samuel DuBois Cook, recalling his days as a Morehouse student, remembered how vigorously Mays pushed the students to reach higher, to do more. Later as a faculty member in the Atlanta University Center, Cook also witnessed the same kind of vigor in Mays as he pushed his faculty and staff. Cook described Mays's enthusiasm this way:

> Dr. Mays was a hard taskmaster. I sometimes thought that it was easier to please God than Dr. Mays. His standards for himself and others were inordinately high, lofty, and demanding. Truly they could never be satisfied—thank God. He kept us stretching, striving, aspiring, and always looking up.[35]

Though Mays was demanding, he "asked no more than he gave." Whatever he asked of his students or faculty, he had done or was willing to do himself. He was therefore able to advise his faculty "don't drink, don't smoke, [and] don't borrow money."[36]

He was more than qualified to ask his faculty to get advanced degrees and to conduct research. Mays was well aware of how difficult that could be after having had to postpone obtaining his doctorate because of many delays and several professional opportunities. Nevertheless, he did go back to graduate school to obtain his doctorate, which was something he encouraged all of his non-terminal degree holding faculty members to do.

Additionally, he continued to produce significant research throughout his professional career. His research was always done at such a high level.

---

[34]*Disturbed About Man* (Richmond: John Knox Press, 1969), 120.

[35]50. Samuel DuBois Cook, Funeral Eulogy for Dr. Benjamin E. Mays, March 31, 1984. The entire text of Dr. Cooks' eulogy of Mays can be found in *Morehouse College Bulletin: Founder's Day Issue* 46 (Winter 1984), 14-16.

[36]Butler T. Henderson, "Bennie Mays and Morehouse, *Bates College Bulletin* 116, (January 1969), 1.

The account of the 1898 Phoenix Riot which Mays included in *Born To Rebel* prompted historian O. Vernon Burton to remark, "[It] is first-rate historical investigation combining techniques of oral history with the more time-tested traditional sources." Burton also cited Mays's *The Negro's God as Reflected in His Literature* and a collaboration with Joseph W. Nicholson, *The Negro's Church* as the starting point for studies of Black religion.[37] With these kinds of credentials, coupled with numerous affiliations with civic, cultural, and civil rights organizations, it is easy to see how Mays could ask so much of his students and staff.

Few people knew of Mays's frequent generosity to students, faculty members, and others in need, and to the college. He often assisted both faculty and students who were in need of financial help. However, since he advised against borrowing money, in most instances he would simply offer his assistance as a gift. In 1961, when Mrs. Mays saw that student Lonnie King was ill and without a winter coat, she had her husband's personal tailor make a coat for him. Mays knew that as a student leader, Lonnie appeared in public often. He therefore suggested that a good suit be made for Lonnie, as well. King recalled that he was overwhelmed by their concern for his well being and appearance, and equally amazed that the suit was worth $300 and the coat was worth $500.[38]

Tobe Johnson reported that in later years, "Mays gave most of his salary back to the College." Johnson added, "[N]o one was more benevolent than he."[39] Mays merely gave what he had, hoping that the people he affected might take heed of his actions and do the same.

---

[37]Burton, in his introduction to Mays's *Born To Rebel* (revised edition), 1986, xxxiii, xl-xlii.

[38]Lonnie King interview. It was interesting to find out that a man who appeared to be so miserly would have a personal tailor. King pointed out that although it appeared Mays owned only a couple of suits, he actually owned several suits that were very similar in style and color. They were of the finest quality and since they were tailor-made they lasted for a very long time. Thereby, allowing Mays to wear them year after year.

[39]Tobe Johnson interview.

CONNECTIONS

Mays had numerous connections outside of Morehouse. These connections included people who had no direct relationship to the college, as well as those who had a casual involvement. He also maintained strong ties with countless others who were either former faculty members or students, parents of Morehouse students, or major contributors to the college. These connections extended from coast to coast and around the world. They came from all walks of life with many of them being leaders in the fields of religion, politics, civil rights, sports, and entertainment. A glance at the speakers and pallbearers for Mays's funeral would reveal such friends as Martin Luther King, Sr. and Jimmy Carter among the speakers and people like Henry Aaron, Ralph Abernathy, Lerone Bennett, Coretta Scott King, Charles Merrill, and Charles V. Willie among the honorary pallbearers. Most of these friendship were cultivated long before these people became famous.[40]

Mays's skillful use of such relationships helped him to meet many of the college's needs. To be able to call on a Ralph Abernathy or a Henry Aaron to address a student body or to be able to call on successful authors like Bennett and Willie to help spread the word of the conditions at Morehouse was an advantage that Mays enjoyed and used. To be able to write to a friend like Charles Merrill and request funds for the college was a distinct advantage for Mays. Sometimes no requests were necessary. Just having Mays as a personal friend often left a fondness and appreciation for Morehouse's success on the hearts and minds of these contacts. Many influential individuals were so inspired by Mays they would often perform unrequested gestures of generosity.

Former Georgia Governor Jimmy Carter who was awarded an honorary doctorate from Morehouse College cherished the degree which was bestowed upon him prior to his election to the presidency. He often went to Mays for advice which in later years indirectly resulted in favorable considerations for Morehouse. Following an unsuccessful run for Governor of Georgia, Carter sent shock waves around the state and the country as he made his 1971 inaugural speech at the conclusion of a second, and victorious, gubernatorial

---

[40]*Morehouse College Bulletin: Founder's Day Issue* 46 (Winter 1984), 6.

campaign. Many of his critics were astounded when they heard him say, "No poor, rural, weak, or black person should ever have to bear the additional burden of being deprived of the opportunity for an education, a job, or simple justice." With those words, Carter ushered in a new day for black educational opportunities in the state of Georgia.[41]

When Carter's policies implemented his statements, it was clear that his relationship with black higher education would be harmonious. Although policies made by the governor could have little direct impact on a private college such as Morehouse, the indirect effects of those policies greatly affected the college. State supported financial aid and scholarships were used by Morehouse students. Also, the governor's appointive power and his many social invitations enabled persons connected with Morehouse to participate in various activities. Carter's relationship with Mays helped to keep him informed about the needs of black higher education. It was a relationship they continued through Carter's term as President. In recognition of their friendship and his unique relationship to Morehouse, Carter was asked to speak at Mays's funeral. There he recounted an amusing prophecy that Mays once gave him, ". . . You may be the first Morehouse Man in the White House, but you won't be the last."[42]

Mays had many loyal friends and he was loyal to them as well. The loyalty he received often established loyal ties to the college. Although this most often developed unintentionally, Mays wanted it that way and it nearly always produced favorable results for Morehouse. McGrath suggested in 1965 that since black colleges were "[h]eavily dependent on the good will of influential private benefactors or local political powers, they have tended to remain 'presidential' institutions."[43] This tendency required a strong leader who could "win friends and influence people." Mays had that ability.

INTEGRATION, AND OTHER CONCERNS

Following the historic 1954 *Brown v. Topeka Board of Education* much talk and debate centered around the black colleges. Some educators were

---

[41]*Current Biography Yearbook 1977* ed. Charles Moritz (New York: H. W. Wilson Company, 1977), 102.
[42]*Morehouse College Bulletin: Founder's Day Issue* 46 (Winter 1984), 5.
[43]McGrath, *Predominantly Negro Colleges*, 124.

curious as to what would be the black colleges' response to the Supreme Court's ruling. Others questioned the necessity of the black college amidst this removal of racial barriers and this new day of equality. History has proven that these latter concerns lacked a great deal of insight as neither equality nor the removal of racial barriers immediately followed this ruling. Nevertheless, these were pressing questions of the day.[44]

Always full of sound advice, Mays gave the students plenty of ammunition with which to address these questions and problems. He challenged his students to overcome the evils of the day. Typical of the advice was the wisdom he shared with his students on how to.deal with segregation. Mays explained:

> I pointed out to the Morehouse students that the only way they could be free in a rigidly segregated society was by consistent refusal ever to accept subservience and segregation in their own minds. As long as a man registers some form of protest against that which is obviously wrong, he has not surrendered his freedom, and his soul is still his own.[45]

This was the type of message that Mays repeated on many occasions. There was a solution to every problem, and he challenged his students always to seek it out. He was challenged as well; many times by himself. While pondering the complexities of the racial climate, he composed the following reflective question: "How should the president of a black college behave when his sense of right and righteousness is assaulted by the interracial wrongs in the society in which he lives?" Mays's response to his own question demonstrated wisdom and insight into the difficulty of leading a traditionally black institution, such as Morehouse, during a period of tremendous racial inequity. He suggested that there is no single definitive answer. According to him it was a question that "must be answered over and over again in a world where the problem of race is omnipresent, as close to a black man as the beating of his heart."[46]

---

[44]Ibid., 5-10.
[45]*Born to Rebel*, 196.
[46]Ibid.

Mays wrote *Born to Rebel* with the hopes that it would bring about some understanding of the modern problems related to race. Interwoven with his story are countless tales and references describing and questioning the "omnipresent problem," its affect on people, and how they dealt with it. As he did for his students, he offered numerous strategies for combating what he called the "ridiculous manifestations of segregation." Most of these solutions were straightforward and serious, but a glimmer of impishness appeared in more than one solution. In reference to segregated drinking fountains, Mays reported, "[T]here were a few devilish ones like me, who, though unmistakably black, just had to have a sip of 'white water' once in a while just for the fun of it."[47] As with so many other challenges that he faced, Mays was able to find a logical and successful strategy for meeting the challenge and accomplishing his goals.

Among the many questions that were directed at Morehouse, was the question of integration. When asked in the late 1950s to define Morehouse's position on integration, Mays pointed out that the Morehouse faculty had always been integrated and that the college's charter prohibited the exclusion of worthy students solely on the basis of race. He added:

> . . . The President of the College believes that integration is not the chief concern of Morehouse. Our chief concern is quality education—to attract a faculty so excellent and a student body so able that no one would ever need to raise the question of integration. If we succeed in doing this, in due course, students of all races will find their way to Morehouse. We would like to say here once and forever: that if the quality of work we do at Morehouse is not good enough for members of any race, it is not good enough for Negroes. Our aim is to make a good college better and a better college the best.[48]

Mays's opinions on this issue were passionate, although always insightful and logical. He was particularly disturbed about the apparent "overnight" inferiority that was presumed of black colleges immediately

---

[47]Ibid., 85.

[48]"The Goal: To Make a Good College Better and a Better College Best," pamphlet circa 1959, 10. G.A. 157. Box 62. Folder 543. Rockefeller Archive Center.

following the *Brown* decision. Referring to the distasteful thoughts of many an educator of the period, Mays wrote,

> Colleges that were good enough for brilliant Negro students prior to May 17, 1954, ceased to be so immediately after. Black colleges, in the thinking of many, are not academically strong enough to train bright-minded blacks, but a white college—any white college—is so qualified."[49]

This type of thinking infuriated Mays as he noted time and again, the disparity with which funding was directed toward black colleges. He noted that despite his numerous efforts and contacts with white philanthropy, there remained a great discrepancy between how Morehouse was treated and how white colleges were treated. In his later years, after he had left the presidency, Mays had stern words for these philanthropists when he stated, "When it comes to the support of black institutions, it takes philanthropy a long time to make up its mind, even when the appropriation is relatively meager." This discrepancy also was quite pronounced in terms of government funding. Mays found it strange that a country could "willingly make reparations to the enemy and yet feel little or no moral obligation to compensate its own citizens for decades of shameful and savage treatment."[50]

Mays pointed out that whether they accepted it or not, the black colleges' financial well being were inextricably linked to white support. He noted that thirty-three United Negro College Fund colleges after having set a fundraising goal of $100,000,000 could not garner enough support for their goal and had to readjust this goal to half of that amount. Even this goal was not met as only $30,000,000 was raised. Meanwhile, in just three years, a single institution, the University of Chicago, was able to raise over five times the amount of money that these thirty-three black colleges collectively had raised. In Mays's opinion this was a clear case of white philanthropy supporting what it wanted to support. Mays would go on to

---

[49]*Born To Rebel*, 192.
[50]Ibid., 193.

suggest if white America truly wanted to help black higher education, it had better put its money where its mouth was.[51]

Tremendous changes took place regarding opportunities for blacks during the twenty-seven years Mays was president. One of his strengths was his ability to adapt to change or to speak about the dangers that even good change brought. His warning about the presumed "overnight" inferiority of black colleges and his chastisement of white philanthropists were not statements he likely would have made public before the late 1960s. He continuously advised his students and faculty about the changing times, yet he chose his words carefully when making controversial public statements relative to these changes. In spite of the fact that some of the students and faculty thought of him as "old fashioned," it appears that Mays was quite up to date. He was able to read the winds of change, knowing when it was safe to speak his mind in order to challenge or chastise the white community without fear of offending it to the point of losing support.

Like so many other American Negroes, Mays found it peculiar and unfortunate that he would be accepted more readily outside of his native land. Over the years he traveled outside of the country extensively, including trips to India, Ethiopia, Switzerland, Italy, and England. He went as a representative of the World Council of Churches, the YMCA, and on several occasions, the United States government.[52] This was the same country that was so hesitant to treat him as a full citizen.

What Mays learned from his travels, among other things, was that a global view was necessary to realize a better world. He also realized that if Morehouse was to be a great college, it would have to expand and become involved at an international level. This involvement was accomplished both directly and vicariously. Several efforts were begun to increase travel funds (including international travel) while at the same time international students began to attend and international faculty began to teach at the college. Sixteen years after his departure, the Morehouse student newspaper was crediting Mays with developing an international flavor on campus. In retrospect, the paper stated, "Under his leadership the College earned international recognition as scholars from other countries joined the faculty,

---

[51]Ibid, 194.
[52]Jones, *A Candle in the Dark*, 327-328.

growing numbers of foreign students enrolled, and fellowships and scholarships to study abroad became available."[53]

One crowning achievement for Mays was never realized during his administration, yet the majority of the necessary groundwork had been completed during his tenure. In a letter dated September 1, 1967, Hugh Gloster wrote to the Rockefeller Foundation informing them that Morehouse had been approved for a Phi Beta Kappa chapter.[54] The chapter was established in January of the following year and the first Morehouse initiates were welcomed four months later. Beginning in 1953, the approval process for the nation's best known honor society had taken fourteen years of appeals and requests from Mays. He wrote to the national offices, and he contacted the foundations looking for support for a Phi Beta Kappa chapter at Morehouse. After several rejections over the course of the years, a site visit was designated in 1967, and Morehouse was subsequently approved on the same day that Notre Dame and Michigan State were accepted. In his announcement letter, Gloster acknowledged the diligence with which Mays had pursued this recognition immediately prior to his retirement.[55]

Mays who was turned down for membership into Phi Beta Kappa as a student at Bates, but was later admitted in 1935, felt that perhaps race had something to do with his earlier rejection. Nevertheless, Mays always knew that acceptance into this organization was a clear indication of academic success; he wanted it for himself, and he wanted it for Morehouse. John Hope was a member as were several other faculty members, yet none of them pursued the acquisition of a chapter for Morehouse as aggressively as did Mays. In the end, both he and Morehouse had achieved another symbol of success and respectability.[56]

MAYS STEPS DOWN

Mays retired as president of Morehouse on 30 June 1967. He had originally planned to resign in 1965, but was requested by the Board of

---

[53]*The Maroon Tiger* 58, 17 February 1983, 3.

[54]Hugh Gloster to Joseph Black of the Rockefeller Foundation, 1 September 1967. General Education Board. Box G.C. 565. Rockefeller Archive Center.

[55]*Born To Rebel*, 187-188; Gloster to Black, 1 September 1967.

[56]*Born To Rebel*, 137, 158; Jones, *A Candle in the Dark*, 82, 210.

Trustees to stay on another year so that he could serve during the College's centennial anniversary year. Upon his retirement he was named President Emeritus of Morehouse. From 1968 to 1969 he was a visiting professor at Michigan State University.[57]

On 11 October 1969, following a serious illness, Sadie Mays, his constant companion and helpmate, died. Gloster said of her death, "they seemed to relate well and be happy together. He was never the same after she died."[58] Although disheartened by her loss, Mays continued as a member of the Atlanta Board of Education, serving as its President from 1969 to 1981. In that capacity "he urged young people to have a great love of learning, a burning desire for excellence, and a genuine compassion for humanity."[59]

On 28 March 1984, Mays died of pneumonia in an Atlanta hospital. It was said of him that he was always available with a word or a phrase of inspiration. These words were nearly always obtained from a portion of his deeply rooted Christian training and faith. Further, more often than not he had practiced what he preached. For his role in developing and leading Morehouse College, there is no less fitting example than the following advice that he gave:

Whatever one touches, his aim should always be to leave that which he touches better than he found it.[60]

[57]Mays to J. G. Harrar of the Rockefeller Foundation, 27 November 1964. General education Board. G.A. 157. Box G.C. 482, Rockefeller Archive Center. In this letter Mays announced his plans to retire on June 30, 1965; *Morehouse College Bulletin: Founder's Day Issue* 46 (Winter 1984), 7.

[58]Gloster interview.

[59]*Morehouse College Bulletin: Founder's Day Issue* 46 (Winter 1984), 18.

[60]*Quotable Quotes*, 4.

18

THE QUEST FOR STUDENTS: RESHAPING AFRICAN-AMERICAN MINISTRY

Charles Shelby Rooks

College campuses were the first target of the revolution I envisioned. The trumpet was sounded with a letter from President Nathan M. Pusey of Harvard, chairman of the Fund for Theological Education, Incorporated (FTE). The letter was directed to the presidents of all the African-American colleges and universities in the nation. A second letter was sent to the theological seminaries affiliated with the American Association of Theological Schools. Both letters announced the creation of the Protestant Fellowship Program and my appointment as the staff person responsible for managing it. Each college president was asked to name a faculty member or senior administrator who would serve as liaison with the Fund in publicizing the program. The intention was to establish a network of college and university personnel to inform students about the fellowships and interest them in ministry. Such a network was vital to the success of the Fund's efforts. It was impossible to cover three fellowship programs and all the colleges and seminaries in the United States and Canada with a two-person staff. No similar network was required for seminary campuses, because most seminaries are much smaller than colleges and the president or dean could be the effective liaison.

GETTING THE ATTENTION OF HIGHER EDUCATION

This approach was similar to the organization of the Trial Year in Seminary Program. At the outset of that program, a similar letter had been written by Pusey to colleges and universities all over the United States and Canada. The colleges responded by naming persons with whom the staff of the FTE could correspond. Participants in the program were known as Trial Year representatives by students and faculty at their schools. These representatives arranged for visits of the FTE staff with faculty and students on their campus, organized publicity about the program for students, and created faculty committees to screen nominees whose names were sent to the FTE. They were the very heart of the program, believers and evangelists who gave tremendously important service gratis to this effort. Some of these persons were already located on African-American college campuses. We hoped to expand this network significantly on such campuses.

Pusey's letter was directed to African-American colleges for two reasons: (1)s there was no need to duplicate the Trial Year in Seminary Program network because it could also be used to promote the Protestant Fellowship Program; and (2), and more important, by far the majority of African-American college students in 1960 were in the segregated African-American schools. Statistics estimated that there were between 120,000-180,000 African Americans enrolled in all U.S. colleges. Because the total African-American population was 20 million, this was a very small percentage of the eligible population to begin with. Further, desegregation was still ahead for most institutions of higher education. Most of the African-American students were therefore enrolled in African-American schools located mostly in the South.

The prestigious colleges and universities in the East and Midwest had few if any African Americans enrolled. Princeton University, for example, had no African-American students in 1960. Other Ivy League schools were not much better. This story was duplicated everywhere in the United States. Public colleges and universities were just beginning to admit African-American students reluctantly, and a handful of private schools in the South had such students in greatly limited numbers. In Virginia in 1960, for instance, African Americans of that state had only five colleges from which to choose—two public and three private. Similar patterns existed elsewhere. In the East, Midwest, and West, a small percentage of the large universities had a handful of African-American students. In those regions of the nation, they went either to colleges in the South or to teachers colleges or city colleges in urban areas near them. Large numbers of African-American high school graduates didn't go to college at all. Because the Protestant Fellowship Program offered fellowships for the senior year of college and the three years in seminary studying for the Master of Divinity degree, the Fund obviously would need to direct its efforts to African-American colleges in order to locate nominees for the Protestant Fellowship program in any numbers. Our focus and travel, therefore, would be principally in the South, where most of the African-American schools were located.

Our approach to the seminaries was different. African Americans already in seminary were eligible for these fellowships. Most seminaries had someone responsible for student aid. It was a simple matter to write to the president, the dean, or some other easily identifiable person and request that nominations be made. When I accepted the appointment to the staff of the FTE in June, I was introduced at the annual meeting of the American Association of Theological Schools during its sessions at the Episcopal Theological Seminary in Virginia. Most of those who attend meetings of ATS are heads of seminaries. The program was announced, and I was introduced to them. They evidenced great interest in this new program. During the fall I had only to remind them about the beginning of the program and the method of making nominations. It was an easy network to develop and cultivate, largely because the program was in the best interests of the seminaries anyway.

Searching for Students

We had much to do in a short time. I began work at the Fund on September 1, 1960. In many places, the fall semester had already begun or would soon begin. The letter to the college presidents had to be sent quickly so we could learn from them who were the liaison persons to whom I would travel in person to discuss the program. The application process we established required that nominations for the program be made by a college or seminary faculty person by November 20 of each year. No one could apply directly. This was deliberate. It provided a very important initial screening for us. We wanted to establish the necessity for excellence in the minds of faculty and students. With a maximum of forty fellowships per year to offer, we obviously expected to locate and support the most talented and promising men available. (In 1960 all programs of the FTE were open to men only. Before the decade was over, however, the Fund became more sensitive to the issue of feminism and women's rights and opened its programs to women.) The FTE would be criticized later for what was admittedly an elitist approach, but we felt it important to establish in the minds of everyone the expectation and requirement that African-American ministers should be highly able, creative, and well-educated persons. Anyway, we would never compromise on excellence if Benjamin Mays had anything to do with it! I agreed completely.

The second step in the application process required completed applications to be returned to the FTE by December 15. All persons who appeared to have a competitive chance were scheduled for interviews with a committee of persons in the general geographic region of their colleges. The FTE paid the cost of travel to the interviews. These committees usually consisted of three persons; they were chaired by either Walter or me, and included two college or university faculty members or administrators known to us largely through the networks we maintained. The interviews were conducted all across the United States and Canada during January and February. Normally, a committee would interview applicants for both the Trial Year in Seminary and Protestant Fellowship Programs. In March a national committee for each program, composed solely of FTE directors, met to review recommendations of the interview committees and to select the persons they nominated for election as Scholars by the full board of directors in April. In late April or early May, notices would go to the Scholars selected, to their colleges, and to the seminaries they planned to attend. I had to learn all the details of this highly organized process very quickly.

Visiting Campuses

I also had to establish some travel patterns immediately. I served as associate director for all activities of the Fund and would not be limited just to management of the Protestant Fellowship Program. Because most of the candidates for the Protestant Fellowship Program would undoubtedly be in the South, I contacted all the faculty the Fund would visit in the South, and I would be present for all the interview committees in that region later in the year. In the period from October 1 to November 20 I traveled throughout the South, visiting both colleges and universities I knew well and many I knew only by name.

It was a vital learning experience for me. Benjamin Mays's travels ranged from Delaware to Texas and many places in between. Most people have forgotten how difficult travel in the South was for an African American in 1960. Everything was still radically segregated. For that reason I couldn't even visit some campuses where our representatives were located. When I went to Tuscaloosa, Alabama, for example, I went to Stillman College, not the University of Alabama campus. Hotel accommodations weren't available in most places, and I usually stayed in facilities provided by African-American colleges. Often this meant sleeping on a cot in a dormitory. Meals were also a problem. Our normal approach was to ask our campus representative to arrange a meal, at the Fund's expense, with a significant group of faculty members to whom I could talk about Christian ministry and both the Trial Year in Seminary and Protestant Fellowship Programs, because African-American students were eligible for each. That sounds easy, but it wasn't, principally because we couldn't go to public restaurants in most of the South. Our meetings were therefore confined to what a college campus could offer. In many cases this was very limited.

The Fund reimbursed the colleges for the hospitality provided in their dining rooms, but it was not the level of hospitality we were able to offer in later years, when segregation in public accommodations finally ended. The issue has less to do with personal comfort than with the desire to demonstrate that this effort to recruit and support prospective Christian ministers was first class in every way and had resources to be so. This was one aspect of our attempt to change attitudes and ideas about African-American ministry. In 1960 segregation would not permit that kind of subtle but important demonstration.

I was well received on every campus I visited. I'm sure my name helped, especially on African-American campuses. At first some faculty people thought my father was about to visit them. Many people on African-American campuses knew my father either from his days of teaching English Bible at Lincoln University, his preaching at St. James Presbyterian Church in Harlem, or his marriage to Dorothy Maynor. Because they didn't know about me, some college people actually thought my father had accepted the job at the Fund. Thus, my name gave me entree in a variety of places.

The more important name was Rockefeller! We were very deliberate in associating the Rockefeller name with the Protestant Fellowship Program. We did that by always announcing in our publicity that the program was funded by Sealantic Fund, Inc., "established in 1938 by John D. Rockefeller Jr." This was a revolutionary statement in itself. Not only were significant major new resources available to support an enterprise directed toward the African-American community, but those resources supported the ministry. That grabbed attention about Christian ministry on African-American college campuses as perhaps nothing else could do. At the time, no other profession open to the African-American community had any comparable resources available.

Negative Images of Ministry
Among Faculty and Administrators

The revolution was directed initially toward administrators and faculty of African-American colleges and universities. In my travels that first fall, I discovered how very important this was. Faculty members tended to look negatively upon students who openly declared themselves for the Christian ministry. The Student Christian Association or its counterpart, the extracurricular activity in which most preministerial students could be found on campus, was often regarded by the majority of faculty as unworthy of their attention. Many college professors thought it a total loss if a young man with academic promise decided upon a church vocation. One college dean was almost in tears that year when one of his most promising mathematics students accepted a fellowship from the Fund. Another dean of one of the most highly regarded African-American colleges, a college still receiving support from a Christian denomination, told me quite openly, "I don't see why you're looking for such outstanding boys for the ministry. The average fellow can do quite well in that field." I found that attitude to be the predominant one among college administrators and faculty. Clearly, a revolution in these attitudes was necessary if the future of African-American ministry was to change for the better.

Some attitudes of faculty resulted from ignorance about both the church and preparation for ministry. Many faculty people had studied little if anything about religion in general, and even less about the particular historical contributions of African-American churches to their people and society. When I went to Virginia State College in the 1940s, at least one class in what was called "Negro History" was required for everyone's graduation. That requirement was admittedly unusual. Many teachers in African-American colleges in 1960 had not taken any such course. Thus, they knew little about the history of their own people or about the history of African-American Christianity. They had a negative image, however, of the churches in their community. With a few exceptions, those churches seemed to persons in an academic environment excessively emotional and anti-intellectual, and they did not think that conditions would change. They were also ignorant generally about educational qualifications for ministry required increasingly by Protestant churches. Some teachers didn't know that a first professional degree in ministry requires seven years of higher education. As a result, large numbers of African-American college teachers were either ignorant about education for ministry and church vocations or simply did not believe either religion or ministry was a rigorous intellectual discipline.

Further, in 1960 not many African-American colleges were consciously attempting to direct their students toward graduate education of any kind. A few did so very deliberately and very well, and the results were impressive. However, most did not. In most cases, administrators and professors spent little time acquainting themselves with the millions of new dollars in scholarship and fellowship monies being offered in a wide variety of fields. They also gave scant attention to the vocational opportunities suddenly beginning to open for African-American students for the first time. In the majority of colleges, no one had yet thought to appoint a faculty committee or administrator to stay abreast of graduate study opportunities or new vocational possibilities. Thus, curricula managed by such faculty showed little evidence of the flexibility or adaptability required in an era of remarkable and growing change in the prospects of African Americans.

I was greatly saddened to discover just how extensive was the lack of real intellectual interchange between students and faculty on many campuses. In some places, students' grades were even lowered for asking questions of the teacher. This was principally because of the unusual circumstances of that historical moment. It was also more true of faculty in some state colleges than in private ones, but I found it true to a degree in each. During the "sit-ins," college faculty found themselves challenged by their students for leadership of the communities in which faculty lived and worked. Sometimes faculty members were intimidated by state boards of education or by governors who made them uncertain of their personal futures and the very survival of their institution as integration approached. Many teachers responded by withdrawing or retreating from the leadership role they understood themselves to have. In an attempt to regain their leadership role, some teachers attempted to stifle students and would permit no challenge to their control of the one place left, the classroom. This swirl of events and emotions made difficult any creative intellectual interchange between faculty and students.

Finally, administrators and professors in most African-American colleges had yet to understand their personal responsibility to the college, to their students, and to themselves in connection with encouraging graduate education and competition in national fellowship programs by their graduates. The Protestant Fellowship Program was a good example. The Fund asked college faculty to do several things in connection with the program: (1) establish a process on campus whereby students could learn about the program and become interested in it; (2) develop faculty committees to screen students and help them compete better for the fellowships they sought; (3) make certain that students completed and returned applications; and (4) write careful and helpful recommendations when requested.

All of that seems very elemental. It was not. Unfortunately, in a segregated educational system only a handful of professors and administrators in African-American colleges had any experience in such matters in 1960. They would need to accept this additional responsibility if the African-American community was to prosper. They would also need to learn how their students compared with other college students. Isolated as they were, most teachers in African-American colleges had no way of making comparisons. Consequently, their nominees sometimes fared poorly in national competitions, and the faculty did not know why. Part of my task was to help them develop new determination about their tasks and gain this knowledge and experience. It was another side to the quiet revolution. I addressed it by visiting campuses annually and reporting my findings and observations.

In the predominantly white colleges with a few African-American students, we had other problems. Some attitudes exhibited by African-American college faculty were evident among their counterparts elsewhere in higher education. For instance, the image of ministry in the African-American community was negative for most white faculty. They also didn't believe that the most able African-American students should go into the profession. The most fundamental attitudinal problems with white faculty, however, had to do with overcoming the racism that existed everywhere. In many colleges, white professors and administrators were openly hostile to African Americans.

The academic community is not always the objective place it claims to be. Even at its best, the racism was demonstrated by either fundamental ignorance about the African-American community, low expectations about the ability of African-American students to do graduate study, or basic lack of interest in nearly everything outside white society and its preoccupations. Most of these teachers spent their energy on promising white students. They were blissfully unaware that African-American students might have academic and vocational needs or interests different from white students. In later years, when African-American students began to demand "Black Studies," the idea of such study as legitimate intellectual inquiry came as a shock to most white faculty. What was there to study? they asked. If they had an aim at all, it was simply to prepare African-American students for the kind of future their other students would have. It didn't occur to most of them that the future wouldn't be the same for African Americans as it was for whites for many years to come. A revolution was definitely required also in the thinking of most white faculty about ministry in the African-American community. Many were even more surprised than teachers in African-American colleges when an African American arrived on their campus looking for able and talented African Americans, offering opportunities for graduate study for the ministry, of all things, and waiving dollars from the Rockefeller family.

LEARNING ABOUT AFRICAN-AMERICAN STUDENTS FROM THE FIRST NOMINEES

After reviewing the applications and evaluating the interviews, we realized that dramatic changes would be needed in the thinking and attitudes of college students about Christian ministry, graduate study, and competing in national fellowship programs. By December 1, 1960, 102 nominations for the Protestant Fellowship Program had been made by college and seminary faculties. This number is significant when viewed against the total enrollment of 387 African Americans in 66 seminaries during the 1958-59 academic year reported at the Seabury Consultation by Harry Richardson, but it is not as good as it appears at first glance. The unfortunate news was that 41 of the 102, or roughly 40 percent, either did not apply after the forms had been sent or sent in such a small portion of their applications that we could not continue them in the competition.

A few statistics from the first year of the program are indicative of patterns that would be generally repeated during the next 15 years. In the fall of 1960, 21 private colleges or universities nominated 38 persons. Fourteen public colleges or universities nominated 23 students. Seventeen seminaries nominated 41 men. The 101 nominees had taken, or were taking, their college training at 30 African-American colleges or universities and only 11 white schools.

By far the largest denominational representation among the nominees was Baptist, 27 making application after being nominated. Next in order were the African Methodist Episcopal Church with 7, the Methodist Church with 6, and the Episcopal Church and the Christian Methodist Episcopal Church with 4 each. Nine denominations scattered 13 nominees among them. These statistics, with small variations from year to year, would be repeated in future years.

In the fall of 1961 I reported to the Institute of Religion at the Howard University School of Religion about the efforts of the first year of the program. The Institute of Religion was about the only forum for the discussion of religion in the African-American community at the time. I had participated in it while a pastor in Washington and knew most of its members well. They invited me back after my first year away to report on what I was doing. During my fourteen years at the FTE, I would wrestle continually with some of the problems and concerns I articulated in that report. They are worth noting here.

The report was published by the School of Religion under the title "The Image of the Ministry as Reflected in the Protestant Fellowship Program."[1]

1. The majority of men nominated were already seminary students. This meant simply that the Protestant Fellowship Program was not a signal success in enlisting new manpower. Actually, only nine out of 24 fellows [finally selected] represent new blood.

---

[1]Charles Shelby Rooks, "The Image of the Ministry as Reflected in the Protestant Fellowship Program," *Journal of Religious Thought* 18(Fall 1961): 139-140.

2. The private colleges and universities tend to produce a much higher percentage of men for the Christian ministry than do public institutions. This has been borne out over a six-year period by other programs offered by the Fund for Theological Education. The fact is, however, that public institutions are enrolling an increasing percentage of the college population, and a good deal more time and effort will have to be exerted on such campuses lest we fail in our purpose. [This is still true.]

3. The bulk of Negro ministerial candidates receive their college training in Negro institutions. This is not really news since the majority of Negro college students are in such schools, a fact which is likely to be true for some time. [Actually, this changed much more quickly than I predicted.]

4. The majority of Negro ministerial candidates are Baptist by denominational preference. The Methodist groups together produce only two-thirds the number of Baptist nominees. No one will be startled by that statement, but it poses real problems, particularly in the matter of placement, because the Baptist congregational organization, as contrasted with an episcopal structure, is still a handicap to the young man seeking his first pulpit. Note also that the African Methodist Episcopal Zion Church nominated only one man for our program. Add to that fact that less than half-a-dozen A.M.E.Z. men are now enrolled in accredited seminaries and you have a serious shortage of adequately prepared men in that denomination. The predominantly white denominations are in trouble, too. The two Presbyterian bodies, the Congregationalists, and the Episcopalians nominated only ten men, and only two of these received fellowships.

5. The great bulk of these nominees came from southern states. Again, this is not news. This was partly because we concentrated on the South, believing that most of the Negro students would be found there and , would therefore be easier to contact. It is true, however, that large numbers of Negroes are now attending the public universities of the East and Midwest, with an increasing number doing the same in the South. The problem is how to get at them for enlistment purposes since so many of these schools no longer keep records by race.

6. A large number of the nominees either made no application after the forms had been sent, or did not complete their forms: 36 out of 102 or roughly one-third. This is a most unfortunate statistic and we are at some pains to discover the reason for such a statistic. Certainly it is obvious that the persons making nominations need to follow through much more carefully on them.[2]

So much for statistics. This pattern was not to change substantially until the mid-1970s. What it pointed to, however, was the scope of the revolution required.

RESHAPING STUDENT ATTITUDES

The revolution was thus aimed substantially at the ideas and attitudes of students. Their thoughts and convictions about ministry determined whether they chose the profession themselves and often whether their peers did do.

Negative Images of Ministry

The first attitude requiring change was similar to the problem with faculty; a negative image of ministry in the African-American community. The fundamental aim of the Protestant Fellowship Program was to encourage men to enter the ministry with the intention of becoming pastors of local churches. Many applicants that first year were openly rebellious against the image of the ministry they saw in their pastors and other clergy with whom they were acquainted. Over and over again, in both the written papers that were part of their applications and in their interviews, they told how much they had been repelled by the lack of training their pastors had, by dull and uninteresting sermons, by the seeming unconcern of their churches with the problems of this life, and by what they regarded as open exploitation of the church by pastors they knew. They were also largely uninspired by their college chaplains, many of whom were uninteresting teachers and uninspiring preachers. Although most applicants had not

---

[2]Ibid., 139-140.

developed their own vision of what ministry could be, they had begun the process. The main problem for the aspirations of the FTE was not so much our nominees as those other students on campus who might never overcome the antipathy toward ministry caused by their equally unhappy observations of the profession. That first year of competition had thus identified and confirmed the necessity for revolution in negative student attitudes about ministry in African America.

Commitment to Academic Excellence

Another attitudinal revolution had to do with insufficient concern among ministerial students about academic excellence. Of the sixty-one men who applied in the fall of 1960, eighteen were rejected without making the interview stage. Nineteen were rejected after being interviewed. That means that less than one-third of those who completed their applications were qualified for the Protestant Fellowship Program awards. We funded twenty-four persons that first year, but had fiscal resources to support about forty. We would have been delighted to offer additional fellowships, but simply did not turn up sufficient numbers of persons who met the program's standards.

This situation continued far into the life of the Protestant Fellowship Program. It was largely because too many aspirants for graduate theological study and ordained ministry didn't have the cumulative grade average of at least a "B" which was the minimum standard for the program. Benjamin E. Mays, B. Julian Smith, and I had agreed that the program should operate as a distinguished graduate study program. The minimum standard for admission to and continuing in most graduate degree programs is a cumulative grade average of "B." Mays insisted that we should find candidates academically eligible for whatever seminary the Scholar chose among the member schools of the American Association of Theological Schools. Our fellowship would provide the financial means to attend Harvard, Yale, Union, and so forth, as well as the Howard University School of Religion or the Interdenominational Theological Center, the two fully accredited African-American seminaries. We were determined that every Scholar's grades and academic standing should be sufficiently high to guarantee admission to any seminary. We wanted to be certain that Scholars were free to exercise their choice and that no one would turn them down for academic reasons. Again, we were convinced that the Protestant Fellowship

Program should be first class in every way.

In the first and subsequent years of the program, some college faculty didn't understand this requirement. Sometimes they nominated persons who weren't fully eligible academically. I frequently received complaints about our minimum standard when I visited college campuses. I always recalled for students, faculty and myself Benjamin Mays's quiet but stubborn comment when we looked at results of the interviews the first year. I had brought to the national selection committee (consisting of Mays, Smith and myself) a person with less than a "B" average. I tried to indicate my belief that the man had unrealized potential. Mays looked at me and said insistently, "But, Mr. Rooks, this man doesn't have a "B" average!" End of the matter. I never forgot Mays's comment. I had been forcefully reminded that the Protestant Fellowship Program was neither a simple financial aid nor a compensatory education program. Both financial aid and compensatory education might be required by African-American students, but the Protestant Fellowship Program was expected to serve a much larger purpose. Through the persons selected and the awards offered, it would establish a new vision about a highly educated ministry in African-American churches and provide an example of the superior kinds of persons required for the ministry of those churches. We were betting on unusual people to be the leaders of the future.

The significant and continuing problem with this conviction about the program was that many college faculty and their students had no vision of ministers as professionals who were exceptionally qualified academically and intellectually. They really didn't believe it was necessary, therefore, to work at producing the outstanding grades that were the usual measure of a passion for excellence in academic circles. The FTE would need to find a way to foster a revolution in attitudes about the academic performance of college students contemplating study for Christian ministry.

Entering National Competitions

The third change in student attitudes concerned preparation for national academic competitions. Nineteen applicants were rejected that first year in the interview process. I have to admit that the Fund's interview process was completely foreign to the experience of most African-American college students in those days. A committee of three persons would interview about ten applicants in the course of a single day. The entire application consisted of a brief biography, a writing sample, a registrar's transcript of grades, a budget for the fellowship year and recommendations from three persons. This information was duplicated and sent in advance to committee members. Interviews were scheduled for thirty-minute intervals. We talked with an applicant for about twenty-five minutes. Each committee member then made individual judgments about him, recording these on forms provided by the FTE. There was a minute or two to review papers for the next candidate, and the new interview began. At the end of the day, committee members compared notes and made a collective decision about their recommendations, finally ranking the nominees they recommended.

This was a rigorous process for both the interviewees and interviewers. All the interviewers with whom I worked during my fourteen years with the FTE took their responsibility very seriously. They read the materials carefully, asked thoughtful questions, and listened to the persons being interviewed very attentively. What made the responsibility awesome was the knowledge that career decisions and even the future of human beings might be determined by the decisions made, and those decisions had to be made quickly. Twenty-five minutes is not a very long time upon which to base a judgment about any person. It was the time available however.

What made this situation at all just or tenable were the checks and balances of the system: (1) the considerable amount of information received in the application, including recommendations from college professors who knew the applicant; (2) a review of the application by both FTE staff persons; (3) a personal interview with a committee of distinguished educators and clergy who compared judgements with each other; (4) another review by a committee of FTE directors; and (5) a vote by the full FTE Board of Directors. The system was evaluated constantly to keep us all sensitive to the need for both compassion and justice. We spent hours each year, for instance, developing the content of letters to applicants who had been rejected. No is a hard word for anyone, but we wanted to be sure we said it with as much compassion and support as possible. We also developed methods to introduce those turned down for PFP fellowships to seminaries that might offer them admission and financial aid. It was a way to increase the total number of qualified seminary students.

I'm certain the interview had to be even more difficult for the interview-ees. Sometimes the interviews were held in impressive surroundings that were foreign to the student. For instance, in January 1961 few, if any, African-American students in Texas had ever been near the office of the Chancellor of Texas Christian University. That was where we conducted interviews that year, however, for students from all over Texas. Sometimes the interviewers themselves were impressive. It wasn't often in those days that African-American students ever talked personally with the legendary Benjamin Mays, but Benny was always an interviewer in Atlanta, sometimes in his own office. It is not surprising, then, that many African-American students were exceedingly nervous about the interview. My task as chairperson of the interview committee was to put them as much at ease as possible so they could make their best showing. Over the years I worked hard to learn how to do this. As I reported to my colleagues in the Institute of Religion, however:

> A good many of our nominees did not show up well in interview at all. These students showed no indication of ever having read anything of significance outside of their required reading. Many did not retain the title and author of textbooks currently used! Most of them did not show much ability to think for themselves in their major field of study. They simply repeated what they had gotten from their teachers! Too often they did not react quickly or decisively to questions directed toward them.[3]

Of course, there are reasons for this. Desegregation of the educational system had been decreed by the Supreme Court only six years earlier (1954). In the segregated society and educational system under which our nominees had grown up, few African-American students had been exposed to those disciplines that produce quickness and incisiveness of mind, disciplines others in our society take for granted. The majority of African-American children, even those from so-called better homes, were not acquainted daily with the arts, theater, philosophy, history. They were not taught to develop wholesome reading habits, and reading is a basic activity of graduate education. The purchase of books, or even the newspaper, was the exception rather than the rule.

---

[3]Ibid., 140.

What struck me in the interviews every year was the contrast between the white and African-American applicants. On the whole, the white student showed up far better in his ability to react to ideas quickly, in his training to think for himself, in his knowledge of what was going on in the world at large, and in his overall understanding of his major field. During those initial years I saw many African-American students who may have had tremendous potential for ministry, but who had not been exposed to experiences and disciplines that produce sharp and carefully reasoned thought. Thus, they did not demonstrate their potential for graduate study. These deficiencies, which resulted from segregation, would haunt me throughout my years with the Fund.

I was always torn, on one side, by the desire to help African-American students reach their promise and, on the other side, by the necessity, for the fundamental good of the order, to hold up the banner of excellence. I always came down on the side of excellence, in the conviction that the long-term future of African America is dependent upon the ability to produce people who can compete with anyone in any arena. For nearly a quarter century, the word I proclaimed on college campuses everywhere was about the necessity for college teachers to train their students for competition more deliberately and help them develop the vision and attitudes to compete well in every academic arena. I had no doubt that the students could do so if challenged correctly and given the opportunity and experience required.

Proper Completion of Applications

Finally, we discovered African-American students required assistance in learning to complete application forms with competence. During every one of the fourteen years I was with the Fund, most students simply did not communicate well in writing. Almost everybody was highly articulate verbally, but only a few could transfer that skill to paper. Applications for the Protestant Fellowship Program required a writing sample. Standard questions were asked of everyone. They were designed to demonstrate the applicant's thinking and writing ability. This would give the interviewer an insight into the applicant as a person, some notion about academic skills, and would suggest questions the interviewers might ask the candidate to elaborate upon during the interview. The writing sample was very important, therefore. The questions weren't technical or really tough, yet most applicants had difficulty discussing themselves or their ideas in writing. They were unable to elaborate or expand upon their responses to the questions. Too often we received one or two sentence responses instead of thoughtful answers that demonstrated intellectual interests and academic competence. There was little evidence of reflecting upon contemporary problems in society. What made this distressing, obviously, is that graduate education is so highly dependent upon a student's ability to write. Verbal skills, at which African-American students were very adept, don't count for much at graduate level. Reading and writing are the primary occupations of graduate students—in seminary or anywhere else. The inability to write with clarity and competence is a tremendous handicap even for the most verbal candidate. This competence usually determines whether a person will gain admission to and remain in graduate school or receive a national fellowship.

The other part of the application that African-American students did not complete well was the budget for the anticipated award year. The Protestant Fellowship Program did not offer the same stipend to each Scholar. We knew students would inevitably have very different needs and completely dissimilar resources available to them. Originally, the program provided support for the senior year of college and the three years of seminary. We wanted to encourage the schools to become partners with us in supporting each student. It would help them develop more awareness of their responsibilities to the entire African-American community. Most of all, we wanted to be as just and as fair as we could be in the distribution of the funds available to FTE.

For all these reasons, the application required each candidate to fill out a budget. It was not surprising that most had difficulty doing so. Students couldn't be entirely certain what their expenses would be and didn't know what to expect in financial aid from the schools in which they were enrolled or would attend. They weren't sure what the FTE would provide either. They were also uncertain about their personal resources. The information provided on the budget, therefore, was usually not very reliable. How could it be? Few of these students had ever been fortunate enough to have adequate funds available to them. They learned to live on whatever they had, often working at several jobs to make ends meet.

One of the Fund's aims was to relieve them of financial worries so they could concentrate on their studies. That's the major benefit of a graduate fellowship. In order to help them adequately, we needed enough financial information to make a reasoned judgment about the amount of each fellowship.

I learned a good deal during those fourteen years about creative budgeting. During every interview, I tried to clarify my basic budget questions. That's when the creativity really started. I finally began to understand that African-American students were highly skilled, not at budgeting, but at taking what they received and making it work—somehow. My job, therefore, was to make the best educated guess I could about the costs a student would incur in a particular school during a given year, what resources the student might develop, and how much money the Fund should provide. It would have been helpful if each of us could have been more precise, but the outcomes worked despite inadequate and incomplete information. Fellowships ranged from $500 to $8,000 during my years with the Fund. It was significant financial help based upon each person's need.

Regular Campus Visits

I attempted to get at the revolution with faculty and students in a number of ways. For every one of the fourteen years I was with the FTE, I visited college campuses regularly. Through our representative I arranged meetings with key faculty persons—usually at dinner or luncheon. On some tours I would have lunch with faculty in one school, drive or fly to another town for a dinner meeting, and go on somewhere else for a breakfast meeting to start the next day. It was a grueling schedule, but gradually over the years I could begin to see some headway. I discovered what I had learned well in the parish ministry, namely, that there is no substitute for face to face conversation. Such discussion is enhanced by the simple fact of eating a meal together. That's not a new discovery in the history of the world, but it is an important one to remember. The table is a great place for revolution!

Sometimes we gathered faculty people from several colleges at the same time. It was a way of enlarging the conversation and helping professors compare notes with each other on a broader basis than their own campus. In all these instances, the FTE paid all the necessary expenses of faculty and administrators to travel and be together.

I also lectured and preached on college campuses throughout the nation, and particularly in the South. In those days, there were two major religious platforms available on campus: the college chapel and what was known as "Religious Emphasis Week." I preached in college and university chapels all over the United States—from Rutgers University in New Jersey to Stanford Memorial Chapel in Palo Alto, from Rankin Chapel at Howard University, Washington, D.C., to Lawson Chapel at Dillard in New Orleans. Many of these engagements were repeated over and over. For instance, my friend Evans E. Crawford, dean of Rankin Chapel at Howard University, had me on a regular schedule of annual and biennial Sunday morning preaching engagements. I was also guest preacher and lecturer at religious emphasis week programs in many colleges. I became a familiar speaker, particularly on African-American campuses. It was a way to model ministry and arouse interest in it among faculty and students.

I spent much time writing as well. I discovered early that one way to arouse and keep the attention of faculty was to publish. One good method to do that was to speak from a manuscript and have it in hand just in case someone wanted to print it. Of course, the manuscript must be prepared with both readers and listeners in mind, and that's not always easy to do. Still, during my fourteen years with the FTE I was able to publish articles in many of the important periodicals and journals in the United States. We frequently distributed reprints of those articles as a means of keeping attention focused on African-American ministry.

REGIONAL CONFERENCES ABOUT MINISTRY

One of our more imaginative undertakings was to arrange regional student conferences to discuss visions of African-American ministry. In the fall of 1961, one year after I began my work with the FTE, I persuaded three seminaries to permit the FTE to hold a conference on the ministry on their campuses. The three schools were the Interdenominational Theological Center in Atlanta; the Divinity School of Duke University in Durham, North Carolina; and Perkins School of Theology at Southern Methodist University in Dallas, Texas.

The choice of schools was interesting. One was an African-American school; the other two were white and in the United Methodist Church. I would gladly have conducted these conferences primarily on African-American seminary campuses, but that was not to be for very complex reasons. In the first place, the FTE directors insisted, as a matter of principle, that all our fellowships be given for study at fully accredited schools. At that time only two African-American seminaries, the ITC and the Howard University School of Religion, were full members of the American Association of Theological Schools, and were the only African-American seminaries available. Because we wanted to cover as much of the South as possible, which we did, Howard University was located a bit too far to the northern end of the target region. It was eliminated for that reason.

ITC and Duke were therefore our best choices when, under the circumstances, our choices were very limited. We knew ITC would draw students from Georgia, Alabama, and Florida. Duke's location would permit conferees to be recruited from colleges in Virginia, as well as from North and South Carolina. Students could come to Perkins from Texas, Louisiana, and Mississippi. That was the best we thought we could do. In addition, we were determined to revolutionize the prevailing practices of segregated theological education and a segregated ministry. In that part of the nation, seminaries and the rest of higher education were still segregated. There weren't many schools to which we could go. We believed it would be an important demonstration to hold some of these conferences on the campuses of white schools. It would open African-American students to a completely new experience, and their presence and visibility would dramatically arouse the attention of white students and faculty on their own campuses.

In some ways it was remarkable that Duke and Perkins agreed so enthusiastically to permit us to hold our conferences there. It was a pioneering moment for them because, at the time, they had no African-American students enrolled anywhere in the universities. The experience encouraged the two Methodist seminaries to develop their own resources to recruit and educate African-American students. Duke was able to secure a grant from the Mary Reynolds Babcock Foundation, which provided scholarship monies for African Americans, and began to seek such students actively. Perkins did so as well, but without foundation funding.

The program of each conference was designed to introduce students to three major themes: images of ministry, the purposes of the church, and what a call to ministry is. At the 1961 gathering at ITC, for instance, in the panel discussion about images of ministry, Professor Ralph Williamson of ITC described the range of contemporary images of ministry; President Frank Cunningham of Morris Brown College talked about the minister as a leader of social reform; the Reverend Ezekiel Bell, an African American who had been a Trial Year Scholar, discussed the image of the local pastor; and President Benjamin Mays of Morehouse College spoke of the function of the seminary in relation to these images. The other conferences followed a similar pattern.

We asked the colleges to send us both students who were not committed to the ministry as a vocation and those who were. The meetings always began on Saturday at 1:00 p.m., and ended on Sunday after a midday dinner. This meant the students were away from their campus and classes only on the weekend. The program included a tour of each seminary so students could see the physical surroundings. The conference participants attended Sunday morning chapel in both the Duke and SMU chapels. The ITC didn't hold Sunday worship because it was not on a university campus and its students were away doing fieldwork, but a special service was arranged for the conference.

Another principle under which we operated was to give the faculty of each school an opportunity to be visible. In each section of the agenda, professors of New Testament, Old Testament and Theology spoke to the students. At both Duke and SMU, this was a learning experience for the faculty as well as the students. In those days, African-American students were rarely in touch with white theology professors. They learned much from each other! We also made it an objective to help the students enlarge their images of ministry by having them meet and interact with scholars of the FTE whenever possible. At both Duke and ITC, two scholars of the FTE spoke about ministry. Even more important, they were a visible model of an educated ministry. Finally, we wanted the students to see seminary education as unsegregated; that is to say, we wanted the experience of the weekend to include both African Americans and white people. To this end, the program at each seminary included persons from both backgrounds. I attended each conference annually to be a presence from the FTE, to talk about our programs, and to ensure that our hopes were realized. These were absolutely unique events in higher education during that period. I know they were the subject of much conversation and inquiry, and they succeeded greatly in permitting new ideas about ministry to be discussed and to develop among African-American students. I was always exceedingly grateful to President Harry V. Richardson at ITC, Dean Robert Cushman of Duke Divinity School, and Dean Joseph D. Quillan Jr., of Perkins for their farsighted and enthusiastic support of the meetings. They were faithfully present at each conference to give the opening address.

STRENGTHENING COLLEGE CHAPLAINCIES

Another notable but limited experiment in enlarging the insights and vision of African-American students had to do with college chaplains. In 1964, *Presbyterian Survey*, the magazine of the Presbyterian Church, U.S. (the Southern Presbyterians), published an article I wrote titled "We Can't Ignore the Negro Campus." In it I talked about the conditions on college campuses contributing to the critical shortage of African Americans studying for the ministry. Among those who read the article were Lawrence Bottoms and other officers of that denomination who invited me to discuss how they might be of assistance. As a result, we formed a small committee to experiment with placing African-American college chaplains on state university campuses.

With funding from members of the Reynolds Aluminum Company family, we targeted two campuses: North Carolina A. & T. College in Greensboro and Southern University in Baton Rouge, Louisiana. I served as secretary for the committee and helped to find persons to serve on both campuses. One member of the committee was Felton G. Clark, president of Southern, which, with ten thousand students, claimed to be the largest of the African-American colleges.

Our aim was simple—to enable students on public university campuses to encounter religious experience under the leadership of a dynamic young minister. African-American state colleges had few full-time persons in religion available to them either in class or in extracurricular settings. State funds could not support a chaplain because of the separation of church and state. Our committee provided funding for the entire salary and benefits of the ministers we placed on these two campuses, as well as limited money for program. One highly visible result of this program was the development of Jesse Jackson's interest in ministry, partly as a result of his encounters with A. Knighton (Tony) Stanley, a former Trial Year Scholar at Yale Divinity School, who served as the chaplain at A. & T. and was supported by our committee. Unfortunately, we could not find sufficient funds to expand that significant, but small experiment.

PROTESTANT FELLOWSHIP PROGRAM SCHOLARS:
A DISTINGUISHED NEW ROLE MODEL

In the effort to revolutionize the attitudes and thinking of both faculty and students—and eventually churches—about ministry, our best weapon was the Scholars of the Protestant Fellowship Program. They were an impressive group, and we always tried to make them as visible as possible. The first class was typical. These were the survivors of the initial competition during the 1960-61 academic year who received awards for the 1961-62 academic year. Because the program was brand new, we thought we would be lucky if we could find a dozen Scholars. We found twenty-four. They had every qualification for which we could ask. One Scholar already held a master's degree from Harvard University. Another had spent a year studying at the University of Edinburgh in Scotland under a Merrill grant. A third was working on his master's degree at Fisk University in a Danforth Foundation program.

The 1961-1962 Scholars came from a variety of denominational and college backgrounds. Morehouse College had educated the most (five) followed by Bishop, Howard, Shaw, and Wilberforce with two each. Eleven colleges had one Scholar each. Fourteen were Baptist; four were A.M.E.; and one each came from the C.M. E., United Methodist, Congregational Christian, Episcopal, United Holy Church of America, and Church of God denominations. Fourteen Scholars came from the South, six from the North, and four from the Midwest. Fifteen were already enrolled in seminary, six were college seniors at the time of selection, two were college juniors, and one was in graduate school.

These award recipients attended twelve seminaries during the 1961-62 year. Four (the largest contingent) were enrolled at the ITC in Atlanta, three each at Boston University School of Theology and Colgate Rochester Divinity School, two each at Howard University, Yale Divinity School, and Union Theological Seminary in New York. Seven seminaries each had one PFP Scholar.

Statistics do not tell the story of these men, however, The FTE has not been able to track their activities consistently over the years because of lack of staff and funds. Some facts are known about that first class, though. For one thing, given the intention of the program to educate men for the parish ministry, it is significant that, to my personal knowledge, twenty-one of the twenty-four either were or are parish ministers. The most famous of the pastors is James A. Forbes Jr. now senior minister of The Riverside Church in New York City. Forbes became a pastor of United Holy Church of America congregations in North Carolina and Virginia after completing his studies at Union Seminary. His preaching became legendary across the nation, and he finally became professor of preaching at Union Seminary before his call to The Riverside Church. One Scholar, John R. Pearson, became an Army chaplain. Two received Ph.D. degrees but continue to be pastors. One, Harry Starks Wright, was dean of the chapel and later president of Bishop College. He is pastor of Cornerstone Baptist Church in Brooklyn, NY. Two persons in the first class are now deceased, but both served significantly in local churches as far apart as Phoenix, Arizona, and Newport News, Virginia.

This profile of the 1961-62 Protestant Fellowship Program Scholars is typical of the succeeding classes. All the Scholars were strongly committed to parish ministry. They envisioned their ministry in diverse ways, of course. Perhaps the most famous Scholar is Jesse Jackson, who attended the Chicago Theological Seminary during the 1964-66 academic years. He was the regional director of the Southern Christian Leadership Conference and organized Operation PUSH on the south side of Chicago while still a student. Operation PUSH was Jesse's singular form of ministry, holding services on Saturday morning and involving him in numerous acts of attempted social transformation the rest of the time. Another nationally known Scholar was William Gray III, a Scholar at Drew University Theological Seminary in the class of 1965-66. He later served as Majority Whip in the U.S. House of Representatives in the 101st Congress, while continuing to be pastor of the Baptist Church in Philadelphia founded by his grandfather and served by his father. This combination of politics and ministry of a large congregation is a familiar one in the African-American community. He now serves as the president of the United Negro College Fund. Bill Gray has brought ministry to new levels of possibility. Protestant Fellowship Program Scholars hold important pulpits across the nation. Charles G. Adams and Nicholas Hood III, in Detroit; William P. DeVeaux and H. Beecher Hicks Jr. in Washington, D.C.; Calvin Butts and Harry Starks Wright in New York City; and Peter J. Gomes at Memorial Chapel of Harvard University come immediately to mind. One Scholar, Eddie S. O'Neal, teaches preaching at Andover Newton Theological Seminary. These are a highly distinguished body of men. The story of their ministries is a ripe subject for further examination and recording.

The Protestant Fellowship Program ended in 1976 after funding from the Sealantic Fund ran out. It has continued as the Benjamin E. Mays Fellowships for Ministry since then, with funding by the Lilly Endowment, and is available for both men and women. During the period from 1960 to 1976, the Protestant Fellowship Program gave a total of 456 grants to 251 persons in the total amount of $1,003,989. Considering the fact that the program intended originally to support approximately forty Scholars per year, plus fund all the other things required to stir interest in ministry, and began with a grant of $75,000 per year for three years, its accomplishments are remarkable. It was possible mainly because both college and seminary education was considerably less expensive in 1960 than it is now.

THE BENJAMIN E. MAYS SCHOLARS IN MINISTRY

In 1976 this aim of the FTE was given a boost with its new name and funding. It was altogether fitting that the name of Benjamin E. Mays should be attached to it. He had been a director of the FTE from the very beginning. Even more important, this already legendary college president was the one African-American president with consistent energy for the church and active concern about its ministry. Mays ranked at the top of the educators in his era, along with such persons as Fred Patterson at Tuskegee, Mordecai Johnson at Howard University, Charles Johnson at Fisk University, Albert Dent at Dillard University, and Felton G. Clark at Southern University. It was a very small but very distinguished group of people. Among them, Mays had the strongest and most visible interest in the church and its ministry. He was dean of the School of Religion at Howard University before becoming president of Morehouse College in 1960. In both places he was an extraordinary inspiration to students. He never permitted them to relax in the struggle for excellence.

When the Howard University School of Divinity, as it was renamed, dedicated a building in his memory in 1987, the program included this quotation from Mays: "It is not environment, it is the quality of minds, integrity of souls, and determination of wills that determines futures and shapes lives." Interestingly enough, Mays said very little about his passion for the church and its ministry in his autobiography, *Born to Rebel*. He sent me a copy of the manuscript for comment before its publication, and I insisted he include a section about all he had done for the church, but he chose not to. When I was inaugurated as president of the Chicago Theological Seminary in 1975, I asked Mays, a Ph.D. graduate of the neighboring University of Chicago, to deliver the principal address. His scholarly and provocative speech was titled "The Durability of the Church and Its Priestly and Prophetic Role in the 1980s."

At the remarkable love-in that was his funeral at Morehouse College on March 31, 1984, I made it my business to report on the Mays influence in Protestantism. Among the impressive array of distinguished speakers, I was the one person to do so. Naming this fellowship after "Buck Benny," as his students lovingly called him, is one way to honor both Christian ministry and Benjamin Mays. It also establishes the vision of educated ministry that he supported and helped the FTE develop in higher education across the United States. Through the spirit of Mays and the ministries of African-American Scholars in two national programs, the revolution in Zion continues in both higher education and the church.

19

BLACK MALE ROLE MODEL OF THE CENTURY: A FUNERAL TRIBUTE TO DR. BENJAMIN E. MAYS

Hugh M. Gloster

Morehouse is a close family as well as a first-class college, and today we are facing the most trying experience that a family can confront—the death of a loving and beloved parent.

For 44 years—from 1940 when Dr. Mays became President of Morehouse College, to 1984, when he passed during his sleep at Hughes Spalding Community Hospital—he has been a father to the students who have attended this institution. He motivated us in his office, at his home, in the chapel, and in the community; and after we graduated, he visited us in our homes and at our jobs in order to check up on us and see if we were living up to his standards and expectations. He helped to develop in us the Morehouse mystique, which demands that we be successful in college and in later life, that we rise to the top in our professions, that we serve our fellow man, that we be loyal to each other and to Alma Mater, that we have self-confidence and self-respect, and that we use Christian and democratic principles in the solution of social and racial problems.

On Wednesday Dr. Mays left us and joined Mrs. Mays, his devoted wife who passed in 1969. Since Dr. and Mrs. Mays had no children of their own, they adopted Morehouse men. They are our parents, and we are their sons. Therefore, in view of the great achievements and contributions of Dr. and Mrs. Mays, I urge each Morehouse man: "Do as your great progenitors have done, and by your merits prove yourself their son."

One of the miracles of our time is how Bennie Mays, a son of former slaves, lifted himself from a sharecropping farm in South Carolina and became one of the nation's outstanding leaders in education, religion, and civil rights. As he made his upward climb, poverty could not delay him, discrimination could not discourage him, segregation could not block him, and oppression could not intimidate him. Despite all these formidable barriers, he persevered until he earned his high school diploma at South Carolina State College, his B.A. degree and Phi Beta Kappa key at Bates College, and his M.A. and Ph.D. Degrees at the University of Chicago. As most of us know, it is a long way from milking a cow and pushing a plow to earning a Phi Beta Kappa key and getting a Ph.D. degree.

After Dr. Mays gained the best possible training for a career in education and religion, he dedicated his life to helping others and eventually served as Dean of the School of Religion at Howard University from 1934 to 1940, as President of Morehouse College from 1940 to 1967, and as president of the Atlanta Board of Education from 1969 to 1981. Throughout his career he urged young people to have a great love of learning, a burning desire for excellence, and a genuine compassion for humanity.

Benjamin E. Mays was a man of deep compassion and wide experience; and he had several institutional loves including South Carolina State, Bates, the University of Chicago, Howard, Paine, Benedict, and Morehouse; but the greatest of his loves was Morehouse, where he spent thirty years of his professional career—there as a teacher from 1921 to 1923 and twenty-seven as president from 1940 to 1967.

The love affair between Dr. Mays and Morehouse began in 1921, when he came to the College to teach mathematics and psychology and learned about the spirit of Morehouse from the great Triumvirate—John Hope, Samuel H. Archer, and Benjamin G. Brawley—as well as from other great Morehouse men such as Charles D. Hubert, John W. Davis, and Mordecai Johnson. At Morehouse Dr. Mays coached a great debating team consisting of James Nabrit and Howard Thurman, and he learned that Morehouse not only demanded academic excellence of its students but also taught them never to accept segregation and always to seek the overthrow of the vicious Jim Crow system in which they lived. It was at Morehouse that Dr. Mays began his long career of teaching and preaching against segregation and training able young men to go out into the country and struggle to establish Christianity and democracy on this planet.

After leaving Morehouse in 1923 to seek his M.A. degree at the University of Chicago, Dr. Mays did not return as an employee until 1940, when he resigned from the Deanship of the School of Religion of Howard University to accept the presidency of Morehouse College.

Dr. Mays had his finest hour as President of Morehouse, where he became a living legend. At the time of his appointment in 1940, Morehouse had suffered eleven years of decline largely as a result of her contributions to the Atlanta University Affiliation that was launched in 1929. The school suffered other financial problems caused by the stock market crash of the same year. In order to help the graduate school get off to a good start, Morehouse sacrificed President John Hope, some of her ablest professors, her front campus along the west side of Chestnut Street, Quarles Hall, and classroom space in Merrill Hall and Sale Hall. During the Great Depression, the College suffered sharp enrollment declines, serious financial problems, and subordinate status in the Affiliation. In other words, when Dr. Mays assumed the Presidency in 1940, Morehouse was a weak and failing school; but, when he retired in 1967, he had laid a firm foundation for the future growth and improvement of the College. He had doubled the enrollment, tripled the endowment, expanded the physical plant, increased the proportion of faculty Ph.Ds to 52 percent, and qualified for a Phi Beta Kappa Chapter—one of only three in black colleges and one of only four colleges in Georgia.

This is a good point at which to discuss my long friendship and association with Dr. Mays, who was my predecessor in the presidency of Morehouse College. I first met him during my undergraduate years when he was a National Student Secretary of the YMCA. At that time his job was to visit colleges and strengthen YMCA programs on campuses. I vividly remember him as an eloquent speaker who supported Christianity and democracy and opposed segregation and disfranchisement. More than a decade later—during Dr. Mays's first year as President of Morehouse—he invited me to join the Faculty as a Professor of English; and I accepted. During my brief service at Morehouse Dr. Mays seemed to like me and appreciate my work. In any case, he helped me to complete study for my Ph.D. degree, appointed me to several important Faculty committees, made me editor of the official school publication, and called on me to proofread some of his articles and speeches. On one occasion he helped to get me out of jail in Tupelo, Mississippi, after I had been arrested, beaten by police, and thrown in prison because I had protested against a conductor's refusal to seat black women on a segregated train that was going from Atlanta to Memphis. In 1943, when it became obvious that I would have to leave teaching and enter war-related work, Dr. Mays recommended me for an

administrative appointment with the USO. In 1943-1944 I served a year
as a USO Regional Executive with headquarters in Atlanta and became the
first black to have an office downtown on Marietta Street. After Governor
Eugene Talmadge attacked the USO for giving me this downtown office,
I feared that I would lose my life during the war on the front lines here in
Atlanta. Because of our close friendly relationship, Dr. Mays was disappointed when I left Morehouse in 1946 to accept the directorship of the
division of Language and Literature at Hampton Institute, which I
considered as an opportunity to head a challenging academic program.

Despite my departure from Morehouse in 1946, Dr. Mays and I kept
in touch with each other; and I always had the feeling that I would
eventually return to Morehouse in some capacity. Around the middle 1960's
Dr. Mays told me that he was planning to retire from the presidency during
the centennial celebration of the College and that I would likely be one of
those to be considered for appointment as his successor.

In 1967, after I had received and accepted the appointment, Dr. Mays
and I met in New York, Washington, Richmond, and Atlanta for long
conferences during which he introduced me to every phase of the organization and operation of the College. He wanted to be sure that I would be well-
acquainted with the College and would not have any problems because of
lack of information. But during this period he did more than brief me for
a new position: He took advantage of every opportunity to motivate me by
challenging me privately and publicly at least to equal if possible, or to
surpass his record as president. During the Morehouse Centennial Banquet
at the Biltmore Hotel in Atlanta on 17 February 1967, I responded to one
of Dr. Mays's challenges with the following statement, that won warm
applause and frequent reference: "Socrates had his Plato, Plato had his
Aristotle, Hope had his Mays, and Mays will have his Gloster."

To be sure that I would not loaf on the job, Dr. Mays left me with a
fundraising campaign having a goal of $11 million. I knew exactly what Dr.
Mays was doing in his challenges: He was motivating me to work to the
limit of my capacity so that Morehouse would survive and succeed.

After his retirement in 1967, Dr. Mays continued to show his love and
affection for Morehouse by supporting the College in every possible way. He
served on the Board of Trustees. He was available to me for advice and
cooperation. He declined lucrative out-of-town speaking engagements in
order to attend commencement exercises and other college programs.

Moreover, he backed up his love for Morehouse with generous contributions to the College. For example, he established two endowed funds at Morehouse—a $25,000 endowed fund to maintain the Sadie G. Mays Lounge in Mays Hall and a $25,000 endowed fund to provide scholarships for talented and needy students. Moreover, whenever the College had a fundraising campaign, Dr. Mays would lead off with a generous gift. For instance, in the current campaign he made a kick-off contribution of $6,000. In addition, in response to an inquiry from the College, Dr. Mays said that he would be pleased if Morehouse would establish an endowed chair in philosophy and religion in his honor. During the years that lie ahead, therefore, the College will seek to raise endowed funds for the Sadie G. Mays Lounge, the Benjamin E. Mays Scholarship Fund, and the Benjamin E. Mays Chair in Philosophy and Religion.

It was at Morehouse that this giant of a man became a national role model who furnished living proof that impoverished black youth could get an education if they really tried. On the Morehouse campus he was a father figure who attracted admiration and respect. Born to lead and not to follow, he did not know his African roots, as did Alex Haley; but his ancestors must have included great men of superior talent and brilliant leadership. Tall and erect, he was a natural aristocrat who was emulated because of his charisma and competence, his intelligence and integrity. Throughout the nation young black Americans tried to walk like him, talk like him, and even look like him.

Dr. Mays was the best role model that I have ever seen or known. Here at Morehouse we admired him because we knew that he had been tested in the fires of human experience. We knew that he had been born in 1894 to a poor black family on a sharecropping farm in South Carolina and that he aspired to get an education and serve his people. We knew that—despite poverty, prejudice, and persecution—he tirelessly struggled to get his high school diploma at South Carolina State, his B.A. degree at Bates College, and his M.A. and Ph.D. degrees at the University of Chicago. We knew that he gave the best years of his life as Dean of the School of Religion at Howard University, as President of Morehouse College, and as president of the Atlanta Board of Education. And we knew that he often left the halls of academe to flight discrimination, segregation, disenfranchisement, lynching, and all the other ordeals through which black people have had to pass in this country.

Dr. Mays is a shining example of the kind of man Morehouse is trying to develop. He not only got an excellent education leading all the way to the highest degree in his field, but he used that education to help and lift people who were less fortunate than he was. A Morehouse man who uses his education to exploit his people is not following in the footsteps of Dr. Mays.

I think that two of Dr. Mays's greatest honors were to receive the Order of the Palmetto, the highest award that the State of South Carolina can bestow, and to have his portrait placed in the South Carolina State House in Columbia in 1980. In earlier years South Carolina had honored many men for their defense of slavery and segregation, but in 1980 South Carolina was wise enough to honor its leading champion of freedom and justice.

Although all Morehouse Men admired and respected "Buck Benny," as we affectionately called him, only a few—like Dr. Thomas Kilgore Jr.—followed his rigid code of conduct. Buck Benny abhorred hard liquors and addictive drugs. He never smoke cigars, cigarettes, or pipes; and he would not supply ashtrays for others. He did not like expensive clothes, cars, and houses. In this connection I recall one occasion when someone was teasing him about the wide lapels of his old-fashioned tuxedo and he replied, "This tux is in good shape, and it meets my needs quite well." He was a loyal fan of the Atlanta Braves, Falcons, and Hawks and the Maroon Tigers; but he seldom attended games. He had no favorite sports like tennis, golf, hunting, and fishing; and he was not attracted to card games like whist, bridge, and poker. He was a firm believer in Christianity and democracy; and, as a teacher and as a preacher and as a writer and as a speaker, he used these two philosophies to attack racial and social injustice. But, most of all, he was a workaholic, a prolific writer who not only authored numerous articles, books, and speeches but always had new ones in mind. Only a few weeks ago, for example, he told me that he planned to write at lest three more books. Truly, he was a seeker of "The Impossible Dream," which Oliver Sueing will describe later in his song during today's program; and he indeed lived this philosophy which he expressed as follows:

It must be born in mind that the tragedy of life doesn't lie in not reaching your goal. The tragedy lies in having no goal to reach. It isn't a calamity to die with dreams unfulfilled, but it is a calamity not to dream. It is not a disaster to be unable to capture your ideal, but it is a disaster to have no ideal to capture. It is not a disgrace not to reach the stars, but it is a disgrace to have no stars to reach for. Not failure, but low aim is a sin.

Dr. Mays had to wait a long time to see the demise of disenfranchisement and segregation in Georgia. He was fifty-two years of age and had been President of Morehouse for six years before he was finally able to vote in local and state elections, and he was seventy-two and nearing retirement at Morehouse before he finally saw segregation fade away in this state.

The overthrow of segregation in Georgia required a massive effort, and at the forefront of that effort were many students of Dr. Mays. Hamilton Holmes was one of the first two blacks to gain admission to the University of Georgia. Martin Luther King Jr. upset segregation first in Montgomery and finally throughout the country, and then went on to receive the Nobel Peace Prize and become the nation's greatest civil rights leader. Lonnie King and Julian Bond, Morehouse students, led the sit-ins that integrated restaurants and hotels in Atlanta. Maynard Jackson became the first black Mayor of Atlanta, and honorary alumnus Andy Young succeeded him in that office. In addition, Michael Lomax was elected as the first black Chairman of the Fulton County Commission; and Leroy Johnson as the first black member of the Georgia Senate since Reconstruction. Horace Ward was appointed as the first black Federal Judge in this state.

Dr. Mays's life was a long history of overcoming obstacles. He overcame obstacles in order to gain a first-class education for himself, and he overcame obstacles in order to train black youth to seek academic excellence in colleges and universities and to overcome bigotry and brutality in this country and aborad. Dr. Mays's struggle against obstacles was perhaps the most dramatic during his campaign against age and death. Refusing to retreat or fall before the relentless advance of Father Time and the Grim Reaper, Dr. Mays accepted Tennyson's view of that "Old age hath yet its honor and its toil. Death closes all; but something ere the end, Some work of noble note may yet be done."

Since Dr. Mays regarded the years of senior citizenship as a period when one should labor and achieve rather than rest and relax, he shared the following sentiments of Browning:

Grow old along with me.

The best is yet to be—
The last of life for which the first was made:
Our times are in His hand Who saith,
"A whole I planned, Youth shows but half; trust God; see all,
    nor be afraid!"

Again like Browning, Dr. Mays welcomed the contest of death and
vowed to make it his bravest effort.

I was ever a fighter, so—one fight more.
The best and the last!

In conclusion, I would like to borrow the words of John Donne and say,
"Death be not proud" because of your encounter with Bennie Mays.
Practicing the courage that he preached, he fought death to the bitter end.
When age and disease bent him, he did not break. He was an active writer
and speaker until the last year of his life. Again and again he pulled himself
out of his bed and, wearing his cowboy hat and waving his walking cane, he
fared forth by plane to speaking engagements in all parts of the country—from New York to California and from Minnesota to Texas. When he
reached the point where he could not walk, he went by wheelchair; and at the
end death, which could not conquer him in open combat, slipped up on him
when he was asleep yesterday morning. Dr. Mays was the embodiment of the
kind of man who said,

Let me die working,
Still tackling plans unfinished, tasks undone
Clean to the end, Swift may my race be run—
No laggard steps, no faltering, no shirking,
Let me die working.

Let me fare forth, still with an open mind,
Fresh secrets to unfold, new truths to find.
My soul undimmed, alert, no question blinking.
Let me die laughing.
Let me die thinking.

No sighing o'er past sins, they are forgiven;
Spilled on this earth are all the joys of Heaven,
The wine of life, the cup of mirth still quaffing,
Let me die giving.
Let me die aspiring.
Let me die laughing.

A Partial Bibliography of the Writings of Benjamin E. Mays

A. Books

The Negro's Church (Co-author with Joseph William Nichelson). New York: Institute of Social and Religious Research, 1933; Reprint: Salem, NH: Ayer Company, Publishers, Inc., 1988.

The Negro's God as Reflected In His Literature. New York: Atheneum, 1938; republished 1968.

Seeking To Be Christian in Race Relations. New York: Friendship Press, 1957.

A Gospel for the Social Awakening: Selections from the Writings of Walter Rauschenbusch. Compiled by Benjamin E. Mays, New York: Association Press, 1950.

The Christian in Race Relations (pamphlet). West Haven, CT: Publication of Promoting Enduring Peace, 1956. One of the Henry Wright Lectures given at Yale University Divinity School.

Disturbed About Man. Richmond, Virginia: John Knox Press, 1969.

Born to Rebel. New York: Charles Scribner's Sons, 1971.

Lord, The People Have Driven Me On. New York: Vantage Press, Incorporated, 1981.

Quotable Quotes of Benjamin E. Mays. New York: Vantage Press, 1983.

B. Chapters and Sections in Books

"The New Negro Challenges the Old Order." In *Sketches of Negro Life and History in South Carolina*, by A. H. Gordon, W. B. Conkey and Company, 1929; reprint, Columbia: University of South Carolina Press, 1971), 192-212.

"Race." In *Christus Victor*, edited by Danzig Patrick. Geneva, Switzerland: World Committee of YMCA, 1939.

Numerous articles in *Encyclopedia of Religion*, edited by Vergilius Ferm. New York: The Philosophical Library, 1945.

"The Inescapable Christ." In *Representative American Speeches*, edited by A. Craig Baird. New York: H. W. Wilson and Company, 1944-45.

"The Inescapable Christ." In *Best Sermons*, edited by G. Paul Butler. New York: Harper and Brothers, 1946.

"The Obligations of the Individual Christian," In *The Christian Way in Race Relations*, edited by William Stuart Nelson. New York: Harper, 1947.

"Christian Light on Human Relationships." In *Baptist World Alliance—Eighth Congress*. Valley Forge PA: Judson Press, 1950.

"The Case of Integration." In *Contemporary Civilization*. New York: Scott, Foresman and Company, 1959.

"Race III: The Negro Perspective." In *The Search for America*, by Huston Smith. Englewood Cliffs NJ: Prentice-Hall, Inc., 1959.

"Materialism and Secularism." In *The Christian Mission Today*. Nashville: Abingdon Press, 1960.

"The Christian in Race Relations." In *Rhetoric of Racial Revolt*. Denver: Gordon Bell Press, 1964.

"The Challenge to Religion as It Ponders Science." In *Religion Ponders Science*, by Edwin P. Booth. New York: Appleton Century, 1964.

"I Have Been a Baptist All My Life." In *A Way Home*. New York: Holt, Rinehart & Winston, 1964.

"The Moral Aspects of Segregation." In *Black, White, and Gray*, New York: Sheed and Ward, 1959.

". . . and the Pursuit of Happiness." Washington DC: National Urban League, 1951.

"Why I Believe There Is A God." In *Why I Believe There Is A God*, edited by Howard W. Thurman. Chicago: Johnson Publishing Company, 1965.

"The Genius of the Negro Church." In *The Black Church in America*, by Hart M. Nelson. New York: Basic Books, 1971.

C. JOURNAL AND MAGAZINE ARTICLES

"After College, What? for Negroes." *The Crisis* 37 (December 1930).

"Realities in Race Relations." *The Christian Century* 48 (March 25, 1931).

"Education of the Negro Ministry." *Journal of Negro Education* 2 (July 1933).

"The Color Line Around the World." *Journal of Negro Education* 6 (1937).

"Christianity in a Changing World." *The National Educational Outlook Among Negroes* 1 (December 1937).

"The Church Surveys World Problems." *The Crisis* 44 (October 1937).

"World Churchmen Score Prejudice." *The Crisis* 44 (November 1937.

"Oxford." *A.M.E. Zion Quarterly Review* (July 1938).

"The American Negro and the Christian Religion." *Journal of Negro Education* (July 1939).

"Christian Youth and Race." *The Crisis* 46 (December 1939).

"The Training of Negro Ministers." *The National Educational Outlook Among Negroes* (December 1939).

"The Most Neglected Area in Negro Education." *The Crisis* (August 1938).

"Benjamin Griffith Brawley." *The National Education Outlook Among Negroes* (February 1939).

"Yesterday and Tomorrow in Negro Leadership." *Missions* (1940).

"The Religious Life and Needs of Negro Students." *Journal of Negro Education* 9 (July 1940).

"The Negro Church in American Life." *Christendom* 5 (Summer 1940).

"Amsterdam on the Church and Race Relations." *Religion in Life* 9 (Winter 1940).

"The Negro and the Present War." *The Crisis* (May 1942): 160-165.

"Yesterday and Tomorrow in Negro Leadership." *Missions* 33 (February 1942).

"Interracial Leadership in this Time of Crisis." *Georgia Observer* (March-April 1942).

"The Role of the Negro Liberal Arts College in Postwar Reconstruction." *Journal of Negro Education* (July 1942).

"Negroes and the Will To Justice." *Christian Century* 59 (October 1942).

"The Eyes of the World Are Upon America." *Missions* 35 (February 1944).

"Why Go To Student Conferences?" *Intercollegian* 6 (April 1944).

"The Inescapable Christ." *The Pulpit* 15 (June 1944).

"When Do I Believe in Man." *International Journal of Religious Education* 21 1 September 1944).

"The Unique Demand in Negro Education." *Religious Thought* 4 8 (October 1944).

"The Time Is Always Ripe." *The Women's Press* 39 (March 1945).

"Veterans It Need Not Happen Again." *Phylon* (Third Quarter 1945).

"Democratizing and Christianizing America in This Generation." *Journal of Negro Education* 14 (Fall 1945).

"Obligations of Negro Christians in Relation to an Interracial Program." *Journal of Religious Thought* 2 (Autumn-Winter 1945).

"Democratizing and Christianizing America in This Generation." *Howard University Bulletin* 25 (October 1 1945).

"The Present Crisis and Relationships of People." *Christianity Meeting the Crisis of Our Time* (1946).

"The Hazen Conference and Warren Wilson College" *Women and Missions* 22 11 February 1946).

"The Colored Races in the Postwar World. *Missions* 37 (February 1946).

"What Does It Matter What I Believe?" *Highroad* 5 (March 1946).

"Financing of Private Negro Colleges." *The Journal of Education Sociology* 19 (April 1946).

"How Religious Is the Negro College?" *Christendom* 11 (Winter 1946).

". . . Religious Forces of the South are Politically Impotent." *Prophetic Religion* 8 (Spring 1947): 1-3.

"Seeking to Be Christian in Race Relations." *The Methodist Woman* 7 (February 1947).

"The Negro Rural Church." *Christendom* 13 (Winter 1948).

"How America Exports Race Hate." *Negro Digest* (1949).

"World Aspects of Race and Culture." *Missions* 147 (February 1949).

"Conflict in Czechoslovakia." *Christian Century* 66 (November 1949).

"Segregation in Higher Education." *Phylon* 10 (Fourth Quarter 1949).

"Improving the Morale of Negro Children and Youth." *Journal of Negro Education* (1950).

"How Christian Can I Afford To Be?" *Southern Baptist Home Missions* 21 (August 1950).

"Why An Anti-Segregation (Atlanta School) Suit?" *New South* (October 1950).

"The South's Racial Policy." *The Presbyterian Outlook* 132 (November 6, 1950): 2-6.

"What's Wrong With Negro Leaders?" *Negro Digest* (1951).

"Have You Forgotten God?" *Our World* (November 1952).

"The Present Status of and Future for Racial Integration in the Church Related White College in the South." *Journal of Negro Education* 21 (Summer 1952).

"The Second Assembly of the World Council of Churches." *Journal of Religious Thought* 10 (Spring-Summer 1953).

"Religious Roots of Western Culture." *Child Study* 30 (Fall 1953).

"Democracy . . . in the U.S.A. and in India." *The Presbyterian Survey* 43 (November 1953).

"The Church and Racial Tensions." *Christian Century* (1954).

"I Am Glad I Could Report Progress." *World Call* 36 (February 1954).

"I Am Glad I Could Report Progress." *The Presbyterian Life* (February 1954).

"Progress in Race Relations." *The Presbyterian Life* 7 (February 1954): 8-9.

"Democracy . . . in the U.S.A. and in India." *World Call* 36 (February 1954).

"Progress in Race Relations." *Gospel Messenger* 103 (February 1954).

"I Am Glad I Could Report Progress." *Gospel Messenger* 103 (February 1954).

"I Report Progress." *Lutheran Woman's Work* 47 (February 1954).

"We Are Unnecessarily Excited." *New South* 9 (February 1954).

"Christianity and Race." *The Pulpit* 25 (May 1954).

"The Church Will Be Challenged at Evanston." *Christianity and Crises* 14 (August 9, 1954): 106.

"The Second Assembly of the World Council of Churches." *The Journal of Religious Thought* (August 21, 1954).

"The Church and Racial Tensions." *The Christian Century* 71 (September 1954).

"The Supreme Court Decision and Our Responsibility." *The Y.W.C.A. Magazine* 48 (October 1954): 8-9.

"Benjamin E. Mays Addressed the Second Plenary Assembly of the World Council of Churches at Evanston Illinois August 21 1954" *Journal of Negro History* 39 (October 1954): 338.

"The Church Amidst Ethnic and Racial Tensions." *African Methodist Episcopal Church Review* 10 (October-December 1954): 86-88.

"The Faith of the Church." *The Intercollegian* 72 (December 1954).

"Of One Blood." *The Presbyterian Life* (February 5, 1955).

"The Gulf Between Our Gospel and Our Practice." *The Presbyterian Survey* (April 1955).

"Why An Anti-Segregation Suit?" *Changing Patterns In the New South* (July 1955).

"A Recent Supreme Court Decision How Decisive?" *The Chicago Review* 9 (Fall 1955).

"In Behalf Of All We Affirm the Fatherhood of God and the Brotherhood of Man." *Wesley Quarterly* 15 (January-March 1956).

"Why I Am a Life Member (NAACP)." *Crises* 63 (February 1956): 96.

"The Moral Aspects of Segregation." *Journal of Educational Sociology* 29 (May 1956).

"The Road to Blessed Immortality." *The Pulpit* 28 (January 1957).

"A Negro Educator Gives His Views." *Christian Science Monitor* 49 (January 1957).

"Moral Aspects of Segregation." *Christian Community* 9 (February 1957).

"Full Implementation of Democracy." *New South* 12 (March 1957).

"I Believe in God." *The Message Magazine* 23 (May 1957).

"A Dream Comes True." *African Methodist Episcopal Church Review* 14 (July-September 1958): 55.

"I Am Glad I Could Report Progress." *The Messenger* 19 (February 9, 1959).

"The Role of the 'Negro Community' in Delinquency Prevention Among Negro Youth." *Journal of Negro Education* (Summer 1960).

"The Significance of the Negro Private and Church-Related College." *Journal of Negro Education* 29 (Summer 1960): 245-251.

"The Only Way to Make The Youth 'Sit Down Protest' Effective." *Worker* 23 (July-September 1960).

"A Plea for Straight Talk Between Races." *Atlantic Monthly* 23 (December 1960).

"What is the Future of Negro Colleges?" *Southern School News* 17 (April 1961): 11-13.

"The Future of Negro Colleges." *Saturday Review* (November 18, 1961): 53.

"Why I Believe There Is a God." *Ebony* 17 (December 1961): 139.

"Does Integration Doom Negro College?" *Negro Digest* 11 (May 1962).

"What's Ahead For Our Negro Schools?" *Together* 6 (June 1962).

"The New Social Order When Integrated." *Religious Education* (March-April 1963).

"Scientists Have Repudiated Concept of Superior Inferior Races." *St. Louis Post-Dispatch* (August-September 1963).

"The Tragedy of School Dropouts." *The Message* 29 (October 1963).

"The Churches Will Follow." *Christian Century* (1964).

"In Pursuit of Freedom." *A.M.E. Church Review* 80 (January-March 1964).

"The Role of the Schools in a Social Revolution." *Teacher's College Record* 65 (May 1964).

"Why I Went To Bates." *Bates College Bulletin* (January 1966).

"The Achievements of the Negro Colleges." *Atlantic Monthly* 217 (February 1966).

"The American Negro College." *Harvard Education Review* 37 (Summer 1967).

"A Centennial Commencement Address: Higher Education and the American Negro." *Journal of Religious Thought* 24 (1967-1968).

"Letter to an Average Man." *The Equalizer* 1 (January 1968).

"Eulogy of Dr. Martin Luther King Jr." *Pan-African Journal* 1 (Summer 1968).

"Crisis and Challenge." *The Pilot Magazine* 19 (October 1970).

"The Diamond Jubilee of the National Association." *Journal of the National Medical Association* 62 (November 1970).

"The Church New Challenges for Survival." *Tuesday Magazine* 9 (February 1974).

"Comment: Atlanta Living with Brown Twenty Years Later." *Black Law Journal* 3 (1974).

"The Challenge of Our Unseen Witnesses." *Boule Journal* 37 (Summer-Fall 1974).

"A Look At The Black Colleges." *Foundations* 17 (July-September 1974).

"Black College: Past Present and Future." *The Black Scholar* 16 (September 1974).

"Education Is . . ." *Going to College Handbook* 30 (1976): 3.

"Coming to Chicago." *The University of Chicago Magazine* 71 (Spring 1979).

"Meeting Tomorrow's Challenges Today with Academic Moral and Spiritual Preparation." *AM-African Journal of Research and Education* 1 (Spring 1981): 1-6.

D. ARTICLES IN THE *MOREHOUSE COLLEGE BULLETIN*

"The Needs of the College." Morehouse College 1942. (booklet).

"The Financial Future of Morehouse College." Morehouse College Seventy-Fifth Anniversary, 1867-1942. Souvenir Program, (February 13-18, 1942, 16-17.

"A Crises as Challenge an Opportunity." 11 (July 1943): 21.

"Frederick Carrigon Gassett: A Eulogy." and "We Carry On." 11 (November 1943): 2, 16.

"The State of the College." 12 (March-April 1944): 22-23.

"Dr. Charles D. Hubert Great Soul Passes." and "Greater Things Than These We Must Do." 12 (July 1944): 2, 20.

"We Shall Not Falter." 12 (November-December 1944): 20.

"Radio Address of Dr. B. E. Mays on Seventy-eighth Anniversary of Morehouse College." and "We Drive Toward the Stars." 13 (March-April 1945): 3-4, 27.

"The Unawareness of Man." 23 (March 11, 1945).

"The President's Page." 13 (July-August 1945): 20.

"Let Us Finish This Job!." 13 (November 1945): 12.

"Radio Address (Station WGST) 11:15 P.M." and "We Face a Dilemma." 14 (April 1946): 6-7, 20.

"The President Message." 14 (July 1946): 12.

"James B. Adams the Unselfish." and "Why 860?" 14 (November 1946): 6-7, 12.

"Radio Address for Eightieth Anniversary" and "Our Needs Are Great." 15 (March-April 1947): 9, 24.

"The Future of Morehouse is in the Laps of the Alumni." 15 (July 1947): 28.

"The President's Page." 13 (November 1947): 12.

"We are Grateful." 16 (March-April 1948): 20.

"The End of an Era." 16 (July 1948 20.

"Three Million Dollars." 18 (April 1950 20.

"In and Around Morehouse." 18 (April 1950): 20.

"The President's Message to Black High School Graduates." Student Life, 1952.

"The Class of 1922 Proposes." 20 (July 1952): 24.

"The Price of One Book." 20 (November 1952): 16.

"The Chemistry Building and the Ford Scholarship." 21 (March 1953): 24.

"Where You Can Help the College Best." 21 (July 1953): 28.

"The President's Page." 21 (November 1953): 15.

"The President's Page." 22 (November 1954): 19.

"The Status of the Physical Education and Health Building." 23 (July 1955): 32.

"Why Morehouse Men Should Support the United Negro College Fund." 23 (November 1955): 12.

"Our Ninetieth Anniversary." 24 (July 1956): 28.

"I Don't Mind Getting Beat But . . . ." 24 (November 1956): 19.

"Goodby Mr. Scandal!!." 25 (March 1957): 28.

"So the Alumni Who Have Not Contributed." 25 (July 1957): 24.

"Reminder of the Proposed Plaque and Honor Book for Contributors to the Building Fund." 25 (November 1957): 15.

"Challenge to the Graduating Class of 1958." 26 (July 1958): 20.

"The President's Page 27 (March 1959): 19.

"A Fairly Good Year." 27 (July 1959): 24.

"Education To What End?" and "The President's Page." 28 (March 1960): 3-8, 20.

"The President's Page." 28 (November 1960): 15.

"Merrill Faculty Student Awards." 29 (March 1961): 24.

"The President's Charge to the Graduating Class of 1961." 28 (July 1961): 31.

"The President's Page." 29 (November 1961): 20.

"Tribute to Mrs. Catherine Hughes Waddell 1898-1961" and "Morehouse College and The United Negro College Fund." 30 (March 1962): 11-12, 20.

"Acceptance Speech for Christian Culture Award by Assumption University (Catholic) in Windsor, Canada, April 17, 1962." and "The President's Charge to the Class of 1962." 30 (July 1962): 26-28.

"The President's Page." 30 (November 1962): 20.

"Morehouse College and the United Negro College Fund." 31 (July 1963): 32.

"Three Things in Three Minutes." 31 (July 1963): 32.

"The Late John F. Kennedy." 31 (November 1963): 20.

"The President's Charge to the Class of 1964" and "An Explanatory Statement from President Mays About the Ford and Rockefeller Grant." 32 (1964): 17 and 40.

"The 100th Anniversary." 32 (November 1964): 36.

"The President's Page $500000!" 33 (March 1965): 32.

"The President's Charge to the Class of 1965" 33 (July 1965): 19-38.

"Tribute to Gladstone Lewis Chandler" and "Into the Second Century." 34 (Fall 1965): 3-4 and 36.

"The Alumni and $66666.66" 35 (Spring 1966): 36.

"The President's Charge to the Class of 1966" 34 (Summer 1966): 48.

"Once in a Century." 35 (Fall 1966): 28.

"Dr. Mays' Centennial Convocation Statement: 'Et Facta Est Lux.' " 36 (Spring 1967): 60.

"Eulogy of Dr. Martin Luther King Jr." 136 (Summer 1968): 8-12.

"Twenty-Seven Years of Success and Failure at Morehouse." 35 (Summer 1967): 29-32.

"The Predominantly Negro College: What Next?" 36 (Spring 1968): 17-18.

"Prisoner in Hairness Hall." 37 (Summer 1969): 30.

"Eulogy for Samuel Woodrow Williams." 38 (Fall 1970): 5-6.

E. NEWSPAPER ARTICLES

"It Costs Too Much." *Tampa Bulletin*, 7 April 1928.

"Howard University Dean of Religion Begins a Series of Articles Telling of Vast Subjects Tackled." *Norfolk Journal and Guide*, 25 September 1937.

"Members of Oxford Conference's Economic Committee Able Group (Conflicting Theories Advocated By Those There)." *Norfolk Journal and Guide*, 16 October 1937.

"Brotherhood Key to Oxford Conference." *Norfolk Journal and Guide*, 6 November 1937.

"Hitler Would Be 'God.' to Germans Asserts Dr. Mays." *Norfolk Journal and Guide*, 13 November 1937.

"How Americans Are Blamed For Color Discriminations Abroad." *Norfolk Journal and Guide*, 20 November 1937.

"Christian Youths Confer: 'World's Youths Soberly Consider Ills of World's Church and Society.' " *Norfolk Journal and Guide*, 9 September 1939.

"Racial Problems (Nature of Problems and the Jew a Challenge to Christianity)." *Norfolk Journal and Guide*, 16 September 1939.

"Segregated Churches (The Relationship of the Church to the So-Called 'Color' Question)." *Norfolk Journal and Guide*, 23 September 1939.

"Fear of Intermarriage (Will Christian Fellowship in the Church and Home Lead to Intermarriage?)." *Norfolk Journal and Guide*, 30 September 1939.

"Points of Agreement (Race Prejudice Acquired Through Social and Not Biological Heredity)." *Norfolk Journal and Guide*, 7 October 1939.

"Amsterdam Appraisal (Race Problem One of the Great Challenges Facing Christian Youth Today)." *Norfolk Journal and Guide*, 14 October 1939.

"Fifty Years of Progress in the Negro Church." *Chicago Defender*, 1950.

"Fewer and Fewer Men Are Training for the Ministry." *Chicago Defender*, 1955.

"Howard University's Offer is Best." *Atlanta Constitution*, 21 August 1977.

F. Unlisted Writings

From 1 June 1946 to 7 March 1981, Mays wrote 1,595 weekly column for the national edition of the *Pittsburgh Courier*

800 unpublished addresses, lectures, and sermons

A voluminous correspondence file, not yet catalogued

CONTRIBUTORS

Lerone Bennett Jr., D.H.L., Secretary of the Board of Trustees, Morehouse College, Executive Editor, Ebony Magazine, Chicago, Illinois.

Robert James Branham, Ph.D., Professor of Rhetoric, Bates College, Lewiston, Maine.

Noel C. Burtenshaw, Former Director Catholic Communications and Editor of *The Georgia Bulletin*, Atlanta, Georgia.

Orville Vernon Burton, Ph.D., Professor of History, University of Illinois, Urbana, Illinois.

Lawrence Edward Carter Sr., Ph.D., Dean, Martin Luther King Jr. International Chapel, Professor of Philosophy and Religion, Morehouse College, Atlanta, Georgia.

Mark L. Chapman, Ph.D., Assistant Professor, African American Studies, Fordham University, New York, New York.

Freddie C. Colston, Ph.D., Professor of History and Political Science, Georgia Southwestern College, Americus, Georgia.

Samuel DuBois Cook, Ph.D., President Emeritus, Dillard University, New Orleans, Louisiana.

Illya E. Davis, Ph.D. candidate, University of Chicago Divinity School, Chicago, Illinois.

Miles Mark Fisher IV, D.Min., Distinguished University Professor of the University of the District of Columbia

Doris Levy Gavins, Ph.D., Assistant Professor of Speech and English, Dillard University, New Orleans, Louisiana.

Hugh M. Gloster, Ph.D., President Emeritus, Morehouse College, Atlanta, Georgia.

Randal M. Jelks, Ph.D., Instructor, Calvin College, Grand Rapids, Michigan.

Barbara Sue K. Lewinson, Ed.D., J.D., Attorney at Law, North Brunswick, New Jersey.

Verner R. Matthews, Ph.D., Senior Pastor, Second Baptist Church, Asbury Park, New Jersey.

Thomas I. S. Mikelson, Th.D., Lecturer in Ministry, Harvard University Divinity School, Senior Minister, First Parish, Cambridge, Massachusetts.

Charles Shelby Rooks, D.D., Former Executive Director, The Fund for Theological Education, New York, New York; Former President, The Chicago Seminary; Former Executive Vice President, The United Church Board of Homeland Ministries.

Dereck Joseph Rovaris, Ph.D., Director of Graduate Placement and Assistant Professor of Education in the Graduate School, Xavier University, New Orleans, Louisiana.

Charles Vert Willie, Ph.D., Professor of Education and Urban Studies, Harvard University, Cambridge, Massachusetts.

CPSIA information c:
Printed in the USA
LVOW06s16483007

448251LV0(